The Heyday of Willie, Duke, and Mickey

The Heyday of Willie, Duke, and Mickey

New York City Baseball's Golden Age amid Integration

Robert C. Cottrell

BLOOMSBURY ACADEMIC
NEW YORK • LONDON • OXFORD • NEW DELHI • SYDNEY

BLOOMSBURY ACADEMIC

Bloomsbury Publishing Inc, 1359 Broadway, New York, NY 10018, USA
Bloomsbury Publishing Plc, 50 Bedford Square, London, WC1B 3DP, UK
Bloomsbury Publishing Ireland, 29 Earlsfort Terrace, Dublin 2, D02 AY28, Ireland

BLOOMSBURY, BLOOMSBURY ACADEMIC and the Diana logo are trademarks
of Bloomsbury Publishing Plc

First published in the United States of America 2026

Copyright © Bloomsbury Publishing, Inc., 2026

Cover design by Devin Watson

All rights reserved. No part of this publication may be: i) reproduced or transmitted in any form, electronic or mechanical, including photocopying, recording or by means of any information storage or retrieval system without prior permission in writing from the publishers; or ii) used or reproduced in any way for the training, development or operation of artificial intelligence (AI) technologies, including generative AI technologies. The rights holders expressly reserve this publication from the text and data mining exception as per Article 4(3) of the Digital Single Market Directive (EU) 2019/790.

Bloomsbury Publishing Inc does not have any control over, or responsibility for, any third-party websites referred to or in this book. All internet addresses given in this book were correct at the time of going to press. The author and publisher regret any inconvenience caused if addresses have changed or sites have ceased to exist, but can accept no responsibility for any such changes.

A catalog record for this book is available from the Library of Congress.

ISBN: HB: 979-8-8818-4257-4
ePDF: 979-8-8818-5445-4
eBook: 979-8-8818-5444-7

Typeset by Deanta Global Publishing Services, Chennai, India
Printed and bound in the United States of America

For product safety related questions contact productsafety@bloomsbury.com.

To find out more about our authors and books visit www.bloomsbury.com
and sign up for our newsletters.

To Sue and Jordan

Contents

Acknowledgments ix

Introduction 1
1. Nine of Major League Baseball's Original Ten Cities and the Negro Leagues 9
2. Baseball in America's Greatest City 19
3. The Veterans Return 31
4. Postwar Baseball as the Negro Leagues Wither 43
5. A New Yankee Dynasty amid the Boys of Summer and Leo's Giants 59
6. New York Baseball Ascends in 1951 69
7. The Yankees and Dodgers on Top as Mantle Returns and Mays Enters the Military 81
8. Franchise Shift and Wait 'Til Next Year Season, Yet Again 91
9. Return of the Say Hey Kid 107
10. The Year the Yankees Lose the Pennant, Willie Mays Targets Ruth's Record, the Catch, and Durocher's Team Wins! 119
11. The Duke of Flatbush 143
12. No More Wait 'Til Next Year for Duke Snider and the Brooklyn Dodgers 155
13. The Commerce Comet 179
14. Stengel's Yankees Rebound as Mickey Mantle Wins the Triple Crown 189

15 A Baseball Era Nears an End 215
16 The New York City Dynasty Winds to a Close 227
17 Legacies 249

Notes 259
Selected Bibliography 293
Index 297
About the Author 315

Acknowledgments

I want to tip my own baseball cap to Jon Sisk for soliciting the manuscript that evolved into *The Heyday of Willie, Duke, and Mickey*. My new editor, Christen Karniski, has proven gracious and supportive in helping to shepherd this book to production. Joanna Wattenberg and Sanjana Premkumar also offered invaluable assistance. In this digital age, I am grateful to the manifold archival materials readily accessible, as well as the too many to be named authors who have helped to mine the history of the national pastime. I do need to acknowledge the good folk at the National Baseball of Fame Library in Cooperstown, New York, particularly Claudette Scrafford, Manager of Manuscript/Photo Archives, and Cassidy Lent, Director of the HOF Library. Additionally, I am thankful to the research staff at the Library of Congress, the National Archives, the New York Public Library, and the Naval Historical Center for making accessible invaluable photographs. I also want to convey my admiration for sabermetricians, whose work I have chosen to draw from to underscore the brilliance of early and mid-20th century professional baseball players. That especially includes the great center fielders of New York City baseball's golden age: Willie Mays, Duke Snider, and Mickey Mantle.

As always, my deepest appreciation is reserved for my wife Sue and my daughter Jordan, my two biggest fans.

Introduction

During the first half-century after the merger of the National League and the American League in 1903, New York City dominated Major League (MLB) Baseball more decisively and more frequently than any other metropolitan area. Initially spearheaded by their fiery skipper John McGraw and right-handed pitching ace Christy Mathewson, the New York Giants stood as Organized Baseball's preeminent team. Then, the New York Yankees, featuring sluggers Babe Ruth and Lou Gehrig, became the sport's most storied franchise, maintaining that status when first, center fielder Joe DiMaggio and then, his eventual replacement, Mickey Mantle, starred in the nation's greatest city.

Following McGraw's retirement, the Giants, under player-manager Bill Terry, won the 1933 World Series but dropped back-to-back matches against the Yankees later that decade. Despite having won a pair of early pennants under Wilbert Robinson's tutelage, the Brooklyn ball club generally foundered before becoming a force to be reckoned with during the Second World War. Eventually, the Dodgers, including the famed Boys of Summer—Jackie Robinson, Pee Wee Reese, Duke Snider, Gil Hodges, Roy Campanella, and Don Newcombe, among others—competed with the crosstown Giants in the National League and against the Yankees in seven World Series matchups in 16 years. The Giants, for their part, fielded their own array of radiant performers, such as Bobby Thompson, Sal Maglie, Monte Irvin, and Willie Mays.[1]

The Giants, Yankees, and Dodgers were hardly the only professional baseball players based in the nation's greatest city. With varying lifespans, six major Black teams competed there between 1905 and 1959: the Brooklyn Royal Giants, the New York Lincoln Giants, the Cuban Stars, the New York Black Yankees, the New York Cubans, and, albeit very briefly, the Brooklyn Eagles, soon merged into the Newark Eagles. Versions of those teams were among Blackball's finest, containing some of its and professional baseball's greatest players, including catcher Louis Santop, second baseman Frank Grant, third baseman Jud Wilson, and shortstops John Henry "Pop" Lloyd, Judy Johnson, and Willie Wells. Other stars included outfielders Buck Leonard, Martin Dihigo, Mule Suttles, and Turkey Stearnes, and pitchers "Smokey" Joe Williams, Satchel Paige, and Leon Day. Those players, manager and former player Sol White, and owners Effa Manley and Alex Pompez were all eventually inducted into the Baseball of Hall of Fame in Cooperstown, New York.[2]

The story of New York baseball and of the game in general has been dramatically recast by recent decisions made by MLB, spurred on by dedicated researchers. On December 16, 2020, Robert D. Manfred Jr., Commissioner of Baseball, declared that MLB would henceforth acknowledge that each of seven Negro Leagues that operated between 1920 and 1948 was in fact "Major League." He indicated, "All of us who love baseball have long known that the Negro League produced many of our game's best players, innovations and triumphs against a backdrop of injustice." Manfred continued, "We are now grateful to count the players of the Negro Leagues where they belong as major leaguers within the official historical record." Referring to the decision, Bob Kendrick, president of the Negro Leagues Baseball Museum asserted, "For historical merit, it is extraordinarily important."[3]

Then, on May 28, 2024, the commissioner announced the incorporation of Negro League statistics into Organized Baseball's record book. "We are proud that the official historical record now includes the players of the Negro Leagues." Manfred declared, "This initiative is focused on ensuring that future generations of fans have access to the statistics and milestones of all those who made the Negro Leagues possible." Kendrick deemed this "a major milestone in baseball history." Larry Lester, a leading Negro League scholar, explained, "The Negro Leagues were a product of segregated America, created to give opportunity where opportunity did not exist."[4]

The fate of the Negro Leagues and Organized Baseball had long been intertwined, as had been the opportunities afforded or denied to some of the sports' greatest performers. As the Second World War wound to a close, the decision of Brooklyn Dodgers general manager Branch Rickey to sign an African American player to a minor league contract would alter Organized Baseball, the Negro Leagues, and the fate of that ballplayer and other Negro Leaguers. Unable to compete in the cancelled 1940 Olympic Games and racially prohibited from playing in the National Football League, the precursors to the National Basketball Association, or, until 1946, Organized Baseball, a brilliant African American athlete, a four-sport letterman at UCLA, broke a decades' long color barrier. Another year down the road, Jackie Robinson, positioned at first place, became the first Black player to appear in a major or minor league game in several decades. Fortuitously, Robinson proved to be a Hall of Famer himself while carving out a path for other Negro League veterans to follow.[5]

The ability of a select few, like Robinson, Larry Doby, Paige, Campanella, and Newcombe, to enter the long all-white minor or major leagues proved a mixed blessing for Black ballplayers and managers, as well as owners, Black or white, such as the Kansas City Monarchs' J. L. Wilkinson, along with other personnel. While some of the finest or most promising Negro League players entered Organized Baseball, and Negro League veteran player-manager Buck O'Neil later became a major league scout and coach, others, including older, aging, or troubled stars such as Josh Gibson never experienced that thrill. Moreover, the raiding of Negro League teams, with little or no compensation afforded team owners, rapidly resulted in a deterioration and the ultimate demise of Blackball, which often proved to be a devastating loss to African American communities. Attendance and valuations of Black franchises plummeted. Sportswriter William C. Rhoden contends, in fact, that integration of Organized Baseball proved crippling for a "black industry, practically eliminating every black person involved in sports—coaches, owners, trainers, accountants, lawyers, secretaries and so on—except the precious on-the-field talent."[6]

The fact that the stunningly talented, handsome, ebony-skinned Robinson had been unable to enter the major leagues until he turned 28 limited his time with the Brooklyn Dodgers, but his playing career spanned a full decade—1947–56—resulting in six pennants and a long-sought World Series championship. It also coincided with most of the 11-year time span, 1947–57, often considered the golden era for New York City baseball and for good reason. Except for 1948, at least one of the three metropolitan area's major league teams—the New York Yankees, the New York Giants, and the Brooklyn Dodgers—made it into the World Series every year throughout that period. Seven times both the American League and the National League pennant winners came from the nation's greatest city. In 1947, when the Yankees and Dodgers met in the World Series for the second time, the next-to-last Negro League World Series saw the New York Cubans defeat the Cleveland Buckeyes four games to one, with an additional tie.[7]

Of no small significance, the Yankee, Giant, and Dodger managers and players exuded star power befitting their sporting prowess and New York City's preeminence. Skippers Casey Stengel, Leo Durocher, and Charlie Dressen were colorful figures all, perhaps because rather than despite frequent malapropisms or inappropriate behavior. Their teams—the Bronx Bombers, Durocher's Giants, or sportswriter Roger Kahn's Boys of Summer—were peerless in their own fashion. How could that fail to be so with players like the Yankees' Joe DiMaggio, Yogi Berra, Whitey Ford, and Mickey Mantle, the Giants' Willie Mays, Sal Maglie, and Monte Irvin, and the Dodgers' Jackie Robinson, Pee Wee Reese, Duke Snider, and Roy Campanella, to name only a few of the manifold stars on those squads.

But as the adage goes, all good things come to an end, and that was true with the reign of New York baseball. Retirements, aging ball players, trades, salary disputes, and down seasons removed stellar figures from the three New York City teams, although rapid-fire turnover of rosters hardly matched what the sport later endured. No matter, the loss of Joltin Joe, Negro League veteran Irvin, and Jackie could hardly be overcome, regardless of who replaced them. Still more striking, franchise shifts involving two of MLB's most historic franchises ensured that New York City baseball dominance could never again be replicated, at least in similar fashion. Even the eventual addition of the New York Mets to the National League, which occurred five years following the Dodgers and Giants move out West to Los Angeles and San Francisco, respectively, scarcely replaced them in the hearts of diehard fans who had experienced a genuinely unique era in baseball history.

While others, most notably Roger Kahn, Harvey Frommer, and Carl E. Prince, have explored that full period, I have elected to concentrate on the final years of that remarkable heyday, starting with the season when the Yankees failed to win the pennant after five consecutive World Series titles. The Giants, in 1954, won their final World Series championship while residing in New York City, while the Dodgers finally captured their first title the following year, beating their hated rival Yankees, after five losses to them in the World Series. The Yankees triumphed in 1956 but lost to the Milwaukee Braves the next year when Dodger owner Walter O'Malley and Giant boss Horace Stoneman completed plans to shut down the gates to Ebbets Field and the Polo Grounds.[8]

During those four critical years, at the very height and later the extreme depth of the postwar New York City baseball dynasty, three luminescent ballplayers competed for recognition as the game's finest. All three deftly played center field, the apex of so many critical moments in the sport, ran the bases with genuine skill, and were high-average power hitters. Each had a season for the ages, making a run at the most storied mark in MLB, indeed, throughout American sports: Babe Ruth's single-season home run record. Each came up short but went on to complete a brilliant season that culminated with his team's triumph in that year's World Series. In 1954, Willie Mays returned from service in the US Army with a splash, becoming the most exciting player in either league while leading the New York Giants to a stunning upset in that year's World Series. The next year, Duke Snider, amid arguably his finest season, helped the Brooklyn Dodgers finally defeat the New York Yankees in the Fall Classic, ending the need for talk of "Wait 'til next year." Then, in 1956, Mickey Mantle fulfilled his seemingly unbounded promise with one of the major league's greatest seasons, through a Triple Crown performance and a major role in the Yankees' return to World Series glory.

Thus, key figures include the great center fielders, Snider, Mantle, and Mays. Then, there is the incomparable Jackie Robinson, along with managers Durocher, Stengel, Dressen, and Walter Alston. But the era also encompasses the Cleveland Indians, the Boston Braves, the Philadelphia Phillies, and the Milwaukee Braves, the teams that broke through the New

York City dominance to win pennants between 1948 and 1957. Such players allowed the New York City preeminence to be contested, interrupted, and eventually terminated.

But that was only possible with age tearing at the fabric of the great Brooklyn Dodgers, Durocher's imploding with the Giants as he had earlier with the Dodgers, the Yankees' too-long disinclination to add Black players, and, as important as any factor, franchise shifts, which began with the move of the Braves from Boston to Milwaukee. Franchise alterations picked up momentum as the St. Louis Browns became the Baltimore Orioles and the Philadelphia Athletics headed for Kansas City. It became complete, at least for the period examined, with the decision of the Dodger and Giant owners to relocate to Los Angeles and San Francisco, respectively, after the 1957 season. That ensured New York City baseball dominance, involving three historic franchises, would never again be possible, certainly in the same fashion that occurred for the 11-year stretch starting in 1947.

Perhaps it was inevitable given the New York Yankees' reluctance to follow the lead established by the Dodgers, Indians, Browns, and Giants, as well as by the Braves somewhat later, to bring on board the finest Negro League players they could find. The tale of New York City baseball's rise and fall is also that of the game's far too belated integration, its reticence in pushing back against the American nation's racial divisions. The decision by some in Organized Baseball to sign Robinson, Doby, Campanella, Don Newcombe, Paige, Minnie Minoso, Irvin, Mays, Aaron, and Ernie Banks to contracts paralleled the budding civil rights struggle to rid the United States of hateful, hurtful, poisonous Jim Crow edicts and discriminatory practices. The athletic brilliance, the startling luminosity of players once relegated to Blackball melded with the legal challenges delivered by the National Association for the Advancement of Colored People (NAACP), through its lead attorney, Thurgood Marshall, and by Black activists. Those activists often paid a heavy price for contesting the American brand of apartheid too many were willing to uphold through horrifically violent acts. That included the use of the politics of assassination, which was eventually wielded against, among others, a young Black minister, a believer in and practitioner of nonviolent direct-action tactics who considered Robinson and the other Negro League pathfinders to have spearheaded the civil rights drive.

What follows is something of the story of New York City ballplayers, particularly Robinson, Snider, Mays, Mantle, and their Dodger, Giant, and Yankee teammates, as a baseball era wound to a close in the face of struggles to transform playing fields and America itself.

1

Nine of Major League Baseball's Original Ten Cities and the Negro Leagues

At various points, although far more briefly, other cities, besides New York City, on the East Coast or in the Midwest—four of which boasted a pair of major league teams—also vied for ascendancy in the sport that was called the national pastime. Boston boasted the Red Sox and the Braves; Philadelphia, the Athletics and the Phillies; Chicago, the White Sox and the Cubs; and St. Louis, the Cardinals and the Browns.

During the first 15 World Series played after the merger of the National League and the American League in 1903, the Boston Americans, soon known as the Red Sox, captured five championships and might have won another but for the refusal, in 1904, of the New York Giants to compete. The team was led by such stars as pitcher Cy Young, center fielder Tris Speaker, and George Herman "Babe" Ruth, the AL's top left-handed pitcher who also managed to tie for the league lead in homer in 1918, when he established a scoreless innings pitched record—29 2/3—during World Series competition, a standard that lasted for 43 years. Following the trade of the game's greatest slugger to the Yankees, however, the Red Sox experienced doldrums—many Bostonians referred to it as "the curse of the Bambino," not winning another pennant until 1946. Also based in Boston, the generally woeful Braves managed to sweep the heavily favored Philadelphia Athletics in 1914.[1]

The Athletics, led by owner-manager Connie Mack, won nine pennants and five World Series between 1905 and 1931, featuring two dynasties in the process. The first, whose top performers were pitchers Eddie Plank, Rube Waddell, Charles "Chief" Bender, and Jack Combs, along with second baseman Eddie Collins and third baseman Home Run Baker, ended with defeat at the hands of the underdog Braves and Mack's decision to sell key players. The second dynasty, which followed two World Series titles amid three straight pennants, concluded in 1932 when the financially strapped Mack again broke up a star-studded lineup that included future Hall of Famers Mickey Cochrane, Al Simmons, Jimmie Foxx, and Lefty Grove. Generally mired in the second division, the Phillies, thanks to home run champ Gavvy Cravath and pitching phenom Grover Cleveland Alexander, took the 1915 National League title but dropped the World Series to the Red Sox.[2]

During the early stages of the twentieth century, both the North and the South Sides of Chicago were well represented in pennant races. Led by manager-first baseman Frank Chance and pitcher Mordecai "Three-Finger" Brown, the Cubs swept three straight pennants, starting in 1906, the year they won a record 116 games but fell to the White Sox, tagged as "hitless wonders" due to a .228 team batting average, in a six-game World Series. The Cubs went on to take the next two World Series, won additional pennants in 1910 and 1918 but were defeated by the A's and the Red Sox to end those seasons. The Cubs, starting in 1916, began hosting games at Wrigley Field, previously called Weeghman Park. There, in 1914 and 1915, the Chicago Whales, managed by Tinker, played in the short-lived Federalist League (FL), winning the pennant during the second year. The Cubs also won circuit crowns in 1929, 1932, 1935, 1938, and 1945—three under Charlie Grimm—but came up short in each of those World Series. Led by catcher second sacker Eddie Collins, third baseman Buck Weaver, outfielder "Shoeless" Joe Jackson, and pitcher Eddie Cicotte, the White Sox took the 1917 and 1919 pennants, winning that initial World Series while ingloriously dropping the next one through what became known as the Black Sox scandal, a fix purportedly involving several players including Jackson, Weaver, and Cicotte, and triggering the team's own prolonged curse.[3]

Baseball-friendly St. Louis featured both the Cardinals and the Browns. Under the tutelage of general manager Branch Rickey, who constructed an elaborate farm system, the Cardinals became the preeminent National League team, winning six pennants and four World Series through 1942, when he moved over to the Dodgers, whom he also shaped into a powerhouse. The first pennant-winning Cardinals team, in 1926, defeated Babe Ruth and the New York Yankees in the World Series. The Cardinals took three pennants during the early 1930s, including the 1934 Gashouse Gang, topped by 31-game winner Dizzy Dean. Having built something of a dynasty in St. Louis, Rickey watched as the Cardinals, with manager Billy Southworth and featuring outfielder Stan Musial, won again in 1943 and 1944, and in 1946 under skipper Eddie Dyer, taking the World Series in the even-numbered years too. The long-suffering Browns, by contrast, won only one pennant, then fell to the Cardinals in the 1944 World Series.[4]

Not surprisingly, single-team cities—Pittsburgh, Cincinnati, Detroit, Cleveland, and Washington, D.C.—tended to do less well in the accumulation of league titles and World Series championships. Led by shortstop-batting champion Honus Wagner and manager-outfielder Fred Clarke, the Pittsburgh Pirates won three straight pennants, starting in 1901, and another in 1909, when they captured the World Series. Pittsburgh bested another superstar-led team, Walter Johnson's Washington Senators in the 1925 World Series, but its next pennant winner was swept by the 1927 Yankees of Ruth and Lou Gehrig.[5]

Taking their first twentieth-century pennant in 1919, the Cincinnati Reds defeated the scandal-laden Chicago White Sox. Managed by Bill McKechnie, they came in first in the National League in both 1939 and 1940, with key performances by catcher Ernie Lombardi, first baseman and 1940 National League Most Valuable Player (NL MVP) Frank McCormick, and pitchers Bucky Walters, the 1939 MVP, and Paul Derringer, getting swept by the Yankees and then beating the Detroit Tigers.[6]

Over in the American League, Hughie Jennings's Detroit Tigers, spearheaded by Ty Cobb, who won even more batting crowns than Wagner, took three straight pennants, 1907–1909, but lost each World Series. Following a quarter-century drought, the Tigers prevailed four more times in the American League during the 1930s and 1940s, fueled by slugger Hank Greenberg, garnering two World Series championships a decade apart.[7]

Notwithstanding the presence of stellar players like second baseman Nap Lajoie, a four-time batting champion,[8] and outfielders Joe Jackson and Tris Speaker, Cleveland usually ended up around the middle of the league for most of its first two decades in the American League. The then-named Cleveland Indians did win both the American League pennant and World Series in 1920 behind playing manager Speaker and 31-game winner Jim Bagby, and fellow pitchers Stan Coveleski and Ray Caldwell. That season, ill-fated 29-year-old shortstop Ray Chapman became the only major league player to die from an injury suffered during a game after behind struck in the head by a pitch from Yankees hurler Carl Mays.[9]

A frequent cellar-dweller but sometimes a competitor, as represented by runner-up finishes in 1912 and 1913 when right-hander Walter Johnson won 33 and 36 games, respectively, the Washington Senators, grabbed pennants in 1924 and 1925, prevailing in their initial World Series appearance. The Senators, fueled by playing-manager-shortstop Joe Cronin, won another pennant in 1933, falling to the Giants, their last title in the nation's capital.

*****

Only recently have Negro League games, according to MLB, been acknowledged as on par with those of the major leagues. This was true even though incredibly skilled athletes, precluded from entering the major or minor leagues, competed in Blackball contests, which sometimes involved going head-to-head against white players from Organized Baseball. The most storied teams, including the Philadelphia Giants, the Chicago American Giants, the Kansas City Monarchs, the Pittsburgh Crawfords, the Homestead Grays, and the Kansas City Monarchs, featured stellar pitchers, hitters, fielders, and managers, equal to the best in the big leagues. Led by playing manager Sol White, white sportswriter H. Walter Schlichter, and Black sports editor Harry A. Smith, the Philadelphia Giants won five Eastern Region Championships over a six-year period during the first decade of the twentieth century. Stars at various points included second baseman Frank Grant, shortstop Pop Lloyd, outfielder Pete Hill, catcher Louis Santop, and pitchers Dan McClellan, Emmett Bowman, and Rube Foster.[10]

Those Blackball teams and performers excelled in the face of relentless pressure. Like their predecessors, they sought their place on the baseball diamond in a sport deemed the national pastime. Writers like Mark Twain and Walt Whitman had waxed eloquent about baseball being such a part of the American experience or even embodying Americana. During a lecture at New York City's Delmonico's restaurant on the evening of April 8, 1889, the author of such classics as *The Adventures of Tom Sawyer* and *Adventures of Huckleberry Finn* asserted, "Baseball is the very symbol, the outward and visible expression of the drive and push and rush and struggle of the raging, tearing, booming nineteenth century."

Quite possibly on that very day, responding to an admirer indicating, "Baseball is the hurrah game of the republic!" the great poet who was ever altering his epic *Leaves of Grass* asserted, "That's beautiful—the hurrah game! well-it's our game: that's the chief fact in connection with it: America's game: has the snap, go, fling, of the American atmosphere—belongs as much to our institutions, fits into them as significantly, as our constitutions, laws: is just as important in the sum total of our historic life."[11]

Such sentiments, albeit seldom expressed so eloquently, were hardly unique during the last several decades of the nineteenth century and well into the twentieth. Perhaps that was true because the sport became the favorite of many writers, who, much like Twain and Whitman, could convey in words what baseball meant to them, and, purportedly, their fellow citizens. Extolled as the national pastime, it unfortunately proved all too representative of a nation deeply splintered along racial lines. The United States was also riven by ethnic and class divides, but with the passage of time, those appeared diminished, in various ways, on the baseball diamond. Not so, the racial schism, particularly the one involving white and Black, which left many of the game's finest practitioners sidelined or compelled to participate in a Blacks-only version.

Little helping matters was the racism that long afflicted American society and became embedded within the fabric of the nation even following the Civil War waged, in large part, to end slavery. The Confederacy's demise failed to vanquish forces drawing on repellent ideas and abhorrent practices, like those of the Ku Klux Klan, ensuring that some Americans and new immigrants were treated as "others." With the ending of Reconstruction that had once promised to restructure the American South and genuinely emancipate the Freedmen, the nation shifted course, a process abetted by the US Supreme Court. Judicial rulings, topped by the infamous *Plessy v. Ferguson* decree in 1896 sustaining "separate but equal" edicts, facilitated an American system of apartheid supplanting slavery while adopting semblances of its dreadful ways. The ever-present American readiness for violence did likewise, with vigilantism helping to crush the hopes engendered by the Thirteenth, Fourteenth, and Fifteenth Amendments terminating slavery, calling for equal protection of the laws, due process, and a safeguarding of privileges and immunities, and seemingly shielding voting rights for eligible Black Americans. Black codes, legislatively drawn mandates and prohibitions, even restricted Black individuals' literal movement, including from the very plantations where many had been held in bondage.[12]

Supposedly sacrosanct rights were thus delivered but then unceremoniously removed. One of those, the right to vote, was steadily withdrawn from southern Blacks, virtually altogether. So too was the ability to hold political office, as a surprising number of African Americans did after the Civil War. The right to an education, increasingly guaranteed in state constitutions, proved to be nominal or non-existent for many. The employment opportunities for Black people were sorely limited. Housing availability, particularly reasonably priced, adequate housing, was likewise severely restricted. In an age following slavery's literal demise, a kind of new subjugation ensued involving too easy incarceration, debt peonage, and the constant threat of violence. Most frightening, lynchings proved a favorite tactic in too many communities, with thousands slaughtered over a several decades' span of time.

No matter how romantically depicted as the national pastime, baseball, at least at the professional level, hardly proved immune to the turn toward segregation, Jim Crow practices, discriminatory realities, and the persistent debasing, across much of the country, of people considered to possess African ancestry. Little helping matters was the influence and vicious race-baiting of key figures like Cap Anson, longtime first baseman-manager of the Chicago White Stockings. Anson took the lead in refusing to allow his team to play against any club that had African American players, including well-regarded ones like Toledo's catcher Moses Fleetwood Walker and batterymate George

Stovey. Purportedly, Anson declared, "I will never step on the field" against a Black player. Soon, players as skilled as Walker, Stovey, Bud Fowler, and Frank Grant were excluded from Organized Baseball.

As white leagues, including those considered to be at the highest levels, refused to allow African Americans to participate in official competition, enterprising Black players, managers, and entrepreneurs established their own teams and attempted to devise circuits like those in Organized Baseball. That was incredibly difficult, no matter the brilliance of early figures like Octavius Catto, Sol White, Walter S. Brown, and Frank Leland. Nevertheless, proponents of Blackball persevered, ironically frequently encountering white teams and players barnstorming during off-seasons or even through exhibitions on off-days from league play. By all accounts, Black players more than held their own during games conducted outside the United States, with Cuba, Mexico, and other locales in Latin American favorite destination spots, or back in the States.

While the play was often stellar, Blackball games were frequently performed under less-than-ideal circumstances, far removed from the baseball diamonds found in the major or even the minor leagues. African American players and teams often lacked adequate resources and experienced uneven conditions on and off playing fields. Sol White, author of the classic *History of Colored Baseball* (1907), nevertheless contended that the game "should be taken seriously by the colored player. An honest effort of his great ability will open the avenue in the near future wherein he may walk hand-in-hand with the opposite race in the greatest of all American games—baseball."[13]

What came to be known as the Great Migration resulted from the deteriorating conditions for Black people in the South. Beginning around 1910 and continuing for decades, millions of African Americans voted with their feet, leaving the South, with many congregating in large cities in the North, Midwest, and, later, out West. Another early impetus was the First World War, which afforded unprecedented opportunities for Black Americans in industrial plants. Even the early stages of the Great Migration resulted in substantial concentrations in metropolitan centers like Chicago, New York, Boston, Philadelphia, and Pittsburgh, enabling Black institutions, including newspapers and the baseball teams they publicized and supported, to emerge.[14]

Long led by manager Rube Foster, at one point Sol White's teammate and the best pitcher in Black baseball, who later founded the Negro National League, the Chicago American Giants loomed large from the team's founding in 1910 through the middle of the 1930s. They captured numerous unofficial championships before the NNL's emergence, then won a series of league titles and a pair of Negro League World Series crowns. In addition to Foster, the American Giants' roster contained, at various points, stars like Pop Lloyd, Pete Hill, William Foster, and "Cannonball" Dick Redding. After mental illness afflicted Rube Foster, his replacement, David Malarcher, led the American Giants to those Negro League World Series championships.[15]

Initiating operations in 1920 and continuing into the last half of the 1950s, the Kansas City Monarchs, owned by J. L. Wilkinson, a white businessman, won 13 league titles and a pair of Negro League World Series. Its star players included Bell, Turkey Stearnes, Newt Allen, Wilber "Bullet" Rogan, Hilton Smith, and Paige. The 1945 lineup had 26-year-old Jackie Robinson, who played first base and shortstop, hit .375, and topped the Negro American League's abbreviated season in doubles, homers, and WAR (indicates how many more wins a player is "worth" than a replacement player at the same position), while making the famed All-Star Game featuring the best Negro Leaguers.[16]

The Crawfords existed for a much briefer period—1933–40—but won three NNL championships, including, most notably in 1935 and 1936. The 1935 team had catcher Josh Gibson, an 11-time home run champ in 13 full seasons, first baseman-manager Oscar Charleston, who held that distinction on five occasions, third sacker Judy Johnson, and center fielder Cool Papa Bell. Owner Gus Greenlee's squad added Satchel Paige, who declined to play for Greenlee in 1935 owing to a salary dispute, to the next year's roster. That season's version of the Crawfords saw Gibson lead the NNL in homers and runs batted in (RBIs). Lefty Leroy Matlock helped to make up for Paige's absence, topping the league in wins, win-loss percentage, and earned run average (ERA). The next year, Gibson won the batting triple crown, hitting .389, Matlock again won the most games in the NNL, as the returning Paige went 8–2, resulting in the best win-loss percentage, while nearly striking out the most batters.[17]

Also initially based in Pittsburgh but later playing in Washington, D.C., too, Cumberland Posey's Homestead Grays performed in the Negro Leagues for nearly two decades, winning nine NNL titles and three Negro League World Series championships. Playing at the Pirates' Forbes Field and the Senators' Griffith Stadium, the Grays also boasted Gibson, Johnson, and Bell, in addition to Buck Leonard, Martin Dihigo, "Smokey" Joe Williams, Luke Easter, and playing manager-outfielder Vic Harris. Many baseball historians view the 1931 Grays' team, with Gibson, Charleson, Jud Wilson, Williams, and Foster, as the greatest ball club, amassing a 143–29–2 record during a season when the recently formed American Negro League, which the Grays initially joined, collapsed amid the Great Depression. Others claim that distinction for the 1935 Crawfords, but a case could also be made for the 1938 or 1943 editions of the Grays. Batting .370 in 1938, Gibson was again the NNL home run and RBI leader, while Leonard topped with a .420 BA and a .740 slugging average. Both Ray Brown (14–0) and Edsall Walker (10–0) went undefeated for manager Vic Harris's team that compiled a 41–13 record. Candy Jim Taylor's 1943 squad, Negro League World Series winners, went 53–14–1, with Gibson leading the league in homers and RBIs one more time. Johnny Wright (18–3) was tops in wins and ERA, aided by 40-year-old Spoon Carter (14–2). Forty-five hundred fans attended the Grays' last NNL game of the season at Griffith Stadium in Washington, D.C., with a testimonial to Gibson, labeled by Washington Senators' owner Clark Griffith "one of the great hitters of baseball."[18]

Excelling more briefly, the St. Louis Stars, who captured titles in 1928, 1930, and 1931, included, at different stages, catcher Biz Mackey, center fielder Oscar Charleston, slugging outfielder Mules Suttles, shortstop Willie Wells, and center fielder Cool Papa Bell, considered perhaps the fastest man in baseball. The Bacharach Giants, situated in Atlantic City, New Jersey, won three Eastern Region NL championships (1926–28) but disbanded a year after the last of those. Ed Bolden's Hilldale Athletic Club, operating out of Darby, just outside Philadelphia, won four Eastern-region titles (1923–1925, 1931) and the 1925 Negro League World Series championship. Team members included Martin

Dihigo, Louis Santop, Biz Mackey, Judy Johnson, Pop Lloyd, and Oscar Charleston. Abe and Effa Manley's Newark Eagles, who existed from 1933 to 1951, won the 1946 Negro World Championship. Among its stars were pitcher Leon Day, Biz Mackey, Mules Suttle, Willie Wells, third baseman Ray Dandridge, center fielder Larry Doby, and left fielder Monte Irvin.[19]

2

Baseball in America's Greatest City

Thus, at various points, Pittsburgh, Chicago, Boston, Philadelphia, and St. Louis in particular could lay claim to preeminence in professional baseball. No matter, New York City, due to its stature and the presence of three ball clubs in the National League and the American League, often grabbed the bulk of attention regarding Organized Baseball. Dating back to the 1880s, the New York Baseball Club, first known as the Gothams, was led by manager Jim Mutrie, catcher Buck Ewing, first baseman Roger Connor, shortstop John Montgomery Ward, and pitchers Tim Keefe and Mickey Welch. They captured two NL titles and World Series championships in 1888 and 1889, acquiring the nickname of the Giants. Starting in 1889, the team played at a site soon called the Polo Grounds, located at 155th and 157th Streets along 8th Avenue between the Harlem River and Coogan's Bluff.[1]

The Giants achieved an early dominance, amassing an array of pennants—ten, altogether—under John McGraw, although frequently stumbling in the World Series. McGraw and team owner John T. Brush refused to participate in the second World Series, which would have matched Giants pitchers Christy Mathewson and John McGinnity against Boston hurler Cy Young, whose Red Sox had defeated the Pirates the previous year. Ironically, the Giants, McGraw, Mathewson, catcher Roger Bresnahan, and outfielder Mike Donlin experienced among their most glorious moments in the 1905 World Series when they contested Connie Mack's Athletics. Each game was a shutout with the Athletics' Chief Bender winning Game Two, McGinnity beating Eddie Plank in Game Four, and Mathewson pitching expertly in Games One, Three, and Five, tossing two four-hitters and then a five-hitter in the final contest. In three additional World Series—1911–1913—Mathewson pitched deftly but was too often a hard-luck loser as the Giants failed to repeat their 1905 triumph. The Giants lineup included left-handed pitcher Rube Marquard, catcher Jack "Chief" Meyer, and second baseman Larry Doyle, the 1912 NL MVP.

Starting in mid-1911, the Giants hosted games at the newly reconstructed Polo Grounds with a seating capacity of 34,000 for that year's World Series; 11 years later, almost 55,000 fans could be seated. Homers easily flew across the fence near the short left and right field foul poles, but dead center required a mammoth clout, ranging between 433–505 feet from home plate over the next 46 years. From 1913 to 1922, it also served as the Yankees ballpark.[2]

In 1914, the Giants failed to win the NL pennant for the first time in four years, falling ten and a half games behind the surprising Boston Braves. After finishing in the league basement the next year as Mathewson foundered, and fourth in 1916, their great pitcher's final season, the Giants, fueled by outfielder Benny Kauff and pitchers Ferdie Schupp and Slim Sallee, rebounded to take the pennant in 1917, although once more losing the World Series. Three consecutive runner-up finishes followed, before McGraw fielded his last great team, which won four straight pennants, along with the World Series in both 1921 and 1922. Its stars included first baseman George Kelly, second baseman Frankie Frisch, outfielders Ross Youngs and Irish Meusel, and pitcher Art Nehf.[3]

Over the next several seasons, the Giants, still managed by McGraw, generally did well, other than the 1926 season, finishing second or third. McGraw retired early in the 1932 season, when he was replaced by first baseman Bill Terry, who, two years earlier, became the last National Leaguer to bat over .400. Terry led the Giants to the pennant and a World Series title in 1933, backed by slugging outfielder Mel Ott and southpaw pitcher Carl Hubbell, who led the league in wins (23) and ERA (1.66) on the way to an MVP award. After coming in second and third in subsequent years, the Giants again won pennants in 1936 and 1937 but dropped the World Series to the Yankees each time. Ott was the NL's home run champ (33, 31), while Hubbell remained the pitching ace, topping the league in wins (26, 22) and ERA (1936, 2.31), and finishing first and third in MVP races.

After coming in third during 1938, but only five games behind the first-place Cubs, Terry's Giants slid further over the next three years before he was replaced by new player-manager Ott. During his first year as Giants' skipper, Ott won his sixth NL homer title, first baseman Johnny Mize added more power, and the Giants rebounded with an 85–67–2 record, good for third place. Starting in 1943, however, the Giants fell to the league bottom, winning only fifty-five games and finishing forty nine and a half games back of the Cardinals. The final war years saw the Giants in fifth, but they again plummeted to last place in 1946 despite Mize's continued artistry at the plate.

As part of the agreement to pair the National and American leagues, AL president Ban Johnson was allowed to place a team in New York City. Playing at Hilltop Park, situated in Washington Heights between 165th and 168th Streets, the New York Highlanders, soon to be called the Yankees, performed erratically over their first several years. They managed three runner-up finishes—1904, 1906, and 1910—coming particularly close during their second year in the American League, when Hall of Fame outfielder Wee Willie Keeler had his final great batting campaign. Relying on both a spitball and a slower pitch, Jack Chesbro won 41 games, including 14 straight at one point, but hurled a wild pitch in the ninth inning on the season's final day, resulting in a crushing defeat to Boston, which won the pennant.[4]

Stumbling through most of the 1910s, the Yankees, who included Home Run Baker, future MVP shortstop Roger Peckinpaugh, and 20-game winner Bob Shawkey, and by 1918, managed by Miller Huggins, went 80–59–2 in the abbreviated 1919 season, finishing in third, seven and a half games behind the about-to-become infamous Chicago White Sox. More importantly, early in the off-season owners Jacob Ruppert and Tillinghast L. Huston engineered one of the two most significant transactions in MLB history, the other involving the signing of Negro league player Jackie Robinson to a minor league contract 25 years later. On January 5, Colonel Ruppert, the Yankees team president, announced the purchase of George Herman "Babe" Ruth from the Red Sox. Financially strapped Boston owner Harry Frazee received a $300,000 loan, with

Fenway Park standing as collateral, and a $100,000 payment doled out in four equal increments, one immediately and the others during the next three years.[5]

Whatever the actual expense, the amount required to acquire the game's most legendary figure was, effectively, repaid innumerable times as Ruth quickly helped to turn the New York Yankees into the most successful American sports team, athletically and financially. Beginning in 1920, Ruth's performance on the playing field proved epochal as he altered MLB altogether. Turned into a full-time player, Ruth helped to end the majors' dead ball era, characterized by low-scoring contests, middling batting averages, and a paucity of homers. Baseball researcher David J. Gordon indicates that from 1901 to 1919—that last season when Ruth first established a new home run mark—AL and NL teams amassed a .254 batting average while garnering "3.9 runs, 8.4 hits, and 0.15 home runs per" game. Ruth and those who attempted to follow his lead offered a new "power... free-swinging approach" at the plate. Helping to pump up batting and slugging averages were balls with a "lighter cork core" and a readiness to discard "dirty or damaged balls," particularly following the Chapman tragedy. But the new core had arrived a decade earlier and Ruth's latest assault on the home run record preceded Chapman's death, which occurred from an injury late in the 1920 season.[6]

Ruth's unprecedented performance at the plate led others, including Rogers Hornsby, Ken Williams, and soon, teammate Lou Gehrig, to go for the fences, while maintaining high batting averages. The new Yankees batting feats in 1920 and 1921, followed by more than an additional decade of dominance, transformed MLB for more than the next century of play. Setting a bounty of records during his first season with the Yankees and then breaking many of them the next year, Ruth led the league in runs scored (158, 177), RBIs (135, 168), walks (150, 145), on-base percentage (OBP) (.532, .512), slugging (.847, .846), on-base plus slugging (OPS) (1.379, 1.359), on-base plus slugging with ballpark and league averages considered (OPS+) (255, 239), and, of course, homers (54, 59). After his 388 total bases in 1920 fell 11 short of George Sisler's mark, Ruth set a new total bases (TB) record in 1921 with 457. MLB would never be the same as team batting averages, slugging percentages (SLG), and run scores jumped over the next decade.[7]

With Ruth also receiving salaries of an unprecedented sort—reaching $80,000 in 1930 and 1931—his team, more importantly, became a force to be reckoned with, indeed the standard by which other ball clubs evaluated themselves. After a third-place finish in 1920—winning 95 games left the Yankees just behind both the Indians and the White Sox—Ruth and his teammates ended atop the AL three years running. The roster included first baseman Wally Pipp, third baseman Home Run Baker, outfielder Bob Meusel, and pitchers Carl Mays, Waite Hoyt, Bob Shawkey, Bullet Joe Bush, Sad Sam Jones, and Herb Pennock. After losing to the Giants in both 1921 and 1922, Miller Huggins's Yankees won the franchise's first World Series title in 1923, with Ruth, who hit .393 during the regular season, his highest average ever, belting three homers and batting .368, while Pennock picked up a pair of victories.

Despite Ruth's leading the league in both homers (46) and batting (.378), the 1924 Yankees finished in second, two games back of the Senators. The next year, plagued by physical and emotional issues, Ruth stumbled, as did the seventh-place Yankees, who compiled the only losing record during his tenure with the team. The 1926 Yankees again won the pennant, with Ruth taking back the home run (47) and RBI (153) titles, and batting .372, while second-year man Lou Gehrig, who had replaced Pipp at first base, drove in over 100 runs, as did second baseman Tony Lazzeri. Twenty-three game winner Pennock, Urban Shocker, and Hoyt led the pitching staff. While that version of the Yankees fell to the Cardinals in a seven-game World Series, the next two editions swept the Pirates and the Cardinals.

Considered MLB's greatest team, the 1927 Yankees won 110 games, 19 games ahead of the improving Philadelphia Athletics. Scoring 158 runs, driving in 165, and batting .356, Ruth set a new single-season home run record, smacking 60. This occurred following a torrid September that ended spirited competition with Gehrig, who hit 47 homers, drove in 173, and batted .373 following Ruth in the vaunted Yankees lineup. Lazzeri again drove in over 100 runs, as did Meusel, while center fielder Earle Combs batted .356. Once again, Hoyt, Pennock, and Shocker were the top pitchers, but 30-year-old rookie Wilcy Moore surprised with a 19–7 record and a league-leading 2.28 ERA, often finishing Yankees contests. The Yankees swept the Pirates in four games, then did the same to the Cardinals the next year. Ruth delivered

54 homers and 146 RBIs, one behind Gehrig's top in the league mark, George Pipgras and Waite Hoyt were 20-game winners, Pennock added 17 wins.

Despite Ruth and Gehrig's remaining MLB's top slugging duo, the Yankees dropped to second, third, and second over the next three seasons, far behind the front-running Athletics. The 1932 Yankees won 107 games, 13 games in front of the Athletics, a team—particularly the pitching staff—that was starting to age. Thirty-seven-year-old Ruth had a fine season, although beneath his usual standard, while Gehrig delivered another stellar campaign. Lazzeri and Combs contributed too, as did catcher Bill Dickey, outfielder Ben Chapman, and pitchers Lefty Gomez, Red Ruffing, Johnny Allen, and Pipgras. New York swept the World Series for the third straight time, pummeling the Cubs with Ruth, Gehrig, Combs, Dickey, and Lazzeri, along with 38-year-old left-handed pitcher Pennock, leading the way. Gehrig topped all hitters with three homers, eight RBIs, and a .529 BA, but Ruth, as he did so often, stole the show, having pointed—or not—to where he intended to park Charlie Root's pitch before doing so during Game Three at Chicago's Wrigley Field on October 1, 1932. Root denied Ruth had called the shot.[8]

Experiencing another relative drought between 1933 and 1935, the Yankees, with Ruth worn down and then released, finished second each time, then experienced another and, at the time, unprecedented surge. Winners of four straight AL pennants, the Yankees also took the World Series each time, losing only three games in the process while completing a pair of sweeps. Now headed by MVP Gehrig, New York also had Dickey, Lazzeri, shortstop Frankie Crosetti, third baseman Red Rolfe, and outfielders George Selkirk, Jake Powell, and Joe DiMaggio, along with pitchers Lefty Gomez, Red Ruffing, Monte Pearson, and Johnny Murphy, in a star-studded, power-packed lineup. Twenty-one-year-old DiMaggio, a native of San Francisco and the Pacific Coast League, soon became the centerpiece of the latest Yankees dynasty, one that endured for his too brief 13-year career, shortened by three years of wartime military service and injuries. During his actual playing time, New York won ten pennants and nine World Series. By 1938, second baseman Joe Gordon, outfielder Tommy Heinrich, and pitcher Spud Chandler also starred, while the next season, outfielders Charlie Keller and George Selkirk, along with pitchers Bump Hadley, Atley Donald, Oral Hildebrand, and Steve Sundra, also became top contributors. Tragically, the 1939 campaign witnessed Gehrig's retirement following 2130 consecutive games played as the disease named after him continued to ravage his body.[9]

Following a third-place finish in 1940, albeit only two games behind the Tigers, the Yankees ran off three more pennants and a pair of World Series titles from 1941 to 1943. Having added shortstop Phil Rizzuto, the 1941 Yankees are most remembered for not only their victory over the Dodgers in the World Series but DiMaggio's record 56-game hitting streak that led to his receipt of the MVP despite Ted Williams's .406 batting average. Along with MVP Gordon, DiMaggio, and Keller, pitchers Tiny Bonham, Hank Borowy, Red Ruffing, Chandler, and Donald helped carry the Yankees to the next year's pennant, but the team fell in five games to the Cardinals. A patchwork Yankees squad, with DiMaggio in military uniform, led by Keller, Chandler, Bonham, and Murphy, wreaked revenge on St. Louis during the 1943 World Series. Two decidedly mediocre seasons followed, while even the return of the Yankee Clipper, Rizzuto, Heinrich, and Gordon from military service—Keller missed only the 1944 season—failed to prevent New York from finishing third in 1946, 17 games behind Boston.[10]

The team that became the Brooklyn Dodgers—after being called the Bridegrooms, Grooms, the Superbas, and the Robins, to name a few—experienced early mediocrity, pennants, doldrums, occasional success, extended stays in the second division, and rare season-long triumphs before attaining, during the Second World War, general excellence. The American Association's Brooklyn Bridegrooms won the pennant in 1889, as did the Bridegrooms, now in the National League, the next year. The top hitters were outfielders Darby O'Brien and Thomas Burns, the best pitcher, 40-game winner Bob Caruthers, in 1889. The following season, O'Brien, Burns, first baseman Dave Foutz, and third baseman George Pinkney led at the plate, with Caruthers, Adonis Terry, and 30-game winner Tom Lovett the leading pitchers. The 1889 Bridegrooms dropped the World Series to the New York Giants. The 1890 version inconclusively split the Series with the Louisville Colonels.

After a lengthy stretch of poor performances, the now-named Brooklyn Superbas won the National League pennant in both 1899 and 1900, managed by Ned Hanlon and featuring outfielders Willie Keeler and Joe Kelley, and second baseman Tom Daly, along with 20-game winners Jay Hughes, Jack Dunn, Brickyard Kennedy, and Joe McGinnity. Following third- and second-place finishes, the Superbas landed in the second half of the division for 12 straight years. Having inched up to fifth under new manager Wilbert Robinson in 1914, the Brooklyn Dodgers, as the franchise, now playing at Ebbets Field, was temporarily called, ended in third before the renamed Brooklyn Robins captured the 1916 pennant with a 94–60 mark, finishing two and a half games up on the defending champion Phillies. First baseman Jake Daubert, outfielder Zack Wheat, and 25-game winner Jeff Pfeffer guided the Robins into the World Series, which they lost in five games to the Red Sox. Brooklyn, in 1915, also featured the Tip-Tops, a Federal League team that finished seventh with a 70–82 record but had the circuit's top star, center fielder Benny Kauff, a two-time league batting and stolen base champion—the first year with the Indianapolis Hoosiers; Kauff later joined John McGraw's Giants.[11]

Tumbling to seventh before twice ending up in fifth, the Robins again won the pennant in 1920, their 93–61 record seven games better than McGraw's Giants. Wheat remained the top hitter, while Pfeffer and especially 23-game winner Burleigh Grimes contributed from the pitching mound. The Robins fell in the World Series to Tris Speaker's Indians. Other than a close runner-up finish in 1924, the Robins slid to the second division throughout the remainder of the decade, before amassing three straight winning records that at least placed them in the NL's first division. From 1933 to 1938, the once again Brooklyn Dodgers foundered mightily, then became more than respectable under their fiery player-manager, shortstop Leo Durocher, who guided them to third and second place, respectively.

In 1941, Brooklyn won its third title since the two leagues joined, winning one hundred games, a total only surpassed by the 1899 Superbas pennant winners. The Dodgers lineup included home run and RBI champion Dolf Camilli, the first baseman named MVP, who nosed out teammate Pete Reiser, the 22-year-old second-year batting champion, and fellow outfielders Joe Medwick and Dixie Walker. Both Kirby Higbe and Whit Wyatt won 22 games, while Hugh Casey anchored the relief staff. In a tense World Series, despite ending in five games, the Dodgers lost out to the Yankees.[12]

The 1942 Dodgers were even better, winning a then franchise-record 104 games, despite a career-altering injury suffered by Reiser, coming up two games short of the Cardinals. After finishing third, the Dodgers, crippled by the loss of key players to military service, plunged almost to the cellar before finishing third in 1945.

*****

New York City baseball was even richer than the game presented by the Giants, the Yankees, and the Dodgers. As indicated earlier, the great metropolis was also home to Blackball teams, including several fine ones with exceptional ball players. The Brooklyn Royal Giants, founded in 1904 and lasting into the early part of the Second World War, having lost considerable stature, did include notable players, among them Pop Lloyd, Smokey Joe Williams, and Louis Santop. The team's managers were among the greatest names in Black baseball: Grant Johnson, Sol White, Lloyd, Santop, and Cannonball Dick Redding. The Royal Giants were proclaimed champions of Eastern Blackball in 1909, 1910, 1914, when they dropped a five-game series to the Chicago American Giants, the Western champions, and 1916. In 1923, the Royal Giants, led by the white booking agent Nat Strong, joined the Eastern Colored League, became independents again in 1928, then briefly joined the Negro National League.

Beginning in 1911, their first season in a history that spanned almost three decades, the New York Lincoln Giants roared to a 108–12 record, fueled by catcher Santop, shortstop Lloyd, and pitchers Williams and Redding. That year, the Lincoln Giants captured the first of three consecutive titles, however unofficial, among Eastern Blackball clubs; second baseman Johnson, a high-average power hitter, joined the team in 1913, when the team bested the Chicago American Giants, Rube Foster's Western championship team. Skippers of the Lincoln Giants, who entered the Eastern Colored League in 1923 but switched to the Negro National League six years later, included White, Lloyd, and Williams. A strong Lincoln Giants team in 1930 fell to the Homestead Grays in an Eastern championship playoff.

Beginning during the mid-1910s, the Cuban Stars, stationed in Queens, began a 17-year run; their top performers included the dual threat Martin Dihigo, a brilliant pitcher and hitter, and outfielder Alejandro Oms, a three-time batting champion in the Cuban League. The team joined the Eastern Colored League in 1923, compiling the circuit's top record in 1928, but moved over to the American National League the next year.

Established in 1931, the year following the demise of the Lincoln Giants and the brief existence of the Harlem Stars—managed by the legendary Lloyd, who as a 47-year-old played first base—the New York Black Yankees would also run for almost 30 years. Initially financed by Bill "Bojangles" Robinson, the famed Black dancer and actor, and by James "Soldier Boy" Semler, a Harlem-based tailor and numbers runner, the team had Satchel Paige, George "Mule" Suttles, Willie Wells, and Ted "Double Duty" Radcliffe, a pitcher and catcher on the roster, however temporarily. Among the managers were Lloyd and Wells. The Black Yankees, frequently based at Yankee Stadium or the Polo Grounds, joined the Negro National League during the second half of the 1936 season, remaining in the circuit through 1948, after which the team opted for independent status.[13]

Playing at Ebbets Field in 1935, the Brooklyn Eagles, co-owned by Effa Manley, were led by star pitcher Leon Day, then merged with the Newark Dodgers to become the Newark Eagles. Resurrected from the Cuban Stars, Alex Pompez's New York Cubans, who started out as an NNL team in 1935, were outside the league in both 1937 and 1938, rejoined it in 1939, but wound down as a Negro American League squad in 1949 and 1950, briefly featured Dihigo, who managed for the first three years, third baseman Minoso, or Tiant, all Cuban born. The squad operated out of the Polo Grounds and became one of Blackball's powerhouse units, winning second-half championships in 1935 and 1941, then capturing the Negro League World Series championship in 1947.

One reason for the greater receptivity to New York City's Blackball was the growing percentage of African Americans residing within the metropolitan area. During the first decades of the Great Migration, that percentage jumped from 1.92 percent at its start in 1910 or so to 6.15 percent by 1940. In terms of sheer numbers, almost 92,000 African Americans were city residents in 1910, leaping to over 458,000 within three decades. Then, during the 1940s, the increase would continue with almost three-quarters of a million Black residents, comprising 9.47 percent of the population, dwelling in New York City by the end of the decade. If welcomed at Ebbets Park, the Polo Grounds, or Yankee Stadium, African Americans could boost National League and American League attendance.[14]

3

The Veterans Return

During the 1946 season, more players returned from military service, some with baseball skills diminished, others able to pick up right where they had departed. *Baseball Digest* displayed a cover with Bob Feller and another with Ted Williams and Joe DiMaggio, all AL superstars back from the military. Author Steve Treder indicates that 71 major leaguers "missed the 1942 season, 219 in 1943, 342 in 1944, and 384 in 1945." With rookies also returning from military service, fierce competition existed for limited MLB roster spots.[1]

The Yankees continued their recent less-than-stellar play, finishing third, seventeen games out of first place. Longtime manager Joe McCarthy, who, after leading the Cubs to a pennant, had guided the Yankees to eight pennants and seven World Series titles, quit 35 games into the season, replaced by first Bill Dickey and then Johnny Neun, as the Yankees went 87–67. More positively, their attendance total of 2,265,512 spectators topped the American League, in keeping with soaring numbers experienced during the first full season following the end of the Second World War. In blowing past the two-million mark, the Yankees shattered the previous record of 1,485,166 set by the Chicago Cubs in 1929. Attendance jumped 63 percent as both leagues set records.[2]

Military veterans were sprinkled throughout the Yankees roster and those of many other teams. Having missed three full seasons, DiMaggio was back in center field and managed 25 homers and 95 RBIs but missed several games, while batting .290, his first time below .300. He also finished 19th in MVP balloting, easily his weakest showing yet. Other returnees performed even more poorly, as second baseman Joe Gordon, playing in only 112 games, delivered 11 homers, 35 runs scored, 47 RBIs, and a .210 BA, each far and away the worst of his career. Shortstop Phil Rizzuto also appeared in only 126 contests, batting a mere .257. Playing in a career-high 150 games, outfielder Tommie Heinrich scored 92 runs and batted in 83, hit 19 homers, but batted .251, also his lowest mark ever. By contrast, Charlie Keller, who returned near the end of the previous season, had a largely solid campaign, scoring 98, driving in 101, and slamming 30 homers, with a .275 BA, which was below his standard. Thirty-eight-year-old Spud Chandler, back from almost two full years in the US Army, went 20–8 with a 2.10 ERA.

Continuing their recent lackadaisical or poor play, the 1946 New York Giants plunged to the bottom of the National League, with a 61–93 record placing them 36 games behind the front runners. After three years in the military, Mize suffered a broken toe, limiting him to 101 games, but he hit 22 homers, only one behind the league leader, and batted .337. Also returning from the military, outfielder Sid Gordon hit .293, albeit with little power. Despite their weak showing, the Giants drew 1,219,873 fans, third best in the NL.

Far more successful, Leo Durocher's Brooklyn Dodgers, welcoming 1,796,824 to Ebbets Field, finished the regular season tied with the St. Louis Cardinals at 94–60. Outfielder Dixie Walker led the Dodgers with 116 RBIs and a .319 BA, while military veterans Pee Wee Reese and rookie outfielder Carl Furillo both hit .284. Another veteran, reliever Hugh Casey, bolstered the pitching staff, going 11–5 with a 1.99 ERA in almost 100 innings of work. Also returning from military service were third baseman Cookie Lavagetto, Pete Reiser, Kirby Higbe, and rookie catcher Bruce Edwards. Unfortunately for Dodgers fans, their favorites dropped two straight to the Cardinals in the majors' initial best-of-three game playoff series.

Led by Williams and Stan Musial, the game's greatest hitters, the Boston Red Sox and the St. Louis Cardinals prevailed in their respective leagues, then faced off in a tight, seven-game World Series. The Red Sox, with skipper Joe Cronin, swept through the American League, winning 94 games, placing them 12 ahead of the Tigers and 17 better than the third-place Yankees.

Leading the charge, of course, was Williams, the Splendid Splinter returning from military service, who hit 38 homers, drove in 123, batted .342, and led the league in runs scored (142), walks (156), total bases (343), slugging (.667), OBP (.497), OPS (1.164), and OPS+ (215). He finally was named AL MVP. Another veteran, 24-year-old Dave Ferris delivered 25 victories for the team, while yet another returnee, Johnny Pesky, batted a career-best .335 batting average with a league-high 208 hits.

Taking their fourth pennant in five years, the 98–58 Cardinals, managed by Eddie Dyer, faced the Red Sox in the World Series. League MVP Musial played first base and dominated his league in runs scored (124), hits (228), doubles (50), triples (20), batting average (.365), slugging (.587), total bases (366), OPS (1.021), and OPS+ (183). Third sacker Whitey Kurowski hit .301, a point better than outfielder Enos Slaughter, whose 130 RBIs were tops in the league. Twenty-one game-winner Howie Pollet headed the pitching staff, depleted by the loss of Max Lanier, who had gone 6–0 with a 1.93, before bolting to the Mexican League. Winning their third recent World Series, the Cardinals were led by outfielder Enos Slaughter, who, running from first base, scored the winning run following an eighth-inning double by Harry Walker, with starter Harry Brecheen picking up his third win in relief.

On the playing field, MVP recipients Williams and Musial led their respective leagues and MLB in offensive WAR, while Cardinal shortstop Marty Marion topped the NL in defensive WAR and Red Sox second baseman Bobby Doerr tied White Sox shortstop Luke Appling in the AL. The Tigers' Hank Greenberg, with 44 homers and 127 RBIs, bested Williams in both those chases, although Williams beat out Greenberg in slugging percentage. The Indians' fireballer, Bob Feller, who lost almost four full years to military service, including naval combat in the Pacific Theater of Operations, and the Tigers' Hal Newhouser, turned down from the US military because of a heart murmur, were the top pitchers in baseball, each winning 26 games. Feller posted a brilliant 2.18 ERA, but Newhouser's 1.94 was the finest in the game. Newhouser struck out 275 batters, Feller 348, a new major league record, one that stood for almost two decades.[3]

*****

Both more and less attention than previously would be afforded Blackball, which like the major leagues, had been dramatically impacted by the Second World War. Throughout much of the conflict, the Grand Alliance, made up of the United States, Great Britain, with its global empire, and the Soviet Union, battled against the Axis powers, Nazi Germany, fascist Italy, and militarist Japan. No matter the evil they confronted, the members of the Grand Alliance had serious problems of their own. Joseph Stalin's communist dominance within the Soviet Union proved even more despotic than that of his predecessor, Vladimir Lenin. Great Britain presided over colonies exploited and dominated from outside. The US remained, at best, an imperfect democracy, beset by the stain of racism affecting people of color and even European immigrants viewed as less than ideal.[4]

On January 6, 1941, President Franklin Delano Roosevelt delivered his vision of a future world that would safeguard the very freedoms threatened by authoritarian regimes extolling war, militarism, and tyranny. Articulating a clear rationale for contesting the Axis, FDR's Four Freedoms address extolled freedom of speech and expression, worship, from want, and from fear, globally.

As the US participated in what many, including President Roosevelt and Vice President Henry A. Wallace, considered a war to save democracy from right wing totalitarianism, the American nation remained beset by terrible contradictions. Swedish economist-writer Gunnar Myrdal fastened onto "The American Dilemma": race. The war's advent and first, the increased likelihood of US engagement, and then, the nation's actual participation only heightened concerns about race relations.[5]

Activists led by the socialist and union activist A. Philip Randolph insisted that American defense plants must desegregate. He threatened a march on Washington unless the federal government halted Jim Crow practices in plants producing war materiel. Responding, President Roosevelt issued Executive Order 8802, declaring, "There shall be no discrimination in the employment of workers in defense industries and in Government, because of race, creed, color, or national origin."[6]

Shortly following US entrance into the war, the *Pittsburgh Courier*, one of the great African American newspapers, initiated the Double Victory Campaign, demanding a defeat of fascism overseas and of segregation at home. The journalist Edgar T. Rouzeau's article, "Black America Wars on Double Front for High Stakes," published on February 7, 1942, asserted:

> Where white Americans must fight on foreign soil for the salvation of the United States and for the preservation of "democracy," Black Americans must fight and die on these same battlefields, not merely for the salvation of America, not merely to secure the same degree of democracy for Black Americans that white Americans have long enjoyed, but to establish precedent for a world-wide principles of free association among men of all races, creeds and colors. That's the black man's stake.[7]

In May 1942, a small band of young people—some Black, some white—led by James Farmer, an organizer for the pacifist Fellowship of Reconciliation, engaged in a sit-in at the segregated Jack Spratt Coffee House located on East 47th Street in Chicago. This followed a sit-in at the Alexandria Library in Alexandria, Virginia, almost three years earlier. The protestors there, unlike those in Chicago, faced charges of disorderly conduct.

Notwithstanding Roosevelt's action and the framing of the war as a fight against fascism, the ugly reality of racism continued to surface, resulting in antidemocratic practices and waves of violence. The Roosevelt administration, despite its liberal cast, engaged in wholesale violations of the civil rights and civil liberties of Japanese Americans and Japanese citizens residing in the United States. Approximately 120,000 individuals of Japanese descent landed in ten concentration camps run by the War Relocation Authority, an action fueled by egregious ethnocentrism and racism.[8]

During the summer of 1943, a series of race riots erupted, including in Los Angeles, Detroit, and Harlem. The first, starting on June 3, was triggered by sailors claiming to have been attacked by zoot suiters, young Mexican Americans wearing suits that supposedly violated rationing restrictions. Over several days, zoot suiters, who included Black and Filipino American youngsters, were assaulted, with more than 500 individuals arrested. The worst race riot that the nation had experienced since the First World War's immediate aftermath broke out in Detroit, resulting in three days of violence—June 20–23—involving looting and arson, leading to 34 deaths, all but nine of whom were African Americans. Seventeen Black Americans died because of police intervention. Eventually, federal troops quelled the riot. In Harlem, another race riot occurred at the beginning of August, following a white policeman's shooting of an African American soldier, Robert Bandy. As rumors swirled that Bandy, who attempted to intervene when a Black woman was being arrested for disorderly conduct in a hotel, had been killed, a riot ensued. White-owned businesses were targeted, leading to six deaths, hundreds of injuries, and nearly 600 arrests.[9]

The US military continued to adhere to segregation practices throughout the Second World War. The Army, Navy, and Marine Corps ushered in African Americans—1.2 million altogether—but placed them in units apart from other soldiers. The Army often put white, Southern-born officers in charge of Black soldiers engaged in combat. Further indignities awaited African American soldiers, with US military "blood banks, hospitals or wards, medical staff, barracks and recreational facilities" segregated. The historian Matthew Delmont deems the experience "very dispiriting for a lot of Black soldiers," who referred to "being in slave-like conditions and being treated like animals." Frequent racial slurs came their way, basic respect and civility were often absent, and assigned tasks conformed to racial stereotypes.

Still, as the war dragged on and casualties mounted, the US military turned to African Americans to serve in combat roles, including "as infantrymen, officers, tankers and pilots." The Buffalo Soldiers, members of the 92nd Infantry Division, became the first Black soldiers waging combat during the Second World War in helping to drive German troops into Northern Italy. A Black division, the 761 Tank Battalion, helped Patton's Third Army liberate portions of France from Nazi control. The African American Tuskegee Airmen, operating for the US Army Air Corps, flew combat missions over Italy and Sicily. Although initially resistant, General Dwight David Eisenhower, supreme commander of Allied troops in Europe, established African American volunteer platoons that provided invaluable assistance during the brutal Battle of the Bulge in the winter of 1944–5.[10]

*****

Not surprisingly then, a push to integrate Organized Baseball continued, fueled largely by Lester Rodney, editor of the *Daily Worker*, the communist newspaper, and Black sportswriters Sam Lacy of the *Chicago Defender* and Wendell Smith of the *Pittsburgh Courier*. Scores of Negro Leaguers served in the US military during the war, including slugger Willard Brown, outfielder Monte Irvin, and pitchers Leon Day and Joe Black. Nevertheless, like the NL, the AL, and the minor leagues, Negro League play continued with Josh Gibson, Buck Leonard, and Satchel Paige remaining among the game's greatest stars. Indeed, prior to the start of the 1945 season, Kansas City Monarchs owner J. L. Wilkinson revealed, "Negro baseball last year had its greatest attendance. There seems to be a big demand for it. It's the only amusement that a lot of folks seem to get. We're going to play if it is at all possible."[11]

One young player joined the Kansas City Monarchs following acquittal in a court-martial proceeding. That resulted from his refusal to adhere to segregation practices on a bus near the base in south Texas where he was stationed. Lieutenant Jackie Robinson, his commission obtained following heavyweight boxing champion Joe Louis's assistance in his entering Officer Candidates School, was, like the great Black boxer, a nationally known athlete prior to his military service. A four-sport varsity athlete at UCLA, Robinson played a single 34-game season with the Kansas City Monarchs and was named to the prestigious East-West All-Star Game held in Chicago's Comiskey Park on July 29, 1945. Robinson went hitless in the contest, which lacked two of Blackball's greatest stars: Paige and Gibson. A financial dispute precluded Paige's participation, while the Homestead Grays had suspended Gibson, afflicted by alcoholism and drug usage.[12]

Gibson's growing instability and age—he turned 34 later in the year—precluded Branch Rickey from selecting him as the player to break Organized Baseball's color barrier, which had held firm since the late nineteenth century. Age and his independent, idiosyncratic ways undoubtedly prevented Paige, nearing 40 years of age if not already past that mark, from becoming chosen. Other possibilities included 23-year-old catcher Roy Campanella, the 1944 Negro National League batting champion (.388) and recent RBI leader, and the just turned 19-year-old pitcher Don Newcombe.

Rickey, now the Brooklyn Dodgers general manager, seriously considered Irvin, who had attended Lincoln University in Pennsylvania. Bob Kendrick, the Negro Leagues Baseball Museum president, later indicated, "Monte had the same exact qualities that Jackie had. He was college educated. He was stable.... Monte had everything to be a star. He was just an amazing man who just happened to be a great baseball player. You can make a case that he was a better baseball player than Jackie was at that time." The 26-year-old Irvin, after three years in the NNL, two of which were spectacular, had gone into the military, playing only seven league games between 1942 and 1945. That followed his 1940 and 1941 seasons, when he led the NNL with .380 and .387 batting averages. However, Irvin had experienced combat, particularly during the ferocious Battle of the Bulge, and appeared to be experiencing "shell shock" or "post-traumatic stress disorder."[13]

For a combination of reasons, then, Rickey turned to Robinson, who had excelled in a pair of tryouts with major league teams, one back in 1942 with the Chicago White Sox and another much more recently with the Boston Red Sox. Having received "glowing reports" from Dodger analysts, Rickey invited Robinson to meet at his Dodgers' office, where he grilled him as to whether the Black player was tough enough to withstand racial onslaughts without responding in kind. Robinson questioned, "Mr. Rickey, are you looking for a Negro who is afraid to fight back?" Angered, Rickey responded, "Robinson, I'm looking for a ballplayer with guts enough not to fight back."[14]

Signed to a minor league contract with the Dodgers' AAA team, the International League's Montreal Royals, which Rickey startled the sports world by announcing on October 23, 1945, Robinson, notwithstanding doubters such as Bob Feller, excelled on the baseball diamond. He led the IL in batting (.349), stolen bases (40), and fielding percentage at second base (.985), was named MVP, and helped his team win the Little World Series against the Louisville Colonels. In the process, he battled against racism, including that emanating from teammates and his manager, whom he won over with his showing on the baseball diamond and unwavering but fierce demeanor amid relentless pressure. Drawing fans both in Montreal and on the road, Robinson enabled the Royals to attract more fans than various AL or NL teams recently had.[15]

In an extended column, Red Smith referred to Robinson as "the model Negro infielder of the Dodgers' model Montreal farm." Jackie, he noted, was "a major attraction at home and on the road" as the Royals' attendance soared. Robinson's minor league manager, Clay Hopper, asserted, "I think he's a major leaguer. He goes hard all the time and he has great hands for an infielder." Regarding racist slurs, Robinson indicated, "There's been no trouble at all. I haven't heard anything worse than you hear in college football."[16]

It was vitally important for Robinson to succeed as baseball's "Great Experiment" unwound. Hardly the most accomplished Negro League star—he had played so few games, after all—Robinson was, unquestionably, among the nation's finest athletes. That athleticism allowed him to excel at the top minor league level and, from the vantage point of the Brooklyn Dodgers, hopefully augured well for his entrance into the NL. Along with the virulent racism still enveloping the American nation, the pressure on the still young African American proved to be extreme and unrelenting.

After all, race relations in the United States remained troubled, to put it mildly. African Americans, from former soldiers to members who comprised what W. E. B. Du Bois had referred to as the Talented Tenth, faced intensified efforts to put them "back in their place." Notwithstanding calls for "Victory Abroad and Victory at Home," veterans attired in military uniforms confronted violence, including from mobs angered about their wearing the uniform the soldiers had honored so heroically. Many were denied the benefits to which they were entitled through the Servicemen's Readjustment Act of 1944, the GI Bill; among those benefits were low-interest mortgages for houses, farms, and businesses, tuition and expense stipends, and unemployment compensation.[17]

Certain incidents were simply horrific. Traveling to meet his family in North Carolina, with his honorable discharge after serving in the Pacific theater of the war, 26-year-old Isaac Woodard was forced off a Greyhound Lines bus in Batesburg, South Carolina, on February 12, 1946. Police officers there pummeled Woodard with nightsticks and arrested him for disorderly conduct. The police chief beat Woodard, blinding him with his eyes "gouged out" by a billy club. A subsequent jury trial found the police chief not guilty of the assault. Another honorably discharged World War II veteran, 31-year-old John Cecil Jones, was arrested near Minden, located in Webster Parish, Louisiana, in early August. Beaten by deputies as he and a cousin were jailed despite no charges being leveled, Jones was lynched after being delivered to a mob.[18]

*****

As Baseball's Great Experiment unfolded amid stormy racial currents, 1946 proved notable for other reasons as well. Prior to the start of the season, major and minor leagues confronted a challenge from south of the border. The Pasquel brothers, well-heeled businessmen, engaged in a series of raids of ballplayers to bolster the Mexican League. The Pasquel brothers approached big league stars, including Joe Medwick, the 1937 NL MVP, and Cardinal shortstop Marty Marion, the MVP seven years later. Rumors of massive offers to Feller, Ted Williams, and Stan Musial, floated, while Tiger slugger Hank Greenberg expressed no interest in the Mexican League.[19]

Altogether, 22 big leaguers, half tied to the Giants or the Dodgers, accepted the Pasquels' entreaties. They included stars and lesser-known players, as well as those who would later make their mark in the major leagues, notwithstanding an edict from Commissioner A. B. "Happy" Chandler, the ex-Kentucky governor and senator, that those who jumped would be banned from Organized Baseball for five years. However, the Cardinals' Max Lanier, the NL's 1943 ERA leader, who had helped his team win both the 1942 and 1944 World Series, bolted, as did the Giants' Sal Maglie, whose greatest days on the playing field lay ahead. Actual Mexican League play proved less happy for many jumpers, including Lanier, who produced a league-best 1.93 ERA. "I thought the conditions would be better," indicated Lanier, displeased with inadequate facilities, rowdy fans, and a lack of professionalism.[20]

Salary disputes led to Lanier's decision to leave the Cardinals, although he battled with the Pasquels regarding his contract, too. Many MLB players shared such dissatisfaction, inducing a Harvard-educated attorney, Robert Murphy, to establish the American Baseball Guild, the latest in a series of efforts to convince players of the need to organize. The Guild sought a $7,500 minimum salary, no maximum salary, arbitration of salary squabbles, and half the money delivered to players "sold" to other teams. In early June, Murphy almost convinced the Pirates to strike before a game against the Giants.[21]

*****

In one of the final seasons experts and MLB consider "major," the Negro Leagues, notwithstanding the trickle of players departing for Organized Baseball, continued to perform top-flight ball. Biz Mackey's Newark Eagles won the Negro National League, while the team Robinson left, the Kansas City Monarchs, dominated the Negro American League. During his last campaign, Josh Gibson again produced the most homers and the highest slugging percentage, beating out Larry Doby, Irvin, Henry Kimbro, Willard Brown, and Buck Leonard, although his batting average "slipped" to .318 and his on-base percentage was the lowest of his career. Paige (4–0), said to be 40 years old, had the best win-loss percentage and a league-finest ERA (1.29).

Following the regular MLB and Negro League seasons, Bob Feller's Major League All-Stars, managed by Rollie Hemsley, played a 16-game set against Satchel Paige's Colored All-Stars, led by Frank Duncan. The major leaguers bested their Negro League counterparts 11–5, with Washington Senator first baseman Mickey Vernon starring at the plate, Spud Chandler and Dutch Leonard each winning three contests, while Feller, who started all but two games, lost his only decision despite striking out 39 in 33 innings and putting up a 2.00 ERA. Twenty-year-old Hank Thompson was the batting star for Paige's team, while Satchel went 1–3, whiffing 23 batters in one less inning than that.[22]

Another controversy loomed due to statements made by Feller, notwithstanding his barnstorming that included four games against the Robinson All-Stars, regarding Jackie and other Black ballplayers. "If he were a white man, I doubt they would consider him big league material." When asked if any of the Black participants in the barnstorming tour could make the majors, Feller replied, "Haven't seen one—not one." Reflecting further, he offered, "Maybe Paige when he was young."[23]

That same off-season, baseball experienced the loss of one of its greatest players, albeit one whose feats were not well-known even by most fans of the game. Succumbing to a stroke, Josh Gibson, only 35 years old, died. Newspaper accounts recalled a game against the Negro American League's Memphis Red Sox, played in Zanesville, Ohio, in 1938 when he belted four homers and another hit that flew over 500 feet. Considered the second-highest paid player in the Negro Leagues, Gibson received an annual salary of $6000 with an additional $3000 at times resulting from play in Latin America. Reports referred to "a brief illness," "rundown condition," and "failure to observe training rules" damaging his health. A silent tribute was slated to precede the Washington Grays's home opener.[24]

On December 5, 1946, President Harry S. Truman, responding to the spate of violence directed at African Americans since the end of the war, issued Executive Order 9808, establishing the President's Committee on Civil Rights. The Executive Order authorized the Committee "to inquire into and to determine whether and in what respect current law-enforcement measures and the authority and means possessed by Federal, State, and local governments may be strengthened and improved to safeguard the civil rights of the people."

Days prior to the start of 1947, sixteen men—eight Black, eight white—undertook what came to be known as the Journey of Reconciliation. This followed a Supreme Court ruling, *Morgan v. Virginia*, indicating that segregation on interstate buses violated the US Constitution's Interstate Commerce Clause. Beginning in Washington, D.C., on April 9, and lasting for two weeks, the civil rights activists, associated with the Congress of Racial Equality, the Fellowship of Reconciliation, and the American Friends Service Committee, traveled to Durham, North Carolina, then went back to the nation's capital. Along the way, arrests occurred, with various participants, including the white pacifist Jim Peck, assaulted. Three, including Bayard Rustin, a leader in the threatened March on Washington campaign, toiled for 22 days on a chain gang.

4

Postwar Baseball as the Negro Leagues Wither

Before 1947, New York City baseball teams, individually and in pairs, had established dynastic qualities. During the first decade and a half of the twentieth century, the New York Giants of McGraw and Mathewson threatened to become MLB's greatest but World Series failures, with the exception of 1905, along with the refusal to play the previous year, actually made them less successful than Connie Mack's Athletics or the Boston Red Sox. During the 1920s, for the first time, the Dodgers, Giants, and Yankees all won pennants, the initial such success for both the Dodgers and the Yankees since the National League and the American League merged. That was the decade when the New York Yankees supplanted the New York Giants as the greatest and most lucrative baseball franchise in the major leagues, which it would remain for much of the next century. The dominance established in the 1920s lengthened through the 1930s, when the Yankees became the first MLB team to win three and then four consecutive World Series.

The Second World War brought somewhat greater parity, largely between the Yankees and the St. Louis Cardinals, who threatened, with their latest World Series triumph in 1946, to establish their own dynasty. As matters turned out, the Cardinal pennant bounty was coming to an end, but ones involving the Yankees, yet again, and the Dodgers, for the first occasion in their lengthy history, would soon begin. The Giants too would eventually win a couple of additional NL titles during the 1950s but failed to create anything approaching a dynasty, for a variety of reasons.

This all began in 1947, the second full season for MLB following the Second World War, a time of startling changes impacting the national pastime. For the third straight year, attendance at major league games reached record levels, although the percentile increase from the previous season hardly matched that from 1945 to 1946. It was during the 1945 season when the Second World War came to an end and players, including some of the game's finest like Hank Greenberg and Bob Feller, returned from military service, however late in the campaign. For only the second time, total attendance surpassed ten million, with a record 8,813 fans on average showing up for MLB games that year. Then, pentup energy and complete seasons for Greenberg, Feller, Ted Williams, and Joe DiMaggio, among others, resulted in attendance mushrooming in 1946, with over 18 million fans, nearly 15,000 per game, sitting in big league ballparks. That figure increased to almost 20 million in 1947, with just under 16,000 fans present for MLB, which still offered a fast-played game generally lasting around two hours.[1]

Social chroniclers attribute some of the latest attendance bump to the entry of Negro League players, led by Jackie Robinson, who reshaped MLB in other ways as well. Robinson helped to return speed and a thinking man's approach to the game, both seemingly having disappeared or at least diminished since the long-ball emphasis spearheaded by Ruth and other sluggers. He also contributed mightily as the Dodgers, led by 62-year-old Burt Shotton following Leo Durocher's season-long suspension by Commissioner Chandler for "conduct deemed detrimental to baseball," turned the tables on the Cardinals, beating them out for the National League pennant by five games; Chandler's charge particularly involved Durocher's ties to gamblers. The cover of *Sport* magazine displayed a pensive Leo in the Brooklyn dugout, with the headline, "Durocher—Always on the Spot." The Braves were another three games back, the Giants in fourth, thirteen games behind the pennant winners, who went 94–60.[2]

During the season, the *New York Times*' Arthur Daley analyzed the Dodgers, deeming them "the darlings of the Flatbush Faithful," whose makeup had been shaped by "twin dynamos, Larry MacPhail and Leo Durocher," along with "the pontifical [Branch] Rickey." Now managed "by the sedate and kindly Burt Shotton" and with a diminishing of "the Durocher stamp," the Dodgers exuded "a more respectable mien." They also featured, among their very best players, former Negro Leaguer Robinson, constantly harassed by "curiosity seekers, Negro and white" as well as by photographers and sportswriters. Teammate Pee Wee Reese wondered, "Why don't they leave that kid alone?" But to Daley, Brooklyn had become "the best franchise in baseball" with "bandbox" Ebbets Field attracting "the Flatbush fanatics," who came from all walks of life. Baseball was "almost a religion in this borough of churches and the quaint," Daley observed.

Daley considered the Dodger president "the smartest and soundest organizer in baseball." The team that MacPhail and Rickey had put together, Durocher predicted, would "win seven out of the next ten" once it broke through, a prediction that all but came to pass. Daley deemed "Dodger rooters" who "live in hope" to be "in a class by themselves as the best and most fanatical group of fans in the entire sport." Such yearning continued although the franchise, before 1947, had won a mere three pennants over a time span covering more than four decades. Retaining "their wait-till-next-year slogan," Brooklyn fans accepted "each winning season as it comes."[3]

The Dodgers featured a balanced lineup, with Robinson hitting .297, catcher Bruce Edwards and outfielder Carl Furillo batting .295, outfielders Pete Reiser and Dixie Walker topping .300, and shortstop Reese hitting .284. The pitching staff featured 21-year-old Ralph Branca, a hard-throwing 21-game winner, 17-game winner Joe Hatten, and reliever Hugh Casey. The Dodgers also had a couple of young, still unproven players, catcher Gil Hodges and outfielder Duke Snider, each of whom would, of course, feature prominently in Brooklyn baseball history. But the obvious sparkplug was Robinson, stationed at first base to avoid inevitable physical clashes in the middle of the infield, scoring 125 runs, stealing an NL-best 29 bases, and delivering 31 doubles, a dozen homers, and a league-leading 28 sacrifice hits. He piled up 74 walks, in contrast to a mere 37 strikeouts. All of that led to Robinson's coming in fifth in the MVP race, a spot behind Edwards, another in back of Johnny Mize, the Giant's slugging first baseman. The Braves' third baseman Bob Elliot won the MVP, beating out the Reds' 22-game winner Ewell Blackwell.[4]

In the initial MLB Rookie of the Year contest, devised by *The Sporting News*, Robinson bested the Giants' 21-game winner Larry Jansen. Publisher J.G. Taylor Spink acknowledged that the Black pioneer may "have had more obstacles . . . and . . . perhaps a harder fight to gain even major league recognition" than his competition. However, "the sociological experiment that Robinson represented, the trail-blazing that he did, the barriers he broke down, did not enter into the decision" Spink insisted, however disingenuously. Rather, Robinson was evaluated on "his hitting . . . running . . . defensive play . . . team value." And Jackie "had it all" and "was spectacularly outstanding" when viewed against other first-year players. Even Dixie Walker, initially a reluctant teammate, supposedly ready to refuse to play alongside a Black ballplayer, admitted that Robinson had "done more to put the Dodgers up in the race," except perhaps for catcher Edwards. Robinson, Walker asserted, "is everything that Branch Rickey said he was when he came up from Monteral."

Continuing to laud Robinson, Spink wrote that Jackie had "been a National League eye-popper . . . because he has run the bases like an Ebony Ty Cobb," while "his hotfooting," joined with that of Pete Reiser, "has typed the Dodger play." Such success followed a slow start, charges he wasn't big league material, and getting plunked at the plate. Encouraged by Rickey to "take that extra base every time," Robinson "began to turn it on, with spectacular success." His hitting came alive, nearing the .300 mark.[5]

Robinson's brilliant performance overshadowed how precarious Baseball's Great Experiment actually was. After a brief stint in the Negro Leagues, he moved into Organized Baseball, excelling with first Montreal and then Brooklyn at the plate, in the field, on the basepaths, and through his ability, however unhappily, to tolerate what no player should have had to endure. Confronting the discrimination that the national pastime was still heavily afflicted with and notwithstanding doubters, Robinson succeeded in truly remarkable fashion. Had he not, such a lack of success could have dampened or even halted the readiness of Rickey and other big league magnates to open the doors to Black players, no matter how gifted. His blend of talent, perseverance, and temperament enabled Robinson to defy critics and the kinds of obstacles besetting no other player, at least since segregation beset Organized Baseball.[6]

Well into the season, *Time* magazine placed Robinson on its cover. Opening an extended article, "Rookie of the Year," the *Time* staff referred to a game during which Cardinals' Enos Slaughter spiked Robinson at first base, resulting in a "ripped stocking and bleeding leg." This "might have been an accident, but Jackie didn't think so. Neither did a lot of others who saw the play. Jackie set his teeth, and said nothing. He didn't dare to." Teammates told Robinson, "If they give you the works, give it back to them—and the team will be behind you 100%." Weeks later, the front-running Dodgers and second-place Cardinals met again, with "trigger-tempered Catcher Joe Garagiola" spiking Robinson. A "rhubarb" threatened between Robinson and Garagiola during the next inning, but the umpire intervened. Nevertheless, "it was a sign, and an important one, that Jackie had established himself as a big leaguer. He had earned what comes free to every other player: the right to squawk."[7]

Robinson was experiencing, *Time* indicated, "the toughest first season any ballplayer has ever faced. He had made good as a major leaguer, and proved himself as a man," getting chosen as Rookie of the Year. While *The Sporting News* downplayed the significance of "the sociological experiment that Robinson represented," Jackie did not, recognizing that "he, his teammates and the National League had broken baseball's 60-year color line." This came a mere two years after Hall of Famer Rogers Hornsby indicated, "Ballplayers on the road live close together . . . it won't work." Robinson, "one of the great all-around athletes of his day," had "made it work," hitting baseballs "on the dead run," displaying "daring" on the base paths, "keeping the enemy's infield upset and off balance, and worrying the pitcher."[8]

That same season when Robinson thrived with the Dodgers, Larry Doby, Willard Brown, and Hank Thompson, far more established Negro Leaguers, along with Jackie's teammate Dan Bankhead, also entered major league ball. While outfielder Doby, who had excelled with the Newark Eagles, batting .354 in 30 games, he hit only .156 with a mere five hits in thirty-two official plate appearances for the Cleveland Indians. Brown, a feared, high-average slugger with the Monarchs, managed only a dozen hits in 67 at bats for the St. Louis Browns, during his lone experience in Organized Baseball. Another Monarch power hitter, infielder-outfielder Hank Thompson batted .256 in 78 official at bats with the St. Louis Browns, with only two extra-base hits.

A star hurler, mostly with the Birmingham Black Barons, Bankhead pitched ten innings over four games with a 7.20 ERA.[9]

In contrast to the Brooklyn Dodgers, who hit only 83 homers, topped by Robinson and Reese with 12 apiece, the also-ran New York Giants, blowing past both the previous NL and MLB team records, quashed 221 homers, 100 more than in 1946, when they also topped the National League. Thirty-four-year-old Johnny Mize, the Big Cat, smacked 51 homers, tying the Pirates' Ralph Kiner for the major league lead. Other Giant sluggers included outfielder William Marshall (36), catcher Walker Cooper (35), and rookie outfielder Bobby Thompson (29), with league-leader Mize (138), Cooper, and Marshall each also driving in more than 100 runs. Jansen had a brilliant rookie year on the mound, and Dave Koslo won 15 games, but no other Giant pitcher compiled a win total in double digits.

The 1947 New York Yankees, with the majors' best record of 97–57 finish, 12 games ahead of the Tigers and 14 in front of the defending AL champion Red Sox. Joe DiMaggio topped the Yankees with 97 runs scored and RBIs, 31 doubles, 10 triples, 20 homers, and a .315 batting average, resulting in his third MVP. Ted Williams, despite winning the triple crown and more than doubling DiMaggio's WAR total (9.5 to 4.7), while also easily leading the league in on-base percentage, slugging, and OPS, each far beyond DiMaggio's marks, got only three first-place votes in the MVP race, losing out to DiMaggio by a single ballot. Yankees reliever Joe Page, who went 14–8 with a 2.48 ERA and 17 saves, finished fourth in the MVP contest, but pulled in seven first-place votes, only one back of his teammate. Third baseman Billy Johnson and outfielder Tommy Heinrich drove in 95 and 97 runs, respectively, while Heinrich and second baseman Snuffy Stirnweiss scored more than 100 runs apiece. Allie Reynolds, a hard-throwing right-hander just acquired from the Indians, went 19–8, while rookie Spec Shea was 14–5 with a league-best .737 win-loss percentage. Starting 14 games, rookie right-hander Vic Raschi, a World War II veteran, put up a 7–2 record, the harbinger of even betters things to come.[10]

The Yankee-Dodger clash was viewed as a contest involving power against speed, particularly exemplified by Robinson and Reiser. In a bitterly contested World Series that went the distance and included Game Four, during which

New York pitcher Bill Bevens lost a no-hitter and the game with two outs in the bottom of the ninth, the Yankees beat the Dodgers for the second time. Shea won twice, Reynolds and Page once each, with the Yankees rebounding from an early 2–0 deficit behind the reliever's five scoreless innings, during which he allowed a lone single, and the hitting of shortstop Phil Rizutto. DiMaggio belted a pair of homers in the Series, outfielder Johnny Lindell drove in seven runs, two more than DiMaggio and Heinrich. Both Rizutto and Heinrich batted over .300, as did the Dodgers' Furillo and Reese. Casey won two games and saved another. Robinson, the first Black player in the World Series, contributed seven hits and a pair of steals in a losing effort.[11]

As Robinson's entry into the National League and the World Series garnered massive attention, the Negro Leagues continued during the next-to-last season MLB and baseball historians consider to have been "major." Before departing for the St. Louis Browns, the Kansas City Monarchs' Williard Brown led the Negro American League in batting (.371). Following his abbreviated, unsuccessful stint with the Browns, he won the Triple Crown in the Puerto Rican Winter League. Other top hitters included Sam Jethroe and Hank Thompson, who would also soon enter Organized Baseball. The Monarchs top pitchers were Jim LaMarque, Ford Smith, and 40-year-old Hilton Smith. Nevertheless, Kansas City came in second behind the Cleveland Buckeyes in the Negro American League, while the New York Cubans prevailed in the Negro National League. The Baltimore Elite Giants' Henry Kimbro won the batting crown (.385), beating out teammate Johnny Washington, the Cubans' Minnie Minoso, and the Newark Eagles' Larry Doby.

Top Negro Leaguers gathered at the Polo Grounds for an All-Star contest attended by 38,402 fans. Leading hitters included the Birmingham Barons' Art Wilson, who got four singles, and the Cleveland Buckeyes' Sam Jethroe, who produced two singles, a triple, and four RBIs. Other participants included Bob Boyd, Quincy Troupe, Monte Irvin, Minoso, Luis Tiant, and Joe Black.

Although little acknowledged at the time, New York baseball acquired another notch from the 1947 Negro League World Series. Prevailing in the sixth game of a best-of-seven playoff, the New York Cubans, led by Minoso and Claro Duany, each of whom batted over .400, topped Cleveland, whose Leon Kellman outhit everyone in the short series. Third baseman Minoso's

.356 batting average, shortstop Silvio Garcia's .335, and right fielder Duany's .321 were the leading Cuban batsmen during the regular season, while 40-year-old left-handed pitcher Tiant was undefeated in nine decisions. The Buckeyes, with the finest regular season record, 57–19, included first baseman Archie Ware, right fielder Willie Grace, center fielder Jethroe, and shortstop Al Smith, all of whom hit over .300. Nineteen-year-old southpaw pitcher Webbo Clarke headed the pitching staff.

Although the Negro National League and the Negro American League apparently concluded another successful year, former Negro Leaguer Robinson's incredible display of fortitude and athletic prowess continued to weigh heavily on Blackball. It ensured that National League and American League teams would pursue other Negro League stars. It initiated a considerable dip in attendance at Negro League games, with both Black patrons and Black sportswriters shifting their attention, particularly, to the Brooklyn Dodgers. Negro League team owners recognized their game and livelihood had become more precarious than ever.

*****

On October 29, the President's Committee on Civil Rights issued *To Secure These Rights*. Declaring "the time is now" to implement recommendations, the report urged "elimination of segregation, based on race, color, creed, or national origin, from American life." It pointed to discrimination "in private employment," public and private schools, housing, health care, and the US Armed Forces. The committee called for congressional legislation ensuring no American soldier encountered "discrimination of any kind by any public authority or place of public accomodation, recreation, transportation, or other service or business."[12]

On February 2, Truman delivered a special message to Congress regarding civil rights. American ideals were incomplete, the president contended, while "any American suffers discrimination" due to "race, or religion, or color, or the land of origin." The federal government, Truman insisted, possessed "a clear duty" to protect constitutionally safeguarded liberties and equal protection under the law.[13]

*****

The 1948 season resulted in a rare absence of New York teams from postseason play, along with unanticipated pennant winners in the American and National leagues, and more predictable ones in the Negro Leagues. Perennial powerhouses, the Kansas City Monarchs and the Homestead Grays, were declared winners of the Negro American League and the Negro National League, respectively. But the Cleveland Indians won their first AL pennant in 28 years, the Boston Braves their first NL title in 34.

As their most diehard fans saw matters, the New York Yankees, the Brooklyn Dodgers, and the New York Giants compiled less than satisfactory records. The Yankees, despite a 94–60 record, landed in third place in the American League, costing Bucky Harris his job. DiMaggio had his final great, full season, leading the league in homers (39), RBIs (155), and total bases (355), while batting .320. Fellow outfielders Johnny Lindell and Tommy Heinrich also hit over .300. Heinrich led the league in runs scored (138) and triples (14), slammed 25 homers, and drove in 100 runs. Twenty-three-year-old catcher Yogi Berra belied the supposed jinx involving a sophomore slump, batting .305 and driving in 98 RBIs. Infielder Bobby Brown, the same age as Berra, hit .300. The pitching staff, headed by three aces, boded well for the future. Joining right-hander Allie Reynolds were lefty Eddie Lopat, traded from the White Sox, and Vic Raschi, who had briefly appeared in 1946 and then contributed to the next year's World Series-winning team.

Early stumbling during the quest to repeat their 1947 NL pennant, the Dodgers fired manager Leo Durocher, who had returned from a year's suspension. Burt Shotton again replaced him and the team responded by playing better, just not well enough to beat out the Braves or the Cardinals, the Dodgers' fiercest rivals throughout the decade. Nevertheless, the 1948 version of the Brooklyn Dodgers approached that later heralded, most famously by Roger Kahn, as the Boys of Summer. Twenty-six-year-old Negro League veteran Roy Campanella played just over half the games, many behind the plate where he soon became a Brooklyn fixture. Campanella shared time with Bruce Edwards, the star catcher who had suffered a spring training arm injury. Also breaking into the starting lineup was another still raw but promising player, 24-year-old first baseman Gil Hodges, while 21-year-old center fielder Duke Snider usually rode the bench.

Leading the Dodgers with a .327 batting average in just over 300 official plate appearances was rookie outfielder Marv Rackley, who lacked power, in contrast to fellow outfielder Gene Hermanski, a .290 hitter with a team-high 15 homers. Carl Furillo batted .297 but also displayed little power, while Jackie Robinson, after a slow start, scored 108 runs, collected 170 hits, delivered 12 homers, drove in 85, and batted .296, a mere point behind his Rookie of the Year performance. Rex Barney, Ralph Branca, Joe Hatten, and Preacher Roe were also serviceable starters, with Roe having the best season, delivering a 2.63 ERA. Displaying considerable promise was 21-year-old rookie right-hander Carl Erskine, who went 6–3 with a 3.23 in 64 innings pitched. Slipping badly was Hugh Casey, the once formidable relief stalwart bedeviled by an aging arm and a penchant for heavy drinking.

The middle-of-the-pack New York Giants, who replaced manager Mel Ott with Durocher after Leo was fired by the Dodgers, still relied on the long ball, with the now 35-year-old Johnny Mize, whose 40 homers again tied Ralph Kiner for the NL crown, while Sid Gordon hit a career-high 30 homers and a team-best .299. Once more, Larry Jansen headed the pitching staff, winning 18 games, as Sheldon Jones added 16 victories but no other Giant won more than 11.

In an extremely tight race, the Indians nipped the Red Sox by one game, with the Yankees two and a half games back. The Braves were six and a half games better than the Cardinals, seven and a half up on Dodgers, eight and a half ahead of the Pirates, and thirteen and a half in front of the fifth-place Giants. Cleveland only won the pennant following a one-game playoff against Boston, in which the Indians prevailed, 8–3. Indian manager-shortstop Lou Bourdeau hit a pair of homers as 27-year-old rookie starter Gene Bearden won his twentieth, while surprise starter Denny Galehouse, a 36-year-old journeyman Red Sox manager Joe McCarthy inexplicably handed the ball to, fell to 8–8. Bourdeau went four for four, scoring three times, while third baseman Ken Keltner got three hits, including a homer, and drove in three. Second baseman Bobby Doerr homered for the Red Sox, but Ted Williams went only one for four, dropping his league-leading average to .369.

The MLB regular season was dominated by St. Louis outfielder-first baseman Stan Musial, Williams, and Bourdeau at the plate and the Braves' Johnny Sain, the Tigers' Hal Newhouser, and the Indians' Bearden on the mound. In his greatest season, Musial led the league in runs scored, hits, doubles, triples, RBIs, batting average, total bases, OBP, slugging average, OPS, and OPS+. While batting .376, slugging at a .702 clip, and amassing 429 total bases, NL MVP Musial just missed out on the triple crown, falling one homer—a career-best 39—behind co-league leaders Johnny Mize and the Pirates' Ralph Kiner. Topping the AL in doubles, walks, slugging average, OBP, OPS, OPS+, and batting average, Williams came in behind Bourdeau and DiMaggio in the MVP balloting. Bourdeau had career-best totals in runs scored, homers, RBIs, batting average, and slugging percentage.

Boston Post sports editor Gerald Hern helped popularize the notion, "Spahn and Sain and pray for rain," as the Braves raced to a surprising first-place finish in the NL. Sain won a major league high 24 games, completed 28 games, and tossed over 300 innings, while his pitching partner, left-hander Warren Spahn, actually had one of his weaker seasons, winning but 15. Newhouser won over 20 games for the fourth and final time to lead the American League, one better than 20-game winners and teammates Bearden and Bob Lemon. Five-time 20-game winner Bob Feller fell one short of that mark, as prolonged military service and pitching usage wore down his magnificent pitching arm. Arguably, nobody pitched better than the Cardinals' Harry Brecheen in 1948, as he went 20–7 with a league-leading 2.24 ERA and 7 shutouts.

The pennant-winning Indians had three top-flight starters and a fine relief staff, which included Satchel Paige, a 42-year-old American League rookie who went 6–1 with a 2.48 ERA while tossing a pair of shutouts. The well-balanced lineup had second baseman Joe Gordon's 32 homers and 124 RBIs, Ken Keltner's 31 homers and 119 RBIs, and .300 plus hitters Bourdeau, outfielder Dale Mitchell, and outfielder Doby, rebounding from his aborted rookie year. Outfielders Tommy Holmes, Jeff Heath, and Mick McCormick all hit above .300 for the Braves, as did middle infielders Al Dark and Eddie Stanky, while Bob Elliot drove in 100.

MLB set an attendance record in 1948, averaging 16,912 fans during the regular season, although the games were longer than ever, lasting an average of 2 hours and 23 minutes per contest. The Cleveland Indians established several attendance marks with 72,562 individuals appearing for a nighttime battle against the Washington Senators on August 3. Altogether, 2,620,627 fans watched Indian home games; the 33,173 average per game attendance beat out the Yankee Stadium mark of 30,830. On October 2, 86,288 fans watched Game Five of the World Series at Cleveland's Municipal Stadium.

In six games, the Indians beat the Braves in the 1948 World Series, despite longtime ace Feller dropping both the opener and Game Five. Led instead by Lemon's two well-pitched outings, the Indians also relied on catcher Jim Hegan's five RBIs, while the Series' hitting star, Elliott, slammed a pair of homers in batting .333.[14]

*****

During the middle of the 1948 season, Jackie Robinson's face appeared on the cover of *Ebony*, the monthly magazine targeting an African American audience, issued by John H. Johnson, who headed the Chicago-based Johnson Publishing Company. Alongside the Dodger's image was a small box indicating "'WHAT'S WRONG WITH NEGRO BASEBALL?' By Jackie Robinson." The feature article was a scathing indictment of the brand of baseball that had set the stage for Branch Rickey's pursuit of Robinson. Acknowledging his stay in Blackball had been "short," Robinson nevertheless felt certain "Negro baseball . . . needs a housecleaning from top to bottom." "The bad points," he contended, "range all the way from the low salaries paid players and sloppy umpiring to the questionable business connections of many of the team owners." Robinson blasted uncomfortable travel conditions, cheap, "dingy and dirty" hotel accomodations, "lax" rules, and "the failure to enforce the rules." But Robinson also revealed the racism he confronted in Organized Baseball at both the minor and major league levels.[15]

Indeed, for several years after a trickle of Negro Leaguers integrated the NL and the AL, those players confronted segregation whenever their teams trained in the South or Cuba. Other than the Dodgers, who admittedly assigned four Negro League players—Robinson among them—to a different hotel from where their teammates stayed in Havana, that was true even for MLB facilities. The historian Louis Moore indicates,

Black players on all other squads had to lodge with Black families or at a Black-owned motel. They could not eat with their teammates, and if they wanted to to eat at a Black restaurant instead of taking their meals outside of a white establishment, they had to take a Black taxi. Some teams would not even mix the laundry.

Stadiums throughout spring training retained segregated seating, enraging Black players, their wives, and Black fans.[16]

*****

On July 26, President Truman had issued Executive Order 9981, a decree addressing some of what Robinson encountered during his military service. Truman indicated, "There shall be equality of treatment and opportunity for all persons in the armed services without regard to race, color, religion or national origin." The policy was to be implemented "as rapidly as possible."[17]

Truman also presented Executive Order 9980, declaring that American principles demanded "a policy of fair employment" in the federal sector. Each executive branch department or agency required a Fair Employment Officer.[18]

Three days later, Truman became the first president to deliver a speech to the NAACP, gathered for its 38th Annual Conference; the speech was piped out to a nationwide radio audience. Praising the organization, he declared, "It is my deep conviction that we have reached a turning point in the long history of our country's efforts to guarantee a freedom and equality to all our citizens." The federal government, Truman indicated, needed to stand as "a friendly, vigilant defender of the rights and equalities of all Americans."[19]

The twin directives and the address to the NAACP were presented amid mounting pressure from opposite sides of the political spectrum on Truman, who was involved in a bid for election to a full term as president. The segregationist Dixiecrats had bolted from the Democratic Party. From the left, A. Philip Randolph informed Truman that many Black Americans might defy Selective Service directives should the Armed Forces remain discriminatory. Newly elected Representative Leo Isacson, who was tied to former vice president Henry Wallace's Progressive Party presidential bid, also insisted Truman initiate civil rights action.[20]

*****

Responding to criticisms of the Negro Leagues, Effa Manley, the Newark Eagles' co-owner with her husband Abe, indicated, "I charge Jackie Robinson with being ungrateful. He is where he is today because of organized Negro baseball. I believe that he never would have been noticed if it were not for the people and the teams he derides." Refuting Robinson's indication that Branch Rickey "was fair and democratic," Manley claimed the Dodger executive "paid the Kansas City Monarchs nothing for Robinson." By contrast, the Cleveland Indians handed the Manleys $15,000 for Larry Doby.[21]

Less than a week earlier, the Homestead Grays won the last Negro League World Series, beating the Birmingham Black Barons in five games. The Grays nipped the Baltimore Elite Giants, with a .636 win-loss percentage just hundreds of a point better than the second-place finisher. Thirty-six-year-old Lester Lockett of the Elite Giants had the top batting mark (.362), ahead of the Philadelphia Stars' Frankie Austin, the Newark Eagles' Bob Harvey, and the New York Cubans' Minnie Minoso. The Elite Giant's Bill Byrd, Joe Black, and Jonas Gaines were among the top pitchers, as was the Eagles' Max Manning.

The Black Barons nipped the Kansas City Monarchs in the Negro American League, where Birmingham's Artie Wilson led all of Black baseball with a scorching .433 batting average. The Monarchs' Willard Brown also topped .400, a mark the Black Barons' Piper Davis just missed. Top NAL hurlers included the Monarchs' Jim LaMarque and the Black Barons' Jimmie Newberry.

The normal excitement generated by the Negro League World Series proved somewhat muted, tempered by the introduction of Black players into the National and American leagues and their upcoming World Series, in which Satchel Paige and Larry Doby would play. The 1948 Negro League World Series did feature the Grays' slugging first baseman Buck Leonard, left fielder Luke Easter, right fielder Bob Thurman, and pitchers Tom Parker and Wilmer Field. It also exhibited the Black Barons' second baseman Davis, shortstop Wilson, right fielder Ed Steele, and pitchers Newberry, Alonzo Perry, and Bill Powell. The Barons also had on their roster a 17-year-old outfielder, whose playing skills were still being honed: Willie Mays.[22]

Blackball's fate was apparent with the NNL's termination following the 1948 Negro League World Series. The Grays opted to barnstorm, which proved an unsuccessful endeavor. The New York Black Yankees ceased operations. The Newark Eagles, sold by the Manleys, headed for Houston, Texas. "We are not quitters," Effa Manley stated, "but it is just impossible for us to continue." Criticizing Branch Rickey, Manley also attacked "the gullibility and stupidity of Negro baseball fans themselves in believing that he has been interested in anything more than the clicking of the turnstiles."[23]

After the AL-NL World Series, publisher J.G. Taylor Spink, writing in his "Looping the Loops" column for *The Sporting News*, produced a subheading, "Doby's Play Make the Eagles Scream." That referred to Doby's having led the Cleveland Indians with a .318 batting average. During a conversation with Manley, Spink listened to her exult, "I knew he would do it, and just watch him for the next two years." Pleased with Doby's success, Manley emphasized "the matter of the Negro players' efforts to get stronger representation in the National and American leagues, on an honest basis." She declared, "You know, I think that fate arranged it all, sent Doby to us here, and made me a sort of agent in this vital, this very involved situation having to do with the Negro in the major leagues. And the effort to solve the complex problems of social mixing in the American pastime."[24]

The Negro American League soldiered on but lacked the aura of legitimacy that had previously sustained it. Blackball suffered too from some of what Jackie Robinson had recently criticized. Another factor, one that would begin to impact Organized Baseball, was the ability of fans to take in National League and American League games on television. As the year neared an end, another Negro League star, Monte Irvin, whose Newark Eagles had disbanded as he starred in the Cuban League, signed a contract with the Dodger's farm team in St. Paul, Minnesota.[25]

Meanwhile, President Truman, to implement Executive Order 9981, appointed the Fahy Committee, formally known as the President's Committee on Equality of Treatment and Opportunity in the Armed Forces. In mid-January 1949, its seven members met with the president, as well as the Army, Navy, Air Force, and Defense secretaries. At the beginning of the session,

Truman referred to the executive order's insistence "on the better treatment—not 'fair' treatment—but 'equal' treatment in the Government Service for everyone, regardless of his race or creed or color." He wanted the committee members to "actually carry out the spirit, as well as the letter, of the order," pertaining to the military and "all the branches of the Federal Government."[26]

5

A New Yankee Dynasty amid the Boys of Summer and Leo's Giants

On October 12, 1948, President Dan Topping named 57-year-old Casey Stengel the new manager of the New York Yankees, with the understanding that the former Braves and Dodgers skipper would receive a two-year contract paying $50,000. Stengel had played in the major leagues from 1912–25, attaining his greatest success as a part-timer with the pennant-winning New York Giants in 1922 and 1923, ironically particularly excelling in the latter's year World Series battle against the Yankees.[1]

A nine-year managing career with NL teams in Brooklyn and Boston had proven uneventful and largely unsuccessful with two fifth place finishes and a single winning season—that by a mere game—the top performances. Let go by the Braves following the 1943 season, Stengel began managing in the minors, including, in 1945, for the AA Kansas City Blues, tied to the Yankees. The next year, he began skippering the Oakland Oaks of the Triple-A Pacific Coast League, leading them to the pennant and a playoff victory in 1948, resulting in *The Sporting News*' designating him Minor League Manager of the Year. Yankees general manager George Weiss explained the decision to annoint Stengel as the Yankees' 13th manager. "We combed the lists of everybody in baseball—major and minor leagues—for our new manager, and Stengel proved the most capable. He's got great patience with young players. He gets along well with his players and he's a 24-hour manager." For his part, Stengel indicated, "We've got a great bunch of players."[2]

Dan Daniel of *The Sporting News* considered Stengel to be confronting the toughest task of any new Yankees skipper since 1918, the first season of the then new manager Miller Huggins. Indicating that Weiss was going to offer little assistance, Daniel suggested that "infielders are finished, outfielders won't do, the catching is in need of help, the pitching looks sickly." Still stunned by his ouster, outgoing manager Bucky Harris wondered, "Why did I get fired?" As the start of the 1949 season loomed, purported experts viewed the Yankees as shaky at best, predicting a fourth-place finish behind the Red Sox, the Indians, and even Connie Mack's Athletics.[3]

Notwithstanding Daniel's assessment of the Yankees' roster and the less-than-favorable predictions, what followed over the course of the next five years was still unanticipated and unprecedented as the Yankees, under Stengel, began a run of five consecutive AL pennants and World Series championships. In pushing past the previous mark established by the 1936–9 Yankees of McCarthy, Gehrig, and DiMaggio, the latest Yankees dynasty beat out Ted Willliams's Red Sox, the Detroit Tigers and Hal Newhouser, the Cleveland Indians with general manager Hank Greenberg, an old Yankees nemesis, and Al Lopez's Chicago White Sox, often in tight pennant chases. Their World Series triumphs came against the Dodgers on three occasions, a surprising Phillies team, and the Giants.[4]

In the process, the Yankees might well have prevented another dynasty from fully flowering the one based in Brooklyn's Ebbets Field. But for Stengel's Yankees, the Dodgers, who won pennants in 1949, 1952, and 1953, and missed out on two others—in 1950 on the last day of the season and the next year, when they fell in a best-of-three playoff to the Giants—might have been the era's super team. By contrast, New York City's other team, those Giants, were far more inconsistent, ranging from a 73–81 fifth-place record in 1949 to a 86–68 third-place mark the next year to winning the pennant in 1951. Finishing runner-up in 1952, they slid to a fifth place, 70–84 record in 1953.

With DiMaggio suffering from an inflamed heel that limited him to 76 games, the 1949 Yankees lineup, devised by Stengel often in platoon-like fashion, relied on steady performances as many hit in the .270s or .280s range.

It lacked the power of many previous Yankees squads, producing only 115 homers. As injuries continued to mount, Red Smith indicated that "no team ever succeeded in the face of greater adversity than the Yankees . . . with their sixty-odd disabling injuries."[5]

Thirty-six-year-old Tommy Heinrich still delivered 24 homers and 85 RBIs while hitting .287. Twenty-four-year-old Yogi Berra became a star behind the plate, adding 20 homers and a team-best 91 RBIs. Finishing second in the MVP race, shortstop Phil Rizzuto anchored the infield, while scoring 110 runs. With only 272 official at bats, DiMaggio managed 14 homers, 58 runs, 67 RBIs, and a 1.055 OPS. The Yankees continued to rely on their three top-flight starting pitchers—Allie Reynolds, Eddie Lopat, and the now 21-game winner Vic Raschi—and added Tommy Byrne, all backed by reliever Joe Page.

A game behind with two days left in the regular season, the Yankees went head-to-head with the front-running Red Sox, featuring shortstop Vernon Stephens, who ended with 39 homers and 159 RBIs, and Ted Williams, with a career-best, league-leading 43 homers and 159 RBIs, along with a .343 batting average that left him just shy of a third triple crown. Left-hander Mel Parnell won 25 games, two more than Ellis Kinder.

But on October 1, before 69,551 fans at Yankee Stadium, Boston's Parnell squandered an early 4–0 lead and a chance to clinch the pennant, as the Red Sox went scoreless during the final six innings to fall 5–4.; Williams managed a single in three official at bats. The next day, with 68,055 watching, the Red Sox's inability to score continued into the final frame, allowing the Yankees to win the AL title, 5–3, with Williams going hitless, costing him the battle crown and what proved to be his last opportunity to be on a second pennant-winning team. Having endured years of doubts regarding his managerial ability, Stengel stated, "I want to thank all these players for giving me the greatest thrill of my life."[6]

The Red Sox debacle resulted in the second Yankee-Dodger World Series in three years and the third during the decade. Burt Shotton's Dodgers also prevailed in an exceedingly tight pennant race, their 97–57 win-loss record, identical to that of the Yankees, one game in front of the Cardinals. Despite blowing leads of 5–0 and 7–4 on the last day of the regular season, Brooklyn defeated the Philadelphia Phillies 9–7 after Duke Snider drove in Pee Wee

Reese and Luis Olmo plated Snider in the top of the 10th, before Jack Banta got through the bottom half of the inning.[7]

The 1949 Brooklyn Dodgers were, at last, genuinely close to being the Boys of Summer, later effectively mythologized. The starting lineup was potent, with the notable exception of the left fielder, which often proved a sticking point for years to come. Behind the plate, Roy Campanella had settled in nicely, while popping 22 homers and driving in 82 runs. First baseman Gil Hodges had his first big season, swatting one more homer than Campy, and 115 RBIs, with a .285 batting average. Center fielder Duke Snider matched Hodges's home run total, scored 100 runs, drove in 92, and batted .292. Shortstop Pee Wee Reese scored a league-best 132 runs, drew 116 walks, and hit 16 homers. Also starring for the initial time, right fielder Carl Furillo produced 18 homers, 106 RBIs, and a .322 batting average. Part-time outfielders Gene Hermanski and Marv Rackley were right around .300, with Hermanski again offering more power. The Dodgers had a number of solid starters, including youngsters like Ralph Branca, Rex Barney, Jack Banta, Carl Erskine, and former Negro Leaguer Don Newcombe, who logged the most innings, completed 19 games, tossed a league-high 5 shutouts, and went 17–8. Newcombe would be named the National League Rookie of the Year by *The Sporting News*, which departed from its previous practice of naming one honoree to select a recipient from each league.[8]

But the brightest star in the Dodger firmament remained Jackie Robinson, whose stature was exemplified by his appearance on the cover of the August 1949 issue of *Sport* magazine. During the season, Robinson scored 122 runs, drove in 124, stole a league-leading 37 bases, produced 313 total bases, and got 203 hits, 38 doubles, 12 triples, and 16 homers, while batting .342, tops in the NL. He had moved over to second base the previous season, forming a dynamic duo with Reese, what the *New York Times*' John Lardner called a "team within a team." When asked if he would trade Robinson, manager Shotton quipped, "Sure. For two pitchers who were certified to win thirty games apiece." Robinson's production, coupled with his leadership qualities, fiery personality, and charisma, led to his and not runner-up Stan Musial's receipt of the MVP. That narrow victory paralleled a similar slight advantage over Musial in WAR totals, 9.3–9.1, which would, much later, prove meaningful to baseball analysts.[9]

Offering a mediocre brand of baseball during their first full season under Leo Durocher's tutelage, the New York Giants did, nevertheless, experience a few bright spots. Although age at last appeared to catch up with slugger Johnny Mize, outfielders Willard Marshall, Whitey Lockman, and Bobby Thompson all hit over .300, with Thompson hitting 27 homers, one more than third baseman Sid Gordon, and contributing 109 RBIs. Struggling at the plate was Monte Irvin, who had won three Negro League batting titles and one home run crown. The Giants' topline pitchers, even Larry Jansen, foundered, with only Sheldon Jones, at 15–12, managing a winning record.

The *New York Journal-American*'s Frank Graham quoted Giants' manager Leo Durocher as exclaiming, "This isn't my kind of ball club." That franchise, "once the proudest and most powerful of the three New York Clubs," the one that had "ruled the National League and won World's Series," had become "a bad third." At mid-season, power-hitting All-Star catcher Walker Cooper, traded to the Cincinnati Reds, expressed discontent with Durocher's treatment of players, indicating that Leo's "fiery manner" had alienated several players. "I've always felt Durocher would ruin any good ball club. He's just too outspoken. I'm not saying that because I can't take it myself, but there's a certain type of men you got to handle a different way to get the best out of them. There's a lot of feeling on the Giants about the way Durocher handles men and pops off."[10]

Durocher and the Giants could only watch as the other New York City teams met in the 1949 World Series. Reynolds shut out the Dodgers on two hits in Game One, won on a ninth-inning homer by Heinrich off Newcombe, who to that point had struck out 11. The Dodgers' Roe beat Raschi in Game Two by the same 1–0 score. Ralph Branca pitched brilliantly until the ninth inning of Game Three, relinquishing three runs, which enabled the Yankees to prevail despite reliever Page's giving up homers in the bottom of the frame to Luis Olmo and Campanella. Back-to-back three-run innings in the fourth and fifth allowed Lopat to survive his own shaky outing in Game Four. Reynolds got the final ten outs for the Yankees. In Game Five, DiMaggio and the Yankees pounded Barney and the Dodgers, 10–6, although Raschi relinquished six runs and had to rely on reliever Page. Leading the way for the Yankees were infielder Bobby Brown, hitting .500, and Page, who picked up a win and a save, while holding the Dodgers to six hits and two runs in nine innings. Hermanski batted .308, but ace Newcombe dropped both his starts, the beginning of an inauspicious World Series career. Robinson scored and drove in two runs each but stole no bases and batted only .188. Snider went homerless, drove in no runs, and hit .143.[11]

Following the World Series, Rickey expressed dismay about the latest Dodger loss to the Yankees, insisting his "good, young team" would get better in its quest for a World Series championship. Yankees general manager Weiss proceeded to deride Brooklyn's fabled farm system, which Rickey helped to cultivate. He then pointed to three former Negro Leaguers as the Dodgers' most important: Robinson, Campanella, and Newcombe. Slapping back, Rickey denied "raiding the Negro leagues" and pointed to the general dominance of Dodger farm teams over those of the Yankees.[12]

Garnering plaudits for his handling of the Yankees was manager Stengel. *Morning Telegraph* sportswriter Tom Meany contended that the Yankees prevailed despite being "a poor insurance risk." Meany credited Stengel, who praised his players for capturing the pennant, for maintaining the team's "great spirit" enabling them to overcome the favored Red Sox. "Ball players don't hustle for a manager unless he has their admiration and respect." To Meany, Stengel drew on lessons he learned under the tutelage of both John McGraw and Wilbert Robinson. And his "handling of DiMaggio," Meany noted, proved "extremely tactful," allowing the star to inform him when he "felt ready to play," not using him "as a one-legged pinch-hitter." Stengel had been heard to say, "DiMaggio has been too good a ball player to be wasted trying to pinch-hit on one leg."[13]

*****

Once again, the supposed experts picked the Red Sox and the Dodgers to win pennants, this time still more emphatically. No matter, the 1950 regular season concluded differently than the previous one and the three that immediately followed with only one New York team—the Yankees—ending up in the World Series. While the Yankees, at 98–56, repeated in the American League, nipping the Tigers by three games, the Red Sox by four, and the Indians by six, with all winning over 90 games, the surprising Philadelphia Phillies won their first pennant since Grover Cleveland Alexander's heyday back in 1915. The Phillies (91–63) edged out the two New York area National League teams, the Dodgers and the Giants, by two and five games, respectively. Clinching the pennant, Philadelphia so-called "Whiz Kids" defeated the surging Dodgers on a three-run tenth-inning homer by Dick Sisler, the son of the former great St. Louis Brown, before 35,073 fans at Ebbets Field. The winning pitcher was 24-year-old Robin Roberts, his twentieth; the loser, Don Newcombe, who failed in a bid to match Roberts and sustain Brooklyn's pennant hopes.[14]

An ailing, aging Joe DiMaggio still managed a team-high 32 homers, scored 114 runs, drove in 122, collected 307 total bases, and batted .301, despite enduring an astonishing week-long benching following a slump. When Stengel sat DiMaggio down, Red Smith wrote simply, "DiMaggio was benched. Nothing like that ever happened before." Yogi Berra had his first great season, scoring 116 runs, getting 192 hits, swatting 28 homers, gathering 124 RBIs, amassing 318, and batting .322, only two points better than Hank Bauer. In only 274 official at bats, Johnny Mize, picked up from the Giants, produced 25 homers and 72 RBIs. Team sparkplug Phil Rizutto, 33-years old at season's end, scored 125 runs, got 200 hits, and batted .324 on the way to the MVP, with Berra coming in third behind Red Sox infielder Billy Goodman, the batting champion at .354. That was the first of seven straight years that the Yankees catcher finished in the top four in the AL MVP contest. Allie Reynolds, Vic Raschi, Eddie Lopat, and Tommy Byrne remained the top four starters, but the Yankees, never suffering from an embarrassment of riches, added a brilliant young southpaw, Whitey Ford, who went 9–1 with a 2.81 ERA. Joe Page continued to lead the bullpen but suffered the worst season of a career that was winding down.[15]

Eddie Sawyer's Phillies featured a lineup with only one player, first baseman Eddie Waitkus, having turned 30. It included catcher Andy Seminick who hit 24 homers and batted .288, 24-year-old Willie Jones who scored 100 runs, hit 25 homers, and drove in 88, Sisler, with a .296 batting average, and outfielders Del Ennis, 25-years old, and Richie Ashburn, two years younger, both hitting over .300 with Ennis providing the power, 31 homer and 126 RBIs. Former bonus baby Roberts led the pitching staff, which included 21-year-old left-hander Curt Simmons, still more acclaimed as a bonus baby, and closer Jim Konstanty, went 16–7 with a 2.66 ERA in 152 innings in a league-high 74 games pitched, resulting in his beating out Stan Musial as the National MVP.[16]

The seemingly far more potent Brooklyn Dodgers managed to come in second, perhaps due to a failure to find a third mainstay in the pitching rotation. The everyday lineup included three 30-homer batters—Roy Campanella, Duke Snider, and Gil Hodges—three 100-RBI men—Carl Furillo, Snider, and Hodges—and three hitters who batted over .300—Furillo, Snider, and Jackie Robinson. Five Dodgers scored more than 90 runs: Pee Wee Reese, Hodges, Robinson, Furillo, and Snider at 109. Snider, with a league-best 199 hits, along with 31 doubles, 10 triples, and 31 homers, produced 343 total bases, tops in the NL. Coming off his MVP season, Robinson had another terrific season, scoring 99 runs, getting 39 doubles, hitting 14 homers, and batting .328. His face, topped by a baseball cap, graced the cover of *Life* magazine, with an inside story on a movie, *The Jackie Robinson Story*, he starred in about his life. Newcombe and 34-year-old Preacher Roe each won 19 games, while 22-year-old Carl Palica added 13, but Joe Hatten and Rex Barney both neared an end while youngsters Carl Erskine and Ralph Branca struggled. Ex-Negro Leaguer Dan Bankhead, during his second MLB stint, went 9–4, a deceptive record given his 5.50 ERA.[17]

Brooklyn's team president Walter O'Malley, who was also the majority owner, pushed aside Branch Rickey, who soon moved over to the Pittsburgh Pirates, and manager Burt Shotton, despite his having guided the Dodgers to two pennants and a close, runner-up finish in three full seasons. Replacing Shotton was Chuck Dressen, a former major league infielder who had been a less-than-successful manager with the Cincinnati Reds during the mid-1930s. Not going away quietly, Rickey charged Dodger players with "complete satiety," as well as "complacency."[18]

As the pennant race wound on, *The Sporting News* displayed an image of an overweight character, with the label "Dodgers" on his chest, holding a block of melting ice, with a line indicating it represented "that promised pennant," the water flooding an August 1950 calendar. He was crying out, "MIS-TER RICK-KEY!"[19]

Markedly improving on their 1949 campaign, the third-place New York Giants, playing ball more to manager Durocher's liking, were led by scrappy second baseman Eddie Stanky, who scored 115 runs and batted .300, while walking a NL-high 144 times with a league-best .460 on-base-percentage. The next two top Giant hitters, with Johnny Mize traded, also lacked much power, outfielder Whitey Lockman and Don Mueller, but both hit in the .290s. Bobby Thompson had 25 homers, Wes Westrum, 23, former Negro Leaguer Hank Thompson, 20, along with 91 RBIs and a .289 batting average. Beginning to star as he received more playing time was Monte Irvin, who in 374 official at bats had 15 homers, 66 RBIs, and a .299 batting average, inching closer to some of his marks in Blackball. Rebounding, Larry Jansen won 19 games with a 3.01 ERA, while Jim Hearn went 11–3 with a 1.94 ERA, albeit in only 125 innings (which did not make him eligible for the ERA title). Most promising of all, Sal Maglie, despite his relatively advanced age of 33, returned from the Mexican League and suspension, won 18, losing only 4, for an NL-leading .818 win-loss percentage along with a league-best 2.71 ERA and 5 shutouts.

Undoubtedly due to television's soaring popularity, MLB attendance dropped noticeably during the 1950 regular season as overall attendance was down almost 3.5 million fans from the record set two years previously. That amounted to a loss of almost 3,000 fans per game. And the attendance slide was hardly complete, as major league owners, over the next several years, would discover.

For the sixth time, the Yankees swept the World Series, although the first three contests were won by a single run apiece. At Philadelphia's Shibe Park, Raschi shut out the Phillies, allowing only a pair of singles in Game One, beating surprise starter Konstanty, who was opening a contest for the first time all season. Konstanty gave up just five hits, but the Yankees pieced together the game's lone run in the top of the fourth thanks to a double by Bobby Brown and fly outs by Hank Bauer and Jerry Coleman. In Game Two, Reynolds beat Roberts 2–1 on a tenth-inning homer by DiMaggio. Back at the Stadium for Game Three, the Yankees rebounded from a 2–1 deficit by scoring single runs in both the bottom of the eighth and the ninth, beating reliever Russ Meyer. Tom Ferrick, in relief of Lopat, picked up the victory. In the most high-scoring affair, the Yanks won, 5–2, all their runs scored in the initial two innings, as

Ford outpitched his fellow rookie Bob Miller, removed after retiring only one batter in the opening frame.[20]

Along with Robinson, Campanella, Thompson, and Irvin, other former Negro League players were adapting to play in the National League or the American League. Thirty-five-year-old Luke Easter, a home run king with the Homestead Grays, made a splash with the Cleveland Indians during the 1950 MLB season playing left field and first base, hitting 28 homers, driving in 107, and batting .280. Two years younger, center fielder Sam Jethroe, a fine player for the Cleveland Buckeyes during and after the Second World War, became Rookie of the Year as he scored 100 runs, hit 18 homers, stole a league-leading 35 bases, and batted .273 for the Boston Braves.

Early in the season, the Fahy Committee had issued its report, *Freedom to Serve: Equality of Treatment and Opportunity in the Armed Services*. In the "reasonably near future," the committee indicated, the US Armed Forces would be fully integrated. Opposition reportedly existed within the military regarding integration, with the contention that "a lowering of over-all morale" would result. However, the report noted that enlisted men appeared "'far more ready' for integration than officers had believed." Expressing appreciation for the committee's work, President Truman also continued to support a Fair Employment Practices Bill, which appeared doomed to defeat in the US Senate. Southern Senators conducted a filibuster, preventing its passage.[21]

6

New York Baseball Ascends in 1951

One of baseball's most iconic seasons, 1951, had all three New York City teams on full display, with the Brooklyn Dodgers and the New York Giants battling for the National League pennant and the New York Yankees fighting for their third consecutive American League title under Casey Stengel. It also proved to be Bob Feller's last great season and the year Joe DiMaggio decided to call it quits. It was the rookie season of two center fielders in America's greatest city: the Yankees' Mickey Mantle and the Giants' Willie Mays, who had played with the Birmingham Barons. Other Negro Leaguers making their debut included Luiz Marquez, Ray Noble, Artie Wilson, Harry Simpson, Sam Hairston, Bob Boyd, and Sam Jones, as the number of Black players began to inch upward, however inadequately.[1]

But most strikingly, New York City baseball, starting in 1951, reached heights it would never quite attain again as its three major league teams finished the regular season in first place, ensuring an all New York World Series for the ninth time once a NL playoff series was completed.

During spring training, a teenager raised near Commerce, Oklahoma, generated excitement in the Yankees' camp. Mickey Mantle, a 19-year-old shortstop who had scorched the Class C Western Association the previous year with a league-leading .384 batting average, was initially not included on the team's roster but was expected to land there soon as DiMaggio's eventual replacement. Former Yankee great Bill Dickey sang the praises of the home run hitting youngster, referring to "his amazing speed" and ability to switch-hit with power. Writers, scouts, and coaches began to call him a "boy wonder" and termed him the "greatest prospect I've ever seen" or "a once-in-a-life-time boy." He hit .402 during spring training, with 9 homers and 31 RBIs, both tops on the Yankees.[2]

The Sporting News contained a front-page cartoon image of Mantle by Willard Mullin, titled "He'll Pass," with another character grinning with his fingers opened, "A Natural: Snap" and a pair of dice coming up seven. In his column, "Looping the Loops," J.G.T. Spink spun the story of "meteoric" Mantle's ascendancy to the Yankees' outfield. Revealed was an old football-induced injury that resulted in chronic osteomyelitis in his left leg and entitled Mantle to 4-F draft status after an examination by his draft board, preventing military service. Controversy continued to swirl about the exemption. Prior to his pre-induction physical, Mantle indicated, "I'll play baseball for the army or fight for it, whatever they want me to do, but if I don't go in the army, I want to play baseball." A second examination, taking place just before the start of the regular season, also indicated Mantle "was physically unqualified for military duty."[3]

Casey Stengel's Yankees, with a 98–56 record, won their third pennant in a row, five games better than the Indians, whose longtime ace, Bob Feller, had his sixth 20-game season, pitched his third no-hitter, and was named American League pitcher of the year by *The Sporting News*. Still led by the peerless Ted Williams, the Red Sox landed in third place, 11 games behind. With both the Cardinals and Braves having settled into mediocrity and the Phillies, defending NL titleholders, ending up with a losing record and in the second division, the two New York area teams undertook a spirited battle for supremacy. As late as August 11, Brooklyn retained a huge thirteen and a half lead on the New York Giants but that evaporated as the two teams ended the regular season tied with identical 96–58 records, necessitating a best-of-three playoff series.[4]

Catcher Yogi Berra had another fine season, scoring 92 runs, hitting 27 homers, producing 88 RBIs, and batting .294, as he was named American League MVP. While infielder Gil McDougald batted .306, resulting in the receipt of the AL Rookie of the Year Award, and outfielder Hank Bauer, .296, the rest of the Yankees performed adequately but hardly spectacularly at the plate as Stengel continued platooning. Young outfielder Jackie Jensen displayed considerable promise, but 36-year-old Joe DiMaggio finally performed like the aging player he had become in what proved to be his final season, producing the worst numbers for his career: 12 homers, 61 RBIs, and a .263 batting average. That last mark was 62 points below his lifetime average. Displaying remarkable promise but dismaying inconsistency that resulted in a temporary return to the minors, Mantle, in 341 official at bats, scored 61 runs, hit 13 homers, some of prodigious length, drove in 65, batted .267, and struck out far too frequently, constantly exasperating Stengel.

The remarkable, seemingly hydra-headed Yankees pitching leaders—Allie Reynolds, Vic Rashi, and Eddie Lopat—remained superlative, with the first two winning 21 games apiece, and Reynolds leading the AL with seven shutouts while also mopping up several contests in the post-Joe Page era. He also tossed two no-hitters. Rookie Tom Morgan went 9–3 with 16 starts. Coming over from the Senators, Bob Kuzava was 8–4 with a 2.40 ERA. Missing from the Yankee roster was lefty Whitey Ford, who had been called into service as the Korean War required a beefing up of the US military.

Holding the National League lead for much of the season, the Brooklyn Dodgers possessed an everyday lineup far more potent than that of the AL champions and a pair of top-flight starting pitchers. New York sportswriter Joe King, in fact, deemed the Dodgers "the finest baseball club since the pre-war Yankees and Cardinals." He also said the Brooklyn team was "probably the most valuable ... in history, at a $2,500,000 to $3,000,000 value tag in today's inflated bucks," while representing "one of the game's all-time bargains." Branch Rickey signed second baseman Jackie Robinson, catcher Roy Campanella, and pitcher Don Newcombe "as free agents from the colored leagues." He grabbed third baseman Billy Cox and Preacher Roe from the Pirates as "practically throw-ins." Pitcher Ralph Branca, first baseman Gil Hodges, center fielder Duke Snider, and pitcher Clyde King had received "nominal bonuses." Outfielder Andy Pafko was obtained in a trade, $5,000 was paid for right fielder Carl Furillo, pitcher Carl Erskine was signed for $8,000. Larry MacPhail did hand the Red Sox $40,000 for the rights to shortstop Pee Wee Reese.[5]

Former sportswriter Garry Schumacher, a New York Giants' official, referred to the Dodgers as "the best National League team since the Cubs of 1929." Topping the roster, Campanella, soon to win his first MVP, beating out Stan Musial, scored 90 runs, got 33 doubles and 33 homers, drove in 108, and batted .325. Hodges had 118 runs scored, 40 homers, 103 RBIs, and 93 walks. Robinson scored 106 runs, collected 185 hits, doubled 33 times, and homered 19, drove in 88, stole 25 bases, had a .429 on-base percentage, and hit .338. Reese scored 94 runs, got 176 hits, drove in 84, and batted .286. Snider ended up with 96 runs, 29 homers, and 101 RBIs. Furillo scored 93 runs, produced 197 hits, got 32 doubles, drove in 91 runs, and hit .295. With the ever-steady Cox holding down third base, left field remained the weak spot, although Pafko, traded from the Cubs, did hit 18 homers and have 58 RBIs in 277 official at bats. Once more, Newcombe and the seemingly ageless Roe, now 35 years old, led Dodger pitchers. Newcombe went 20–9, Roe, 22–3, for the NL's top win-loss percentage (.880). Branca finished 13–12, closer King, 14–7, and Erskine, 16–12, despite an unsightly 4.46 ERA.[6]

A star in the Negro and Mexican leagues, a key contributor after joining the Brooklyn Dodgers during the middle the 1948 season, an All Star the next year, Campanella was now, like Robinson, a mega-star. Campy's 1951 campaign proved to be his finest yet. Already, he had matched the feat of Gabby Hartnett and Walker Cooper of belting at least 20 homers more than once while serving as a National League catcher. Branch Rickey turned to the great Oscar Charleston, among others, for advice about Campanella, who had been schooled behind the plate by another Negro League great, Biz Mackey. In addition to his prowess as a hitter, Campanella was "an iron man" who wanted to play everyday, with a cannon for an arm, according to Reese.[7]

Virtually matching the Dodgers in the power realm, the New York Giants included utility man Bobby Thompson, who scored 89 runs, hit 32 homers, drove in 101, and batted .293, and catcher Wes Westrum, outfielder Monte Irvin, and rookie center fielder Willie Mays, all of whom slammed 20 or more homers. Like shortstop Alvin Dark, whose 196 hits included an NL-most 41 doubles as he piled up 114 runs, Irvin batted over .300, while scoring 94 times and driving in a league-best 121 runs, in placing third in the NL

MVP contest. Like the Yankees' Mantle, Mays was a young—20-year-old—outfielder with boundless promise and the need for his game to still be refined as early struggles sapped his confidence. Encouraged by manager Durocher, he rebounded, hit 20 homers, drove in 68 runs, batted .274, and displayed less of a propensity than Mantle to whale away at the plate. Thirty-four-year-old Sal Maglie and 30-year-old Larry Jansen each won an NL-high 23 games, while former Cardinal Jim Hearn went 17–9.

After a troubled start when he flailed away during his first three games, going hitless with two walks before homering off Boston's Warren Spahn, Mays had proven to be stellar both at bat and in the field on his way to winning the NL Rookie of the Year Award. Some referred to him as the "best kid ball player to come up in years" or indicated, "He's got a chance to become the greatest Negro ball player of all time." The legendary sports columnist Grantland Rice called Mays the "kid everybody likes," who exuded "a quiet, rock-like confidence that would be amazing even in a seasoned veteran." Tom Sheehan, the leading Giant scout, indicated, "That kid is the best-looking young ball player I've ever seen. I saw DiMaggio and all the rest, but this kid's tops."

Durocher stated, "This is the best-looking rookie I've seen in 25 years in baseball," and compared Mays to Reiser, while admitting that the latter was the better runner. But then he said, "Okay, but that's all. There nobody in the league got a better arm than this kid. There's nobody got more power. There's nobody can go get them any better than he can." Moreover, Leo continued, "And what a lift he's given this team. Since he's been with us we've come to life. And he's just a baby. In two years, Mays is going to be the greatest ever to lace on a pair of spiked shoes." Soon-to-be Hall of Famer Al Simmons seemingly agreed. "The best kid I've seen in years . . . look at that stance at the plate . . . look at that poise. He's got everything." The young journalist Clay Felker referred to Mays, "the Giants' answer to Jackie Robinson," as the player, unlike Irvin, Thompson, and Noble, who might attract Black fans and "overcome the magic dazzle of the Dodgers' Robinson, Roy Campanella and Don Newcombe."[8]

Had it existed at the time, Maglie would have previously won, and by a landslide, the Comeback Player of the Year Award. After going 5–4 with a 2.35 ERA in ten starts and three relief appearances for the New York Giants in 1945, the 28-year-old Maglie, who had pitched in the minors and worked at a defense plant, bolted to the Mexican League. Starring for the Giants in 1950—he threw four straight shutouts and 45 consecutive scoreless frames at one point—he excelled once again throughout the 1951 pennant chase. "The Story of Sal Maglie," Joe King wrote midway through the season, "is a romance of baseball" involving an expendable, an "outcast," and then "a shopworn 'senior'" who may have become "the most effective pitcher in the majors."[9]

After winning two of their first three games in mid-April, the Giants underwent a tailspin, dropping 11 straight contests to fall to 2–12. Former players of Durocher like Walker Cooper and Jackie Robinson, excelling in early games against the Giants, taunted him. Durocher accused Robinson of "a bush stunt" for bunting off Maglie, who had brushed him back, thereby threatening to run into the Giant pitcher. Jackie responded, "If it was a bush stunt he is a bush manager, because he taught him to do it." Recalling barbs by Durocher, Robinson also "led a virtual crusade against The Lip. He jockeyed endlessly. His yack-yack was never stilled, and grew in venom the further Durocher plunged into defeat. He led the jubilation in the Dodger dressing room. Above all, he was a great player on the field."[10]

Their powerful bats, it appeared, might let the Dodgers "romp" to the pennant. For a period, they were smashing homers at a pace that would surpass the mark set by the 1947 New York Giants. Brooklyn sluggers appeared to be a "Modern Murderers' Row" akin to the Yankees of previous generations. All of this occurred despite continued receipt by Robinson of hate mail and death threats, which necessitated at least one conversation with FBI agents. Pee Wee Reese offered, "I think we will all wear 42 (Robinson's uniform number) today, and they will have a shooting gallery." Robinson countered, "That would be too much trouble for you fellows, because you would have to darken up, too." He revealed having "received dozens of" threatening letters and indicated the team had probably "had hundreds."[11]

As late as June 7, the Giants were resting at 25–25, and by August 11, they were just eight games above .500 at 59–51. Then, probably with the assistance of stolen signs, the Giants began surging, winning 16 straight times; although inexplicably, attendance at the Polo Grounds lagged, with less than 9,000 fans appearing as the team attempted to maintain the streak. Over the last 62 games, the Giants, whether fans showed up or not, lost only a dozen times. Victories in the regular season's final seven games resulting in a deadlock with Brooklyn. By contrast, the Dodgers, who sat at 87–47 on September 8, went 9–11 over their final 20 regular season games, which included a pair of wins over the Phillies at the very end, to limp into the playoff against the Giants.[12]

In Game One, played at Ebbets Field, the Giants, behind Jim Hearn, won 3–1, beating Ralph Branca. The Dodgers scored first, on a homer by Andy Pafko in the bottom of the second. But in the top of the fourth, Bobby Thompson powered a homer, driving in Monte Irvin, who had been hit by a pitch. The final run came in the eighth when Irvin homered. Game Two, at the Polo Grounds, saw Clem Labine, a rookie right-hander in only his sixth start, shut out the Dodgers on six hits. Brooklyn collected thirteen, four of them homers—one each by Jackie Robinson, who had once again just appeared on the cover of *Sport*, Gil Hodges, Pafko, and backup catcher Rube Walker. The decisive Game Three, also played at the Polo Grounds, drew 34,320 fans, but that was more than 4,000 fewer than the previous day. Don Newcombe and Sal Maglie dueled to a 1–1 tie until the top of the eighth, when the Dodgers plated three to grab a seemingly insurmountable lead, particularly after the Giants went down in order in their half of the inning. Brooklyn went one-two-three against Jansen, pitching in relief of Maglie.[13]

Newcombe gave up singles to Alvin Dark and Don Mueller leading off the last of the ninth, followed by Irvin popping out. Lockman doubled, driving in Dark, with Mueller advancing to third. In doing so, Mueller injured his ankle and had to be replaced by Clint Hartung. Dressen finally took out a clearly exhausted Newcombe, calling on Branca, who was relieving after going all the way in Game One. He was facing Thompson, who had homered off him in Game One; on deck was the rookie sensation, Willie Mays. After a called strike on a fastball, Branca hurled another one. Thompson drove the ball over the fence, propelling the Giants to the pennant. In a soon-to-be well-remembered response, Russ Hodges, New York's radio announcer, cried out, "The Giants win the pennant! The Giants win the pennant! The Giants win the pennant! The Giants win the pennant!" Others would refer to Thompson's homer as "the short heard 'round the world.'"

Later reports would indicate that Thompson, like the other Giants, knew what pitches were coming because of a coach located in center field able to capture the catcher's signals and pass them on to the batter. Thompson denied knowing what pitch was coming in his last at bat of the regular season. He later admitted, "We did steal signs and I did take some, and I don't feel good about it. But I didn't get the sign on that pitch." The journalist Joshua Prager broke the long percolating story in a *Wall Street Journal* front-page article, "Was the '51 Giants Comeback a Miracle, or Did They Simply Steal the Pennant?" appearing on January 31, 2001.[14]

Nevertheless, the mythology surrounding the Giants' surge toward the NL pennant and Thompson's heroics remains as firm for many as it did in real time for the great sportswriter Red Smith, writing in the *New York Herald Tribune* the day after about the "Miracle of Coogan's Bluff." "Now it is done. Now the story ends. And there is no way to tell it. The art of fiction is dead. Reality has strangled invention. Only the utterly impossible, the inexpressibly fantastic, can ever be plausible again."[15]

The Giants and the defending champion Yankees met in the World Series for the sixth time. Still riding a high, the Giants prevailed in Game One, 5–1, before 65,673 fans at Yankee Stadium. Thirty-one-year-old Dave Kelso, a journeyman pitcher with only a 10–9 regular season record, outpitched one of the three Yankee aces, Allie Reynolds, who gave up eight hits, five earned runs, walked seven, and uncharacteristically notched only a single strikeout. All three Yankee outfielders—Joe DiMaggio, Hank Bauer, and Mickey Mantle—went hitless. Irvin rapped out four hits, Westrum and Dark, a pair each, with Dark swatting a three-run, sixth-inning homer off Reynolds. The Yankees rebounded in Game Two, with Eddie Lopat besting Larry Jansen 3–1, although Irvin got three more hits and scored the only Giant run. Mantle got his first World Series hit, DiMaggio and Bauer remained hitless, and Joe Collins homered off Jansen.

During the fifth-inning, three men who, following their careers landed in the Hall of Fame as power-hitting center fielders, converged in dramatic fashion. Mays skied to DiMaggio, who waved to the onrushing Mantle, then playing right field, to back off. As Mantle attempted to do so, an exposed drain ensnared the youngster's spikes, badly damaging his knee, forever altering the trajectory of the man viewed by many as the fastest in the game. The front page of the *New York Times* displayed DiMaggio awaiting the ball, with Mantle, only a few feet away, sprawled on the field. An inside-the-paper headline read, "Yanks' Joy Over Triumph Is Tempered by Loss of Mantle for Remaining Games." Mantle was now afflicted with a torn anterior cruciate ligament, known in common parlance as an ACL.[16]

The Giants regained the Series lead in Game Three, winning 6–2 behind Hearn, thanks to a five-run, fifth-inning explosion, aided by sloppy Yankee defense, off Raschi, before 52,035 in attendance at the Polo Grounds. DiMaggio continued his struggles behind the plate, while Lockman belted a three-run homer off Vic Raschi and Mays got his first two World Series hits and initial RBI. The Yankees bounced back in Game Four, also winning 6–2, with Reynolds recovering from his Game 1 debacle to outpitch Maglie. The winning team's 12 hits included a pair by DiMaggio, who blasted a two-run shot, fifth-inning shot off the Giants' starting pitcher; Bauer and third baseman Bobby Brown also got two hits apiece. The Yankees exploded in Game Five, shelling Jansen and the Giants, 13–1, with another dozen hits, including three by DiMaggio and homers by Gil McDougald—his was a grand slam off Jansen—and Phil Rizutto. Back at the Stadium for Game Six with nearly 62,000 fans present, the Yankees won the World Series in a tight contest, 4–3, with Raschi the winner pitcher and Dave Koslo the loser. The biggest hit was a triple with the bases loaded by Bauer off Koslo, breaking a 1–1 tie in the bottom of the sixth. This was the Yankees fourteenth World Series title in eighteen appearances.[17]

Batting .417, Dark got ten hits; batting .458, former Negro Leaguer Irvin got 11 hits, batting .458. Mays went only 4 for 22, a .182 batting average with no extra-base hits. The steadier Yankees lineup was led by Brown, who batted .357, and Rizutto, who scored five runs, and hit .320. Playing only into the second-inning of Game Two, Mantle went one for five, while DiMaggio batted .261 with a homer and five RBIs as a key figure in the Yankees' ninth World Series titles in ten appearances during his career. Game Six was the final one in the Yankee Clipper's historic run, one abbreviated by an injury that delayed his entrance into the majors by a year and three years of wartime military service.

*****

As attested by their performances in both the regular season and the World Series, former Negro League players Irvin and Mays continued the pattern initiated by Jackie Robinson during 1947, starring at the game's highest levels. Robinson, Campanella, and Newcombe continued doing so for the Dodgers, while the Yankees remained lily-white. Other ex-Negro Leaguers had more mixed results in 1951. The Indians' Larry Doby had another fine season, with 20 homers, 101 walks, a .295 batting average, and selection as an All-Star for the third straight time. Also back in the AL was Minnie Minoso, who after his trade to the White Sox, began hitting like he had for the New York Cubans. Scoring 112 runs, Minoso had 34 doubles, a league-leading 14 triples, ten homers, 76 RBIs, and an AL-high 31 steals. The Indians Luke Easter delivered 27 homers and 103 RBIs. The Braves' Sam Jethroe scored 101 runs, got 18 homers, and again led the league with 35 steals. The Giants' Hank Thompson struggled at the plate, returned to the minor for several days, did little better after being called back up, but was pressed into World Series duty because of the injury to Mueller. The Dodgers' Dan Bankhead also foundered in 14 innings pitched as his major league career ended. Returning to the American League after a year's absence, Satchel Paige, now pitching for the Browns, hardly looked like the Satchel of old.

During the offseason, sportswriter Roger Birtwell of the *Boston Globe* explored the impact of Black players in MLB. As he noted, with the exception of 1950 when the Yankees faced the Phillies, each of the five previous World Series included former Negro Leaguers. "The Negro race," Birtwell wrote, "has produced exceptional ball players." He wondered if ball clubs that refused to employ them would "suffer from the handicap." During the recently played World Series, an all-Black outfield—Monte Irvin, Willie Mays, and Hank Thompson—appeared for the first team. Birtwell also noted that three of the top six vote-getters in the NL MVP race were Black players: Roy Campanella came in first, Irvin, third, and Jackie Robinson, sixth. The AL MVP contest included Minnie Minoso, who was fourth.[18]

Among those supporting Organized Baseball's changed stance regarding the inclusion of Black players was Ty Cobb, long viewed as rabidly racist. However, Cobb declared, "Anyone who qualifies as a gentleman is qualified anywhere, regardless of his color, and the Negro should be accepted not grudgingly but wholeheartedly." Black players in baseball, he declared, "have to date qualified not only as to their deportment but their ability. No trouble has been encountered."[19]

Notwithstanding Cobb's perspective, far too often forgotten amid a remembrance of him as a mean-spirited racist, that type of mindset was hardly absent, in spite of the gains, however belated and incomplete African Americans appeared to be making, including in the national pastime. The easy resort to violence, long employed to restrain, encumber, and debase Black Americans, was scarcely infrequent. At the time, as was the case earlier and later still, some were ready to resort to the politics of assassination to get rid of both well-remembered and too little recalled figures.

Two such victims were Harry T. and Harriette Moore, a married couple known for their civil rights activism. On Christmas Day, a powerful bomb placed underneath their bedroom in the small Florida town of Mims took their lives. The educator Harry T. served as the NAACP's state coordinator; Harriette was a school teacher. Investigators later determined that four individuals, all tied to the KKK, were involved in the assassinations.[20]

7

The Yankees and Dodgers on Top as Mantle Returns and Mays Enters the Military

Both the Yankees and the Dodgers remained potent teams during the 1952 and 1953 seasons, while the Giants, with Willie Mays called into military service and Monte Irvin injured, still managed a second-place finish that first year before falling into the second division awaiting the return of the Say Hey Kid. Under Stengel's tutelage, the Yankees won their fourth consecutive pennant, despite Whitey Ford's continued absence due to military service, and then their fifth straight after the lefty returned to the starting rotation. Through it all, their pitching Big Three—Reynolds, Raschi, and Lopat—a Big Four, with Ford available, and batterymate Yogi Berra still proved stellar, while the young Mickey Mantle, back from a devastating injury during the 1951 World Series, became a star in his own right as well as an extraordinary replacement for the seemingly irreplaceable but now-retired Joe DiMaggio.

Mantle was fortunate that his draft board refused to mandate another physical examination. That decision was made after Sidney Gaynor, who served as the Yankee physician, informed the board Mantle's bone infection demanded virtually daily treatment. In mid-August, Dr. Gaynor was attending to Mantle's leg, which was red and swollen. The Yankee player was required to wear "a papier-mache guard" to shield his damaged appendage. However, a month later, Mantle was slated for a fourth examination, scheduled for October 6, when the World Series would be played.[1]

More than any other major league team, the Brooklyn Dodgers, managed by Chuck Dressen, retained the bulk of their everyday lineup, which now included several players at the peak of their careers, led by Jackie Robinson, Pee Wee Reese, Roy Campanella, Duke Snider, Gil Hodges, Carl Furillo, Carl Erskine, and Preacher Roe. After Pafko was traded to the Braves following the 1952 season, left field was once again a conundrum, and the pitching staff hardly matched that of the Yankees. Nevertheless, the Dodgers clearly were the cream of the National League with the 1953 version one of the finest ever. Unfortunately, during October of both years they confronted a juggernaut in Stengel's Yankees, who went on to take a record-tying fourth straight and then an unprecedented fifth consecutive World Series championship.

Gamely holding on in 1952 notwithstanding the losses of both their great outfielders, the Giants, still managed by the ever controversial Leo Durocher, could well have joined their National League brethren in crying out, "Wait 'til next year!" What they awaited was Mays's return to their roster, while Irvin had a remarkable comeback during the 1953 season. Unfortunately, Mays missed nearly two full seasons, just obtaining his discharge from the US Army on March 1, 1954, as the Giants readied for spring training in Phoenix, Arizona.[2]

The Giants" hopes of retaining their National League title foundered badly with the departures of both Mays and Irvin by the early stages of the 1952 season. The first to go was Irvin, who broke his ankle sliding into third base during a spring training game. The absence of Irvin's bat was viewed "as incalculable." Next to go was Mays, the now 21-year-old center fielder, who had gotten off to a slow start in his sophmore year, batting only .236 after 34 games, with but four homers. He had managed to drive in 23 runs, suggesting a pace that have resulted in over 100 RBIs during a full year of work. This came after an off-season during which Mays initially failed the Armed Forces Qualification Test but was subsequently "administratively accepted" because he was a high-school graduate. His mother, Annie McMorris, expressed a desire for her son to be exempted "because he was such a help to me and my children." One of nine siblings, Mays reportedly had helped his mother care for several of those children.[3]

The Giants' fierce rivals, the Brooklyn Dodgers, got back promising rookie pitcher Billy Loes from the military but suffered a setback of their own when star pitcher Don Newcombe, who had won 17, 19, and 20 games in successive seasons, was called into service. Newcombe's absence, the *New York Times*' sports columnist Arthur Daley indicated, delivered "a violent blow to Dodger pennant hopes," with no adequate replacement available. Daley reasoned that even the possible loss of "the "Mazing Mays"" offered scant comfort to the Dodgers. He pointed to the Phillies' departure of southpaw pitcher Curt Simmons to the Army National Guard near the end of the 1950 pennant race. That proved, Daley wrote, "a fatal blow" for Philadelphia's World Series hopes.[4]

Similar departures had proven less damaging to the powerful Yankees, who had overcome Whitey Ford's induction into the military to win the 1951 World Series. Third in the Rookie of the Year balloting in 1949, the World War II veteran Jerry Coleman became an All-Star infielder the next year, in the midst of helping the Yanks win three straight World Series championships. After a blazing start in 1952, he too would be recalled back into military service as a Marine pilot. Having batted .439 in four World Series competitions amid his completion of medical training, Dr. Bobby Brown served in Korea for 19 months. Red Sox great Ted Williams, who had been a Marine Corps naval aviator and instructor during the Second World War, served in combat during the Korean conflict; the veteran bomber pilot John Glenn asked for Williams to serve as his wingman. Kansas City Monarchs shortstop Ernie Banks was yet another player who went into the military for two years as US troops fought in Southeast Asia.[5]

Not surprisingly then, the *Washington Post*'s Will Grimley bemoaned the fact that the US military was "hitting [the] big leagues hard." By February 1, 55 major leaguers, including several top-flight performers, had already been called up or appeared likely to be in the military during the early stages of the upcoming season; eventually over 100 served. They included Browns hurler Bob Turley, Tigers pitchers Art Houtteman, a 19-game winner in 1950, and Ray Herbert, Braves pitcher Robert Buhl, Braves catcher Del Crandall, Reds catcher Ed Bailey, and Indians outfielder Jim Lemon. Public pressure resulted in a third physical examination of Mantle, but his torn ACL again led to an exemption.[6]

For the second straight year, the Yankees battled the Indians for the American League pennant, with the race even closer as a mere two games separated the teams at season's end. Going 8–2 over their final ten games, the Yankees, with a 95–59 record, eased out the Indians, who finished 9–1. The White Sox, Athletics, and Senators also finished above .500 but 14 to 17 games out of first. The Red Sox fell to sixth, followed by the Browns, and the Tigers, who were at the bottom of the standings, only two years after fighting for the AL title.

With a record of 96–57, the Dodgers beat out the Giants by four and a half games, with the Cardinals and Phillies also in the first division. The Cubs split their games to land in fifth, with the Reds, Braves, and Pirates bringing up the rear. Pirates' vice president and general manager Branch Rickey, so used to winning ways during his lengthy tenures with both the Cardinals and Dodgers, had to have been appalled at his team's 42–112 record.

During the 1952 regular season, Mickey Mantle, having healed from his World Series injury, avoided conscription due to that injury and other physical afflictions, and feeling less pressure, replaced the now-retired DiMaggio as both the center fielder for baseball's greatest team and its biggest star. Finishing third in the MVP race behind teammate Allie Reynolds and the winner, Athletic pitching ace Bobby Shantz, Mantle scored 94 runs, collected 171 hits, hit 37 doubles, 7 triples, and 23 homers, drove in 87 runs, walked 75 times, and batted .311, with a league-leading .924 OPS. Returning MVP Yogi Berra finished fourth this time, scoring 97 runs, homering 30 times, and driving in 98 runs. Outfielders Gene Woodling and Hank Bauer batted .309 and .293, respectively.[7]

With the entire team producing only 129 homers, the pitching staff, including its aging aces, remained instrumental in the Yankees" ability to repeat in the American League. Reynolds went 20–8 with a league-leading 2.06 ERA, 6 shutouts, and 160 strikeouts, and completed 24 games. Raschi was 16–6 with a 2.78 ERA, Lopat, 10–5 with a 2.53 ERA, and Johnny Sain, recovering from a poor year in 1951, was 11–6 with a 3.46 ERA, starting 16 games and finishing 15 others in relief.

Outhomering the Yankees by 24, the Brooklyn Dodgers were still guided by Jackie Robinson, who scored 104 runs, knocked out 19 homers, drove in 75 runs, batted .308, got 106 walks, and had a league-leading .440 on-base percentage. Duke Snider, the National League's hottest hitter over the last five weeks of the regular season, had 21 homers, 92 RBIs, and a .303 batting average. In a full season for Brooklyn, Andy Pafko contributed 19 homers, 85 RBIs, and a .287 BA. Roy Campanella fell off from his MVP year, hitting 22 homers, driving in 97 runs, and batting .269. While Gil Hodges' batting average descended to .254, he hit 32 homers and knocked in 102 runs, while amassing 107 walks. Pee Wee Reese stole a league-leading 30 bases and scored 94 runs. Substitute outfielder George Shuba hit 9 homers, scored and drove in 40 runs, and batted .305 in only 256 official at bats.

With Don Newcombe no longer available, Carl Erskine and Billy Loes served as replacements of a sort, the first going 14–6, including a no-hitter, with a 2.70 ERA, while the second was 13–8 with a 2.69 ERA. Thirty-six-year-old Preacher Roe was 11–2 with a 3.12. But the pitching phenom for the 1952 Brooklyn Dodgers was 28-year-old Joe Black, who went 15–4 with a 2.15 ERA, while finishing a league-tops 41 games. The Negro League and World War II veteran became NL Rookie of the Year and finished third in MVP voting. Black matched winner Chicago outfielder Hank Sauer's eight first-place ballots, ending up just three points behind runner-up Robin Roberts of Philadelphia, who was but 15 votes and a single first-place ballot short of Sauer.

Almost matching the Dodgers in the power department and record-wise, the New York Giants' top hitters for average were infielders Al Dark (.301) and Whitey Lockman (.290), while Bobby Thompson—he of the 1951 pennant-winning heroics—had the most homers (24) and RBIs (108). When Irvin finally returned to the lineup, he hit well—.310—but only managed 126 official plate appearances, one more than the conscripted Willie Mays. Don Mueller came back from his season-ending injury, batting .281, with a dozen homers. Seeking to compensate for the loss of Irvin and the anticipated departure of Mays, the Giants, in April, had traded for 35-year-old Bob Elliott, a former perennial All-Star third baseman and the NL 1947 MVP, but his glory days were over as he slumped at the plate with the Giants.

Sal Maglie, also 35 years old, had another stellar year, going 18–8 with a 2.92 ERA and 5 shutouts. Jim Hearn was 14–7 and Dave Koslo was 10–7, but Larry Jansen dropped to 11–11 with a 4.09 ERA. Helping to keep the Giants competitive was 29-year-old Hoyt Wilhelm, Purple Heart recipient and veteran of the Battle of the Bulge. Having bounced around in the minors, Wilhelm made the major league team with few expectations he would succeed. Relying on a knuckleball, he led the league with 71 games pitched, an .833 win-loss percentage based on his 15–3 record, and a 2.43 ERA. Traded for Eddie Stanky, Max Lanier, the former Cardinal star who had jumped to the Mexican League, disappointed with a 7–12 record and a 3.94 ERA, easily the worst of his career.

As the Yankees and Dodgers readied to face off for the fourth time in the past dozen years, the Bronx Bombers appeared to have three major advantages: their previous success against Brooklyn, their now extended period of success under Casey Stengel, and their trio of aging but still excellent starting pitchers. John Drebinger, who covered New York baseball for the *Times*, emphasized the continued presence of Reynolds, Raschi, and Lopat. By contrast, Brooklyn's top pitchers appeared weaker than in the recent past, with Newcombe in the military, Ralph Branca's "arm ailment" rendering him "virtually useless," and even Preacher Roe "no longer . . . the formidable southpaw of yore" despite possibly "capable of one supreme performance." The Dodgers' other top starting pitcher was Carl Erskine, but Stengel's staff was deeper and included "a surprisingly rejuvenated Johnny Sain." Like Philly skipper Eddie Sawyer, who had slotted reliever Jim Konstanty in the 1950 World Series opener, Dodger manager Chuck Dressen appeared ready to send his closer, Joe Black, to the mound to start Game One.[8]

Black delivered, holding the Yanks to six hits, enabling Brooklyn to win 4–2 at Ebbets Field. McDougald swatted a triple and a third-inning homer, and Mantle went two for four, but Berra and Bauer were hitless. Also getting only six hits, the Dodgers managed a trio of homers, one each by Robinson, Snider, and Reese, with both Duke and Pee Wee going two for four. This after "the Bums" had only managed seven homers in their five previous World Series appearances. For Snider, who also delivered a double, his performance amounted to "revenge" for the three times Reynolds struck him out in the 1949 World Series opener. "I swore I'd get even, and I did today."[9]

The Yankees bounced back in Game Two, scoring five times in the top of the sixth inning to knock out Erskine, while Raschi shut down the Dodgers on three singles, while striking out nine. Mantle went three for five, including a double, and scored twice. Berra was two for three, with an RBI. But the big contributor at the plate was the normally light-hitting second baseman Billy Martin, who had become a regular in the Yankees lineup during the regular season. Martin got two hits in four at bats, swatting a three-run homer off reliever Billy Loes. Erskine's shaky performance and lack of control, leading to six walks, may have been impacted by a locker-room injury he suffered before the game, banging his head and reinjuring a knee. But Robinson admitted, "We probably couldn't have won no matter how well we played" because Raschi "was never as sharp as he was today."[10]

Regaining the Series lead, the Dodgers won Game Three at Yankee Stadium, 5–3, with Roe outdueling Lopat. Berra was three for four, including an eighth-inning homer, but the Yankees outhit the Dodgers 11–6, with Robinson and Pafko getting two hits and Reese, three. With both teams collecting only four hits, Reynolds evened the Series by shutting out the Dodgers 2–0 with Robinson called out on strikes three times, even though Black gave up only three hits and one run in seven innings of work; 71,787 fans were in attendance. Only Reese managed a pair of hits for Brooklyn, while the nearly 40-year-old veteran Johnny Mize got a double and a fourth-inning homer off Black. Mantle scored in the eighth after a 450-foot triple off reliever Johnny Rutherford. The Dodgers moved to within a game of their first World Series championship, beating the Yankees in 11 innings, 6–5. Despite another shaky outing, Erskine went all the way, while Yankee starter Ewell Blackwell was replaced in the sixth inning by Sain, who pitched credibly for the final six frames but was the losing pitcher. Most of the scoring occurred in the fifth, when the Dodgers notched three runs, only to be topped by the Yankees' five. Cox and Snider both got three hits, while Duke homered off Ewell, and ended the game by doubling to drive in Cox, his fourth RBI of the game. Eking out only five hits, the Yankees were again led by Mize, who smacked a three-run homer off Erskine.

Back at Ebbets Field, the Yankees needed to win Game Six and Game Seven to retain their World Series title. They did so, winning two tight contests, 3–2 and 4–2. With Reynolds getting the last four outs, Raschi won for the second time in Game Six, beating Loes as the Yankees came back from a 1–0 deficit after six innings. Berra and Mantle homered off Loes, and both Gene Woodling and Irv Noren got two hits apiece, matching the total of the Dodgers' Cox and Snider. Each of Snider's hits was a homer, giving him four for the Series. Game Seven, which saw Lopat and Black face off, was scoreless for the first three innings, followed by the next two, when each team scored once in each inning. Lopat departed in the fourth inning, replaced by Reynolds, who went three innings before being replaced by Raschi for one out, followed by Bob Kusava, who lasted two-and-two-thirds innings. The Yankees inched ahead with another run in the top of the sixth, knocking out Black, added another the next inning, and held for a 4–2 victory—Reynolds got his second win—and their fourth straight World Series title, enabling Stengel to tie Joe McCarthy's record. The Dodgers got a pair of hits each from Cox and Campanella, while the Yankees got two from McDougald, Mantle, Mize, and Woodling. Both Woodling and Mantle homered off Black.[11]

Mantle delivered two homers and a .345 batting average, while Mize hit three homers, drove in six, and batted .400. Berra also got two homers, Woodling hit .348, and Noren, .300. While Lopat foundered, both Raschi and Reynolds picked up a pair of victories, and Reynolds added a save. Snider excelled for the Dodgers, getting ten hits, including the four homers that tied a mark set by Ruth and Gehrig, setting a new standard with 24 total bases, and hitting .345. Reese also got ten hits and batted .345, while Cox hit .296. But the Dodgers were outhomered 11–6, and some of their best players failed to deliver. Campanella hit only .214 with no extra-base hits or RBIs. Furillo and Robinson each batted .174. Pafko hit .190. Most surprising of all, Hodges was hitless in 21 official at bats, scoring only one run and driving in one. Black pitched his heart out, winning Game One and throwing another gem in a losing Game Four, but he displayed a tired arm by Game Seven.[12]

According to Robinson, "They didn't miss Joe DiMaggio. It was that Mantle, that Mickey Mantle killed us. If it hadn't been for him I think this would have been a very different Series." Jackie contended, "We came so close. We had so many opportunities. But Mantle was the difference." Dodger manager Dressen agreed that Mantle and Johnny Mize "hurt us in the long run." However, he argued, "In the long run it was Reynolds who gave us the most trouble. He's big and strong, a great pitcher."[13]

With the World Series wrapped up, Mantle received his delayed physical examination for the US Army in Oklahoma City. Following that exam, Mantle was compelled to go to Fort Sill for additional exploration of his chronic bone disease. On November 3, the Army Surgeon General, Major General George E. Armstrong, declared Mantle "unfit for military service because of a chronic knee defect."[14]

While Willie Mays and Monte Irvin missed most of the 1952 regular season and Newcombe was serving in the military, other former Negro Leaguers like Robinson and Campanella continued making their mark in the major leagues. Larry Doby delivered another All-Star performance, scoring a league-high 104 runs, 32 homers, and .541 slugging average. Hank Thompson rebounded from a poor showing in 1951, hitting 17 homers and driving in 67 runs. Also named to the All-Star team, Satchel Paige went 12–10 with a 3.07 ERA for the St. Louis Browns, finishing an AL-best 35 games while getting a pair of shutouts in only half-a-dozen starts. All-Star Minnie Minoso won the AL stolen base crown. Luke Easter produced 31 homers and 97 RBIs, leading *The Sporting News* to name him AL Player of the Year. Thirty-five-year-old Sam Jethroe managed 28 stolen bases but failed to retain his NL title and slid to a .232 batting average.

8

Franchise Shift and Wait 'Til Next Year Season, Yet Again

Major League Baseball (MLB) experienced both continuity and change in 1953. Continuing a trend that began, however slightly, with the 1949 season, attendance figures at major league games had dropped each year since. The 1952 season had seen 14,633,044 fans at the 16 big league ballparks, an average of 11,810 per game. Those numbers were markedly lower than in 1948, when MLB attendance records were established. Minor league attendance also were in a downward spiral that heightened markedly as major league games became televised. Many blamed the medium that was quickly becoming a staple in American households for the decline in attendance at both major and minor league contests.

Even winning teams like the Yankees and the Dodgers saw fewer fans at home games. In 1945, Ebbets Field welcomed just over one million fans to watch a third-place team. The next year, attendance jumped to almost 1.8 million through a heated pennant race. Brooklyn, now with Jackie Robinson attracting a new crop of boosters, bumped up to just over 1.8 million, as the Dodgers won their first pennant in six years. But another third-place finish resulted in over 400,000 fewer fans, although over half that number came back as Brooklyn won again in 1949. The heartbreaking 1950 and 1951 seasons again saw fewer fans than in peak attendance years, and the 1952 pennant-winning Dodgers drew less than 1.1 million, barely more than in 1945.

With a mediocre record spanning the period from 1945–9, the New York Giants began that period by attracting nearly as many fans to the Polo Grounds as the Dodgers did at Ebbets Field. Despite finishing in the league cellar in 1946, the Giants' attendance jumped to over 1.2 million during the first full year following the war and continued to soar, as did that of many other major league teams. It went past 1.6 million but began dipping in 1948, falling to almost 1.46 million, followed by another drop to just under 1.22 million the next year. Leo Durocher's third-place team in 1950 barely drew one million to the Polo Grounds, as did the pennant-winning squad in 1951. A second-place finish the next season failed to prevent the Giants from attracting fewer than one million fans for the first time in eight years.

The third-place Bronx Bombers, sorely missing a bevy of stars, attracted fewer than 800,000 to Yankee Stadium in 1944. That number jumped about 100,000 for Joe McCarthy's weakest Yankee squad in 1945, which ended up in fourth place, but then soared in 1946 with the veterans back. Almost 2.27 million went through the Stadium's turnstiles, even though the Yankees only came in third. A slight drop in attendance accompanied the Yankees' pennant in 1947, but an increase to just below 2.4 million followed the next season, when New York dropped to a close third in a hotly contested American League pennant fight. Stengel's first Yankee team in 1949 was about as popular, but a decrease of over 200,000 fans went along with a second straight championship. Stadium attendance fell below two million in 1951, in spite of a third title, then slid more than 300,000 during the fourth year of the latest Yankee dynasty, falling to just under 1.63 million.

Other major league teams, even competitive ones, were also experiencing attendance shortfalls, some of an egregious sort. Boston's Fenway Park's attendance ranged from almost 604,000 in 1945 to a high of nearly 1.6 million in 1949, before dropping to about 1.16 million by 1952. Boston's Braves Field started at a bit more than 374,000 in 1945, peaked at about 1.46 million three years later—when the Braves won the NL pennant—before plunging to around 487,000 in 1951 and barely more than 281,000 the next year. The pennant-winning Chicago Cubs drew over 1 million to Wrigley Field in 1945, increased that number to 1.364 within two years, slipped to 894,000 in 1951, before rebounding to approximately 1.025 million in 1952. The 1945 White Sox had about 658,000 at Comiskey Park, shot up to just over 1.364 million by 1951, then dropped by over 100,000 the next year.

The Philadelphia Athletics' Shibe Park saw around 463,000 fans in 1945, reached a high of around 945,000 three years later, then fell to less than 310,000 two years later, moving back to around 465,000 and 627,000 in 1951 and 1952, respectively. The Phillies, also hosting at Shibe Park, barely drew 285,000 in 1945, shot up to over 1 million the next year, reached a high of 1.217 million in the pennant-winning 1950 campaign, before sliding to barely over 755,000 within two years. The St. Louis Browns, playing at Sportsman's Park, managed only around 483,000 in 1945, scant fewer than in their previous year's lone successful pennant drive. Never achieving the boom other major league teams experienced after the war, the Browns drew just over 300,000 in 1947 and in 1948, fewer than that number for the following three years, with a low of 247,131 in 1950, before bumping up to around 519,000 in 1952. Playing in the same ballpark, the infinitely more successful Cardinals went from around 595,000 in 1945 to over 1 million in their pennant-winning 1946 campaign, had as many as 1,430,676 fans in 1949, but slid to just over 900,000 by 1952.

Single-team cities experienced similar attendance rises and collapses. Cleveland Stadium's attendance went from nearly 560,000 in 1945 to over a million and to more than 1.5 million within the next year. Then, in 1948, its turnstiles recorded a record 2,620,627 patrons during the year when the Indians won their first pennant since 1920. Remaining above 2.2 million in 1949, that figure began dropping sharply, by over a half-million the next year, then down to around 1.45 million by 1952. Cincinnati's Crosley Field had a mere 290,070 fans in 1945, while a postwar high of just around 900,000 fans took place in 1947. Attendance went as low as 539,000 by 1950, inching back to 604,000 in 1952. Playing at Briggs Stadium, the Detroit Tigers had a robust 1.28 million in winning the pennant in 1945, shot up to 1.951 million by 1951, but fell to just over a million within two years. The Pittsburgh Pirates, playing at Forbes Field, started at 605,000 in 1945, mushroomed to 1.517 million three years later, then fell as low as 687,000 by 1952. The Washington Senators, based at

Griffith Stadium, had 653,000 fans in attendance in 1945, then reached a high of 1.027 million the next year, falling to just below 700,000 annually from 1950–52.

Thus, it was clear that overall attendance at major league games had peaked, soaring to unprecedented levels from 1946–1949, then slipping to its lower point since the end of the war. More significantly, several franchises, some having experienced temporary attendance gains, including of a noteworthy sort, fell into the doldrums as the costs of running franchises continued to increase. The Braves, Browns, and Athletics appeared particularly troubled and the kind of rumors that had long floated around the major leagues only mounted. Those involved the possibility of franchise shifts, something MLB had avoided for decades.

Certain possibilities had hardly seemed conceivable, yet received airing, nevertheless. During the summer of 1947, talk was heard of moves by both the St. Louis Browns and the St. Louis Cardinals. The Browns, assisted by Babe Ruth, were supposedly heading to Los Angeles. Sam Breadon, owner of the World Champion St. Louis Cardinals, winners of four pennants and three Series titles in the past five years, refuted talk that a move to Chicago might be impending. "I don't plan to move the Cardinals," Breadon insisted. "As long as I am in baseball, they will be here. The St. Louis public has patronized the club well." National League president Ford Frick purportedly floated the idea, thinking a Cubs-Cardinals rivalry in Chicago could match that of the Dodgers and Giants.[1]

Los Angeles Times sportswriter Al Wolf considered a move to the West Coast highly unlikely, requiring a unanimous vote by whichever league would be directly involved. However, shortly after Breadon's denial, *Washington Post* sports columnist Shirley Povich predicted attendance records would fall "when major league baseball come to Los Angeles, as it surely will some day." Opening-day attendance would reach 99,000, Povich indicated. Big league owners were already anticipating "the richer revenue from Los Angeles." Fans along the Pacific Coast wanted to view hometown players like "the DiMaggios and Bobby Doerr and Ted Williams and Gordon . . . in a big league setting, not in the after-season exhibition games out here."[2]

Big bumps in attendance muted talk of franchise shifts, but as those numbers dropped substantially by 1950, discussion of such developments recurred.

With St. Louis Browns president Bill DeWitt issuing such a threat, the *New York Times* Arthur Daley had difficulty taking him seriously. Mockingly, Daley noted that DeWitt was claiming "offers from Los Angeles, Dallas, Houston, Baltimore, Milwaukee and Kansas City." St. Louis, Daley agreed, was unable to back more than a single big league team. Thanks to Branch Rickey, the Cardinals had become a model, ever-competitive franchise able to attract "crowds," while the Browns offered "shoddy merchandise" and "couldn't draw flies."[3]

Testifying before the House Judiciary Committee on October 15, 1951, Clark Griffith, owner of the Washington Senators, conveyed his continued resistance to placing a major league team "in the South, the Southwest or the Far West." Denying that Pacific Coast teams deserved entrée, Griffith also considered the West Coast to be "too remote for established teams to work out schedules." Moreover, he said, "You're not ready for it on the West Coast. Where are you going to get the ball parks, the revenue, the ball players? There aren't enough good ball players for the two major leagues now. You'll just have to grow. You're not big enough."[4]

MLB's executive council, whose spokesperson was the new commissioner, Ford Frick, established guidelines "for circuits desiring to advance to big league status," while also knocking down proposals to expand the National or American leagues. Projected metropolitan areas required substantial populations, a recent three-year record of favorable minor league attendance, ballparks with a 25,000-person seating capacity at a minimum, $2 million pension fund payments, and both unanimous consent by and compensation to impacted minor league teams.[5]

Less than a month before the 1953 regular season was to begin, new rumors circulated regarding possible movement of one or more franchises. The Browns were apparently considering Baltimore, while the Braves were targeting Milwaukee. Such developments, the *Washington Post*'s Shirley Povich prophesied, would kill "California's chances of getting a big league ball club, perhaps forever." Commissioner Frick reminded Browns' owner Bill Veeck and Braves' owner Lou Perini that each required approval from the affected minor leagues and then from the appropriate major league. Key political and business operatives expressed displeasure with the Braves' perceived move. Deeming the big league season's opening too close at hand, AL owners refused to deliver the requisite three-fourths vote to allow the Browns' transfer to Baltimore, a stab at St. Louis' controversial owner Veeck. By contrast, NL bosses unanimously okayed the Braves' departure to Milwaukee.[6]

Having more than a million dollars on his baseball team, Perini indicated that television had helped to compel his team's move. He admitted, "the enthusiasm of the fans waned considerable." Milwaukee, Perini believed, was "a major league city in every sense of the word" and had "facilities for a major league club." The decision to relocate, he indicated, established a "trend" that could be replicated.[7]

*****

Thus, the first franchise shift since the NL-AL merger 50 years earlier unfolded, as one two-team city lost one of its ball clubs although St. Louis remained MLB's furthest point westward. The Braves fared better in their new destination both at the box office and on the playing field than they had in Boston, their home since 1876. A crowd as large as 80,000 greeted the Braves as their caravan traversed downtown Milwaukee on April 8, 1953. "This is marvelous, just marvelous," owner Perini exclaimed. "There was never anything like this in Boston," not "even in 1948, when he won the pennant. . . . This is just out of this world."[8]

The Braves' new found popularity helped to prevent MLB from experiencing another major drop in attendance. Playing in County Stadium, they drew 1,826,397 fans, a league record, and a massive increase over the 281,278 that visited Braves Field during the 1952 season. In the process, the Braves went from being the worst attended team in the NL to its most popular, catapulting from a per game attendance figure of 3,653 to 23,119. As early as their 13th home contest, the Braves surpassed the previous year's attendance mark.

Rebounding from an abysmal seventh place finish and 64–89–2 record, the Braves, relying on a healthy mixture of veterans and young players guided by new manager Charlie Grimm, finished second to the Dodgers, albeit 13 games behind. Thirty-two-year-old lefty Warren Spahn went 23–7, winning the most games and the ERA title (2.10) in the National League, while 24-year-old Bob Buhl was 13–8 with a 2.97 ERA, and 26-year-old Lew Burdette was 15–5 with a 3.24 ERA. Twenty-three-year-old Del Crandall, hitting 15 homers in 382 official at bats, became a fine, power-hitting catcher. First baseman Joe Adcock, two years old than Crandall, hit 18 homers, drove in 80 runs, and batted .285. Twenty-five-year-old second baseman Jack Dittmer batted .266. The 27-year-old shortstop, Johnny Logan, scored 100 runs, while outfielder Bill Bruton, the same age, stole 26 bases. Veteran outfielder Sid Gordon, now 35 years old, delivered 19 homers and 75 RBIs, and 32-year-old Andy Pafko, traded from the Dodgers, hit 17 homers and batted .297. Twenty-nine-year-old utility outfielder Jim Pendleton, formerly of the Chicago American Giants, hit .299.

The Braves' batting star was third baseman Eddie Mathews, a 21-year-old heartthrob, who, before the season began, was on the cover of *Baseball Digest*. An article by Harold Sheldon, "Long Distance Mathews," indicated that "the home run king of the near future could well be" the young Brave, "the greatest threat to pitched leather that has entered the National League since Ralph Kiner." Mathews, "the National League's answer to Mickey Mantle," managed 25 homers in his rookie campaign, placing him fourth in the NL. More noticable was "the way that he hit them that has excited Bostonian. Every one of the blows was tagged with authority." Viewed as "a natural," Mathews led the majors with 47 homers during the 1953 season, scored 110 runs, drove in 135, hit .302, and finished second in the MVP race.[9]

The New York Yankees and the Brooklyn Dodgers repeated as pennant winners, and the Yankees once again prevailed in the World Series, winning for a record fifth straight time. The Yankees had their best record yet under Casey Stengel, with a 99–52 record that again beat out the Indians, this time by eight and a half games. The White Sox and Red Sox rounded out the first division, followed by the Senators, Tigers, Athletics, and the Browns, who landed in the cellar with a 54–100 record, forty six and a half games behind the Yankees. Behind the Dodgers and the Braves in the National League came the Phillies and Cardinals, tied for third. The New York Giants topped the second division, having fallen to 70–84, ahead of the Redlegs, Cubs, and Pirates. Cincinnati's team had been renamed in the charged atmosphere of the postwar red scare with "Reds" temporarily discarded for the more innnocuous "Redlegs."[10]

Catchers Yogi Berra and Roy Campanella, 1951 MVP winners, became second-time recipients. Twenty-one-year-old Mickey Mantle remained among the game's brightest young stars, while Jackie Robinson continued to excel at the plate, on the bases, and in the field. On April 17, Mantle, batting right-handed, powered a drive off southpaw pitcher Chuck Stobbs 565 feet, landing it beyond Griffith Stadium's left field wall. Yankee coach Bill Dickey, a former teammate of both Ruth and Gehrig, declared, "I saw Babe and Lou hit balls out of parks all over the country. Also I was catching when fellows like Jimmie Foxx were blasting pitches a good country mile. Frankly, I never thought I'd see their like again, but now I've changed my mind." Dickey continued, "For sheer power, Mickey ranks with the best of them and what is more important is that—unlike those other sockers—he can belt from either side of the plate. I think he may eventually be rated at the tops of all time."[11]

Before the season started, sportswriter Charles Dexter asked, "Can Mickey Carry a Big Load?" Having had a fine year in 1952, "the only question remaining to be answered about Mickey's ability to bellwether the Bronxites for many years to come lies in his development as a man of baseball distinction and character." Dexter wondered, "Will Mickey Mantle, like Babe Ruth, Lou Gehrig, and Joe DiMaggio, his distinguished predecessors as Yankee superstars, be able to carry the awesome load?" After all, Dexter explained, "Baseball occupies a niche almost alongside religion in the American scene today." Therefore, "the superstar, if Mickey is one, must be much more than a baseball player. He must be an example to American youth, a public speaker and TV personality . . . a husband, father and friend of the small fry everywhere." The switch-hitting Mantle had "the level swing, the co-ordination of body and arms . . . speed in breaking from plate and . . . remarkable power." Mantle, "a beautiful piece of baseball machinery," and "at 21 the path to glory spread wide and open before him," offered the possibility that "he may eventually become the superest-star of them all." *Sport* magazine placed Mantle on its April 1953 cover along with the declaration "New Pride of the Yankees."[12]

Continuing his torrid hitting from the World Series, Duke Snider vied with Mathews as the NL's top slugger. Returning from military service, Ted Williams hit as if it were 1941, when he was the last .400 hitter, albeit in only 91 official at-bats, while his NL counterpart, Stan Musial, failed in his effort to four-peat as batting champion, despite hitting a point higher—.337—than the previous season. Whitey Ford also came back after two years in the US Army, allowing the Yankees to have a Big Four starting rotation as in the latter stages of the 1950 campaign. Or more accurately put, a Big Five, due to the addition of Johnny Sain. The difference now was that Ford, still only 24 years old, became arguably the top pitcher among Stengel's lustrous crop of starting pitchers.

Experiencing somewhat of a drop in attendance and finishing behind Milwaukee in the number of fans attending home games, the New York Yankees still topped the American League with over 1.5 million ticket holders. Berra and Mantle led Yankee batters, the catcher contributing 27 homers, 108 RBIs, and a .296 BA, the center fielder scoring 105 runs, getting 21 homers, driving in 92, and batting .295. Gene Woodling batted .306, two points higher than Hank Bauer. Gil McDougald hit .295. The Yankees again relied on its top starters, headed by Ford, who went 18–6 with a 3.00 ERA. Eddie Lopat was 16–4 with a league-best .800 win-loss percentage and 2.42 ERA. Vic Raschi added a 13–6 record and 3.33 ERA. Still both starting and relieving, Allie Reynolds was 13–7 with a 3.41 ERA, while another dual threat, Johnny Sain, was 14–7 with a 3.00 ERA.

The team with the best record in the majors, the Brooklyn Dodgers, included some lineup changes, with Pafko traded, former Baltimore Elite Giant Jim Gilliam replacing Jackie Robinson at second base, and Robinson stationed in left field. As a team, the Dodgers, with a slight bump in attendance that placed them well behind the Braves, hit 208 homers and batted .285. In his finest season, Campanella scored 103 runs, delivered 41 homers, drove in 142, and batted .312. Despite finishing third in the MVP contest, Duke Snider outhit his teammate, scoring a league-high 132 runs, collecting 198 hits, swatting 38 doubles, smacking 42 homers, driving in 126 runs, and batting .336. He also led the NL in total bases (370), slugging (.627), and OPS 1.046. Gil Hodges' batting statistics included 101 runs, 31 homers, 122 RBIs, and a .302 BA. Robinson's were stellar too: 109 runs, 12 homers, 95 RBIs, 17 steals, and a .329 batting average. Carl Furillo has his best year, producing 21 homers, 92 RBIs, and a league-leading .344 batting mark. Appearing in only 100 games, Billy Cox still hit .291, while Dodger mainstay Pee Wee Reese scored 108 runs, got 13 homers, and hit .271. Newcomer Gilliam had 125 runs scored, 31 doubles, 17 triples, and a .278 BA, leading to his selection as Brooklyn's fourth Rookie of the Year selection in seven years; all four were former Negro Leaguers. Carl

Erskine again led Dodgers pitchers, with a 20–6 record and an NL-leading .769 win-loss percentage. Russ Meyer was 15–8, Billy Loes, 14–3, the seemingly ageless Preacher Roe, 11–3, Clem Labine, 11–6 with a staff-best 2.77 ERA. Twenty-year-old rookie left-hander Johnny Podres went 9–4 with the kind of ERA characteristic of many Dodger pitchers that year: 4.23. Joe Black was even worse, going 6–3 with a 5.33 ERA in his sophmore year with Brooklyn.

The slumping New York Giants, with a considerable decline in attendance that left them with just over 800,000 fans and still without their star center fielder Willie Mays, nevertheless featured several players who had fine years at the plate. While Wes Westrum never proved comfortable at the plate, other regulars delivered, led by Monte Irvin who had 21 homers, 97 RBIs, and a .329 BA, four points less than Don Mueller. Whitey Lockman and second baseman Davey Williams batted in the mid-.290s, while Bobby Thompson hit 26 homers, drove in 106 runs, and hit .288. Al Dark scored 126 runs, had 194 hits, got 41 doubles, produced 23 homers, delivered 88 RBIs, and batted .300, two points less than Hank Thompson, who had 24 homers. The Giant pitching was middling to poor, with rookie Ruben Gomez, from Puerto Rico, presenting a 13–11 win-loss mark with a 3.40 ERA. Larry Jansen, Jim Hearn, Sal Maglie, Hoyt Wilhelm, and Dave Koslo all posted losing records. Max Lanier's career came to an inglorious end.

*****

Shortly before the World Series began, the long-delayed move of the St. Louis Browns to Baltimore received approval from American League owners. This came after the Browns" Bill Veeck deflected rumors of a possible relocation to Kansas City or Los Angeles. There had even been talk of a move to Toronto or Montreal. Yankees co-owner Del Webb pointed to Los Angeles and San Francisco as the best sites for the Athletics and the Browns, provided long-discussed Coast League plans to obtain major league status failed to come to fruition. "The country has moved West. Business and industry have gone there. It's a great part of the nation." Webb stated. "Why shouldn't the national game go that way, too?" he asked. "Why should the major leagues be concentrated in places so close together as Boston, New York, Washington, Philadelphia, and Pittsburgh?" The Browns franchise, Webb admitted, had become "the plight of the American League. Something must be done about it—and real soon, too." However, Veeck continued to bat down talk of a move to California.[13]

By early September, Veeck reported that seven municipalities—Baltimore, Houston, Kansas City, Montreal, Toronto, and Minneapolis-St. Paul—sought to attract his ball club. Later in the month, a syndicate purchased Veeck's controlling interest for nearly $2.5 million. With that transaction settled, American League owners, delighted to be rid of the talented but mercurial Veeck, unanimously agreed to allow the Browns to resettle in Baltimore. This was to be the AL's first franchise transfer since the merger with the National League 50 years earlier and MLB's second during that time span, following the Braves' move to Milwaukee prior to the start of the regular season. Losing out were investors who sought to relocate the Browns to Los Angeles but failed to amass the necessary capital. One reason for the reticence was a warning by Phil Wrigley, who owned the Chicago Cubs and the Cubs' minor league team in Los Angeles, who indicated that both LA and San Francisco required major league teams to be viable.[14]

*****

Paired again and meeting for the fourth time in the past seven World Series, the Yankees and Dodgers opened at Yankee Stadium, where the home team won the first two games, 9–5 and 4–2. Neither starter lasted long, Erskine gone after the first-inning, Reynolds knocked out in the sixth, when reliever Sain blew a save. But Sain held on long enough to notch the victory, with Dodger reliever Labine taking the loss. Breaking out of his World Series slump from the previous year, Hodges went three for five, including a homer. Gilliam got a pair of hits, one a homer, and pinch hitter George Shuba also homered, the third of three homers off Reynolds, normally a World Series stalwart. Snider and Cox each got two hits, one a double. Matching the Dodgers' 12 hits, the Yankees were led by Martin with three, and two each by Collins, Bauer, and Berra. Both Berra and Collins homered.

With both Roe and Lopat going the distance in Game Two, the Yankees outhit the Dodgers 9 to 5. Reese, Hodges, and Furillo had two hits apiece, with Cox driving in two runs. Martin had a pair of hits, one a game-tying, seventh-inning homer, while Mantle also homered off Roe, a two-run eighth-inning smash that proved to be the game winner.

Back in Ebbets Field, the Dodgers also won two straight, by 3–2 and 7–3 counts. Erskine outdueled Raschi in Game Three, striking out fourteen Yankees to set a new World Series mark, while scattering six singles. Robinson led the Dodgers with three hits, while Campanella delivered a game-deciding blow in the bottom of the eighth. Going eight innings, Loes gave way to Labine in the ninth, while Ford lasted only through the first. Berra and Martin managed two hits each, and McDougald delivered a two-run, fifth-inning homer. Outhitting the Yankees 12–9, the Dodger batters included Gilliam and Snider with three hits each, Gilliam driving in a pair of runs, while Snider doubled twice and homered off reliever Sain in the sixth, producing four RBIs.

Coming back in Game 5, the Yankees left the Dodger faithful dismayed at Ebbets Field, wielding 11 hits to produce an 11–7 victory that overcame 14 hits by the losing team. Sometime starter Jim McDonald got the win despite relinquishing twelve hits and five earned runs, with Bob Kuzava and Reynolds each getting a pair of outs to wrap up the game. Podres was knocked out in the third, having allowed five runs, although only one was earned. Berra, Martin, and McDougald had two hits each, while Woodling, Mantle, Martin, and McDougald homered, Mickey's a grand slam off reliever Russ Meyer in the top of the third. Campanella had three hits, while Gilliam, Snider, and Hodges had two each. Cox drove a three-run homer, eighth-inning homer off McDonald, while Gilliam delivered a solo shot off Kuzava in the ninth.[15]

Back in the Bronx, the Yankees handed Stengel a fifth straight World Series title, three involving whipping the Dodgers. Ford skillfully navigated through seven innings, giving up only a run, but Reynolds got the win in relief after blowing the save. Erskine lasted only four innings, with Labine again losing in relief, after the Dodgers scored twice in the top of the ninth on a Furillo blast off Reynolds to tie the game. Martin delivered the walk-off RBI, driving in Bauer in the bottom of the frame. Furillo had three hits and Robinson a pair as Woodling, Berra, Martin, and Rizzuto managed two hits apiece for the Yanks. Martin, called "My Boy" by Stengel, starred throughout the Series, getting twelve hits, eight RBIs, and batting .500. Mantle and McDougald matched his two homers, while Berra hit .429 and Rizzuto, .316. Hodges's pyrric redemption was virtually complete as he batted .364, while Furillo hit .333. Robinson and Snider, who hit his fifth World Series homer, tying a National League record, batted .320, Cox, .304.[16]

*****

With more former Negro Leaguers playing in the National League and the American League than ever, the finest performers, other than those whose playing skills had ebbed, continued to excel, including those on the three New York City teams. A broken foot curbed the playing time of the Indians' Luke Easter, who managed 7 homers and 31 RBIs with a .303 BA in only 211 official at bats. Satchel Paige pitched decently for the Browns but received no support in putting up a 3–9 mark despite a respectable 3.53 ERA. Now reputedly 47 years old, Paige would not throw again in the majors until he tossed a scoreless 3 innings for the Athletics at the age of 59. The White Sox's Minnie Minoso got 15 homers, 104 RBIs, a .313 batting average, a league-leading 25 stolen bases, resulting in another All-Star selection along with a fourth-place tabulation in the AL MVP race.

Three future stars, two of them former Kansas City Monarchs, Ernie Banks and Elston Howard, and a third, Vic Power, a veteran of the Puerto Rican League, readied for the 1954 season. Shortstop Banks, after two years of military service, rejoined the Monarchs, hitting .347, before making his initial appearance with the Chicago Cubs in 1953. In 10 games, he collected 11 hits, including a double, a triple, and two homers, in 35 official at bats, a .314 BA. Catcher Howard, who had spent the past two years in the military, appeared primed to join the New York Yankees as their first African American player. So did Power, a smooth-looking first baseman-outfielder and hitter. Both would be scheduled to report to the Yankees spring training camp.[17]

Dan Topping, the Yankees president, denied that the failure of his ball club to bring up Power or to have any Black players during the 1953 season was due to racism. "Jim Crow, my eye. Who brought up the first Negro football player into the All-America Conference? I did. I signed Buddy Young. How can anyone accuse any organization of which I am the head of Jim Crowism?" Topping added, "The Negro has established himself in the major leagues. We are eager to get a Negro player on the Yankees. But we are not going to bring up a Negro just to meet the demands of pressure groups. We will glad to place on the Yankees any Negro player who can make that place for himself on his ability."[18]

Perhaps it should not have been surprising when the Yankees shipped Powers off to the Athletics as part of a 13-man swap on December 16. The Yankees, who had recently been informed of retirements by Johnny Sain and Johnny Mize, picked up pitcher Harry Byrd, the 1952 AL Rookie of the Year, and power-hitting first baseman Eddie Robinson while sending away Power and benchwarmers Bill Renna and Don Bollweg, with several other players involved in the transaction. Yankee general manager George Weiss indicated that Power, who had just led the American Association in batting, was the key figure in the swap, according to Philadelphia.

Understanding the criticism the Yankees had endured regarding their white-only makeup, Weiss insisted, "Power's color played no part in the . . . decision to let Vic go." Power and Howard had been included on the Yankees roster toward the end of the recent regular season. "It would be weak to hold Power just because we were afraid of censure," Weiss insisted. "We showed our good faith by bringing up Power and Howard and will bring up others to the Yankees when they merit it."[19]

The *New York Times* Arthur Daley thought the Yankees had engaged in "grand larceny," obtaining "two recognized stars for a batch of expendable second-line ballplayers." He suggested New York might flip Robinson to Baltimore, to get Bob Turley, "a strong-armed, fireballing right-hander" viewed as "another Walter Johnson." He was "the guy the Yanks really want," Daley wrote.

The columnist admitted that the deal left "the Yankees exposed at one vulnerable spot," referring to the trade of Power. "This is one of those awkward, delicate things that can provoke rabble-rousing," Daley stated. "The Yanks never had a Negro ballplayer and have been accused of bias. This, of course, has been denied most violently." Rather, "The Bombers were merely waiting, they claimed, for the right Negro to come along and they refused to be panicked into reaching out blinding for anyone." Experts, Daley noted, reasoned "that Howard, a smarter and more tractable performer, will be a better player than Power in the years to come." But Power might have made the Yankees team, while Howard presently had "little chance of" doing so.[20]

*****

That December, the US Supreme Court, with Chief Justice Earl Warren presiding, began rehearing the case of *Brown v. The Board of Education*. The previous year, the Court had consolidated a series of cases involving whether segregation could be maintained in state-sponsored public education. The NAACP's Legal Defense and Education Fund had brought suit on behalf of the parents of school-age children precluded from attending public schools because of racial strictures. Its lead counsel, Thurgood Marshall, a veteran of judicial clashes involving Jim Crow practices in public education, argued the case before the High Court.

The case had arrived at the Supreme Court a year earlier when Fred Vinson was sitting at its head, and no resolution was made concerning the plaintiff's petition. Then, on September 8, 1953, Vinson, a Truman appointee, died, opening a space for the man who would help to transform American jurisprudence, including civil rights. The next month, President Dwight David Eisenhower nominated as Vinson's successor, Earl Warren, who was in his third term as governor of California and the former state attorney general. While Warren had supported the internment of Japanese and Japanese Americans during the Second World War, he would help to recast rulings regarding criminal procedure, representation, civil liberties, privacy protections, and civil rights, in a progressive direction during his tenure as chief justice.

Receiving his formal nomination in early January, Warren awaited confirmation by the Senate, which occurred on March 1. Deftly employing his considerable political skills, the new chief justice had to navigate among his strong-willed and opinionated judicial brethren. They included liberal appointees by FDR—Hugo L. Black, Stanley Reed, William O. Douglas, and Robert H. Jackson—along with Felix Frankfurter, whose progressive stances as a Harvard Law School professor hardly led to similar positions on the bench. Then there were Truman's selections, Harold Burton, Tom C. Clark, and Sherman Minton, whose judicial determinations often titled in a more conservative direction.[21]

9

Return of the Say Hey Kid

Their second straight World Series loss at the hands of the New York Yankees and their fourth in seven years or fifth in thirteen left Brooklyn's top brass befuddled and angry. Dodger vice president Buzzie Bavasi bemoaned the latest World Series setback by "the best team Brooklyn ever had." Only minutes after Billy Martin clinched another title for the Yankees, Brooklyn president Walter O'Malley told the Dodgers, "You all had a good season. You did well and there are no regrets." He then declared, "Once more, we'll have to wait 'til next year."[1]

In a very different manner, Yankee manager Casey Stengel also looked forward to the upcoming season. "The Yankees, as they are now constituted, have a good chance to win the pennant in 1954 unless the other clubs get stronger." Admitting his pitching required an upgrade, Stengel saw no weaknesses in the everyday lineup. "Mickey Mantle should be better. Gene Woodling is an outstanding player and Hank Bauer had a great year. In Irv Noren we have the best fourth outfielder in the league. He'd be playing regularly on another club. The infield and the catching are excellent." Graciously, Stengel indicated, "The Dodgers are the best ball club we played in the past five seasons."[2]

Early predictions had the Yankees and Dodgers meeting again in the 1954 World Series. There appeared to be "no end in sight to the New York Yankee parade." Stengel, deemed "the reigning genius," was speaking of "a sixth straight" title to continue fostering the "'hate the Yankees' crop." Having won 105 during the regular season, Brooklyn appeared primed to be "even better in '54" with the return of pitching ace Don Newcombe. Dressen seemed ready to beef up his pitching staff and outfield.[3]

Then, on October 14, only days following the end of the World Series, Dressen "quit in a huff" as Dodger manager after O'Malley refused his demand for a three-year contract, rather than the typical year-to-year arrangement Brooklyn afforded its field bosses. His franchise, O'Malley pointed out, adhered to one-year contracts for all its employees, from the players to those who worked in the front office. Dodger management clearly was demonstrating its belief that Dressen, however successful, was "entirely expendable."[4]

Pee Wee Reese expressed a willingness to serve as a player-manager and, for a time, appeared to be the front-runner. Also being considered were Walter Alston and Clay Bryant, both managers of Dodgers farm teams. Then, reports indicated that Reese, still desiring to play, turned down the job. In addition to Alston, other names being floated included Vice President Fresco Thompson, as an interim figure until Reese stopped playing, Brooklyn coach Cookie Lavagetto, former batting champion Lefty O'Doul, Bill Terry, and even longtime Yankee star Tommy Heinrich. On November 25, O'Malley informed the press that the 42-year-old Alston had been signed to a one-year deal.[5]

*****

The offseason featured a series of newsworthy events impacting the upcoming season, and others that really did not but were intriguing to many fans, nevertheless. In mid-January, Joe DiMaggio and Marilyn Monroe exchanged vows in the former Yankee star's hometown of San Francisco. The tempestuous relationship proved ill-fated and the marriage failed to last through the end of the year, although DiMaggio long carried a torch for the beautiful Hollywood actress, well past her untimely death eight years later. On February 2, the Baltimore Orioles dumped Satchel Paige, who immediately returned to barnstorming. That same month, the Brooklyn Dodgers, having outbid their crosstown rivals and the Milwaukee Braves, among other teams, signed 19-year-old Roberto Clemente, an amateur free agent outfielder from Puerto Rico.

The most significant decision regarding the 1954 major league season involved the US Army's release of Willie Mays only days prior to the start of spring training. The induction of the 1951 National League Rookie of the Year into the military 22 months earlier possibly prevented the Giants from repeating as pennant winners the next year. What was called "minor surgery" along with the uncertainty concerning his status resulted in Mays's slow start to the 1952 campaign.

But the young center fielder began to heat up and the 1952 edition of the Giants held a 24–8 record on May 26, placing them in first, just ahead of the Dodgers. The Giants had slipped into the NL's lead position following a game played at the Polo Grounds before 40,456 fans, with Bobby Thompson delivering a first-inning, two-run homer off Preacher Roe. Although Mays went hitless, the Giants prevailed, 4–2. In the crosstown series' second contest, Mays got two doubles and a homer as Sal Maglie shut out the Dodgers, 3–0, in front of 28,089 at Ebbets Field. The finale also went the Giants' way, this time by a 6–2 score, despite Willie again going hitless. Less than 16,000 were in attendance.

The legendary Grantland Rice was one of the first to pen a column honoring Mays, in which he stated, "No young ballplayer has shown greater promise in recent years. His day isn't over. He has time enough for baseball when he leaves the Army, around 23." Aware of Mays' departure from MLB, the Ebbets Field faithful delivered "a farewell that was tinged with more affection than any Giant has been accorded in Brooklyn since King Carl Hubbell's bow out," declared the *New York Daily News*. Wendell Smith noted, "The New York Giants won the ball game . . . but in the process lost the guy who is probably the best young ball player to come up to the majors in the past ten years. Willie Mays."[6]

The *New York Herald Tribune*'s Red Smith wrote, "Willie was in Ebbets Field wearing the gray flannels of the Giants for the last time in—a year? Two years? Eternity? Nobody knows?" Giants' manager Durocher, Smith indicated, "has become a genius among defensive managers—with Willie playing practically his whole outfield." One reporter indicated, "Leo's instructions to Willie are to catch anything he can reach, in left or center or right. He has top priority on all fly balls, and it's up to the other outfielders to get out of his way." Even the Dodgers fans at Ebbets Field cheered for him, although Brooklyn was "where 'Giant' is the dirtiest word in the language." As Mays headed into the dugout at the end of the game, the organist Gladys Goodding signaled, "I'll See You in My Dreams."[7]

Arthur Daley delivered his own "Farewell to Willie" in his sports column for the *New York Times*. "One year ago yesterday a scared kid of 20 made his first major league hit. Willie Mays hammered a majestic blast over the Polo Grounds roof against Warren Spahn. It was typical of Willie the Wonder that his flair for the spectacular should evince itself so early in his career," began Daley. However, Mays's career had, for now, come to an end. Later, Daley would also indicate that "the remnants of Giant pennant hopes" went "with him."[8]

The affection between Mays and his teammates, Daley noted, was "quite extraordinary. The Giants are crazy about him." Durocher lamented, "It's gonna be lonesome without Willie," then referred to him as "such a wonderful, unspoiled kid. Sure, we're gonna miss him as a ballplayer but we're gonna miss more as a person." Speaking to Dizzy Dean, Durocher declared, "The Giants without Willie would be the same as our old Gashouse Gang without Pepper Martin. He's the fellow you play with and kid. He's always laughing and good-natured, the heart and soul of the ball club."

Dodger players also extolled Mays. Carl Furillo declared, "The man is a menace. I still haven't recovered from the way he threw out Billy Cox at the plate last year on the ball I hit to him. I refuse to believe it's possible, even if I saw him do it all over again. I've made some pretty good throws in my time but there never was one like Willie's. What made it the more incredible was that he threw it all the way on the fly for a perfect strike." Jackie Robinson offered, "Willie is a pistol. Last night he doubled off the right field wall, homered over the right field wall and doubled again off the right field wall." Pee Wee Reese added, "Willie can do everything so well." Agreeing, Robinson said, "He will be truly great some day" and might return to the majors with greater "maturity and poise."[9]

The following March, the Giants received word that Mays's request for a dependency discharge, based on his being "the sole support of his mother, step-father," and nine siblings, had been denied. The Army indicated, the "dependency did not exist to a degree that warrants a discharge." That all but ensured Mays would miss the full 1953 season, which *Washington Post* columnist Shirley Povich soon addressed in a column titled, "Say, Hey, Willie, Hurry Back to Those Giants." Mays, Povich emphasized, "was something different" from other Black players who had entered the National League or the American League. Most "were middle-aged by baseball standards, and even older," prior to being "liberated from the colored circuits."[10]

By contrast, "Willie was the fresh-faced kid player unburdened by any deep social complexes." He became beloved by fellow Giants in a manner "no other colored player had ever commanded from his teammates." Rather than his hitting appealing to the other Giants—although Povich contradicted himself about that—it was "the throws he made, the balls he caught, the bases he stole, the laughs he provided and the tensions he eased; also the stout ticker that beat within his youthful chest."[11]

In late July 1953, Mays was hurt sliding into third base during a baseball game at Fort Eustis, Virginia, where he was stationed. Hospitalized due to a bone chip in his left foot, he was expected to be in a cast for several weeks. His injury and an announcement by the Pentagon as fighting ended in the Korean War underscored the fact that Mays and about 50 other major leaguers would not return to civilian life until their two-year stints were completed. It appeared, nevertheless, that most "big name players" would be eligible for spring training. Some, including pitchers Vernon Law of the Pirates and Erv Palica of the Dodgers were already out, while Ted Williams was to be released on July 28. Combat veterans Jerry Coleman and Bobby Brown, the Yankee infielders, were slated to be out in the fall. Brooklyn's Don Newcombe was scheduled for release in February; Mays, in May.[12]

However, in November, the Army indicated that the Giant youngster and other individuals who had employment contracts outside the military could receive their papers three months early. As that information appeared more reliable by mid-January, Leo Durocher expressed his delight. "Man, oh man, that's good news! That's better than having somebody hand me a 20-game pitcher on a silver platter—and how I need a 20-game pitcher!" Durocher predicted, "Having Willie back for the whole season automatically puts us in the first division." Dismissing the foot injury Mays suffered the previous summer, Durocher then exclaimed, "What a kid! He not only gives me the finest flyhawk in baseball, but a good hitter and an inspirational guy both on and off the field."[13]

On January 28, 1954, Shirley Povich's column, *This Morning*, discussed the presence of Black players in the major leagues, over eight years following the end of the color barrier. Jackie Robinson, Povich noted, "made good in a thumping way," serving as "a boon to the race." He "proved" Black players "could make a place for themselves on their merit, not as mediums of exploitation." Robinson's "experience" impacted the Negro Leagues, convincing players to "cut out their fancy-dan clowning and" play "serious baseball." Now, Blackball had become part of "the regular beat of the league scouts." Thus, in the manner of the Black boxing champion Joe Louis, Robinson had "opened a new vista for Negro athletes."

Soon, baseball moguls discovered "that not all of the Negro players are wonder boys like Robinson, and that any Negro they bring up is as much a gamble as the white player." Povich continued, "The early successes of such as Robinson, Roy Campanella, Doby, Willie Mays, and Don Newcombe could be explained. They were skimmed off the top of the Negro leagues. Beneath them, the colored players were something less than wonders."[14]

In early February, the Army indicated Willie Mays would be released soon, enabling him to join his teammates at the Giants' spring training camp in Phoenix. The Giants were one of four teams—the Cubs, Orioles, and Indians, as well—readying for the season by playing ball in Arizona. Writing in the *New York Herald Tribune*, Red Smith referred to "Mays hitting to all fields and running out from under his cap to pluck line drives off the wall." Smith wrote, "Green though he still is in big league baseball, Willie has a flare that sets him apart from the merely competent. It is impossible to watch him for long without realizing that here is an individual touched with genuine greatness."[15]

With Mays's return and the trade for Antonelli, whom he believed would "become one of baseball's greatest pitchers," Jackie Robinson predicted that the Giants, rather than the Braves, would be the Dodgers' toughest competitors for the National League pennant. He also indicated that a third major league was not in the offing but asserted, "Los Angeles and several other cities could support major league ball." With a good team, he believed that LA "would outdraw many of the others." Robinson indicated too that "one or more franchises sometime will be moved to the Coast."[16]

Roger Kahn, writing in the *New York Herald Tribune*, offered his own commentary on the Giant center fielder. "Willie is ten feet nine inches tall. He can jump fifteen feet straight up. Nobody can hit a ball over his head.

Willie's arms extend roughly from 157th Street to 159th Street," site of the Polo Grounds. Moreover, "Willie's speed is deceptive," appearing "a step faster than electricity." He did "more for a team's morale than Marilyn Monroe, Zsa Zsa Gabor and Rita Hayworth, plus cash."[17]

On March 1, Mays received his discharge papers and prepared to depart for spring training. During his 21-month stay at Eustis, he served as the Base Wheels center fielder, batting .420 the first year and .389 the next. The next day, Mays, who had played but one game after the injury to his left foot the previous summer—that with Robinson's barnstorming group in October—entered an intrasquad contest as a pinch hitter, then smacked a fifth-inning homer measured at 400 feet past the left field fence. Two frames later, "the incredible Willie made a spectacular, one-handed catch" of a ball pounded near "the wall in right center." He then "whirled and fired to first" to double up a runner. That same inning, he "raced back fifty feet and made an over-the-shoulder catch" robbing the batter of a two-base hit. All of this followed Mays's "royal welcome" on arriving in camp with a good deal of "back-slapping and hand-shaking." The next day, Mays homered again and prevented runners from advancing on three occasions. He homered against the Indians in a blowout loss, a game played on March 7 "before an overflow crowd of 7190." The following day against the Orioles, May swatted yet another homer. In another exhibition game against the Indians on March 12, Mays went three for five with a pair of homers and three RBIs. On March 18, Mays got three hits, two doubles and a homer, in four at bats.[18]

Baseball aficionados, *Los Angeles Times* sports columnist Braven Dyer indicated, viewed Mays as "a born center fielder, with wings on his feet for far roaming, the eye and co-ordination of a flannel-panted falcon, and a throwing arm that's more Winchester rifle than human." Regarding such praise, Mays responded, "That's mighty nice for 'em to say those things, but I'm a long way from the best center fielder. I got a lot of things to learn. I saw DiMaggio play, you know. Sure wish I had all the moving pictures ever made of Joe playing center field and batting. I've seen a lot of them, and every time I see 'em I find out something."

Manager Durocher considered Mays "great now, but" pointed out "that right now he is a baby. Just a little boy." Nevertheless, "one can easily gather that Leo sees in Willie a star," Dyer wrote, "that will shed a glowing light on the Polo Grounds for many years to come." The *New York Daily Mirror*'s Ken Smith, who had tracked the Giants for over a quarter-of-a-century, also discussed Mays. "He's not only a naturally great outfielder, but he's a naturally great youngster. No trouble with him. No worrying about where he is and what he's doing." On further reflection, Smith revealed, "No, I take that back, Leo did have trouble finding him several times in 1951. Once he looked for him right after a game and he was nowhere to be found. He sent Luis Pompey, a Giant scout, out to find him. Luis finally located him on a Harlem street, playing stickball with 15 or 20 youngsters."[19]

In *Sports of the Times*, Arthur Daley, after coursing through spring training sites, considered the Yankees and Dodgers likely to repeat. This was despite the fact that Raschi, having refused a substantial pay cut following another fine year on the mound, was sold to the Cardinals for $85,000, breaking up the Yankees' unassailable starting rotation. The Giants, Giants, Daley believed, "undoubtedly will baffle everyone all season long. They have Willie Mays back and they've already saddled poor Willie with an enormous load. He's the panacea for all ills; he'll lead them out of the wilderness; he'll—oh, well. Willie the Wonder can even unscramble mixed metaphors." Then Daley asked, "But can he win the pennant? It's more than a one-man job?"[20]

The Yankees' tight-fisted general manager, George Weiss, charged, "This club is complacent," in revealing the Raschi deal. "Raschi's attitude was like so many other attitudes on this club," he claimed. "There are players among the Yankees who expect you to chase after them so that they may take your money." Success on the playing field had enabled players to "become independently wealthy," fostering "a condition which is the enemy of hustle." Weiss warned, "We are not in a mood to stop winning. We have taken steps to eradicate complacency."[21]

In a front-page drawing for *The Sporting News*, sports cartoonist and creator of the "Brooklyn Bum" Willard Mullin offered "Little Rays of Hope" regarding "Yankee Domination." One beam of light indicated "Mize Gone," another had "Raschi Sold," and a third, "Aging Pitching." Three more pointed to "Mantle's Knee," "Martin Drafted," and "Blackwell Quit." The final two referred to second baseman Billy Martin's impending induction into the US Army and former top-flight pitcher Ewell Blackwell's apparent retirement due to a sore arm. On the other hand, Johnny Sain soon abandoned his plans to end his playing career, coming to terms with the Yankees.[22]

In another game against the Indians on March 31, Mays delivered two hits, including a double, "and electrified 8,230 fans with a great catch." Three days later, Willie went four for four, including a homer, again against the Indians, boosting his spring training batting average to .420 with eight homers. Mays's performance, *Times*'s Louis Effrat indicated, gave "the Giants reason to hope that this will be their year." He considered it "remarkable how" the center fielder's return had "ignited the Giants. With Willie around, there is laughter in the clubhouse, joking in the dugout, and, most important, life on the diamond." The Giants "believe in themselves . . . and credit Mays for having restored confidence" to a team that finished 35 games back of the Dodgers in 1953.[23]

United Press International reporter Carl Lundquist noted how Mays and other former GIs could shake up pennant races more than at any point since veterans returned from the Second World War. NL president Warren C. Giles believed in the likelihood of "the most wide-open" fight for the pennant in some time due to the abundance of fine young players, many back from military service. The playing ability of former soldiers, Giles admitted, was "unpredictable," with some performing at the same or a higher level but "others can't seem to get into the groove again." With teams still losing players to the military, Commissioner Ford Frick contended that former soldiers "should be given every possible consideration, even if the players involved are a little slow getting started again." That would not likely be the case with genuine stars, although Ted Williams, having survived 39 missions during the Korean War, had already broken his collarbone chasing a line drive.[24]

*****

With the regular season about to begin, John Drebinger, a longtime NYC baseball reporter, agreed with the general consensus that the Yankees and Dodgers should be favored to repeat. At the same time, he saw Casey Stengel facing more "perplexities" regarding his Yankees, as evidenced by the team's miserable exhibition campaign. Yankee pitching, seemingly "so deep" that

Raschi was sold, had "yet to hit its stride." Mantle's knee remained troublesome, worrying Stengel; Mickey had recently had a second procedure to remove a bursa from behind his right knee. Viewing Mantle as something of a question mark, the *Washington Post* likened him to Joe DiMaggio as the Yankees "most famous invalid."[25]

Notwithstanding Raschi's departure, the Yankees could still count on ace starters Allie Reynolds, Eddie Lopat, and Whitey Ford. Disatisfied with his previous season's work when he went 18–6 with a 3.00 ERA but lost his only decision in the World Series, Ford indicated he was "going after 25 wins this year." Johnny Sain had rescinded his retirement plans, Tom Morgan had returned from military service, and Harry Byrd had been acquired from the Athletics. "The very formidable Yogi Berra" remained behind the plate, while other veterans included shortstop Phil Rizutto, third baseman Gil McDougald, and outfielders Gene Woodling and Hank Bauer. Stengel could also call on "youngsters" like first baseman Bill Skowron, outfielder Bob Cerv, and pitcher Bob Grim.[26]

Experts disagreed whether Cleveland, Chicago, or Boston—all "outstanding rivals"—would most likely supplant New York should it experience "a crackup." Al Lopez's Indians appeared similar to the previous year's runner-up squad. Frontline starters Mike Garcia, Bob Lemon, and Early Wynn would now be paired with Art Houtteman, the former Tiger All-Star. Home run and RBI champion Al Rosen continued to head the everyday lineup.

The NL, Drebinger reasoned, might produce "a terrific five-cornered struggle." Brooklyn appeared strengthened by the addition of Don Newcombe, back from military service, with "a steadily improving staff of young hurlers such as Carl Erskine, Johnny Podres and Billy Loes." Back too were "all the old favorites—Roy Campanella, Duke Snider, Pee Wee Reese, Jackie Robinson, Carl Furillo and Junior Gilliam—still looking as robust as ever." The Giants' pitching staff had added Johnny Antonelli and Don Liddle to Ruben Gomez, Sal Maglie, Larry Jansen, and Jim Hearn. As Drebinger saw matters, Willie Mays's return provided "a further inspirational lift," possibly enabling Durocher's team to "kick up quite a rumpus."[27]

Charlie Grimm's Milwaukee Braves possessed one of MLB's most daunting lineups, at least potentially. It was led by 22-year-old third baseman Eddie

Mathews, the returning National League home run champion viewed as the current slugger most likely to challenge Babe Ruth's single-season record of 60 homers, set in 1927, and career total of 714. Many considered Mathews, the renowned sportswriter Tom Meany noted, "the second Babe Ruth" and baseball's "greatest home run threat." His wrists, those of "the true slugger," were "admired throughout baseball."[28]

Referring to the Yankees' ability to maintain their championship streak, Casey Stengel admitted, "This one will be the toughest." *The Sporting News'* Dan Daniel pointed to a series of factors that reinforced the Yankee skipper's assessment: Mantle's troubled right knee, the sale of Raschi to St. Louis, and Rizzuto's advanced age. Still, Stengel, who had recently appeared on the cover of *Sport* magazine as its "Man of the Year," remained optimistic: "I believe we are going to win." Stengel mentioned three new ballplayers who had "lifted" his "morale" to the extent he thought "we can make it six straight": first baseman Bill Skowron, outfielder Bob Cerv, and right-handed pitcher Bob Grim.[29]

10

The Year the Yankees Lose the Pennant, Willie Mays Targets Ruth's Record, the Catch, and Durocher's Team Wins!

Confronting unexpected developments, New York City baseball ultimately dominated yet again in 1954 as it would, with one exception, throughout an 11-year-long period starting seven years earlier. After five consecutive American League pennants and World Series titles, Casey Stengel's New York Yankees would lose both crowns, notwithstanding the fact that this edition won more games—103—than at any point during the tenure of "the Ol' Perfessor." Chuck Dressen's seemingly highly successful managerial stint with the Brooklyn Dodgers, including a playoff loss and two pennants in three years, came to an abrupt end over a contractual dispute. A pennant winner in 1951 with the Giants—as he had been twice with Dodgers earlier—but a runner-up and a second division finisher since, Leo Durocher at last ended up with the championship he had long sought in his managerial career, with his New York Giants winning their first World Series title in over two decades.

The Giants prevailed despite encountering the heavily favored Cleveland Indians, winners of a then record 111 American League games and conquerors of the mighty Yankees. Their fate and that of other leading contenders that year—the Dodgers, Braves, Indians, and, finally, the Yankees—was again greatly impacted by the performance of former Blackball participants. Those included Brooklyn's returning MVP catcher Roy Campanella, second baseman Jim Gilliam, left fielder Sandy Amoros, the ever-versatile Jackie Robinson, and Don Newcombe, back from two full seasons away due to military service. In its second Major League year, Milwaukee had center fielder Bill Bruton and a new addition, 20-year-old left fielder Henry Aaron. Cleveland still featured center fielder Larry Doby, who led the AL with 32 homers and 126 RBIs in finishing a close second in the MVP race, at the heart of its lineup. The St. Louis Cardinals displayed 29-year-old rookie right-handed pitcher Brooks Lawrence, who produced a 15–6 win-loss record. Unexpectedly or not, the New York Yankees failed to end its whites-only roster, not adding either Elston Howard or Vic Power, the first again relegated to the minors, the second, considered too flashy and enamored with white women, shipped off to the Philadelphia Athletics.

Other than the Dodgers, no team was more impacted by former Negro Leaguers than the Giants. Returning starters Monte Irvin and Hank Thompson remained threats at the plate, although each suffered a drop-off in batting average. But that was more than compensated by the reappearance at the plate, on base paths, and in the field by Willie Mays, back from having missing most of the 1952 season and all of the most recent one. Appearing in all but three games, Mays excelled at every level during the regular season, then made one of the most breathtaking defensive plays on baseball's grandest stage. In Game One of the World Series, his face-to-the-fence catch of a monstrous Vic Wertz drive and throw back to the infield deflated the Indians and set the stage for a four-game sweep. Simply put, in 1954 Mays became the most electrifying and the best player in MLB, a status he would strive to retain for more than a decade. In the process, he proved to be among the greatest all-around baseball players, entitled to placement within a small circle that included only a handful of others.[1]

*****

On Opening Day, April 13, the new Baltimore Orioles played their first game, as did a pair of promising rookie outfielders, Henry Aaron and St. Louis' Wally Moon. Returning from nearly two years away from MLB, Willie Mays played center field and batted fifth, behind Monte Irvin. At the Polo Grounds, 32,397 fans watched "Leo Durocher's minions" nip "the haughty Dodgers" 4–3, despite only four hits, all off starter Carl Erskine, who lasted only six innings. Thirty-seven-year-old Sal Maglie picked up the win with help from reliever Marv Grissom, who entered in the seventh inning. The Dodgers' Roy Campanella swatted two homers off Maglie, while Alvin Dark, Hank Thompson, and Mays homered for the Giants, Willie's the game-winning shot off an Erskine inside fastball. The passage of time, sportswriter John Drebinger noted, "had in no way curbed" Mays's "flair for bringing grief to Flatbush," delivering "an eye-filling circuit smash of more than 400 feet." Arthur Daley labeled Mays's blast "herculean."[2]

Among the 27,160 nestled into Griffith Stadium was President Dwight David Eisenhower, who settled in for a lengthy—nearly three hours—contest with the Washington Senators scoring twice in the bottom of the tenth to beat the New York Yankees 5–3. Mickey Vernon delivered the game-ending, two-run homer off Allie Reynolds, the fourth reliever following starter Whitey Ford's abbreviated outing. Mantle, Yogi Berra, Gene Woodling, and Gene McDougald went hitless for the five-time defending World Series champs.[3]

On April 15, a crowd estimated at half a million people welcomed the Orioles' reentry into the American League. Schools were closed and municipal workers afforded a half-day off as the team paraded through downtown Baltimore. Attendance included Vice President Richard M. Nixon and his wife Patricia, with Nixon offering "the ceremonial first pitch" at Memorial Stadium, where over 46,000 fans watched their Orioles defeat the White Sox, 3–1 on Bob Turley's seven-hitter.[4]

Beating the Dodgers "for the ninth time in his career," Sal Maglie remained undefeated at Ebbets Field, 6–3 on April 18; his overall record against Brooklyn improved to 20–6. Dropped to sixth in the batting order due to an early season slump, Irvin produced two singles, a homer, and four RBIs, while Mays hit his second homer. Purportedly offering some levity during the eighth inning when he initially darted in too much on a fly ball by George Shuba, Mays was forced "to back-pedal to catch the ball over his head." The Giants win over the Dodgers, their second in a three-game set, evened New York's record at 2–2.[5]

About a week into the new baseball season, sports editor Eddie Burbridge discussed Black major leaguers' status in his column, "Layin' It on the Line," for the *Los Angeles Sentinel*, a leading African American newspaper. Burbridge pointed to two promising rookies: the Cubs' shortstop Ernie Banks, "a good hitter and fair fielder," and the Braves' outfielder Henry Aaron, a "brilliant prospect." Aaron belted his initial major league homer, getting the better of Raschi, who, just over a week earlier, had allowed the young player's first major league hit, also an extra-base hit, a double.[6]

Twin shutouts of the Phillies at the Polo Grounds on Sunday, April 25, by Maglie, putting him at 3–0 with a 2.22 ERA, and Antonelli, now 2–1 with a sparkling 1.13 ERA, kept the 6–5 Giants only a game behind the Dodgers. Giant batters were struggling, with second baseman Davey Williams and Westrum barely hitting, Lockman and Thompson struggling, and Dark, Mueller, Irvin, and Mays below .300. On April 30, Maglie spread out 10 hits in a 14-inning complete game win against the Cubs at Wrigley Field, the clinching run scored on Mays's homer, his lone hit in six at bats. On May 2, the Cardinals' Stan Musial pounded five homers while driving in nine runs in a doubleheader split against the Giants, tying a feat by Cap Anson, Ty Cobb, Tony Lazzeri, Don Mueller, and Ralph Kiner, who did it twice in 1949.[7]

That same day, a subcommittee in the House of Representatives prepared to investigate whether well-known athletes, including Mays and Whitey Ford, had received preferential treatment from the US Armed Forces. Republican representative William E. Hess insisted he was not attacking the athletes themselves but rather "the system that made such favoritism possible." The New York Yankees soon blasted the subcommittee for placing Hank Bauer, not Hank Sauer, among those listed, who now included Billy Martin and Don Newcombe. Demanding an "immediate apology from those responsible," Bauer was a former Marine boasting a pair of Bronze Stars and Purple Hearts for 32 months of service in the Pacific theater during the Second World War. A developing story involved Mays's basic training having been delayed to enable him to play baseball at Fort Eustis. Newcombe, former boxing champion Ray Robinson, and boxer Sandy Saddler were other Black athletes purportedly "coddled" during their military service.[8]

At Crosley Field on May 6, the Cincinnati Redlegs nipped the Giants, 5-4, despite two-run homers by Mays—his fourth—and Thompson, dropping New York into seventh place with a 9-11 record, three and a half games out of first. Only 2,566 spectators watched the action. Two days later, the Giants beat the cellar-dwelling Pirates, 2-1, at Pittsburgh's Forbes Field behind Antonelli's five-hitter, with Mays getting his fifth homer, a second-inning drive off Pirate starter Vernon Law. They evened their record the next day, again defeating the Pirates, with Maglie becoming the first National Leaguer to win five times, relinquishing six hits, prevailing 5-1. Mays had a triple, scored once, and drove in two runs, also linking with shortstop Dark and catcher Ebba St. Claire to pull off a double play.[9]

*****

On May 10, *Newsweek* included sportswriter John Lardner's column, "Lardner's Week," during which the son of the legendary Ring Lardner discussed "The Fifty Per Cent Color Line." Seven years had passed since the NL's color barrier had fallen, setting the path for other Black players. Nevertheless, a "color line" effectively continued, with no more than four African Americans from one team allowed on the playing field at any point. The team that had signed Jackie Robinson and other Negro Leaguers denied such a stricture existed to prevent "too many Negroes playing simultaneously in big-league ball." But pointing to the early abundance of first "Irish and German names," then "Italian and Central European" ones, Lardner insisted that "those groups which have it toughest, which must dig hardest to live, produce—selectively, and for a time, till living gets better—more than their share of athletes." He indicated there was "an obvious cure for" all of this, "and the cure has nothing to do with quotas."[10]

*****

Winning for the fifth straight time, the Giants beat the Cubs, 6-3, before 3,170 spectators at the Polo Grounds on May 13. Irvin homered twice, while Mays, Thompson, and St. Claire had one apiece, helping Jansen go to 2-0. New

York now rested at 14–11, in third place, only a game out of first. Mueller was leading the Giants in batting at .352, Irvin was hitting .276, Dark, .272, Mays, .265, and Thompson, .256. Lockman and Williams were struggling mightily, batting only .193 and .157, respectively. Maglie had a 5–1 win-loss record, just ahead of Antonelli's 4–1 mark. Gomez was winless in three decisions.[11]

After winning the next day to land atop the league for the first time since Opening Day, the Giants fell to the Cubs, 4–3, as both Mays and pitcher Jim Hearn committed throwing errors in the sixth inning. Slipping into third place, the Giants would not again head NL standings for several weeks. On Sunday, May 17, the Giants and Braves split a doubleheader, with Antonelli defeating his former teammates in the second game, 9–2, assisted by Mays, who scored twice, drove in four runs, and homered.[12]

The day before, Ted Williams returned to Boston's lineup, going hitless in two trips to the plate. But on Sunday, Williams went eight for nine in a doubleheader, five for five in the second game with two homers and five RBIs. The AL, columnist Shirley Povich suggested, possessed "a special need of his kind of gate attraction." Since DiMaggio's retirement, the AL had experienced a "growing lack of transcendent stars like the Red Sox thumper." The National League, boasting Musial, Campanella, Roberts, Mathews, Robinson, Kiner, Sauer, Mays, and Snider, Povich contended, provided "more exciting fare," having become "the power league." Only Minoso appeared "close to Williams as a gate attraction," operating as "a helter-skelter type on the bases and in the outfield" with "a bullet arm" and "proving a dangerous guy with the bat."[13]

According to Povich,

> the biggest blow to the American League took was when Mickey Mantle failed it. He was the one who supposedly had no ceiling on his talents. He could a ball farther than anybody else in the league, is a switch hitter, the league's best bunter, the league's fastest man. He was stacked to be its most exciting guy, but he isn't. His exciting prospects seemed to excite everybody but Mantle himself.

Povich was referring to Mantle's terrible start, following surgery, to the 1954 season. Going hitless against the Orioles on May 16, Mantle's batting average fell to .203, his slugging average to .320, his slugging average to .391.

*****

Led by Chief Justice Earl Warren, the US Supreme Court issued a monumental decision, *Brown v. Board of Education*, on May 17, declaring racial segregation in public schools to be unconstitutional. This overturned the 56-year-old doctrine articulated in *Plessy v. Ferguson*, which had laid out the principle of "separate but equal," providing judicial justification for racial segregation. In the unanimous ruling, Warren declared, "In the field of public education, the doctrine of 'separate but equal' has no place. Separate educational facilities are inherently unequal."[14]

The *Brown* case resulted in starkly contrasting determinations. It sparked the readiness of many in the Deep South, in particular, to thwart segregation's dismantling. But it also provided fuel for the modern civil rights movement, one that had already received impetus from changes that Jackie Robinson and his fellow former Negro Leaguers fostered on Organized Baseball's playing fields. Chief Justice Warren's decision came during Baseball's Great Experiment's ninth year.

*****

"Willie Mays put on a one-man show tonight as the Giants downed the Phillies ... 5 to 4," wrote the *New York Times*' John Drebinger about the game at Connie Mack Stadium on May 24. After an earlier single, Mays homered in both the seventh and eighth innings, giving him ten for the season, helping the Giants prevail. He also threw out a runner attempting to score on a fly out to center field. Back at the Polo Grounds the next day, New York routed Pittsburgh 21–4 with an 11-run explosion in the eighth inning. Mays had three hits, including a triple, scored five runs, and drove in one. Willie got two hits in three at bats against the Pirates the following day, driving in two and upping his batting average to .304; it would only drop below .300 for a single day over the rest of the season. Additionally, Mays made the game's "most spectacular play" as he snared a first-inning "blast" by Bob Skinner "to the bleacher screen in center. Willie had his back to the diamond on making the catch."[15]

On May 28, the Giants had another offensive explosion, getting 18 hits in beating the Dodgers, 17–6, before 38,758 fans at the Polo Grounds.

Their sixth consecutive victory kept the Giants in second place, one and a half games out of first, with the Dodgers losing their fourth in succession to fall two games back of their NYC rivals. Lockman, Mays, Williams, Dark, Irvin, and rookie third baseman Bill Gardner all homered, four during an eighth inning, six-run eruption. In the second, Mays got his 11th homer, "a tremendous smack into the upper left tier above the 447-foot marker." Altogether, Willie went four for five, with three runs scored, and four RBIs. On May 30, Brooklyn beat the Giants, 5–3, with a walk-off homer by Hodges off Antonelli, to take the deciding contest of a three-game series. "Willie the Wonder" went two for three, scored twice and smacked a second-inning, two-run homer off Podres. The next day, the Giants split a doubleheader with the Pirates at Forbes Field, New York taking the first game 4–0 behind Gomez's three-hitter, with Mays going two for four, stealing a base, and hitting his fourteenth homer in the second-inning off Bob Friend. Following a relatively slow start in April, Mays had a scorching next month at the plate, hitting 11 homers, driving in 31 runs, scoring 37 times, batting .374 with an .808 slugging average.[16]

A couple of notable transactions occurred as the month of June arrived. The Indians, leading the American League by a full game, traded for Vic Wertz, a power-hitting first baseman-outfielder who had struggled with the Orioles. The Dodgers optioned Joe Black, the 1952 NL Rookie of the Year, to their Montreal franchise.[17]

Both leagues remained highly competitive, with the Indians, White Sox, and Yankees battling in the American League, while the Braves, Phillies, Cardinals, Dodgers, and Giants, "re-inspired by Willie Mays," remained closely bunched in the senior circuit. Mays, in fact, pounded a double and two more homers, one less than teammate Henry Thompson, as the Giants slammed the Cardinals at Busch Stadium, 13–8, on June 3. Thompson went four for four with eight RBIs, while Mays was three for five, driving in the rest of the Giant runs.[18]

On June 9, Antonelli shut out the Braves on seven hits at County Stadium to go to 8–2 as the Giants edged into first place. Hitless in two official at bats against Warren Spahn, Mays walked twice and drove in a run with a sacrifice fly. A tenth-inning loss to the Cubs at Wrigley Field two days later dropped the Giants back to second place. But the following day, the Giants behind Maglie's seven scoreless innings and backed by Hoyt Wilhelm's two innings in relief, blanked the Cubs 5–0, with Mays hitting his 17th homer. Regaining the league lead, New York never relinquished it throughout the remainder of the regular season.

Bob Addie, writing in the *Washington Post and Times Herald*, extolled "the exploits of Willie Mays," indicating they were "beginning to rival those of the legendary Paul Bunyan." Addie wrote, "Willie is supposed to have caught a fly ball 400 feet from home plate and then to have thrown out" Jackie Robinson, requiring an "85 miles an hour" toss.[19]

The June 15 issue of *Look* magazine, with the actress Grace Kelly on the cover, contained an article, "Willie Mays: Spirit of the Giants." A week later, the *Los Angeles Times*' Braven Dyer was wondering how the Giants, 35 games back of the Dodgers a year ago, had become "such a strong pennant threat." After all, Irvin's batting average was 90 points lower than in 1953, with only Mueller and Mays above .300. "Biggest physical improvement," Giants public relations director Garry Schumacher explained, "is the play of Willie Mays and the pitching of Johnny Antonelli." Additionally, "it is more largely a thing of the spirit; the club has the 'feel' of winning again," recalling the drive for the 1951 pennant. Mays "has been an infectious force. . . . he makes his big play in the field pretty much every day and has authored 18 homers"; indeed, Willie had belted another pair the previous day.[20]

New York City, columnist Shirley Povich indicated, "is a city transformed since the surge of the Giants to the top of the league. Baseball talk is being heard again, and it's of the Giants. Talk of the kind that was never inspired by the Yankees, whose pennants have been too routine and thus unexciting." When Mays headed into the US Army, manager Durocher bemoaned, "There goes most of our ball club." Willie was back and, Povich noted, "Never has one man done so much for one club. Yankee fans can have their Mickey Mantle. Willie Mays can forget to bring half his skills to the ball park and still outperform Mantle. Giants fans are willing to believe. In fact, they'll argue that he can."[21]

In a doubleheader against the Braves, Mays smacked a homer in the opening game loss, 5–2, then delivered the Giants' only runs with a second-inning shot, his 23rd of the season, off Spahn into the Polo Grounds' upper left tier. Homering for the fifth straight game on June 26, Mays "just missed the upper deck" with a 430-foot, second-inning drive off the Cubs' Bob Rush that rebounded off the wall. Scampering for an inside-the-park homer, Mays engaged in a "pell-mell dash" amid "oppressive heat" that "took so much of Willie that, feeling woozy and nauseated, he sunk to his knees in center field" at the start of the next inning. Attended to by the Giant trainer Frank Bowman, Mays kept on playing, making "five of his trade-marked "basket" catches." Throughout his career, Willie would be afflicted with medical issues, including fainting spells, which at times led to hospitalizations. The prognosis was generally stress, fatigue, or both.[22]

With the Giants maintaining a slim lead in the National League, the *Los Angeles Times*' Al Wolf also suggested "it's the 1951 story all over again—that fascinating story entitled "Willie Mays."" Unquestionably, Mays's return had "fired Leo Durocher's entire squad, just as it did when he came up from the minors in '51." Willie was "the guy who's making Flatbush flatter," aided by Dodger pitching woes and the injury suffered by Roy Campanella.[23]

Notwithstanding Mays's heroics, *New York Times*' columnist Arthur Daley wrestled with the question of which National Leaguer center fielder deserved to be the All-Star starter. The top candidates were "Willie the Wonder . . . the most incredible character since Abner Doubleday" and the Dodgers' "Edwin Donald Snider, the Duke of Flatbush." True, "the Say Hey Kid is utterly fantastic." However, Snider had been at or near the top of NL batters throughout much of the season, hitting "around .370 or so. He's a home run threat. He can run, throw and field. He's Willie with polish." Although not "as exciting a ballplayer as the Wonder," Snider was "sound and solid."[24]

Shirley Povich might have disagreed with his fellow journalist. He indicated, "Willie's back and he's the hottest article in a major league uniform. The Giants are leading the National League, and Willie Mays is the most exciting ball player in either league." With Mays having swatted a half-a-dozen homers during the week, New Yorkers were "in a stampede to join the growing cult of Willie Mays fans." Presently, Mays had 24 homers, equaling the pace Babe Ruth set in 1927; Willie was also hitting .330. While Mays was "knocking the ball out of park," he was "putting the fans into it, in increasing numbers."

A favorite of Giants' fans, Mays now "captivated them completely with his heroics with his bat, on the bases and in center field." A Giants' spokesman taunted the Yankees' bid "to build Mickey Mantle up to a box-office attraction" by getting out tape measures to gauge the slugger's "long homers and try to make him a big shot personality." He went on to say, "They're trying to build him as the greatest center fielder since Speaker, and what happens? Mantle isn't even the best center fielder in town. He runs a bad third to Mays and Duke Snider." Although some accused Mays of showboating, Cincinnati manager Birdie Tebbets said, "Sure, he make the easy plays look hard, but he makes all the hard plays, too. How can you fault him."

Remaining Mays's biggest advocate, Durocher declared, "I don't know if I ever saw a better ball player. He has all the instincts and all the weapons. He could be the perfect ball player." The Giants' skipper continued, "I rate the perfect player as one who has five points . . . hitting . . . power hitting . . . running . . . throwing . . . defensive ability." Mays "has everything but the proof that he can consistently hit for a good average." Willie liked the notion of being the home run league leader but refused "to worry about breaking Ruth's record." For, as he put it, "If you worry about one thing, pretty soon you start worrying about others. So I don't worry about nothing."[25]

Continuing to sing Mays's praises, Povich indicated that the ballplayer, "close to fabulous," had "customers queuing up to the Polo Grounds gates." Fans "come out to see ball players, not ball teams," Giants' publicist Garry Schumacher indicated. They had returned "but mostly to see Willie and the shows he gives them." Finally, the Giants had someone "to headline our show." The Yankees "always had DiMaggio and now they have Berra and Reynolds and Mantle. . . . The Dodgers got lucky with Robinson and Campanella and Duke Snider." But the Giants "didn't have any exciting personality."[26]

That had all changed. "When Willie steps up the plate," Povich noted, "it's almost electric. Giant fans move to the edge of their seats with an expectancy that only such as Babe Ruth, DiMaggio, Ted Williams and Stan Musial commanded." And "if Willie doesn't hit a fence or clout one over it, they simply settle back and wait for his next time up." Moreover, he didn't need "to hit home runs to satisfy the Giants fans. They get a belt out him otherwise. Everything is a sprint with Willie." Durocher confessed, "I don't want to sound giddy, but who plays this game any better than Willie? No ball player ever did so many things so well as this boy." Furthermore, "there's no ceiling on his ability." Durocher soon indicated he "never had to tell Willie Mays how to do anything on the ball field 'because he has better instincts than any player I ever saw.'"[27]

While lauding Snider, sportswriter Joe King insisted that Mays was "one-of-a-kind." Thanks to "dramatic, fantastic feats," the Giants' Say-Hey-Kid made "it appear as if baseball were waiting all these years for him to catch up with it." Although still "just a baseball baby," he had "color and showmanship, which few possess," particularly the top sluggers. King doubted that any other National leaguer could "match the electrifying quality of Willie's presence." This season, Mays had elevated "the otherwise leaderless Giants into . . . raging fire-eaters."[28]

As if determined to prove such accolades, Mays continued to lead the Giants as they held their lead in the National League. He beat out a double on a hard-hit ball that richoeted the shortstop's glove into short center field, swiped third base, and crossed the plate with the winning run on a pinch single by Bobby Hoffman in the bottom of the tenth to beat the Cubs 3–2 at the Polo Grounds on June 27. New York improved to 45–23, remaining in first place by a single game.[29]

Both New York and Brooklyn were playing brilliantly, with the Dodgers having recently gone 22–6 only to fall a game behind the "even faster" paced Giants. The only steady Brooklyn starting pitcher had been Johnny Podres, while Snider was tearing up the league with a .368 batting average and 19 homers. That put him five behind "the Mazing Mays," who, in Arthur Daley's words, was "an utter delight to watch . . . play ball" with his "cheerful, laughing" nature. Mays was "merely doing what comes naturally." While "no showboat . . . he can't help but dramatize everything and quicken pulses. He could very well be the most exciting ballplayer of this generation."[30]

Durocher kept heaping praise on his young center fielder, who swatted another 10 homers with a .314 batting average in June. Leo indicated, "This is the best-looking kid I've seen in 25 years of baseball. I look at Willie and you know who he reminds me of? Pete Reiser. What could Reiser do that Willie can't? Run, that's all. There's nobody in the league got a better arm than this kid. There's nobody got more power. There's nobody can go and get 'em any better than he can." Then, Durocher said, "I've got no idea just how great this kid can be. He can be another Joe DiMaggio. He's got the disposition, the temperament, the ability." He asked, "Trade him for Stan Musial? I wouldn't trade him for two Musials." Continuing his explanation, Durocher offered,

> The stage always seems to be set for Willie to do something dramatic. He's not content to do things the normal way. He's got to be different. Take the time he hit those homers in five consecutive games. All he did was hit 'em on his first time at bat. He makes mistakes, runs bases wrong sometimes. But I don't tell him anything. I let him do what he wants because, somehow, it always turns out right. . . . There's only one Willie.[31]

Dodger teammates took umbrage at the notion that Willie, playing in only his second full season, was a better ballplayer than Duke Snider. One Dodger stated, "A helluva note that the Duke doesn't get the big headlines until they start comparing him to Willie Mays. Mays ought to be flattered, not the Duke." Dismissing the controversy, Snider flippantly indicated, "If we stay in the headlines long enough, we might both get rich." However, Jackie Robinson revealed that Snider was indeed troubled by the linkage to Mays, whom he was "outhitting . . . by 45 points." Dodgers player denied that Mays could catch balls Snider was unable to grab. They noted, "The Duke has as good an arm, more power, and runs faster." Pee Wee Reese pointed out, "He does all of these things as good or better than Mays without making a production of it." Only Stan Musial, Reese declared, "should be rated with Snider." Robinson also considered the comparisons to be unfair. "He's been a great ball player all these years and now he's having his biggest season, and the papers are trying to say he has to prove he's as good as Willie Mays. Some people are stupid." Reese added about Snider, "He calls attention to" the fact that he was a great player "with the things he does and the way he does them. He dominates the game, like DiMaggio did and like Ted Williams and Musial. He bosses his position whether he's playing the outfield or is up there with a bat." When Mays was asked what he thought about Snider, he responded, "I know one thing. He don't hurt 'em none."[32]

Sportswriter Bob Addie chimed in with a column calling Mays "easily the most publicized athlete since Jackie Robinson." Deeming Mays colorful like Babe Ruth, the columnist reasoned that the public, following DiMaggio's retirement, hungered for "someone to adore." Addie wrote, "This may explain the sudden passion of the baseball world for Willie Mays. New York, a highly competitive town, realizes the value of a super-star. The Yanks tried to jam Mickey Mantle down the throats of the public and it didn't work." Admittedly, Addie noted, "Mantle unquestionably will be a great ballplayer some day, but the average fan likes to think he discovers this fact all by himself." Mays, Addie contended, "will have to survive a lot more seasons of heroics before he will accepted as great," Addie stated.[33]

Noted syndicated columnist Walter Winchell offered his commentary on the game's top center fielders. Fans, he declared, "were getting noisy" pitting Mays against Snider and old timer Tris Speaker. "A Yankee maniac" was said to have complained, "If Willie keeps improving, they may start comparing him with DiMaggio!"[34]

Pulling out of an extended slump, Mickey Mantle raised his average to .311 after hitting .380 during the month of May with 7 homers and 23 RBIs. He hit well again the next month, producing 5 homers, 27 RBIs, and batting .316. But Mays and Snider were performing so brilliantly that Mantle was more lightly covered by the New York press and not favorably compared with the city's other center fielders. As Shirley Povich put it, "Mantle, once hailed as the wonder boy of the majors, is no longer being called the greatest. All that New Yorkers will now concede him is a place as the third best centerfielder in town." Bob Addie saw things differently: "I think Mickey Mantle is a better, all-around player than Willie Mays and I also think the Dodgers' Duke Snider is better than both of them."[35]

In a critical, near mid-season series with Brooklyn, which some thought might help determine if "the Giants" new wonder boy, Willie Mays" were "a better ball player than Duke Snider," New York swept three home games to go up four in the NL standings. The nailbiting opener, which went 13 innings and was played before 51,464 fans, the largest number to attend a National League thus far that year, ended when pinch hitter Dusty Rhodes drove in the winning run off Billy Loes. Backed by homers by Irvin and Williams, Maglie held a 2–0 lead with two strikes on Campanella with two out and Robinson on first in the top of the ninth. The Dodger catcher clubbed a hanging curve to tie the score. The Dodgers took the lead in the top of the thirteenth on third baseman Don Hoak's homer, but Rhode's single scored Lockman and Mays to win the game, 4–3. Marv Grisson pitched the last four innings for New York, picking up the victory to put his record at 8–2, with a 1.53 ERA. Antonelli went to 11–1 with a 2.21 ERA, giving up only one run, with Hoyt Wilhelm mopping up in relief, as the Giants won the second game, 5–2. The Giants, behind Ruben Gomez, took the final contest, 5–2, the second game in a row that Snider missed with an injury. Mays went hitless to conclude a relatively quiet series for him.[36]

In another three-game set with the Dodgers, played at Ebbets Field in early July, Mays went five for eleven, with five runs scored, four homers, and nine RBIs to push his season-long slugging above .700. Once again, the Giants swept, crushing the Dodgers by scores of 5–2, 10–2, and 11–2, giving them a six and a half game advantage at 55–25. Mays's second homer in the third game was his thirtieth of the season, placing him ahead of Babe Ruth's record home run pace.[37]

All of that led Shirley Povich to declare that Mays was "still proving that if he isn't the best ball player in the business, he is at least the most exciting." And yet, the columnist noted, Mays's "hitting isn't as spectacular as his fielding." After all, "every catch Willie Mays makes has to be sensational. He plays center field so shallow he's looking down the hitter's throat, secure in the confidence he can go back for a ball."[38]

Writing in the *New York Times Magazine*, cultural critic Gilbert Millstein discussed the Giants' "Natural Boy," whom he deemed "a baseball property of incalculable if ephemeral value." To Millstein, Mays "probably comes as close as anybody in a dour age to fulfilling all of the specifications of Rousseau's Natural Man." Or, as sports columnist Jimmy Cannon put it, he was a "joyous boy." Prone to receive and dole out "mild practical jokes," the young center fielder exhibited, Millstein wrote, "an engaging naivete, a high-pitched laugh, a great natural dignity and an instinctive ability to create sight gags out of meager materials offered around a ball park." But most notably, as Leo Durocher predicted, "In a year, maybe two at the most, he'll be the best ballplayer we ever looked at. . . . What *can't* he do, that's the way to look at it. . . . He's great—that's the word—only great." Standing 5'10½" and weighing 180 pounds, Mays played with a distinct flair, including a propensity for catching fly balls "as though he were dropping peaches in a basket" and for losing his cap "at crucial moments."[39]

Playing the All-Star Game before 68,751 at Cleveland's Memorial Stadium on July 13, the American League, with 17 hits, ended the National League's four-game winning streak in a slugfest, 11–9. The NL's starting center fielder Duke Snider went three for four, Cincinnati first baseman Ted Kluszewski hit a homer and drove in three runs, and Mays, playing in his first All-Star Game, went one for two, singled, and scored a run. Cleveland third baseman Al Rosen was the star of the contest, delivering three hits, including a pair of homers, and driving in five. Second baseman Bobby Avila, Rosen's teammate on the Indians, was three for three with two RBIs, while the Yankees' Mickey Mantle and Yogi Berra each got two hits.[40]

The syndicated columnist Dorothy Kilgallen indicated that agents and managers were fighting to get Mays's signature on a contract that would enable the ballplayer to deliver testimonials and appear on television and in movies. She reported that "the offers piling in" were "fabulous," with "the percentage boys . . . swooning at the thought of the commissions" that Mays would make possible.[41]

By the end of July, Mays, after another incredibly productive month during which he hit 12 homers, drove in 26 runs, and batted .330, was sitting on 36 homers with a .325 batting average. The 65–37 Giants retained a four-game lead in the National League, with just over a third of the regular season remaining. Mays' notoriety continued to grow, with *Time* magazine having placed him on the cover of its July 26th issue, bat in hand as if readying for a pitch. The article referred to Mays as performing with "boy's glee, a pro's sureness and a champion's flair." Like many analyses of Mays, it indicated that "on the ball diamond, he is in a hurry." It also contended that "with his showman's manner and his in-the-clutch timing, Willie Mays is baseball's sensation of the season." To the dismay of oldtime followers of the game, he was "already being talked of as the equal or even the better of the great Tris Speaker and Joe DiMaggio" while seemingly capable of breaking Babe Ruth's single-season home run record.[42]

In recalling past greats like Speaker and DiMaggio, sportswriter Joe Reichler suggested that MLB presently had more stars positioned in center field "than ever before," including Cleveland's Larry Doby, the former Negro Leaguer. Mays, called "the most electrifying player to hit the Polo Grounds in a long, long time," was said to be "the nearest thing to Speaker" as "an amazing defensive player" while being "a more powerful batter." Snider was viewed as "perhaps the best centerfielder in baseball today" but many believed Mantle "will outrank both within a couple of years." Still only 22 years old, Mantle possessed "great power, tremendous speed, a good arm and is improving as a fielder every day."[43]

As Mays's home run clip remained ahead of Babe Ruth's home run clip during the fabled 1927 season, discussion of whether Willie could match or break the record mounted. The journalist Whitney Martin compared the pursuit, previously undertaken by past sluggers Hack Wilson, Jimmie Foxx, and Hank Greenberg, with Roger Bannister's bid to become the first miler to break four minutes and Bobby Jones's capture of golf's Grand Slam. Mays, Martin warned, would confront a "psychological barrier" and might have to match Ruth's colossal close—17 homers in September."[44]

In fact, purportedly encouraged by Durocher to worry more about his batting average, Mays's home run gallop would soon dissipate, at least for the 1954 season. He failed to homer during the Giants" final three games in July and the first 11 in August. During that period, his batting average fell two points. New York lost two and a half games from its four-game lead, dropping four straight and seven of eight at one point. Mays's 37th homer came against the Dodgers in the last of a three-game set, all won by Brooklyn, which left New York only a half-game in front. This was as close as the Dodgers, who remained in second place from May 30 through September 5, would get.[45]

On August 30, Antonelli, who had lost only three times, became the National League's initial 20-game winner during the 1954 season, yielding only four hits in beating the Cardinals at Busch Stadium, 4–1. No Giant southpaw had accomplished that feat since Carl Hubbell and Cliff Melton did so 17 years earlier. Antonelli and Mays were viewed as the keys to the Giants' rise to the NL's top rung.[46]

His home run pursuit lagging, Mays managed a 21 game hitting streak lasting nearly a month. With only three homers during August, he batted .385, raising his season average to .338. On August 31, Cincinnati's Ted Kluszewski grabbed the major league home run lead from Mays by hitting his 40th and 41st homers; Kluszewski went on to hit 49, the most in either league. No matter, Shirley Povich suggested that as Mays discarded the notion of constantly striving for homers, he had become a "tremendous average hitter"; Povich soon indicated that Mays and his fans had "a new ambition": a batting crown.[47]

In his *Los Angeles Times* "Sportraits" column, dated September 7, Al Wolf envisioned the front-running Cleveland Indians and New York Giants winning their respective pennants. He foresaw the AL likely continuing a pattern established in 1947: the World Series title. The Indians looked particularly strong thanks to their "Big Three" starting pitchers—Bob Lemon, Early Wynn, and Mike Garcia—backed by Bob Feller, Art Houtteman, and Hal Newhouser. The bullpen was strong too, thanks to Don Mossi, Ray Narleski, and Bob Hooper. And while Mays had carried the Giants "with his hitting, his defense and above all his infectious spirit," Wolf questioned "how much better" he was than his center fielder counterpart, Larry Doby.[48]

*****

On September 9, with only two and a half weeks left in the regular season, Wolf's prediction appeared astute. On that day, Cleveland, behind Newhouser, upped its record to 100–40, defeating Philadelphia in 11 innings, 5–4. The Yankees lost to the Orioles, 1–0, dropping their record to 94–45, five and a half games behind the Indians. That same day, W. W. Norton & Co. published John Douglass Wallop III's novel, *The Year the Yankees Lost the Pennant*, slated as a Book of the Month Club selection for September. Wallop spun the story of diehard Washington Senators' fan Joe Boyd, a realtor grappling with middle-age doldrums, and his encounter with a Mr. Applegate, who happens to be the devil. Boyd agrees to sell his soul for a promise to be remade as a young, heroic ballplayer who drives the Senators into a unlikely pennant race with the hated Yankees.[49]

Casey Stengel's actual Yankees, despite their own impressive record, proved unable to keep pace with the front-running Indians, falling eight and a half games behind on September 12. Less than a week later, Cleveland won its third American League pennant, beating the Tigers, 3–2, at Detroit's Briggs Stadium.

The Indians went on to post a regular season mark of 111–43, setting a record for the AL in beating the Yankees by eight games. Willard Mullin's front-page sketch, "Ruins All," in *The Sporting News* displayed an open-mouthed Stengel crying out, "HELP!" as a giant Yankee was toppled from a podium. A box displayed the Seven Wonders of the World, with the last reading "Finally the Yankees, lords of all they survey. At long last I wonder, is come and gone their day?"[50]

*****

Baseball Digest's September cover displayed a smiling Mays holding five bats in his hands. In a magazine article titled "I'd Play for Nothing" and purportedly penned by Mays, as relayed to the journalist Milton Richman, the young star decried other players bemoaning how baseball was "hard work." Willie countered, "To me, it's always been nothing but pleasure" and emphasized how much fun the game was.[51]

On September 20, the Giants, behind Sal Maglie, beat the Dodgers, 7–2, at Ebbets Field with 26,932 in attendance, to win the National League pennant, their 17th overall, their 15th during the twentieth century. With three hits, Mays surpassed Duke Snider for the NL batting lead, with Giant teammate Don Mueller close behind. Thirteen players remained from the 1951 pennant-winning squad. Mays clinched the batting title at .345, with three hits on the final day of the regular season as the Giants beat the Phillies, 3–2, in 11 innings; he went into the game slightly in back of both Mueller and Snider.[52]

The next day, *Look* magazine included an article by the acclaimed actress Tallulah Bankhead, "What is so rare as a Willie Mays?" She would be credited with boldly declaring, "There have only been geniuses in the world. Willie Mays and Willie Shakespeare." Placing him ahead of the other "crack center fielders," Mantle and Snider, she said Mays "does everything with a flourish." Bankhead wrote, "He has the spectacular touch. Everything he does on a ball field has a theatrical quality." She pointed to the pathfinder, Jackie Robinson, who in breaking "the color taboo" allowed democracy to begin "to function in the major leagues." The sport had "unbigoted some bigots."[53]

Finishing 97–57, the Giants, with an attendance boost to over 1.155 million leaving them second in the NL to Milwaukee, ended up five games ahead of the Dodgers, eight in front of the Braves. Mays led the way, with 119 runs scored (3rd in the league), 195 hits (3rd), 33 doubles (10th), 41 homers (3rd), 119 runs scored (3rd), and 377 total bases (2nd), with an on-base percentage of .411 (5th). He had a league-best 13 triples, .667 slugging average, 1.078 OPS, 175 OPS+, 10.4 WAR, and a 2.0 dWAR (defensive wins above replacement for position players). Mueller had an NL-leading 212 hits and a .342 batting average. Alvin Dark scored 98 runs, got 189 hits, hit 20 homers, and batted .293. Hank Thompson contributed 26 homers and 86 RBIs, while Monte Irvin rebounded to end up with 19 homers and .262 batting average. Super-sub Dusty Rhodes, in only 164 official at bats, got 15 homers, drove in 50 runs, and batted .341. Johnny Antonelli went 21–7, with a league-leading .750 win-loss percentage, 2.30 ERA, and 6 shutouts. Ruben Gomez was 17–9 with a 2.88 ERA, while Sal Maglie went 14–6 with a 3.26 ERA. Marv Grissom, 10–7 with a 2.35, and Hoyt Wilhelm, 12–4 with a 2.10 ERA, anchored the bullpen.

During Walt Alston's first year at the helm, the Brooklyn Dodgers, barely attracting one million to Ebbets Field, suffered from the hand injury to Roy Campanella and a mediocre pitching staff, led by Carl Erskine, at 18–15, but with a 4.15 ERA. Other starters included 11–6 Russ Meyer, 11–7 Johnny Podres, and 13–5 Billy Loes, all also with high earned run averages. Don Newcombe disappointed in his return to the majors, going only 9–8 with a 4.55 ERA, and Preacher Roe finally reached the end of a too short but brilliant career, with a 3–4 record and a 5.00 ERA. Top reliever Jim Hughes, 8–4 with a 3.22 ERA, had 24 saves. Playing in only 111 games, Campy had a miserable season, getting 19 homers but hitting only .207. Also struggling was rookie third baseman Don Hoak, who hit but .245 with little power. Jim Gilliam remained solid, scoring 107 runs and batting .282, while 35-year-old Pee Wee Reese was terrific, scoring 98 runs, getting 35 doubles, walking 90 times, and batting a career-best .309. Carl Furillo had 19 homers and 96 RBIs, while hitting .294. Gil Hodges had the best season of his career, scoring 106 runs, plating 130, slamming 42 homers, and hitting .304. Duke Snider scored 120 runs, had 199 hits, hit 39 doubles, 10 triples, and 40 homers, while driving in

130 and batting .341. Operating as an All-Star utilityman, 35-year-old Jackie Robinson managed 15 homers and batted .311.

Coming in second place despite their best record under Casey Stengel, the Yankees, with another loss in attendance that still left them in first place in the AL, again had a solid lineup and frontline pitching; the former St. Louis Browns turned Baltimore Orioles drew 1.06 million fans. Yogi Berra, who would beat out Larry Doby, Bobby Avila, Minnie Minoso, and Bob Lemon to win his second MVP, scored 88 runs, got 179 hits, 28 doubles, and 22 homers, driving in 125 runs while batting .307. New starting third baseman Andy Carey batted .302, and Hank Bauer hit .294. But first baseman Joe Collins offered little power, and Gil McDougald, moved to second base, left fielder Gene Woodling, and above all else, Phil Rizzuto had down years. Despite a terrible start, Mickey Mantle had a league-leading 129 runs scored, in addition to 27 homers, 102 RBIs, 102 walks, and a .300 batting average. Also rebounding from a miserable early beginning, Whitey Ford went 16–8 with a 2.82 ERA. Rookie Bob Grim was 20–6 with a 3.26 ERA, Eddie Lopat was 12–4, Allie Reynolds, 13–4, and Tom Morgan, 11–5. Having postponed his retirement, 36-year-old Johnny Sain only split 12 decisions but posted a 3.16 ERA with a league-leading 26 saves.

Al Lopez's pennant-winning Cleveland Indians, with several weak links in their everyday lineup, did have batting champion, second baseman Bobby Avila (.341), with 112 runs scored, another .300 hitter in third baseman Al Rosen, whose homer and RBI totals dropped from the previous year's league-leading 43 homers and 145 RBIs to 24 big flies and 102 runs driven in. Center fielder Larry Doby scored 94 runs, while leading the league in both homers—32—and RBIs—126, to finish a close second in the MVP contest. Pitching buttressed Cleveland's march to the top of the American League, with both Early Wynn and Bob Lemon winning a league-best 23 games and each putting up a stellar ERA (2.73–2.72). Mike Garcia was 19–8 with an AL-tops 2.64 ERA. Art Houtteman was 15–7, and Bob Feller, 13–3. Hal Newhouser, now mainly a reliever, was 7–2, and bullpen mate Don Mossi, 6–1 with a 1.94 ERA.

Each of the New York City teams drew more than one million fans during the 1954 regular season, with the Yankees topping out at just under 1.5 million, the Giants moving up to more than 1.15 million, and the Dodgers dropping a bit to just over 1 million.

*****

Game One of the 1954 World Series, played at the Polo Grounds on September 29, with 52,571 fans present, ended with pinch hitter Dusty Rhodes's three-run homer off Cleveland starter Lemon in the bottom of the tenth. But the play of the game, perhaps MLB's most famous defensive one ever, occurred in the top of the eight when Vic Wertz, who went four for five, powered the ball 450 feet to straightaway center field. Mays, "already rated the greatest" at that position "of all time by many observers," raced "some 100 feet and made a simply unbelievable over-the-shoulder grab just short of the wall." Immediately, Mays had the presence of mind to hurl the ball to the infield, enabling Larry Doby, tagging up from first base, to advance only to second.[54]

Giant manager Leo Durocher indicated, "I've been watching him make catches like that so long that I couldn't say it was the greatest." Mays acknowledged, "I don't know whether I made a greater catch any time. I just try to get a jump on the ball and go get it. I thought I had that one all the way."[55]

The Giants, who won the first game behind reliever Marv Grissom, proceeded to sweep the Indians, winning the second contest, 3–1, with Johnny Antonelli giving up only four hits and Rhodes cracking another homer, this time off starter Early Wynn. Ruben Gomez, with assistance from Hoyt Wilhelm, beat the Indians and Mike Garcia next, 6–2, as Don Liddle, with Antonelli delivering the save, won the clincher, 7–4, with Lemon taking his second loss. Longtime Indian great Bob Feller never got into a game, ensuring that he, the finest pitcher of his generation, continued to lack a World Series win. Mays went four for fourteen, with a double, four walks, and three RBIs.[56]

A gracious Al Lopez acknowledged, "The Giants played good ball, championship ball. They were much superior to us, offensively and defensively, and Leo managed perfectly." He later added, "I guess losing the first game at the Polo Grounds hurt us the most. We had so many chances when a hit or a long fly would have scored something. Willie Mays made that great catch of Wertz" drive and after that we never were the same."[57]

While there had been several "Giant heroes," the *New York Times*' Arthur Daley indicated, "the fellow whose name was on everybody's list was Willie Mays. He's an exciting ballplayer even when he does nothing—which is rare. But when he makes a catch such as he did on Vic Wertz in the opening game, he also sold a bill of goods to millions of television viewers. After watching that with incredulous eyes they're willing to believe anything they read or hear about this baseball Paul Bunyan." Daley quoted one "old-timer, no stranger to fame" who wished he were Willie Mays as "he's going to make a million dollars because he has more natural talent than any ballplayer I ever saw." Having won the batting title in "his first uninterrupted season in the big leagues," Mays's "potentialities" appeared "limitless."[58]

The Sporting News named Mays the National League Player of the Year; it picked Avila as the AL winner. It chose Antonelli and Lemon as the NL and AL outstanding pitchers, respectively. Mays also won his league's MVP, receiving 16 of the 24 first-place votes. Runner-up Ted Kluszewski got seven, the third and fourth-place finishers Antonelli and Duke Snider, none, and fifth-place Alvin Dark, one. All five were named to the Associated Press' 1954 All-Star team, along with Bobby Avila, Al Rosen, Stan Musial, Yogi Berra, and Bob Lemon. Wally Moon was named NL Rookie of the Year, easily beating out Ernie Banks, Gene Conley, and Henry Aaron; Bob Grim would receive the AL award, topping the Athletics infielder Jim Finigan and Detroit outfielder Al Kaline. The peerless golfer Babe Didrikson Zaharias, winning for the sixth time, was named female Athlete of the Year by the AP; Mays was tagged the male winner, besting Roger Bannister, the first man to run a mile faster than four minutes. Mays received the 1954 Hickok Belt, awarded by sportswriters and sportscasters to the year's top professional athlete. New York Giants swept *The Sporting News*' choices for "the No. 1 Men of the Year in Organized Baseball for 1954": Horace Stoneman was named Major League Executive of the Year, Leo Durocher, Major League Manager of the Year, and Mays, Major League Player of the Year.[59]

11

The Duke of Flatbush

With both the Yankees and the Dodgers rebounding from runner-up finishes to meet in the World Series for the third time in four years, 1955 became the year that the Flatbush faithful no longer cried at season's end, "Wait 'Til Next Year." Counting the three pennants garnered before the NL and AL merged, Brooklyn won its 11th pennant but its first World Series title. This was also the initial championship under Walt Alston's stewardship but the culmination of a nearly decade-long everyday lineup that was quite possibly MLB's finest as well as its most enduring.

The brilliant sportswriter Roger Kahn later drew from a Dylan Thomas poem to write about "the boys of summer" who made up the Brooklyn Dodgers during their final 11 years of existence, a period of repeated setbacks, belated success, and ultimately, heartbreaking loss with the team departing for the West Coast. Written nearly two decades after Kahn tracked the Dodgers throughout the 1952 and 1953 seasons for the *New York Herald Tribune*, *The Boys of Summer* focused on, among others, Roy Campanella, Duke Snider, Gil Hodges, Don Newcombe, Carl Furillo, Billy Cox, Preacher Roe, Clem Labine, Joe Black, and, above all else, Jackie Robinson, whom Kahn befriended.[1]

With Cox traded to Baltimore, Brooklyn's anticipated everyday players included Campanella, hoping to rebound from a terrible 1954 season, first baseman Hodges, second baseman Jim Gilliam, shortstop Reese, third baseman Robinson, left fielder Sandy Amoros, center fielder Snider, and right fielder Furillo. As matters turned out, Campanella had a tremendous comeback year, Snider, Hodges, and Furillo remained at the top of their games, and Reese was still a big contributor. Gilliam and Amoros were weak spots, and Robinson suffered through the worst season of his brilliant career. Snider, whom many viewed as good or better than Willie Mays, had possibly his finest year, probably unfairly just missing out on the NL's Most Valuable Player award. Don Hoak split time with Robinson at third, and infielder Don Zimmer provided some power, but neither hit for average. Newcombe also bounced back; Erskine had a decent year, while Johnny Podres was mediocre at best during the regular season. The young left-hander more than made up for that with a brilliant World Series performance. Billy Loes, Clem Labine, Don Bessent, Karl Spooner, and Roger Craig all contributed. A promising young southpaw, Sandy Koufax, started five games for the Dodgers, tossing two shutouts.

While the devil probably had nothing to do with the Yankees' relative lack of success the previous season—they won 103 games, after all—Casey Stengel was happy to steer his team to another AL pennant. Twenty-three-year-old Mickey Mantle, the Yankee center fielder, became a big star, with catcher Yogi Berra repeating as AL MVP; there, as well, the voters probably messed up with Mickey, who finished a distant fifth, more deserving of the award. Despite missing several weeks due to an injury, first baseman Bill Skowron excelled at the plate, while second baseman Gil McDougald and right fielder Hank Bauer had solid seasons, as did outfielder Elston Howard, the first Black Yankee and a Negro League veteran. Shortstop Billy Hunter, third baseman Andy Carey, and left fielder Irv Noren had disappointing years at the plate, as did seasoned veterans Joe Collins and Eddie Robinson. Mainstays Phil Rizzuto and Jerry Coleman played infrequently. Near season's end, Billy Martin returned from military service. Whitey Ford, Tommy Byrne, Bob Turley, Don Larsen, and closer Jim Konstanty were all excellent on the mound. Bob Grim was unable to repeat the exceptional showing of his rookie season, and the last of the Yankees' Big Three starting pitchers, 37-year-old Eddie Lopat, now ineffective, was shipped to Baltimore.

The New York Giants slid to third place in the NL, far behind Brooklyn and Milwaukee, costing Leo Durocher his managerial post. Center fielder Willie Mays was possibly better than the previous campaign, while right fielder Don Mueller, shortstop Alvin Dark, and left fielder Whitey Lockman remained solid performers. But third baseman Hank Thompson failed to hit, as did new starters like catcher Ray Katt, first baseman Gail Harris, and second baseman Wayne Terwilliger. Dusty Rhodes again contributed off the bench, but former greats Sid Gordon and Monte Irvin saw their careers wind down ingloriously. Johnny Antonelli, Ruben Gomez, and Don Liddle proved unable to repeat their 1954 successes. Sal Maglie pitched pretty well but ended up on Cleveland's roster near the season's end. Coming out of the bullpen, Marv Grissom was again quite good, but Hoyt Wilhelm had his worst year yet.

*****

Interviewed by *Look* magazine, Jackie Robinson reported that Brooklyn's top executive, Walter O'Malley, informed him, "The club wouldn't hesitate to put nine Negroes on the field if they were the best nine available players." The 1955 major league season saw former Negro Leaguers continue to excel, with more Black players on NL and AL teams than ever before. Dodger frontliners included Robinson, Campanella, Newcombe, Gilliam, and Amoros. The Giants had Mays, Irvin, and Thompson. The Indians exhibited center fielder Larry Doby and outfielder-third baseman Al Smith, an All-Star that year, and the White Sox outfielder Minnie Minoso. The Athletics' outfielder Harry Simpson was a light-hitting .300 hitter, while the Braves' first baseman George Crowe hit .281 with 15 homers in a limited role. The Cubs' infield included second baseman Gene Baker and shortstop Ernie Banks, both All-Stars in 1955.[2]

That same year was one of both promise and terror for African Americans in general. In Montgomery, Alabama, on March 2, a 15-year-old African American girl, Claudette Colvin, was arrested for refusing a bus driver's demand that she and three companions relinquish their seats to a white girl. Having learned about the abolitionists, Colvin, unlike her friends, remained in place. The driver demanded, "Why are you still sittin' there," and a white passenger at the front of the bus hollered, "You got to get up!" Margaret Johnson, a girl seated in the back of the bus, exclaimed, "She ain't got to do nothin' but stay black and die." Later, Colvin indicated, "It felt like Sojourner Truth was on one side pushing me down, and Harriet Tubman was on the other side of me pushing me down. I couldn't get up." When a policeman asked why she refused to get up, Colvin defiantly responded, "I paid my fare and it's my constitutional rights." He retorted, "Constitutional rights? No, no," and, aided by another police officer, roughly grabbed Colvin, placed her in a squad car, handcuffing her. Having violated Montgomery's Jim Crow practices, Colvin was charged with disorderly conduct and with assaulting the two police officers who compelled her to leave the bus, supposedly becoming "hysterical" as she "scratched and kicked and screamed" while the arrest occurred. Enduring suggestive comments from the policemen on the way to the station, she feared sexual assault.[3]

Angered by the arrest, civil rights figures, led by Rosa Parks, an African American activist and secretary of the Montgomery chapter of the NAACP, and Virginia Durr, a progressive white supporter, mobilized on Colvin's behalf. Parks remained in touch with Colvin, an NAACP Youth Council member.

*****

Following the 1954 World Series, the major leagues had continued to make headline news. On November 5, 91-year-old Connie Mack, who managed the Philadelphia Athletics for half a century and co-owned the team for a bit longer than that, agreed to allow the franchise to be sold to Chicago businessman Arnold Johnson. The Mack family had been bitterly divided about the sale, but the Athletics' financial status was dire. Johnson proceeded to move the Athletics to Kansas City.[4]

Houston Post sports columnist Jack Gallagher predicted his home city, "the Land of the Big Rich," was the major leagues' next likely destination. Former great Tiger slugger turned Indian general manager Hank Greenberg considered several cities more appealing than Baltimore and Kansas City, where the AL had recently allowed franchises to move. Championing a ten-team league, Greenberg believed a $5 million investment necessary to construct "a suitable park."[5]

Team executives appeared to consider expanding the senior circuit to ten teams, with San Francisco and Los Angeles, home to Pacific Coast League ball clubs, viewed as prime locations. Those said to be involved with such discussions included Dodger owner Walter O'Malley, Giants owner Horace Stoneman, and Bill Veeck, former owner of the Indians and Browns. The two California cities, White Sox general manager Frank Lane prophesied, would get major league teams within the next three years. "It's a question now whether the American or National League will be first to grab the territory, but whichever one it is will be top dog."[6]

With rumors floating about a trade involving Jackie Robinson, O'Malley denied having received such a proposal while acknowledging "older players—not Robinson alone—could be moving into the trading twilight." As he had stated at the end of the previous season, Jackie apparently anticipated being dealt.[7]

Surprisingly, given their past history, Brooklyn fans had not clamored for Walt Alston to be fired despite a disappointing second-place finish. But the 1954 version of the Dodgers, even with Charlie Dressen at the helm, would have had problems retaining their pennant. Don Newcombe, Carl Erskine, Billy Loes, and Preacher Roe, among others, all disappointed. Roy Campanella's injury proved devastating. Carl Furillo "did not get unwound until near the end of the season." And "Junior Gilliam stood still," while "old age" began to creep up on Jackie Robinson. Third basemen Billy Cox and Don Hoak offered only a collective .240 batting average. In Arthur Daley's estimation, "only three regulars held up, Gil Hodges, Duke Snider and Pee Wee Reese."[8]

At the beginning of December, the Yankees and Orioles conducted a massive 18-man swap. Players sent to New York included pitchers Don Larsen and Bob Turley, while Baltimore received, among others, pitcher Harry Byrd, catcher Hal Smith, Gus Triandos, and outfielder Gene Woodling. The Yankees most desired 24-year-old Turley, a hard-throwing right-hander who led the league in both strikeouts and walks while posting a 14–15 record with a 3.46 ERA the previous season; he also led the AL with the fewest hits allowed—6.5—per nine innings. During the middle of the month, Brooklyn attempted to send Roe and Cox to Baltimore, although Roe chose to retire. On December 14, the Dodgers agreed to a contract with 18-year-old Sandy Koufax, making the southpaw pitcher another bonus baby required to join the Dodgers rather than being sent to the minors.

In early January, sportswriter Roscoe McGowen dissected the Dodgers, whose ownership team had signed Alston to another one-year contract. As McGowen saw matters, Brooklyn required "a new Roy Campanella, a new Don Newcombe and a new Carl Erskine." Campanella appeared certain that his left-hand injury had healed, enabling his return to an MVP performance. Not quite as confident, "Big Newk" remained hopeful he would pitch like he did before entering the US military. Erskine, ever self-confident, seemed to have "lost something else" the previous year. "A new Jackie Robinson" also might be possible, and he promised to be in good shape by spring training. "A new Johnny Podres" was on the horizon, lacking the appendix that had curtailed his pitching effectiveness.[9]

Leo Durocher continued heaping praise on his star center fielder, claiming he was "better than Stan Musial." Durocher declared, "If Willie hits .325 or better for the next three or four years, he'll be the best we've ever known." Comparing him with the St. Louis star, Leo indicated, "Mays is a better ballplayer. He is as good a hitter and has as good power. He can outrun, outthrow and out-field Musial." While Musial was both an excellent outfielder and first baseman, Durocher said, "Mays could play . . . any position if he had to . . . . He's the greatest shortstop that ever played center field."[10]

New York World Telegram columnist Dan Daniels foresaw two New York teams meeting up in the World Series: the Giants and the Yankees. Leo Durocher's team would prevail after a "furious" three-team battle in the National League—New York, Brooklyn, and Milwaukee—with Newcombe failing to improve on his previous year's effort. The Indians would have a tough time overcoming "the psychological blow of" their whipping by the Giants, while the Yankees' pitching staff, with the additions of Turley and Larsen, would be "stronger." Primed for big years, Mickey Mantle, Irv Noren, and Yogi Berra appeared ready to help the Yankees overcome the Red Sox, the White Sox, and the Indians. The Giants would again prevail in the World Series. Johnny Antonelli would be the NL's MVP, Mantle the AL's MVP and batting champion. The American League would "invade California," while the National League would "add Montreal and Toronto."[11]

For the second straight year, the New York Yankees experienced the loss of one of their longtime pitching aces. Starting with the 1948 season, Vic Raschi, Allie Reynolds, and Eddie Lopat had provided exceptional frontline pitching for the Yankees as they captured five straight pennants and World Series titles from 1949–53. Then, Raschi was sold to the Cardinals, and now, Reynolds opted to retire, leaving only Lopat on the Yankees pitching staff.

During their time together with the Yankees, the three authored five 20 seasons, 10 additional years of at least 15 victories, and 16 of the 20 Yankee wins, producing five World Series championships. During the consecutive World Series run, Reynolds was "Stengel's right-hand man . . . literally and figuratively," becoming the Yankees' "most reliable starter" and "most effective reliever."[12]

As spring training began, Arthur Daley viewed the Yankees as "the most interesting team," likely to engage in "a two-horse match affair" with the Indians. Like Dan Daniel, Daley saw the Giants, Dodgers, and Braves as the National League "Haves." However, he thought the Yankees, having come "a cropper" despite 103 wins the previous season, provoked more unanswered queries. With Raschi gone, Stengel lacked "solid pitching" or a strong enough bench for "his uncanny juggling act." The recent transaction with the Orioles may have rectified that situation, Daley offered, thanks to the receipt of Turley, Larsen, and shortstop Billy Hunter, with Billy Martin due to be released from the military. One question involved Elston Howard, soon to become the first African American Yankee.

However, Mickey Mantle, "the erstwhile Boy Wonder, now a decrepit old man of 23," represented "the most intriguing question." Earlier "hailed instantly as the next Joe DiMaggio," Mantle was considered "to have even higher potentialities than the famed Yankee Clipper" due to "his greater speed." About to enter his fifth season as a Yankee, Mantle was "only the third ranking center fielder in New York. Both Willie Mays and Duke Snider outrank him." To date, Daley argued, Mantle had "displayed only the physical requisites for greatness." Unfortunately, "he has shown none of DiMaggio's fierce inner pride." Indeed, Tommy Heinrich, Daley asserted, "was twice the ball player Mantle is without half of Mickey's talent. Tommy had rare intelligence and a most inquisitive mind." Admittedly, Daley noted, Mantle's "trick knees have hindered his development" regarding bunting and learning the strike zone. Nineteen fifty-five might well "be a year of decision" for Mantle. His "booming bat" might buttress a rebuilt pitching staff.[13]

Mantle also had yet to win over Shirley Povich, at least wholeheartedly. The columnist called Mickey "the lad who appeared destined to make it . . . a disappointment, which is the greater because he has the native talent to be a tremendous ball player. He hits the ball farther, runs faster; bunts better than anybody else in baseball, but apparently lacks the high resolution to make the most of his skills."[14]

Delivering his National League predictions, Povich picked Brooklyn with New York slated for second, if the team's luck held up, otherwise indicating the Giants could land in sixth. He saw Campanella rebounding "to drive in all those runs the Dodgers left on base last year," and better pitching, thanks to Newcombe and lefty Karl Spooner, who had tossed back-to-back shutouts with 27 strikeouts in two late-season games in 1954. Reese remained the NL's top shortstop, Hodges the best first sacker, and Snider the greatest center fielder "if Willie Mays isn't." Left field remained a sore point. Robinson was still on the roster, and Alston was "a year older and wiser in the business."

In Povich's estimation, New York appeared "well-balanced, an opportunistic club blessed" with the NL's top reliever duo in Hoyt Wilhelm and Marv Grissom. The infield seemed "sharp-fielding, sharp-hitting" other than second baseman Davey Williams. Outfielders Mays and Don Mueller were "superb," although Monte Irvin was "definitely slipping." Questioning the heaping of superlatives on Mays, Povich indicated, "Conviction [is] growing that Mays hit far over his norm last season." He referred to Mays as "the most valuable piece of property in baseball currently," who made his team the National League's most attractive, putting on "the kind of show . . . not available from any other club," as "the most daring ball player since Ty Cobb, though not necessarily a great one." The Giants' starting pitchers appeared "solid," although Sal Maglie was "aging." Their catchers were punchless, but pinch hitter deluxe Dusty Rhodes remained on the roster. Durocher provided "smart handling."[15]

Twenty-eight baseball analysts, Dan Parker reported, forecast a Giants-Yankees World Series. Those same "experts," he admitted, had blown both their previous year's predictions, with few having picked the Giants or Indians. Nevertheless, these experts reasoned that the Giants possessed "the drive" and sufficient pitching, coupled with power and manager Durocher, "to keep rolling." Brooklyn, possessing "awesome power" but "inconsistent pitching," was viewed as a likely third-place finisher. The Yankees, having added Bob Turley and Bill Hunter, were seen as the probable AL pennant winners.[16]

As spring training neared an end, John Lardner discussed the players he considered "most worth watching" during the impending baseball season. He pointed to "the de facto existence of an odd situation in New York baseball. Each of the three resident ball clubs has a prodigious centerfielder." Temporarily, Lardner indicated, Duke Snider and Willie Mays were "rated somewhat above Mickey Mantle." When asked to deliver an assessment, Snider reluctantly responded, "All right. I'm better than Mays. I get more money, don't I?" Reflecting a bit further, Duke said, "Some of the catches that Mays makes are maybe a little easier than they look."

While stating that he did not have to choose between Duke and Willie, Lardner acknowledged, "Snider can be dramatic, as well as efficient. Even Mays has not as yet run straight up a wall to make a game-ending catch, as Snider did in Philadelphia not long ago." Their home ballparks, with varying dimensions, affected how each player responded defensively. Adding Mantle to the list, Lardner noted he was "perhaps the fastest straight-on-runner of the three" and could go "a long way for a ball" despite lacking "May's [sic] suppleness and Snider's grace and sureness." At the same time, Mantle could "hit with great power," particularly batting right-handed.

The base runner who best melded the talents of the great Ty Cobb and Max Carey was Jackie Robinson, Lardner wrote. True, his speed was diminished and "his legs" had turned "brittle," but he remained "the most rewarding runner to watch." Two former Negro Leaguers—Junior Gilliam and Minnie Minoso—were among several players "both faster and" apt to steal more bases but drew on "ideas that Robinson brought back into baseball."[17]

Sports Illustrated's April 11 issue featured Mays, manager Leo Durocher, and Leo's wife, the actress Loraine Day. She stood in the middle, with her arms on Willie's and Leo's shoulders, all grinning widely.[18]

*****

Like various teammates, particularly Robinson, Campanella, and Newcombe, Snider received considerable publicity from the national press. Born in Los Angeles on September 19, 1926, Snider, fondly known by fans and sportswriters as "the Duke of Flatbush," was among the most celebrated and beloved of the Brooklyn Dodgers. A high school all-around athlete, 17-year-old Snider appeared in a pair of games for the Montreal Royals before moving over to the Newport News Dodgers of the Class B Piedmont League. Displaying little power, Snider managed 34 doubles while batting .294 before entering the US Navy. Released in 1946, the still-teenage Snider played for the first-place Fort Worth Cats of the AA Texas League, hitting only .250, but was moved up to the St. Paul Saints of the AAA American Association, where he swatted 12 homers in 269 official at-bats, while batting .316. Appearing in 40 games with the Brooklyn Dodgers toward the end of the 1947 season, Snider went homerless in 83 at bats, hitting .241. Returning to the Montreal Royals at the start of the 1948 campaign, Snider belted 17 homers, drove in 77 runs, and hit .327 in 275 at bats. Back in Brooklyn later in the season, he smacked his first five major league homers, batting .244 in 160 at bats.

In 1949, his initial full year with Brooklyn, Snider proved to be a budding star on the pennant-winning Dodgers, scoring 100 runs (6th in the NL), getting 23 homers (8th), driving in 92 runs, and hitting .292. By 1950, he was already an All-Star, finishing ninth in the MVP race after scoring 109 runs (4th), rapping a league-leading 199 hits, delivering 31 doubles, 10 triples (3rd), and 31 homers (5th), batting .321 (3rd), having a league-high 343 total bases, and producing a slugging percentage of .557 (5th). The next year, Snider scored 96 runs, had 29 homers (8th), 101 RBIs (7th), and a .277 batting average, while again making the All-Star team. His image, along with the declaration, "Baseball's Powerman," fronted *Sport Life*'s September issue. During the 1952 season, when the Dodgers returned atop the NL, All-Star Snider had 21 homers (8th), 92 RBIs (7th), and a .303 batting average (5th), finishing eighth in the voting for MVP.[19]

Appearing on the covers of Dell's *Baseball* magazine for 1953 and *Sports Stars*, Snider, also known as the "Silver Fox" for his prematurely gray hair, became a genuine superstar that year as the Dodgers repeated in the National League. He led the league with 132 runs scored, a .627 slugging average, 370 total bases, and an OPS of 1.046—the first of three straight seasons over 1.000. He also got 198 hits (3rd), 38 doubles (3rd), 42 homers (2nd)—the first of five straight seasons of 40 or more—126 RBIs (3rd), 16 stolen bases (5th), a .336 batting average (4th), an on-base percentage of .419 (3rd), and a 9.1 WAR

(2nd). Named to his fourth straight All-Star squad, Snider came in third in MVP tabulations, behind both Campanella and Eddie Mathews.[20]

Sportswriter Arthur Mann authored an article on Snider for *The Saturday Evening Post*, which appeared in its February 20, 1954, issue. It began with a declaration that the Dodgers had experienced setbacks recently, including another World Series loss to the Yankees, Dressen's departure, and broadcaster Red Barber's moving over to Yankee Stadium. At the same time, they no longer had to deal with "the Duke Snider situation." For a decade, "the center fielder with the high potential and the correspondingly low boiling point" acted "as a problem child." For Snider had become a star and was "no longer a source of official concern. Today he is a man."

Late into the 1952 season, Brooklyn officials were still befuddled by the then 25-year-old Snider. They "wanted the player to realize his high promise." Fortunately, "Duke wanted it, too, and desperately." However, "he failed to see himself as, more often than not, his own worst enemy. He held himself back through impatience and frustration." Snider desired to win so badly he was unable to handle "personal failure and team defeat."

Nearly a decade earlier, Branch Rickey Jr., the son of baseball's famed Mahatma, had to contend with the then-teenage Snider, who appeared not to be hustling through training exercises and was ordered to leave training camp. Pleading he would "hustle every minute," the Dodgers recognized Snider's potential and "had no intention of getting rid of him. . . . He was one of a few in the game's history to be labeled a future great at first glance, because of the steel-spring quality of his lithe body, the savage, uninhibited wing of his bat, his leaping catches and his irrepressible eagerness to play." His remarkable throwing arm, near sprinter's speed, and prodigious power at the plate enthralled Dodger management.

While Duke's temper, displayed in tossing his bat or kicking a base, or inclination to defy an order to bunt, belting a homer instead, continued to befuddle team officials, he also offered examples of his immense talent that amazed even seasoned baseball observers. During one game in 1950, Dodger left fielder Gene Hermanski failed to make "a shoestring catch," with the ball skidding madly away. Racing near the foul line abutting Hermanski's position, Snider barehandedly grabbed the ball and hurled it to third baseman Billy Cox to tag the astonished batter, who thought he had a triple. Branch Rickey Sr. was stunned. "An ordinary ballplayer wouldn't have started from center field to back up the play. Only a great player can do things like that—see them, or feel them before they happen!"

And yet, Snider frustrated manager Burt Shotten and then, his replacement, Chuck Dressen; the skippers resorted to fines and benching. During the 1952 pennant chase as Snider slumped, Dressen sat him down as Duke continued to struggle against curves by left-handers. The *New York Journal-American*'s Mike Gaven saw this as Dressen's "most important" managerial decision. After all, Snider was viewed as "baseball's greatest potential star." Dressen clearly believed Snider had to "supplement his great talent with more effort." The Dodgers, Gaven thought, would likely soon shop Snider.

Instead, Mann indicated, "the lighted fire became a conflagration in several spots," with Duke seeking "to tear the portly Gaven to shreds." Returning to the Dodgers lineup, Snider got hot, helping the Dodgers stave off the Giants for the 1952 pennant, then performed brilliantly in the field in the World Series, while smashing four homers. His next year's performance proved even more exceptional during the regular season, topped off by another excellent World Series.[21]

If anything, Snider was even better in 1954, despite dipping to fourth in the MVP count. An All-Star for the fifth straight time, he led the NL in runs (120) and total bases (378) once again, got 199 hits (2nd), 39 doubles (2nd), 10 triples (3rd), 40 homers (5th), 130 RBIs (2nd), a .341 batting average (3rd), a .423 OBP (3rd), a .647 slugging average (2nd), and a 1.071 OPS (2nd), the highest of his career. At the time, many analysts considered him the finest of the New York center fielders, although several viewed Willie Mays as preeminent, with a smaller number favoring Mickey Mantle.

New York Yankee slugger Babe Ruth establishing home run record, c. 1920. Courtesy of the Library of Congress, Miscellaneous Items in High Demand Collection, LC-USZ62-71763.

Pittsburgh Crawford pitcher Satchel Paige, 1935. Courtesy of the Library of Congress, Farm Security Administration/Office of War Information Black-and-White Negatives Collection, LC-USF34- 007958-ZE [P&P].

All-Stars Lou Gehrig, Joe Cronin, Bill Dickey, Joe DiMaggio, Charlie Gehringer, Jimmie Foxx, Hank Greenberg, Griffith Stadium, Washington, D.C., July 7, 1937. Courtesy of the Library of Congress, Harris & Ewing Collection, LC-DIG-hec-22989.

Yankee center fielder Joe DiMaggio kissing his bat, c. December 15, 1941. Courtesy of the Library of Congress, Miscellaneous Items in High Demand Collection, LC-DIG-ppmsca-18794.

Cleveland Indian pitcher Bob Feller, US Navy Chief Specialist, with 40 mm quadruple anti-aircraft gun mount, circa 1942 or 1943. Official US Navy Photograph, from the All-Hands collection at the Naval History and Heritage Command.

Homestead Gray catcher Josh Gibson, January 9, 1943. Courtesy of the Library of Congress, Miscellaneous Items in High Demand Collection, LC-DIG-ppmsca-89886.

Brooklyn Dodger star Jackie Robinson, circa 1947. National Baseball Hall of Fame Library, Cooperstown, NY.

Brooklyn Dodger second baseman Jackie Robinson and shortstop Pee Wee Reese. National Baseball Hall of Fame Library, Cooperstown, NY.

New York Yankee manager Casey Stengel. National Baseball Hall of Fame Library, Cooperstown, NY.

Brooklyn Dodger second baseman Jackie Robinson, 1950. Courtesy of the National Archives, Records of the US Information Agency, Record Group 306, photo no. 6802718.

New York Giant left fielder Monte Irvin, c. 1950. National Baseball Hall of Fame Library, Cooperstown, NY.

Manager Leo Durocher, March 11, 1966. Courtesy of the Library of Congress, Look Collection, LC-DIG-ds-07374.

Chicago White Sox left fielder Minnie Minoso, c. 1952. National Baseball Hall of Fame Library, Cooperstown, NY.

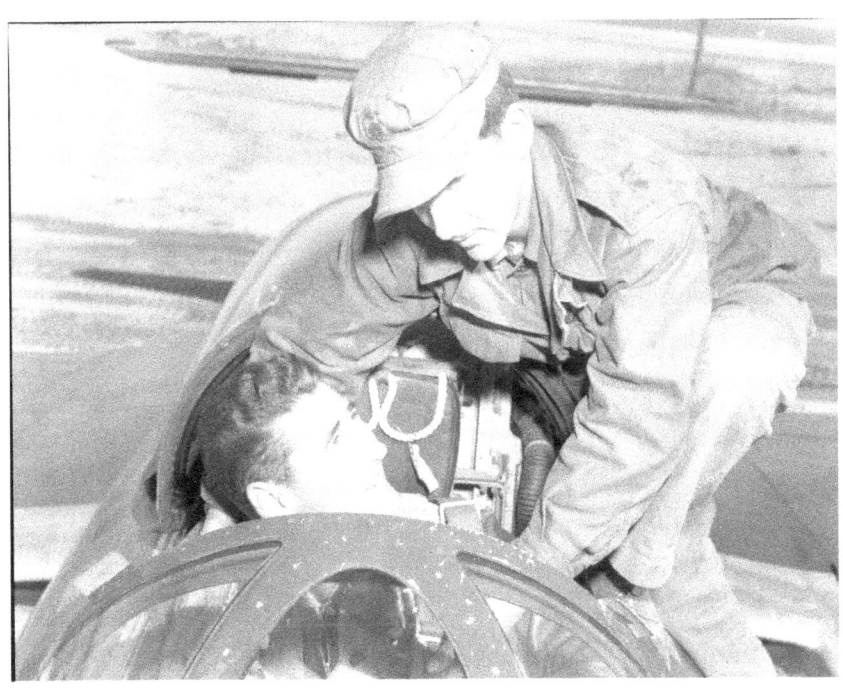

Boston Red Sox left fielder Ted Williams, US Marine Corps captain and pilot during Korean War, March 16, 1953. Courtesy of the National Archives, Records of the US Marine Corps, Record Group 127, photo no. 176250534.

Cleveland Indian center fielder Larry Doby, c. 1954. National Baseball Hall of Fame Library, Cooperstown, NY.

New York Giant center fielder Willie Mays, c. 1954. National Baseball Hall of Fame Library, Cooperstown, NY.

Brooklyn Dodger center fielder Duke Snider, c. 1955. National Baseball Hall of Fame Library, Cooperstown, NY.

Welcome Home Dinner to Brooklyn Dodgers, Hotel St. George, Brooklyn, NY, April 16, 1956. From the New York Public Library.

New York Yankee center fielder Mickey Mantle. National Baseball Hall of Fame Library, Cooperstown, NY.

New York Yankee star Mickey Mantle with Yankee scout Tom Greenwald, May 6, 1957. Courtesy of the Library of Congress, Miscellaneous Items in High Demand, LC-USZ6-2399.

Milwaukee Braves third baseman Eddie Mathews, catcher Del Crandall, right fielder Henry Aaron, c. 1957. National Baseball Hall of Fame Library, Cooperstown, NY.

12

No More Wait 'Til Next Year for Duke Snider and the Brooklyn Dodgers

Opening their 1955 AL season on April 13, the Yankees destroyed the Senators, 19–1 on a Whitey Ford two-hitter. Third baseman Andy Carey got as many hits as did left fielder Bob Cerv, while Ford, first baseman Bill Skowron, and center fielder Mickey Mantle had three each. Ford, Cerv, and Mantle drove in four runs apiece, Skowron, three, catcher Yogi Berra and Carey had two. Skowron, Mantle, and Berra homered. Thanks to inclement weather, only 11,251 were at Yankee Stadium.

The two NL squads from New York City had contrasting opening starts. The Dodgers, with a mere 6,999 fans at Ebbets Field, beat the Pirates, 6–1, as Carl Erskine scattered seven hits. Center fielder Duke Snider went three for three, third baseman Jackie Robinson and right fielder Carl Furillo got two hits each. Second baseman Jim Gilliam and Furillo homered, Carl's a three-run shot. Giving up only three hits, the Phillies' Robin Roberts shut down the Giants, 4–2, with New York's runs unearned although coming off a Monte Irvin double in the top of the ninth inning. Center fielder Willie Mays was hitless in three official at bats, walked once, and struck out twice, although he did manage to steal a base.

The 1955 season, in certain ways, favored Snider as the previous year had Mays and the next would Mantle. His Dodgers, like Snider, got off to a very quick start, winning their first ten games to take a three-game league lead, then, after dropping the 11th contest, going 12–1 to stand at 22–2 on May 10, nine and a half games in front of the Giants, with the Braves another half-game behind.

After completing April with a .345 batting average, 5 homers, 13 runs scored, 19 driven in, 19 walks, a .514 on-base percentage, and a .727 slugging percentage, Snider cooled off a bit over the next eight games. His batting average dropped to .299, although he compiled 10 more runs scored, 4 homers, and 11 RBIs. Throughout the remainder of the month, Snider slumped a bit, batting .280. Nevertheless, he hit 7 homers, scored 25 runs, drove 23, and picked up the same number of walks, while his team stood at 32–11, five and a half games better than the second-place squad, the surprising Chicago Cubs. The 24–21 Giants were nine back, two ahead of the disappointing Braves, who were sitting a game below .500. The three expected top competitors were atop the American League, with the 30–13 Yankees two and a half games ahead of the Indians, the White Sox another game and a half behind.

Surveying the National League, Shirley Povich recalled Leo Durocher's advice regarding the Dodgers' blistering start. "This is baseball, remember? Nothing gets won in early May." He predicted, "They'll come back to us. Nobody keeps up their pace." Despite their lustrous record, the Dodgers had experienced a pair of short losing streaks. Surprisingly, it was Brooklyn's hitting that was coming up short, with the entire team, other than Campanella, slumping, including Snider, Furillo, Hodges, and Reese, with Robinson requesting to be left "out of the lineup." The Braves were suffering from the absence of "their best player, Ed Mathews," because of an appendectomy.[1]

No matter, cartoonist Willard Mullin drew a sketch of Snider regally attired, holding a giant bat, followed by a Brooklyn bum holding Duke's cape, declaring, "GANG WAY! MAKE ROOM F'R ROYALTY!" The companion article in *The Sporting News* by Roscoe McGowen, "Duke Proves Dynamo in Dodger Drive," quoted Philly manager Mayo Smith, who pointed to Snider at the plate and said, "There is a helluva ball player. You can have Willie Mays. I'll take Snider." When informed of Smith's declaration, Dodger boss Walt Alston agreed, "I should say that's about right." Also, Brooklyn shortstop and captain Pee Wee Reese declared, "Duke can do a lot of things. I'll tell you one thing. He comes off that bench swinging. He's ready to take that cut at any pitch he feels he can hit and he has so much power that he can hit 'em out of the park in any direction."[2]

With a month and a half of the season completed, Snider was batting .303, with a .447 on-base percentage and a .619 slugging average. He already had 38 runs scored, 12 homers, 42 RBIs, and 42 walks. His New York City counterparts, Willie Mays and Mickey Mantle, had experienced mixed results to start their seasons. After a blistering start in April, Mays had dropped to a .284 batting average at the end of May, although his long-ball production—9 homers that month—enabled him to match Snider, albeit with a lower on-base percentage (.372) and slugging average (.580). Mantle had a productive April, followed by a torrid next month, elevating his batting average to .329, his OBP to .471, and his slugging average to .678, with a homer total one behind that of both Snider and Mays. On May 13, he hit three homers, one batting right-handed, the other two left-handed, in a game against Detroit at Yankee Stadium, the first time he had accomplished those feats. He also managed, at one point, to get on base 15 consecutive times. The man he replaced in the Yankees lineup in center field, Joe DiMaggio, called Mantle, increasingly celebrated for his "tape-measure homers," "a tremendous ballplayer."[3]

Bob Addie's column in the *Washington Post and Times Herald* referred to Yankees manager Casey Stengel's analysis of New York City's center fielders. "You take the Brooklyn guy, Duke Snider," Stengel indicated. "He's a home run hitter. He can throw and he can field. But can he throw and field and hit home runs better than the kid the Giants have? I mean Willie Mays. You see, we don't know. Mays can do everything, too." Pivoting, Stengel said, "But now you come down to my fella (Mickey Mantle). He could grab it all—I mean be the best of the three. He's a home run hitter, too, from both sides of the plate. He can run and he can throw. Where else do you see so many good centerfielders in one town?"

Agreeing with Stengel, Addie went on to note that "the three New York teams battle constantly for attendance and the only way you draw is with a star." He indicated, "The Yankee dynasty always had a king. There were the golden days of Babe Ruth and Joe DiMaggio. When Mantle came along he was designated as the crown prince." In fact, Mantle, Addie declared, "has a world of talent but has seldom come up to expectations." Although "a good hitter," he was not "a great" one comparable to Stan Musial or Ted Williams. It was true that Mantle was still a youngster, a mere 23 years old with "his most productive years still . . . ahead," while Mays was a year older. Snider was "slightly older" still and in his seventh full season, Mantle in his fifth, and Mays in his third, although the rookie campaigns of the two younger players had been abbreviated.

A regular since the 1949 season, Snider had never driven in fewer than 92 runs, topping the 100 RBI total four times. He was "the best home run hitter of the lot," having twice hit 40 or more, while Mays hit 41 the previous year and Mantle's highest total to date was 27. As Addie saw it, "Mays got all the headlines last year," although "his figures were almost matched by Snider," with Duke scoring one more run and driving in 20 more. Concluding, Addie wrote, "Don't forget—this was a super-performance for Willie Mays while with Duke it was merely routine. It could be that the 'old' Duke is the best of the three. At least, you'll get a strong vote in Brooklyn."[4]

Grabbing the major league lead, Snider squashed three homers—the second time in his career he had done so—and a double, while driving in six, to help Brooklyn beat Milwaukee, 11–8, at Ebbets Field on June 1. This began a three-game stretch during which Snider went eleven for fourteen, with two doubles, five homers, thirteen RBIs, and his batting average lifted to .343. Talk could be heard of Snider's bid for the triple crown, a feat not accomplished in the National League since St. Louis' Joe Medwick in 1937. The *New York Times'* Joseph M. Sheehan contended that the most likely player to lead one of the big leagues simultaneously in batting average, homers, and RBIs was Snider, "big, strong, fleet and in his physical prime at 28."[5]

Duke, "the handsome, prematurely graying Californian" was "more intent and more relaxed than" previously. His recent surge riveted public attention to Snider, but team officials were more pleased by his "sparkling day-in, day-out play" with earlier great promise and expectations coming to fruition. "His booming bat" had produced a soaring 460-foot big fly against the Giants, while a grand slam had helped to edge out the Phillies. "Dazzling catches" included grabbing "Monte Irvin's 440-foot blast to the bleacher wall at the Polo Grounds" and the "jumping spear of" a smash by Willie Jones at Ebbets Field the very day the Dell Publishing Company handed him an award for robbing the Philly player with "the 1954 catch-of-the-year."

Snider, Sheehan admitted, lacked Mays's "flamboyance" or Mantle's "flashing speed and explosive power." Rather, "he went about his business quietly, with much of the almost indolent grace of Joe DiMaggio, making the hardest chores look easy." Notwithstanding "their virtues, proven and potential," the other two New York City center fielders appeared as "Johnny-commy-latelies compared to Snider." Through the end of the previous season, Snider had produced 191 homers while batting .307 in 978 games; Mantle, 84 homers and a .296 batting average, Mays, 65 homers, while hitting .304. Thus, "Mickey and Willie have a long way to go before they can put it on the record that they measure up to Snider." Moreover, "the Duke is complicating their task," playing the best ball of his career over the past two years.[6]

Snider went hitless in two at bats, while Mantle spanked a three-run homer and Mays, like Mickey, got a couple of hits in the 1955 All-Star Game, played at County Stadium on July 12. The National League won, 6–5, when Stan Musial homered off Boston's Frank Sullivan in the bottom of the twelfth.

*****

Continuing to track the success of Black players, the *Los Angeles Sentinel*'s Eddie Burbridge noted the home run prowess of Roy Campanella, Mays, the Indians' Al Smith, and the Cubs' Ernie Banks, who had recently smacked his second grand slam of the season. Top hitters included Campy, Brooklyn's Sandy Amoros, Milwaukee's Henry Aaron, Pittsburgh's Roberto Clemente, and Kansas City's Vic Powers.[7]

Homer "Goose" Curry, a longtime Negro League player who was presently managing the Negro American League's Memphis Red Sox, indicated that acceptance of Black players in the major leagues had all but extinguished Blackball. While he had "played with, against or managed" the likes of "Campanella, Jackie Robinson, Willie Mays, Larry Doby, Don Newcombe and" virtually "all the other Negro major league stars," the Negro Leagues were no longer able to sign such athletes first. Denying that any present Black player was the finest he had witnessed, Curry saved that distinction for Josh Gibson.[8]

Another Negro League veteran, Buzz Clarkson, who briefly played for the Dodgers in 1952, praised Mays but believed Henry Aaron had an even brighter future. "Don't get me wrong," Clarkson stated. "Willie is terrific. I don't think anybody can field with him. And he peps up the whole team. But he goes for lots of bad pitches. And he's so impetuous, such a pepper pot eager to give those balls a ride that he may never learn to lay off." Pointing to the Milwaukee outfielder, Clarkson offered, "Keep an eye on Aaron. There's nothing wrong with his fielding, either. And he's a cold-blooded hitter who don't bite on bad stuff. What wrists, and what action! He practically picks pitches out of the catcher's glove. And can he fly!" Thus, "over the long haul, I wouldn't be surprised if Aaron—he's only 21—proves a more valuable all-round player than Mays."[9]

While Organized Baseball continued making progress through the inclusion of a substantial number of Black players—even the New York Yankees were now finally integrated—American society failed to keep pace. For every separate forward, defenders of segregation proved determined to maintain Jim Crow practices through whatever means were available. On May 7, the Reverend George Lee, a 51-year-old Black minister, grocery store owner, and printer, was shot to death. The assassination resulted from Lee's engagement with the Mississippi chapter of the NAACP, participation in the Regional Council of Negro Leadership (RCNL), and voting rights efforts.

On May 31, 1955, the US Supreme Court issued the implementation order in the case of *Brown v. Board of Education*, declaring that the previous year's ruling that public schools had to desegregate must be adhered to "with all deliberate speed." That pronouncement by Chief Justice Earl Warren proved murky to many, arguably emboldening those determined to resist.[10]

That summer, the resort to violence again surfaced. The victims included a 14-year-old African American boy from Chicago visiting relatives in rural Mississippi, and a 63-year-old First World War veteran who happened to be a farmer and civil rights leader in that state. The youngster, Emmett Till, was abducted, tortured, and murdered by two white men, angered by the boy's purported flirting with one of their wives. His mother, Mamie Bradley, insisted on Emmett's body being displayed during a funeral procession involving

10,000 people in his home city. A jury proclaimed his murderers "Not Guilty" after 65 minutes of supposed deliberation.[11]

Like the Reverend George Lee, Lamar "Ditney" Smith was a RCNL member determined to encourage African Americans to register to vote. That led to his shooting in front of the Brookhaven, Lincoln County, courthouse, and a refusal to allow anyone to take him to a hospital. No prosecution resulted although the killing occurred in broad daylight.

*****

Following another winning streak—this time of six games—Brooklyn stood at 42–12 on June 11, with its largest lead yet, of ten and a half games, over 32–23 Chicago. New York, just two games over .500, was fourteen games behind, a half-game ahead of Milwaukee. The 1954 Giants, the *Los Angeles Times*' Al Wolf indicated, had largely thrived due to Johnny Antonelli's pitching, Don Mueller's hitting, and Willie Mays's "all-around play and sparkplugging." Both Mueller and Mays remained productive, but Antonelli had a losing record, while manager Leo Durocher "appears to be fresh out of genius."

By contrast, the Dodgers might end up being "one of the greatest gangs the game has ever known." Wolf wrote, "You name it—pitching, hitting, power, depth—and the Dodgers have it." Both Don Newcombe and Campanella had made terrific comebacks, while Campy's top competitor for the Triple Crown was "that other destructive Dodger—Duke Snider." Then, there were "Gil Hodges, Jackie Robinson, Pee Wee Reese, Carl Erskine, Sandy Amoros, Billy Loes, Junior Gilliam, Carl Furillo, Clem Labine and Ed Roebuck." The team might be able to overcome "the jinx" dooming Brooklyn to seven straight World Series setbacks.[12]

The Yankees, through the machinations of general manager George Weiss and manager Casey Stengel, appeared to have erected "another juggernaut," replacing veterans with "kids" allowing "the show" to continue "without a hitch." Pitchers Allie Reynolds and Johnny Sain, along with outfielder Gene Woodling, had departed, while Billy Martin was still in the military and both Phil Rizzuto and Eddie Lopat were fading. No matter, pitchers Bob Turley and John Kucks and catcher-outfielder Elston Howard were picking up the slack.

In addition, it remained "business as usual" through "the mayhem business" of Mickey Mantle and Yogi Berra.[13]

Hitting at a .325 clip with 20 homers and 60 RBIs through 57 games, Snider was garnering the kind of accolades Willie Mays had a year before. With the National League race looking like a runaway, sports columnist Shirley Povich indicated, "If Stan Musial is no longer the best ball player in the league, Duke Snider is." Having been annoyed at unfavorable comparisons with Mays, Snider was "out-performing" Willie "by so wide a margin . . . as to admit no dispute of his greatness." Povich wrote, "Snider is the picture player of both big leagues, the very mold of form in all that he does, as handy with a bunting bat as he is with his homerun swing." While not "quite as spectacular as Mays in the outfield," Snider remained "the embodiment of assurance as he gets the job done perhaps as well as Mays." Moreover, "he has a swing that's in the groove, in contrast to Mays who is a helter-skelter swinger."[14]

The *Los Angeles Times*' Al Wolf agreed that Mays was "only the second best center fielder in the National League." Snider, Wolf indicated, was "doing perhaps the greatest all-around job in diamond history." At one point, manager Durocher benched his slumping star, explaining, "He isn't helping the club. He isn't hitting and he's making wrong throws and running bases badly. Maybe he needs a rest and it certainly won't hurt him." Mays, amid a three for twenty-six batting slump, responded, "I don't feel tired but Leo knows more about me than I know about myself. Maybe it'll help. I've never been benched anywhere I've played before." Fans were booing the same player they earlier "cheered his every appearance."[15]

Arthur Daley, the *New York Times*' sports columnist, asked, "Whatever happened to Willie Mays?" indicating that "poor Willie just hasn't lived up to the raves of his personal publicity man, Leo Durocher." Daley seemed pleased that Duke Snider was "finally getting recognition as the superlative ball player he is." The Chicago Cubs' personnel director, Wid Matthews, agreed that Snider was "the best all-round performer in the game today."[16]

Sports Illustrated featured Snider on the cover of its June 27, 1955, issue. The accompanying article, "Duke or Willie?: A Vote for Snider," began with the statement that many viewed Duke as "the most dangerous hitter in the National League." Seemingly little concerned about the purported competition involving Mays, Snider stated, "It's just plain silly, comparing us. I think the real fans know who's the better ballplayer." His larger paycheck--$35,000 to $25,000—seemed justified by "his sensational slugging and his tremendous fielding." Snider was said to be "not as dashing as Willie . . . in center, or as flamboyant, and more confined by the fences of Ebbets Field than Mays is in the Polo Grounds." Instead, Duke recalled "the careful, easy, loping grace of Joe DiMaggio." Moreover, his veteran makeup facilitated "better knowledge of the league's hitters." At the plate, Snider's "hitting form" was probably surpassed only by Ted Williams. Both had "amazing eyes—large, clear, calm and probing." Snider threw "his full 195 pounds" into pitches, relying on "a smooth, lashing motion."[17]

Despite Mays's slamming two homers, including the first grand slam of his career, and driving in all his team's runs during the second of a three-game set at Ebbets Field that the Giants won, 6–1, Brooklyn won the other pair to compile a 52–19 record at the end of June. That placed the Dodgers 13 games ahead of the Braves, who had improved to a 39–32 mark. The fifth-place Giants were at 34–38, eighteen-and-half games back, but only two games ahead of the seventh-place Phillies. His team was "not playing the same kind of baseball" it had in 1954, Leo Durocher admitted. "Nothing we do turns out right. When the players don't foul up, I do."[18]

One reason for the latest superlatives coming his way was Snider's performance during the past month. Batting .327, he hit 12 homers, scored 24 runs, drove in 32, while compiling a .738 slugging average as Brooklyn continued expanding its league lead. That same month, Mickey Mantle managed 7 homers, scored 22 runs, and drove in 17, but batted only .248, while Willie Mays scored only 13 times, drove in 22, got 8 homers, and batted .309. Former major league pitcher Ben Wade, a mainstay with the pennant-winning Dodgers in 1952 and 1953, asserted that Brooklyn was "much too good for the rest of the league," although he considered the 1952 team superior. While the latest iteration of the Dodgers had Don Newcombe, the earlier one possessed Joe Black, Preacher Roe, Andy Pafko, and a "much younger" version of "Jackie Robinson, Roy Campanella, Gil Hodges and so forth." Admittedly, Duke Snider "keeps improving with age."

Wade considered it "a laugh" to compare Snider and Mays as "the better all-around player." The latter, he said, "would never get to play on the same club as Duke, who is just the greatest—and getting greater." Brooklyn dominated due to "a great organization and a great system," melding "one or two kids every spring . . . into the line-up."[19]

*****

After 90 games, Snider already had 31 homers, one more than Cincinnati slugger Ted Kluszewski, both slightly ahead of Babe Ruth's 1927 clip. A year earlier, Mays had been outpacing the Babe, only to fall considerably short. According to Shirley Povich, Snider had possibly "the best chance to beat Ruth's score, even though he did not "hit the ball as hard as Kluszewski, or Stan Musial or Mickey Mantle or even Roy Sievers," the Washington Senator outfielder. He did have Ebbets Field, where the Dodgers played their home games, and Snider could swat "a home run in any direction."[20]

During July, Snider belted 11 homers, giving him 35 for the season, scored 27 runs, drove in 30, and batted .343 with an on-base percentage of .460 and a .758 slugging average. Mantle managed only 5 homers, scored 19 runs, drove in 16, and hit .306; Mays heated up, with 28 runs scored, 26 RBIs, 13 homers, and a .315 batting average. Snider's Dodgers, now boasting a 71–32 record, were thirteen and a half games ahead of the Braves, with the Giants another four games back. After belting three additional home runs in early August, keeping him above the Babe's clip, Snider stated, "I hope nobody ever breaks Ruth's record." His teammate Carl Erskine chimed in, "I hope so, too, but I'm afraid some day, some greedy owner will rig the park so that it will be broken."

Regarding Erskine's concern that a big league mogul would do so "to exploit the gate-appeal of a 'new Babe Ruth,'" Snider indicated, "I sincerely hope not." He did so although many experts considered him the player most likely to shatter Ruth's record-setting single-season total. "If anyone ever does hit more than 60, naturally I would like it to be me," Duke admitted before adding, "But I'd hate to see that record go. Ruth means too much to this game—his mark should stand forever. He made the game great for the kids. He made it great for us. We are benefiting because of him."[21]

At that point, the Cubs' Ernie Banks was also ahead of Ruth's record pace, having briefly tied Snider for the league lead, while having tied the major league mark with his fourth grand slam of the season. During that same game at Wrigley Field on August 5, Snider hit two homers to leap ahead of the Chicago sophomore. By mid-August, Ted Kluszewski, Willie Mays, and Eddie Mathews were also close to both Snider and Banks in their pursuit of homers and, at a bare minimum, Hack Wilson's NL mark of 56. As matters turned out, Duke went into a slump until near the end of the month, going homerless for 19 straight games, during which his batting average also dropped below .300, albeit temporarily. Despite homering in consecutive games in late August, he had only 5 homers, along with 22 runs scored and 20 RBIs, with a .284 batting average, by the end of the month. Even that batting average required Snider's going ten for thirteen during August's final three games. Mantle got hot, scoring 24 runs, driving in 22, hitting 12 homers, and compiling a .333 batting average, as Mays had 27 runs scored, 18 RBIs, 7 homers, and a .324 batting average.[22]

Along with their star center fielder, the rest of the Brooklyn Dodgers underwent something of a tailspin, going 13–14 in August, but their lead, which once stood at fifteen and a half games, remained twelve up on Milwaukee, while the New York Giants had slipped back to fourth, four and a half additional games from first place. As Snider's home run prowess dried up and his batting average dropped, the Ebbets Field faithful responded less than kindly. Stunned by the brickbats he was on the receiving end of, Snider slapped back. "They're the worst fans in the league. They don't deserve a pennant. We're fighting to win the pennant." Taking another shot, Snider threw out a threat of sorts, "That's why we're moving to Jersey," referring to the Dodgers' determination to host several games in Jersey City the following season.[23]

Having had time to cool off, Duke apologized, undoubtedly pressured by Brooklyn management to do so. "I didn't mean all the fans. I'm sorry, in a way, that I popped off. I guess I shouldn't have said what I did." After indicating, "There are quite a few good fans in Brooklyn," Snider smilingly said, as if tongue-in-cheek, "maybe not as many good ones as bad ones, though." It was not only boos that he was on the receiving end of but also projectiles of different sorts, as he indicated. "Just the other day, I felt something nick my shoulder. I looked down, and what do you think it was. A beer-can opener. That's not funny." The booing continued for a spell.[24]

Snider's outburst, the *New York Times*' Arthur Daley remarked, was "completely unexpected . . . from an unexpected quarter." Duke "isn't the type to go around putting the knock on people." But over the course of the past month, he had gone from being a possible Triple Crown winner to a slumping batter. Soon, responding to Snider's eruption, fans were back to cheering him, at least after he got three hits in a game. Daley still considered Duke's response to have been surprising, given he had never seemed "rabbit-eared" in the manner of Red Sox slugger Ted Williams.[25]

*****

Ironically or not, *Sport* magazine's September issue featured Snider on its cover, with an inside story by writer Al Stump. The 8,000-word essay opened with Stump's writing, "The only touches of flamboyance about Duke are contained in the distance he achieves with his screaming home run drives and the unbelievable character of some of the circus catches he makes in center field for the Brooklyn Dodgers. In every other respect he manages, despite enormous publicity, accorded him to play his role in life with dignity and restraint." Stump likened Snider to Joe DiMaggio as being "quiet but proud." He recognized his ability at "smashing baseballs as hard and as often as anyone in the game today."

According to Stump, Snider had "a loose, indolent manner, masking a tightly wound temperament," while some considered him "a perfectionist in the DiMaggio mold." Denying that, Stump indicated that Snider could perform erratically, influenced by his mood, and appeared to require "a tangible challenge." Thus, he hit even better with men on base. Most "baseball people" viewed Snider, not Willie Mays, Stump indicated, as the National League's "best all-around player."

Delivering his own analysis, Ty Cobb asked, "How many years has Mays hit .300 or more for the Giants? In one season, I believe. How many years has he batted in 100 or more runs? One, I think. I also think Snider has four .300 seasons, four years of 100 runs batted-in and something like 1,000 hits to a few hundred for Mays. Hell's bells, at this point the discussion is ridiculous!"

Coming to Snider's defense, Ralph Kiner offered, "He's an acrobat, the same as Mays, but with the difference that he scrambles only when it's necessary. Mays looks like a man in a revolving door. I'd say Duke covers more ground, wastes less motion and is more consistent than anyone since DiMaggio. And in playing the real tough ones, he's very close to Joe." Following a "wall-climbing" grab by Snider at the Dodgers' home ballpark, Alston stated, "I don't think I've ever seen an outfielder who can go so high for a ball while running at full speed. I don't know how he does it. But he catches them, and he never seems to have trouble with the walls."[26]

Duke himself remarked, "The whole thing is no good. I wish it would stop. I can't walk down the street without someone choosing up sides." But happy to be toiling under manager Walt Alston, about whom Duke said, "the best I've worked for because he doesn't pressure you," Snider seemed less prone to sulk or despair.[27]

*****

Over in the American League, no hitter was threatening Ruth's record, but Mickey Mantle was topping the league in homers while his Yankees were perched, alongside the Indians, a half-game behind the White Sox. The Red Sox, with Williams exhibiting his typical hitting heroics, were only five back. This was a different Yankee team, having waived the final member of their longtime Big Three starting pitchers, Eddie Lopat, with his spot in the rotation taken over by 25-year-old Don Larsen. As Arthur Daley put it, Lopat "had outlived his usefulness to a team clawing for the pennant. The Bombers Big Three—Lopat, Allie Reynolds and Vic Raschi, all fine workmen and all fine persons. All are gone now." That meant until their replacements arrived, the Yankees would need "to scramble extra hard for every pennant." Fortunately, sparkplug Billy Martin soon returned from military service.[28]

It was the 23-year-old Mantle, already in his fifth major league season, other players, managers, and owners had unanimously pointed to during the All-Star Game as the "one ballplayer," based "on present performance and potential," they would select. Nevertheless, Ned Cronin, writing in the *Los Angeles Times* in early September, extolled Casey Stengel for keeping the Yankees at or near the top of the American League despite "a spray gun pitching staff and an" inconsistent offense, much of which he blamed on Mantle. Despite Mantle's fine performance the previous two months, Cronin charged that the present season had underscored the fact Mickey "will never make the grade as one of baseball's big guns." While admitting Mantle could powder the ball from either side of the plate, the columnist accused Mickey of transforming "from a tiger to a pussycat," striking out too often and failing to deliver at opportune times.[29]

*****

Roger Kahn presented an article, "The Ten Years of Jackie Robinson," which appeared in *Sport* magazine. "Because Robinson destroyed baseball's shameful racial barrier," Kahn wrote, "there are those who know him as a hero." While Robinson was possibly "no longer baseball's most exciting player," Kahn continued, "he is still its most controversial one" due to his intense, fiery, competitive nature. Former manager Chuck Dressen insisted, "There never was an easier guy for me to manage and there was nothing I asked that he didn't do. Hit-and-run. Bunt. Anything. He was the greatest player I ever managed." By contrast, present manager Walter Alston, in an unguarded moment, said, "Robinson is always conscious of publicity and is always seeking publicity." Teammate Duke Snider pointedly offered, "I'll say this for Jack. When he believes something is right, he'll fight for it hard as anybody I ever saw."[30]

By this point, Robinson had become "the natural captain of the Dodgers." Kahn noted, "He is the team's most aggressive ballplayer" and had the "fire" that "the most respected" player, Pee Wee Reese, lacked. Branch Rickey, the man Jackie viewed as "the finest, in a class by himself," picked him to break Organized Baseball's appalling color barrier. He selected Robinson, Kahn indicated, "with wisdom, that borders upon clairvoyance, to right a single wrong. Robinson had the playing ability to become a super-star, plus the intelligence to understand the significance of his role. He had the fighting temperament to wring the most from his ability and he had the self-control to keep his temper in check."[31]

*****

At the beginning of the new month, the Dodgers righted their ship, winning the first nine games and clinching the NL pennant in smacking the Braves at

County Stadium, 10–2, on September 8 to boost Brooklyn's record to 92–46, 17 games ahead of Milwaukee with New York another two and a half games behind. Arthur Daley lauded the "deft job" by Dodger skipper "Walt Alston, the Quiet Man," who had "bewildered" his team by, at times, putting Reese at second, Hodges in left, "the proud and sensitive" Robinson on the bench, and Campanella eighth in the lineup. Alston was helped by the fact that he probably had "the strongest team in baseball, including the best power hitters." The Dodgers appeared desirous of meeting the Yankees yet again in the World Series, seeking "revenge for past indignities."[32]

Once more attracting just over 1 million fans, barely half of what Milwaukee attained, Brooklyn went on to complete a 98–55 season, with 85–69 Milwaukee thirteen and a half games behind and 80–74 New York eighteen and a half games out of first place. Two games behind Cleveland as late as September 14, the New York Yankees tied for the lead two days later, then grabbed it for good on September 17. Ten victories in eleven games, followed by a meaningless season-ending loss on September 25, left the Yankees at 96–58, three games better than the Indians, five up on the White Sox.

With little to play for other than statistics, Duke Snider tailed off in September, going homerless over the final 16 games, leaving him with only two homers, along with 15 runs scored, 12 RBIs, and a .279 for the abbreviated month. His New York City counterparts, Mickey Mantle, who missed several games due to an injured right leg, and Willie Mays, fared differently. Mantle homered twice, scored 13 runs, and drove in 9 while batting .306 over his final 49 at bats. Mays tore the cover off the ball, hitting 11 homers, including 7 in six games, to become the seventh player to hit 50 or more in a single season, scored 20 runs, drove in 31, and batted .396 in only 23 games.

The Brooklyn Dodgers possessed a fearsome lineup, led by Roy Campanella, Duke Snider, Gil Hodges, and Carl Furillo. Rebounding from his injury-plagued 1954 campaign, Campy hit 32 homers, drove in 107 runs, and batted .318. Although Campanella nipped him in the National League MVP race, Snider had far superior numbers, leading the league in runs scored—126—for the third straight season, hitting 34 doubles (3rd in the NL) and 42 homers (4th), driving in an NL-best 136 runs, walking 104 times (3rd), batting .309 (9th), having a .418 OBP (2nd), a .628 slugging average (2nd), a 1.046 OPS

(2nd), 338 total bases (5th), an 8.6 WAR (2nd), and an NL-high 82 extra-base hits (tied with Ernie Banks and Mays). Snider's performance convinced NL players, managers, umpires, and reporters to name him *The Sporting News* Player of the Year, while the Baseball Writers of America would select both Snider and Campanella to the Associated Press Major League All-Star team. Hodges had 27 homers, 102 RBIs, and a .289 batting average, while Furillo hit 26 homers, drove in 95 runs, and batted .314. Pee Wee Reese scored 99 runs, got 10 homers, and batted .282, but Robinson managed only 8 homers, 36 RBIs, and a career-low .256 batting average in only 317 official at bats.[33]

Don Newcombe bounced back too, going 20–5 for a league-best .800 win-loss record with a 3.20 ERA. Carl Erskine was 11–8, Billy Loes, 10–4, Clem Labine 13–5, and Johnny Podres, 9–10. The high expectations surrounding Karl Spooner bumped against arm difficulties as he went 8–6, but another 24-year-old, Don Bessent, was 8–1 with a 2.70 ERA. A promising youngster, 19-year-old Sandy Koufax, tossed two shutouts, one during which he gave up only two hits while striking out fourteen batters; he went 2–2, with a 3.02 ERA.

The disappointing New York Giants, whose attendance plummeted to just over 800,000 customers, had one brilliant and three solid performers in their starting lineup, along with an equal number of largely inept hitters. Don Mueller had 185 hits, drove in 83 runs, and batted .306, while Alvin Dark hit a solid .282 and Whitey Lockman got 15 homers and batted .273. During his second year back from military service, Willie Mays again excelled, scoring 123 runs (2nd), collecting 185 hits (5th), driving in 127 runs (2nd), batting .319 (2nd), and having a .400 OBP (5th). He led the National League with 13 triples, 51 homers, a .659 slugging average, 1.059 OPS, 382 total bases, and 9.2 WAR; Mays was also selected to the AP Major League All-Star team. Somehow that entitled him to only a fourth-place spot in the MVP tabulations, behind Campanella, Snider, and the Cubs' Ernie Banks. Sal Maglie was 9–5, Don Liddle, 10–4, and Marv Grissom, 5–4 with a 2.92 ERA. But Johnny Antonelli fell to 14–16 with a 3.33 ERA, Jim Hearn had the same win-loss record, Ruben Gomez was only 9–10, and even Hoyt Wilhelm, despite a 4–1 record, had a less than lustrous 3.93 ERA.[34]

While controversy swirled around the selection of Campanella over Snider for NL MVP, with one writer having not included Duke among his ten selections, the *New York Herald Tribune*'s Red Smith wondered why Mays had received so little support. Smith admitted that early in the year, Mays, like the New York Giants, had struggled. In the end, however, many of his numbers looked even better than when he received the MVP, with 3 more runs scored, 17 additional runs driven in, and 10 more homers, although his batting average had fallen 26 points. Mays also stole 24 bases, getting caught only twice, threw out 10 or 11 runners, and was, Smith argued, "a better ball player than" in 1954.[35]

The Giants experienced a different kind of setback as the regular season ended, with Leo Durocher indicating he would not return as their manager. The *New York Post* columnist Jimmy Cannon indicated that Leo the Lip "quit a job he didn't have" as Giants' owner Horace Stoneham had not tendered a contract. One seemingly knowledgeable source disclosed, "It was a face-saving thing all around." Cannon insisted, "It is impossible to denounce Durocher as an incompetent manager. Few are his equal when he has a team that's up close to the leaders." However, "he becomes bored with a club that's drifting aimlessly." Durocher's 16-year record as a manager, to that point, 1,340 wins and 1,051 losses, made for an impressive .560 winning percentage. Equally significant, his teams finished in the top three twelve times, with three pennants and four runner-up finishes.[36]

Back atop the American League, the New York Yankees again led in attendance, virtually duplicating the previous total of almost 1.5 million, with the relocated Athletics finishing second with nearly 1.4 million, but the second-year Baltimore Orioles drew more than 200,000 fewer patrons. New York was led by Yogi Berra and Mickey Mantle, who came in first and a distant fifth in the MVP contest, although Mickey's statistics, even more than Snider's, were far superior to his teammate's. Berra had 27 homers (4th), 108 RBIs (3rd), and a .272 BA. Mantle scored 121 runs (2nd), drove in 99 (6th), batted .306 (7th), produced 316 total bases (2nd), and even had 1.1 Defensive WAR (7th); he also led the American League with 11 triples, 37 homers, 113 walks, a .431 OBP, a .611 slugging average, a 1.042 OPS, and 9.5 WAR. Bill Skowron batted .319, Gil McDougald, .285, and Hank Bauer, .278, with 97 runs scored (8th) and 20 homers. Once again leading Yankee hurlers, Whitey Ford, named to the AP All-Star Team and *The Sporting News*' American League Pitcher of the Year, won a league-high 18 games, lost only 7, had a 2.63 ERA. In his first season as a Yankee, Bob Turley was 17–13 with a 3.06 ERA and a league-leading 177 strikeouts. Thirty-five-year-old Tommy Byrne was 16–5 with a 3.15 ERA, while Don Larsen was 9–2 with a 3.06 ERA. In his one full season with the Yankees, 38-year-old closer Jim Konstanty was 7–2 with a 2.32 ERA and a dozen saves.[37]

*****

Concerns about Mantle's physical condition, which had led him to miss several of the regular season's final games, led scribes to consider favoring Brooklyn in the upcoming World Series. This would be the Dodgers' eighth appearance, five of those against the Yankees, who were in the World Series for the 21st time. Played at Yankee Stadium on September 28 before 63,869 fans, Game One went to New York, 6–5, with Ford lasting until the ninth, followed by Bob Grim, and Newcombe getting knocked out in the sixth inning. Leading the Yankee charge was Joe Collins, who delivered two homers off Newcombe, and Elston Howard, who also homered off the Dodger starter. Furillo had three hits and a homer, while Snider got two hits and homered, with a massive blast into the right field upper deck section, also against Ford. Robinson tripled and scored twice, while Don Zimmer drove in two runs. Robinson stole home in the eighth inning, with Yankee catcher Berra heatedly disputing the call of "Safe!" at the plate. The home plate umpire, Bill Summers, insisted his call was correct.[38]

With 64,707 in attendance, the Yankees went up two games to none, taking the second contest, 4–2, behind Byrne, who beat Loes, who gave up all of New York's runs in the bottom of the fourth. Berra got two hits and scored once, while Byrne singled and drove in two runs. Reese managed two hits and scored once. Snider singled and drove in one run in four at bats.

The Dodgers roared back, winning all three games at Ebbets Field, putting them one victory away from their first World Series championship. As 34,209 looked on, the Dodgers scored twice in the first two innings, again in the fourth, and once more in the seventh, while the Yankees had tied the score in the top of the second, then only plated a single additional run in the seventh to lose, 8–3. Campanella was the batting star, with three hits and a two-run, first-inning homer off starter Turley. Robinson had two hits, one, a double, and scored twice, and Reese drove in a pair. Turley was bombed in the second, having retired only four batters, while Podres, celebrating his 23rd birthday, scattered seven hits. Appearing for the first time in the Series, Mantle homered in four at bats, while Skowron got two hits and scored once.

Brooklyn tied the Series with an 8–5 victory with 36,242 fans present, despite Erskine getting knocked out in the fourth inning. But Bessent and Labine provided adequate relief, while Yankee starter Larsen also was forced to leave the game after he faced one batter in the fifth, and the New York relievers failed to stem the tide. Campanella homered off Larsen, one of his three hits, and scored twice. Hodges also delivered a four-base shot off the Yankee starter, and Snider belted a three-run homer—"Ruthian" in nature—off Johnny Kucks. Duke also made three terrific catches during the late innings to quell potential Yankee rallies. Hodges got three hits and drove in the same number of runs. Jim Gilliam, Reese, and Furillo each had two hits. McDougald homered off Erskine in the first, Martin got two hits and drove in two, and Collins scored twice, while Mantle went one for five.[39]

Game Five, played before 36,796 people, ended up with Brooklyn on top, 5–3, thanks to a solid outing from rookie starter Roger Craig, who had opened only ten games all season; Labine delivered three innings of one-run relief for the save. Yankee starter Bob Grim lasted six innings, giving up four runs, before giving way to Turley. Snider had a huge game, swatting a double and two homers, while Sandy Amoros also homered and drove in two; that made Duke the first player to have as many as four homers in two World Series. Snider now had nine home runs in World Series play, surpassing Joe DiMaggio's total despite having played fewer than half as many games. Only Ruth and Gehrig had more. Hodges scored once and had two hits. Berra provided most of New York's offense, homering off Labine, while pinch hitter Bob Cerv's seventh-inning blast forced Craig from the mound.

With the Dodgers one game away, Snider fielded a question about whether Brooklyn's fans deserved a World Series' title. "I think the players do," he replied. Casey Stengel, wrestling with the fact that his Yankees had fallen behind, acknowledged that Snider provided "the turning point of the fifth game." New York's manager said, "That fellow was the biggest thing they had out there. Nothing else hurt us—just him. Two home runs and a big double." Stengel continued, "I blame myself. We oughtn't let a man hit that many home runs on us, especially when we get two strikes on him. We ought to know how to get him out—but we don't. I take the blame." It also appeared that Mantle was reduced to only pinch-hitting duties, the Yankee skipper revealed.[40]

In a must-win Game Six, New York prevailed, 5–1, in front of 64,022 at the Stadium. Ford, keeping Brooklyn to four singles and getting Snider out in his lone at bat before a knee injury forced him to depart, won his second game of the Series. Young Karl Spooner lasted one-third of an inning, giving up all the Yankees' runs. With Mantle again out of action, New York relied on Skowron, who had a three-run homer, Hank Bauer, who had three hits and an RBI, and Berra, who finished with two hits and an RBI.

Promising to play in the final game of the Series, Snider reported, "My knee popped as soon as I started" as he "stepped in a hole" while going after a fly ball hit by Skowron during the third-inning. "I went on running," able to snare the ball, "but it was the knee I hurt earlier in Chicago," he said. Forced to ask Alston to take him out, Snider, who had undergone whirlpool treatment, pledged to "play even if it's stiff."[41]

The climactic Game Seven, watched by 62,465 fans at Yankee Stadium, concluded with Johnny Podres, named Series MVP, winning his second game, blanking New York on eight hits, 2–0. The loss went to Byrne, who gave up only three hits and one earned run in five and a third innings. McDougald had three hits, and Skowron and Berra each doubled. Mantle bounced out in his seventh-inning, pinch-hit appearance. Hodges drove in Brooklyn's two runs, in the fourth and sixth innings, one on a single, the other through a sacrifice fly. Snider was hitless in three at bats, with two strikeouts, and Robinson did not play, but Brooklyn won its first World Series championship.[42]

Led by Snider, who scored five runs and drove in seven, hit a double and four homers while batting .320, the Dodgers collected nine home runs, one more than their opponents. Campanella had two homers, Hodges amassed five RBIs and hit .292, Amoros hit .333, while both Furillo and Reese batted .296. Podres gave up only two runs in two complete-game victories. Labine, Meyer, and Bessent pitched well in relief. Berra batted .417, Martin .320, Bauer, .429, and Skowron .333, the latter two in more limited action. Mantle only had ten at bats, getting two hits, including a homer. As he had throughout the season, Ford led the pitching staff with two wins and a 2.12 ERA, Byrne split a pair of decisions with an even better 1.88 ERA, but Grim, and especially Larsen and Turley, in starting Games 3 and 4, respectively, had poor outings.

While various teammates denied it, the limited appearances by "the American League's leading slugger" weakened New York, perhaps fatally. Although he belted a homer during his first trip to the plate in Game Three, Mantle had difficulty in the field and was unable to avoid hitting into a double play, something he seldom did. His replacements proved inadequate.[43]

Some of the Yankees admitted, "The Dodgers had the pitching." Stengel declared, "The Dodgers played good baseball," then noted, "I'd have to say that the relief pitcher (Labine), that young man (Podres) . . . and the center fielder (Snider) did the most to beat us. We shouldn't have allowed Snider to hit those four homers."[44]

The Yankee manager thought his team would likely be contending again the next season, while acknowledging that the shortstop position needed to be bolstered, and that Howard might be used to afford Berra "a rest" on occasion. His starting pitching, including Ford, Grim, Turley, Larsen, and Byrne, appeared strong, but he was on the lookout for relievers. The 65-year-old Stengel deflected the notion he might retire.[45]

According to baseball experts, the Yankees looked like a good beat to repeat in the AL during 1956, where they would likely meet the Dodgers yet again in the World Series. Brooklyn appeared likely to make an even bigger shambles of the NL race, with New York rebuilding and Milwaukee lacking "spark and drive." In fact, the Dodgers, The *Los Angeles Times*' Al Wolf indicated, might "be tough to dislodge for the next decade." Their shift to youth seemed to be "paying off," as indicated by Alston's employment of young pitchers Podres, Craig, Bessent, Loes, Roebuck, and Spooner in the World Series. There was also the "bonus slinger," Koufax. Labine, Erskine, and Newcombe had yet to reach 30 years of age. Reese looked about as good as ever, which is plenty good," Hodges and Furillo were displaying "few signs of wear," while Snider was "getting better all the time." Robinson had appeared to gather "his second wind, especially on the base paths." Gilliam, Amoros, and Hoak were "comparative youngsters." The farm system was "loaded with other eager kids."

Only catching, with Campanella no "spring chicken," appeared precarious for his loss could prove disastrous.[46]

The Yankees possessed a mixture of older and younger players. Berra, Bauer, and Byrne continued to play well, while Noren, Collins, Robinson, and Rizzuto were also "getting along." However, New York had "a years-to-come combine" of Skowron, McDougald, Martin, Carey, Cerv, Mantle, Howard, and Berra. Young pitchers included Ford, Grim, Larsen, Turley, Morgan, Tom Sturdivant, Bob Wiesler, Rip Coleman, and Kucks. All of this increased the chances of another Dodger-Yankees World Series meeting.[47]

Like the New York Giants the previous year, the Brooklyn Dodgers captured the top awards issued by *The Sporting News*. Walter O'Malley was selected as the Major League Executive of the Year, Alston as the Major League Manager of the Year, and Snider as the Major League Player of the Year. Deemed "one of the vital cogs in" Brooklyn's unprecedented success, Snider followed his excellent regular season with a strong performance in the World Series. He was also named to his third consecutive All-Star team selected by *The Sporting News*.[48]

*****

Earlier in the year, young Claudette Colvin had been arrested by policemen for refusing to adhere to Jim Crow directives on a bus in Montgomery, Alabama. The woman who came to her assistance and remained her champion, Rosa Parks, ran afoul of those same strictures on December 1, 1955. Ordered to relinquish her bus seat to a white patron, Parks—"tired of giving in"—refused, was arrested, booked, fingerprinted, and charged with disorderly conduct. Defended by Clifford Durr, the husband of her friend and fellow civil rights activist Virginia Durr, Parks was convicted and fined $14.00.[49]

The arrest of the 42-year-old Parks, a well-regarded figure in Montgomery's African American circles and a political activist in her own right, enraged the city's Black community. The same day she was convicted, the Montgomery Improvement Association, spearheaded by Martin Luther King Jr., a young African American minister from the Dexter Avenue Baptist Church, along with a group of women activists, initiated a boycott of the city's buses. The son of Martin Luther King, the pastor of Atlanta's Ebenezer Baptist Church who was one of the most well-regarded Black ministers in the South, King

Jr. insisted on a disciplined, nonviolent campaign. Influenced by the Indian pacifist leader Mahatma Gandhi and Henry David Thoreau, the author of "Civil Disobedience," King convinced Montgomery's Black citizens to adopt the tactics of nonviolent resistance. Behind the scenes, however, the gun culture of the American South and the United States overall was hardly absent from Black homes in Montgomery, including at one point, even King's. Nevertheless, he continued to preach the gospel of nonviolence, even as some supporters demanded vengeance following the bombing of his home.[50]

In mid-February, Dr. Thomas Hency Brewer, physician and civil rights activist, became the latest well-known victim of violence directed at African Americans. A founder of an NAACP chapter in Columbus, Georgia, where he conducted his medical practice, Dr. Brewer had triggered Black voter registration drives there and also helped bring about the hiring of African American police officers. Not unaccustomed to death threats, Brewer also supported the integration of public schools and Columbus' golf course. A white business owner, Luicio Flowers, shot Brewer with two white police officers present, supposedly following a dispute regarding their mutual witnessing of a violent arrest of another Black man. No charges were brought against Flowers.[51]

13

The Commerce Comet

Having twice missed out after five consecutive championships, the New York Yankees rebounded to win the 1956 World Series, acquiring a measure of vengeance in beating the Brooklyn Dodgers. Although Duke Snider had another fine Series, the Yankees prevailed through the long ball, led by Yogi Berra, Billy Martin, and Mickey Mantle, who was able to play all seven games this time, unlike the previous fall. Mantle's World Series performance, which included hitting three homers, was fitting, given this was the year that he fulfilled all his seemingly limitless promise.

Nineteen fifty-four had been the year that Willie Mays became the most electrifying player in MLB. Nineteen fifty-five was when Duke Snider helped to lead Brooklyn to its long-awaited World Series championship. Nineteen fifty-six witnessed the full flowering of the unbounded expectations Mantle, the Commerce Comet, carried. The feats Mickey attained that year led to the 24-year-old Yankee slugger's finally being viewed on a par, at least, with the other great New York center fielders. Debates about their various merits would long range, with a focus on their entire careers but particularly the heyday of New York City baseball, the relatively few years when the three men competed for the hearts and souls of fans and scribes alike. What 1956 also did was display Mantle, notwithstanding the ever-present injury concerns that afflicted him, in his full glory, enabling him to produce one of the Major League's greatest seasons, finer even than the very best of the two brilliant players who called the Polo Grounds or Ebbets Field their home ballparks. Mantle moved into the conversation of who was New York City's and baseball's finest center fielder, and perhaps its greatest player, as well.

That same season was notable in other regards. Brooklyn repeated in the National League, the final title by the Boys of Summer, with Jackie Robinson, after something of a bounce-back year, retiring following the World Series, and Roy Campanella's resplendence fading, but Don Newcombe having his own brilliant campaign, followed by deterioration of his playing skills. While Snider had his fourth straight in a series of remarkable years and Gil Hodges remained one of the game's foremost sluggers, Pee Wee Reese displayed the signs of erosion, which Robinson had done the previous year. More happily, Jim Gilliam, Sandy Amoros, and Carl Furillo performed admirably, and ex-Giant Sal Maglie proved a terrific addition. Carl Erskine had his final solid season. Clem Labine and Roger Craig were steady contributors. Other promising youngsters took a step backward, with Karl Spooner's major league career effectively ending before the season began and Sandy Koufax proving more erratic, although a tall, rookie right-hander, Don Drysdale, displayed considerable promise.

The New York Giants, lacking Leo Durocher's leadership, never really competed amid eroding skills and struggles in the batter's box and on the rubber. Don Mueller tailed off considerably. Rookie first baseman Bill White provided some power but failed to drive in many runs or hit for a decent average. Coming over from the Cardinals, second baseman Red Schoendienst offered little pop, although he remained a consistently high-average hitter. Rookie left fielder Jackie Brandt hit solidly, while Willie Mays remained one of the game's finest all-around players. Johnny Antonelli posted another 20-game season, but other starters had poor to average years. Reliever Hoyt Wilhelm was mediocre at best, unlike 38-year-old Marv Grissom, who remained stellar, but 31-year-old Don Liddle's career wound down.

Although Andy Carey had a poor year, Billy Martin, Elston Howard, and Hank Bauer were steady, with Bauer's power numbers impressive. Bill Skowron and Gil McDougald had fine campaigns, and Yogi Berra performed at an MVP level but still far removed from the season Mantle put together. The bench remained strong with a mixture of young and aging players, although lacking the lightning-strike capabilities of several Yankee teams.

Whitey Ford, Johnny Kucks, Don Larsen, Tom Sturdivant, Tommy Byrne, and Bob Grim pitched well—Ford, exceptionally so—although Bob Turley's ERA mushroomed mightily.

All three New York City teams, and most major league teams, now featured former Negro Leaguers or other players who had competed in the Negro American League since 1948. The Brooklyn Dodgers prominently displayed Robinson, Campanella, Newcombe, Amoros, and Gilliam; the New York Giants, Mays and Thompson; the New York Yankees, Howard. The still highly productive Larry Doby moved over to the Chicago White Sox, a now diminished Monte Irvin to the Chicago Cubs, George Crowe to the Cincinnati Reds, and Bob Boyd to the Baltimore Orioles. Minnie Minoso was again topflight, and Al Smith, unable to repeat a year during which he garnered considerable MVP votes, stayed with the Chicago White Sox. Other productive players, once relegated to Blackball, included the Cubs' All-Star slugging shortstop Ernie Banks and Gene Baker, the Cardinals' Sam Jones, the Redlegs' Bob Thurman, and the Athletics' Harry Simpson, having a career year.

*****

With spring training impending, baseball analysts wrestled with the question of which teams and players were likely to rise or fall. The Dodgers needed, it was said, to avoid the apparent "overconfidence and complacency" that crippled the Giants during the previous season. "Old age" could "finally catch up with the Brook veterans" to bring their "championship reign" to an end. The Giants required new manager Bill Rigney to rally the team's clearly "depleted forces." The Yankees hoped just acquired southpaw Maury McDermott would strengthen their starting pitching staff.

Additionally, there were questions of historical nature, particularly fascinating to baseball aficionados. Might Roy Campanella or Yogi Berra win an unprecedented fourth MVP award? And the query that probably could be heard most frequently was, "Will Mickey Mantle finally make full use of his great potential and reach the heights that will place his name among the greatest stars in the game?"[1]

Baseball experts delivered preseason assessments, with many foreseeing another Dodger-Yankee clash in the World Series. Delivering a subjective evaluation of Major League teams, author Charles Dexter rated the Dodgers as championship caliber across the board, as the *Detroit Free Press*' Hal Middlesworth did for the Yankees. However, despite having "three of the starriest players in the game in Willie Mays, Don Mueller and Alvin Dark," and former 21-game winner Johnny Antonelli, the Giants appeared slated for the second division.[2]

As spring training wound down, big league managers again delivered their analyses of AL teams. Emphasizing that Mantle was "finally beginning to capitalize on his tremendous potential," they noted the Yankees' possession of the American League's "best lefthanded pitching," Martin's presence for the full season, Berra's "greatness," and the "steadiness of Hank Bauer and Gil McDougald." Potential weaknesses included "uncertainty in left field," shortstop, and relief pitching.[3]

Focusing on the National League, the *Washington Post and Times Herald* indicated that Brooklyn had stars like "Roy Campanella, Duke Snider, Pee Wee Reese, Carl Furillo and Gil Hodges." Rookie second baseman Charley Neal, young left-handed pitcher Sandy Koufax, and veteran Jackie Robinson all appeared in good shape, while the team had added third sacker Randy Jackson. Left field remained a trouble spot; there was no real backup for Campanella, and Dodger pitchers seemed beset by an injury bug. New York featured Willie Mays's "all-around brilliance," Alvin Dark's leadership, and Whitey Lockman's versatility, but required a second baseman, a catcher able to hit, a stronger bench, and greater certainty regarding its pitching staff.[4]

Agreeing with the general assessment of his peers, the columnist Shirley Povich picked the Yankees and Dodgers to repeat in their respective leagues. This was in keeping, he indicated, with the general notion that "the teams with the most good ball players win the major league pennants." New York, he reasoned, faced "the greater threat" even though Brooklyn resided in "the better-balanced league." To Povich, the Yankees benefited from the presence of "the same old pros"—Berra, Mantle, Bauer, and Collins—all "spraying destruction with their bats."

Brooklyn was the lone major league team to boast even "more old pros than the Yankees," thanks to Snider, Campanella, Reese, Hodges, Furillo, Robinson, Newcombe, Labine, and Erskine. Exhibiting the National League's "most murderous crew," the Dodgers seemed capable of overcoming pitching woes, such as "the worst epidemic of sore pitching arms that ever afflicted any team." New Giants' manager Bill Rigney "has going for him the wonderful Willie Mays and Don Mueller in the outfield, along with the in-and-outer Dusty Rhodes." Third baseman Hank Thompson, however, appeared "over the hill," second baseman Darryl Spencer had yet to prove himself, shortstop Alvin Dark was "slowing," and "catcher Wes Westrum barely hits .200 every year." Giant pitchers, other than "Johnny Antonelli, Jim Hearn, Ruben Gomez and Don Liddle," did not amount to much.[5]

Thirty experts presented their analyses regarding the upcoming season. All but five selected the Brooklyn Dodgers to repeat in the National League; 19 chose the New York Yankees as the likely American League winners. The *Albany Times-Union*'s Dick Walsh declared, "The Yanks and Dodgers have too much for the rest of the pack." The Dodgers were said to have the sport's finest young pitchers and had added the Cubs' Randy Jackson "to an already power-packed array of Robinson, Snider, Campanella, Furillo, Hodges and even pitcher Newcombe." The New York Giants were reported to have "problems at second base, in left field and on the pitching staff." They did have "Willie Mays, who could overcome most of them," and hoped for "a reincarnation" of Johnny Antonelli's "1954 self." The New York Yankees had added "a full-time Billy Martin" and southpaw pitcher Maurie McDermott to an already loaded roster, particularly Yogi Berra, Mickey Mantle, and their moundsmen, notwithstanding "their "who's-on-shortstop?" situation."[6]

Examining the National League, Roscoe McGowan picked Brooklyn, aided by a likely Rookie of the Year in second baseman Charley Neal, a former Negro Leaguer with the Atlanta Black Crackers, to duplicate its 1955 pennant. Shortstop Pee Wee Reese seemed "ageless," having put together his "two best seasons" during 1954 and 1955. The Dodgers' "disabilities" could be found among its pitchers, with Dr. Harold Wendler, the team trainer, indicating, "Carl is as near normal as he's ever going to be. He'll never be as good as he was before he was hurt." Both Billy Loes and Karl Spooner, seen as "potential first-line pitchers," remained doubtful, Loes suffering from tendon difficulties and Spooner from shoulder problems. Alston admitted, "If Erskine, Loes and Spooner had sound arms, we'd have a helluva staff." Jackson, Jackie

Robinson, or Don Zimmer would likely play third, while left field might see "Gino Cimoli, Sandy Amoros or Junior Gilliam, or . . . a platooning system." Expected regulars included Reese, Gil Hodges, Duke Snider, Carl Furillo, and Roy Campanella. Clem Labine remained the top reliever, while Sandy Koufax was a possible starting pitcher.[7]

Agreeing with most of his peers, Frank Finch chose the Dodgers and Yankees to meet again in the World Series. It appeared, Finch indicated, that Mickey Mantle was "ready to emerge as a star of the first magnitude in the tradition of Ruth, Gehrig, Lazzeri and DiMag." Manager Casey Stengel seemingly "has talent to burn," which should enable him to win his seventh American League pennant in eight years. Although Brooklyn was unlikely to experience another start like the previous season's, no team seemed capable of beating them. The New York Giants' Bill Rigney, Finch wrote, "has Willie Mays . . . plus problems."[8]

*****

According to Casey Stengel, Mantle, baseball's top switch-hitter, should discard batting left-handed, having hit only .279 with a .585 slugging average in 1955. Batting right-handed, he had hit .366 with a .676 slugging average and had belted "his longest homers." But Mantle was already the most powerful switch-hitter in the game's history, with the other top batters who operated from both sides of the plate, like Max Carey and Frank Fritsch, lacking Mickey's ability to hit baseballs as far as any player ever had, probably matched only by Babe Ruth. But then Stengel long viewed "so gifted a player," one capable of tape-measure blasts, as something of a disappointment. What remained unquestioned was Mantle's still untapped vast potential and the power he generated, thanks to "tremendous wrist action."[9]

Typically wrestling with a series of physical ailments during the offseason, Mantle dealt with such issues during spring training, including both "a sore right arm and lame right leg." Nevertheless, he generally appeared in fine form, as when he swatted a 450-foot triple and a 475-foot homer, both left-handed, at St. Petersburg's Al Lang Field against Kansas City on March 17.[10]

A few days later, Shirley Povich penned a column titled, "Mantle Just Bursting into Full Magnificence." It began from the perspective of Stan Musial, racing toward the right-center wall in the bottom of the ninth inning of a spring training contest. After starting to sprint, the St. Louis star "came to a dead halt," then "watched in pure admiration" as a ball slammed by Mantle, hitting from the left side of the plate, soared "out of the park at skyscraper height" to land among kids playing a sandlot game. One sportswriter wryly commented, "There is the only home run that broke up two ball games." As Povich recalled, "There has been nothing like it in Florida training camps since Babe Ruth was pirouetting his power in pitches he liked and knocking home runs all over the fences." Musial indicated, "No home run has ever cleared my head by so much," then was told, "But his power is right-handed, honest."

Povich noted, "Nobody disputes any more the claim that the muscular young Yankee hits the ball farther than anybody else who swings a bat." Moreover, "Mantle's best fans are the other ball players. When it's his turn in batting practice, they watch. He senses that his audience is professional, and goes for the long ball they like to see him hit." Then, Povich indicated that through spring training, with Mantle having already hit five homers, "one feeling has been inescapable. . . . This, you hear on all sides and are willing to believe, is Mickey Mantle's year. This is the one when he'll burst into full magnificence, hit more and longer home runs than anybody else, lead the league in batting, perhaps, and certainly get more extra-base hits than anybody else." Mantle agreed this "could be a very good year for him." Having struck out only once in 36 Grapefruit League at bats, Mickey said, "I'm waiting and making 'em throw my pitch instead of going for theirs."

Already, Povich wrote, "Mantle is, by all odds, the most exciting ball player in the majors," challenged only by Ted Williams. Mantle's "assets can be enumerated quickly. He hits the ball farther, runs faster, bunts better and strikes out more enthusiastically than any other player in the game. Even the lustiness of his strikeouts add (*sic*) up to box office." Prior to his death in late October, Clark Griffith, an inveterate Yankee hater, admitted, "That boy gives me more of a thrill than any ball player I ever saw."[11]

Harking back to the recent World Series, Casey Stengel insisted, "He was the big difference," referring to Mantle's limited appearances against Brooklyn. Extolling his young slugger, Stengel indicated he could be the next .400 hitter, then said, "Don't forget, he's only 24. Been having leg trouble of some kind every year since he's been with us." Then, Stengel stated,

> Now he bats from both sides, remember that. Means he's got to overcome twice as many weaknesses. Ever think of that. Well, he still bats .300 and if he got interested seriously in bunting, that would be 50 more points because nobody ever lived who could lay it down and fly to first base like that boy, and maybe he will.

While some considered Mantle's wrists the source of his power, others pointed to his "powerful forearms." Yankee coach Jim Turner indicated, "Just say, Mickey Mantle has the best physique that ever came into baseball. You see him in the locker room and those 188 pounds show you more symmetrical power than any man I ever saw. That's where the power comes from, from all parts of him."[12]

Bob Addie soon added flattering commentary of his own about the Yankee center fielder. Fellow Yankee outfielder Hank Bauer affirmed,

> Speaking of hitting, I should like to recommend my friend, No. 7—Mantle. We were playing the Dodgers last week in Miami and I swear he hit a line drive which was rising as it went out of the ball park. I remember that home run in Washington he hit off Chuck Stobbs but I'll bet this one was even longer.

Mantle, Addie noted, "seems to have his own fan club right with him. Almost any Yankee will drop what he is doing to talk enthusiastically of his long homers." As Addie saw it, "This is always a sign of greatness-where admiration transcends envy."[13] Yankee coach Bill Dickey, the former great catcher, bluntly stated,

> I get tired of hearing that Mickey Mantle hasn't made good yet. Remember this, he broke in at 19, straight from Class C. He has been a Yankee regular for four years, got married, has two fine children, led the league in homers last season, hits a ball farther than anybody else and has worked himself up to a salary of more than $30,000 and he's only 24. That's my roommate.[14]

The Yankees experienced a sign of relief on learning that Mantle's right leg had only suffered a muscle pull when he slid into second base during a preseason game in St. Petersburg. Reduced to whirlpool treatments, Mantle missed a few games. At the same time, Mantle's maturation appeared to be continuing as he started "to feel his importance as a figure in the game." Furthermore, "it would be hard to ignore him inasmuch as everything else comes to a dead stop on the field when he steps into the cage for batting practice, while the admirers of his muscle watch."[15]

The other New York City center fielders continued to draw attention of their own. Milwaukee outfielder Bill Bruton pointed to Willie Mays as having the best throwing arm among National League outfielders. Second, in his estimation, was Cincinnati right fielder Wally Post, followed by Brooklyn's Carl Furillo. Next were Brooklyn's Duke Snider and Pittsburgh's young Roberto Clemente. To Bruton, Mays and Snider were "the best at charging ball."[16]

Los Angeles Times' sportswriter Frank Finch noted that only five ballplayers—Babe Ruth, Jimmie Foxx, Hank Greenberg, Hack Wilson, and Ralph Kiner—had ever hit more homers than Mays had during the previous year. Ruth had done it four times, while Kiner and Johnny Mize had hit as many as 51. Finch indicated that Mays was generally viewed as the man most apt to break Ruth's single-season home run mark. The *Washington Post* agreed with Finch's assessment, indicating, "This could be the year Willie Mays shatters Babe Ruth's 'untouchable' home run record of 60 in a single season."[17]

During a spring training game in Tucson on March 29, Mays displayed a different kind of spectacular performance on the baseball diamond, which the *New York Times*" Louis Effrat compared with his celebrated catch of Vic Wertz's lengthy drive in Game One of the 1954 World Series. Mays was said to have "played the way he would if a world championship hung in the balance." During the fifth-inning, with New York five runs behind Cleveland, Mays sprinted from center field to right center, ending up 400 feet from home plate, cushioning a potential clash with the wall by bracing it with his right hand as he gloved the ball, preventing two runners from scoring. That followed his delivery of a two-run scoring single in the first and a two-run shot off Bob Feller in the fourth. Two days later, Mays smashed three home runs and a triple, collecting nine RBIs as New York beat Baltimore 27–10, in another exhibition contest. That gave him 11 homers and a .468 batting average for the spring.[18]

14

Stengel's Yankees Rebound as Mickey Mantle Wins the Triple Crown

On Opening Day, April 17, New York pounded Washington, 10–4, as 27,837 fans—among them, President Dwight D. Eisenhower—gathered at Griffith Stadium. New York rookie shortstop Jerry Lumpe got two hits and scored three times. Yogi Berra, swollen finger and all, was four for four, with a homer, a double, and five RBIs. Mickey Mantle, despite "a slight swelling of the hamstring muscle," was two for three, scored three times, drove in four, walked twice, and homered twice—"475-foot blasts"—off Washington starter Camilo Pascual.[1]

Defending World Series champion Brooklyn fell to Philadelphia, 8–6, with just over 24,000 fans at Ebbets Field. Having won 20 or more games for six straight seasons, Philly starter Robin Roberts had a rocky beginning to the new campaign but went all the way, in contrast to the Dodgers' Don Newcombe, who was knocked out in the third-inning. Brooklyn's Pee Wee Reese had three hits, Roy Campanella and Carl Furillo, two apiece, while Campy and Jim Gilliam each homered off Roberts. Starting at third base, Jackie Robinson went hitless.

Alson explained, "When Robinson wants to do something, you can't stop him. He had his mind set to winning the job and he did it." The Dodger manager expressed satisfaction with his team, noting he was relying on rookie

"Don Drysdale, Ken Lehman, Sandy Koufax and Roger Craig to take up the slack from his sore-arm brigade."[2]

A mere 12,790 were at the Polo Grounds to witness New York best Pittsburgh, 4–3, Johnny Antonelli outdueling Bob Friend despite two homers by first baseman Dale Long. Antonelli swatted a homer of his own, while Mays got a double in four at bats, scoring once.

The next day's *Washington Post and Times Herald* included a photo titled, "One for Mickey," with the caption indicating Mantle was "rapidly developing into baseball's new Ruth." Now, the estimates on his opening-day homers were raised to "more than 500 feet" apiece. Calling Mantle "Mr. Wonderful," Bob Addie claimed that Mickey's "booming shots made the other four-baggers look embarrassingly puny by comparison." While the Senators had shortened their spacious left field wall, they "neglected to move out their center-field fence," Addie wrote. "Nobody ever hit two in a game over that long-distance portion of a stadium which has defied the greatest hitters of all time." Throughout the spring, he noted, "there have been strange tales of Bunyanesque homers hit by Mantle," which skeptics dismissed as the latest effort "to build up baseball's newest glamour boy." However, "there was no question about Mantle's prodigious wallops," with "the boys . . . all out of synonyms for the word 'long.'"[3]

"This Morning," Shirley Povich's column, opened with a reflection on Mantle's "massive and magnificent" pair of Opening-Day homers, which outshone Berra's brilliant performance at the plate. Only Babe Ruth was said to have earlier driven a ball over Washington's center field wall, but "not even Ruth hit two in one game. That is a Mickey Mantle exclusive." Povich stated, "The grown-up Mickey Mantle has apparently arrived on the big league scene. This year he seemingly has shed his rookie status. For years he shared the wonderment of the fans at his own prodigious feats in a sort of who-me? reaction to the acclaim of his prowess."

The columnist explained, "Mantle, who came into the majors at 19 and is now 24, only lately has taken on the self-assurance of a veteran, despite the fact that he had more reasons for being cocksure of his future than any newcomer in decades." After all, "nobody of his era has been able to hit the ball as far, run as fast or bunt as well as Mantle, yet he lent himself to the role of perennial rookie." During the recent spring training, "he sort of came of age," viewing Yankee rookies in a "patronizing" fashion. Now, Povich predicted, "this is the year when Mantle could very well burst into full magnificence. The home runs he hits are not only Ruthian in quality, sometimes they're farther than the late Babe's," as coach Bill Dickey, a one-time teammate of the Babe, acknowledged. Reflecting further, Dickey concluded, "Put it this way: Ruth could hit a ball awful high and awful far. Mickey can hit it just as high and just as far."

While three Yankee players currently made more money than Mantle, that would change as he was "blossoming as the biggest box-office attraction since Babe Ruth." Why? "For a reason that is infallibly good box office: The big home run." The *N.Y. Mirror*'s Ben Epstein claimed Mantle's power derived from the "muscles of the neck, shoulders, back and arm. . . . A symphony, that's what." Other players spoke of Mantle's slugging the way players had once referred to the Babe's, pointing to where balls had been belted. During spring training, National League ballplayers, unable otherwise to watch Mantle in person unless their team made the World Series and encountered the Yankees or they made the All-Star team, stopped "to watch him in the batting cage and enjoy their own enthrallment at the things he can do to a baseball."

Many believed Mantle could bump his batting average by 50 points if he chose to bunt more as "nobody can lay them down with such skill or speed down the baseline so fast, either after a push or a drag bunt." Povich recalled such a bunt resulted in a leg injury the previous September. That day, Epstein noted, was "when we won the pennant and lost the World Series. That knee kept Mickey out of the Series, remember?"

As the accolades poured forth, Mantle pushed back, particularly regarding comparisons with Babe Ruth. He declared, "Ruth was Ruth. It's silly to compare me with him. It's just no contest." After stating he simply wanted "to have a good year," Mantle said, "This is bad for me. Sure, I like to hit the long ball but it's just another hit. I never think about the records. I'm in there all the time trying to get on base or move the man around. All I want to do is keep from striking out." His manager indicated, "I don't know if you can talk about Ruth and Mantle the same way. Ruth hit them more often but maybe Mantle hits them farther. I don't know." But then Casey Stengel offered, "Maybe, Mantle hits them better than Ruth left-handed or better than Jimmy (*sic*) Foxx right-handed. Or, maybe even better than Joe Jackson." Mantle recognized that "he's strong. He expects the ball to go 'some distance' when he hits it."[4]

Noting that both Stan Musial and Ted Williams hit for much higher averages during their first several major league seasons than Mantle had, Bob Addie considered it mere "speculation as to the unbounded excitement whenever he steps up to the plate." Addie then wrote, "Of course, there's only one answer—Mantle is the big boom man. Just as in boxing, the customers love to see the knockout wallop. Maybe Mantle doesn't hit them often but he hits them far; yea farther perhaps than any other man who ever lived." Several years younger than Ruth was when during the season he hit 60 home runs, Mantle "at his present rate of development," Addie suggested, "should be in a class by himself." Mantle also retained humility as displayed at a train station in Baltimore, when teammates Yogi Berra, Allie Reynolds, and Hank Bauer ribbed Mantle on their way to the All-Star contest. "A little boy yelled: 'Which one are you?'" Sighing, Mickey responded, "Nobody."[5]

In their fourth game of the season, New York beat Boston at Yankee Stadium, 7–1, to push their record to 3–1. Whitey Ford, in his first outing, went the distance, giving up only five hits to the Red Sox, playing without Ted Williams. Mantle went two for three, with a drag bunt single, a walk, two runs scored, and four RBIs, three on a seventh-inning homer, but departed following the seventh inning due to a leg injury aggravated by the bunt. Expected to miss five days, Mantle was back in the lineup the next day. One reason his teammates came to revere Mantle was his threshold for pain, his ability to play despite injuries that would have confined other players to the bench or working with a trainer while sitting out games. In the game following his latest leg discomfort, Mantle got three hits, including a homer, "another mighty blast," and drove in two runs against Boston.[6]

Casey Stengel, arguably Mantle's greatest critic and champion, responded to his slugger's latest feats by contending Mickey could break Ruth's single-season home run record if he "will only not swing so hard." The Yankee manager remarked, "There is no doubt that maybe he is the greatest distance hitter in baseball history. Only trouble is, what's the difference whether a homer goes 500 feet or only 300 feet? It's a homer either way." Stengel continued, "Mickey has got so much natural power that even when he don't hit the ball so good, he still gets a measly 350-foot homer. So figure it this way: If he cuts down on his swing and just tries to meet the ball, he will get lots more hits and in those hits will be more homers."[7]

On April 21, New York, after blowing an 8–0 lead, defeated Boston, 14–10, in a game featuring seven Yankee homers, including Mantle's fourth, said to be "another characteristic king-sized clout. . . . 415 feet into the right-field upper deck." The next day, Arthur Daley delivered his column devoted to Mantle, whom he called "A Reformed Man." Mickey was quoted as saying, "I've quit trying to hit home runs every time I go to bat. From now on I'm just trying to keep from striking out. All I want to do is meet the ball. If I do that I'll have a good year." While conversing, Mantle tracked Williams's "flawless swing . . . in the batting cage, watching every move with admiring eyes."[8]

Daley referred to Mantle as "a shy young man of 24 who always seems embarrassed at the realization that he is a celebrity" and so "awed by his surroundings" that Stengel's advice was just starting to take hold. "I'm beginning to learn that easy does it," Mantle admitted, then pointed to the two towering shots he recently delivered at Griffith Stadium. "I didn't swing hard at either of them. I did just what I've been trying to do all along—just meet the ball" and avoid strikeouts.

The man whose swing Mickey was admiring analyzed the younger slugger. "As far as I can see," Williams stated, "Mickey has improved every year and he'll continue to improve. My guess is that he's now heading definitely for his peak. Why shouldn't he be great? He has good speed, a good swing and good power. There's no reason in the world why he can't be a .340 hitter and a forty-homer slugger—or maybe better." Williams then said, "I'll tell you one thing. He's the only guy in this league who has a chance of breaking Babe Ruth's home run record. Me? Naw, I'm an old, washed-up has-been." About to return to the plate, Ted tossed out, "Don't worry about Mantle. In another fifteen or twenty years you'll be voting for him for the Hall of Fame."

Next to offer observations about Mantle, Stengel indicated in his typically grammatically free manner,

> A tree-mendous ballplayer. Don't matter what ball park he's in, either. See that last exit in the upper deck in left field. Look. Way up there almost over

the bullpen. They say that nobody ever hit one outta the Yankee Stadium. But if the stands didn't get in the way Mantle's would have gone over the wall because it was still climin' when it smacked the seats.

Moving on to another favorite topic of his, Casey blurted out, "Mantle is the fastest slugger I ever saw." Wrapping up his piece, Daley again referred to Mantle's slugging prowess. He believed "that the Oklahoma kid" most "wants to challenge" Ruth's single-season home run record. Now, Mantle recognized he could do so only if he reduced his strikeouts. Thus, "his new motto is: Easy does it." That led Daley to believe "Mantle's enormous potentialities" might "soon be realized."[9]

Pointing to 21-year-old Detroit outfielder Al Kaline's ability to win the American League batting title the previous year, sportswriter Dan Daniel wondered why the ambidextrous Mantle could not "land the Triple Crown." After all, Mantle had "the power, the speed, the eye, the intense ambition and high determination with which to gain the pinnacle which lies open to his prowess in baseball." To date, however, Mantle had lacked the "mental poise, emotional steadiness," or the ability to cut down on whiffing at the plate. Additionally, Mickey had "been a brittle ball player" even though he was "a picture" of athleticism "with the neck muscles of Praxiteles' Discus Thrower, the look of an athlete." However, "his knees are in bandages. His left shin, where his once highly dangerous osteomyelitis lies dormant, is wrapped up. The cartilage is out of his right knee." Moreover, "No major leaguer within my experience ever got so little out of terrific speed as does Mantle" due to Stengel's "fear" of injury, Daniel stated. But when Mickey went all out as he had during the previous year's pennant race, the likelihood of injury mushroomed.

Notwithstanding a lack of wholesale support from Yankee fans and mixed relationships with the press, "the Oklahoma Kid, with potential terrific, chances amazing," was confronting "his year of decision." According to Daniel, Mantle, who might well "be at his physical peak," would be in the mix of another pennant chase, with "every game, every time at bat" counting. Different paths could unfold, Daniel noted. "Championships, and realization of his tremendous abilities? Failure and disappointment? Or, for one so gifted, the disappointing middle road?"[10]

Despite not hitting any homers over the next six games, Mantle finished April with 10 runs scored, 15 RBIs, a .415 batting average, while slugging at an .805 clip and getting on base during half of his plate appearances. The 8–3 Yankees were a half-game ahead of the White Sox, with the Indians and Senators two behind. The 7–2 Dodgers were off to another fast, league-leading start, albeit not the blistering pace of the previous season, a game and a half ahead of the Braves and the Cardinals, while the 4–5 Giants were tied for fourth, three games back. Duke Snider began the season in a terrible slump, with 6 hits, including only 1 double and no homers, 4 runs scored, 4 RBIs, a .162 batting average with a woeful .189 slugging percentage. Willie Mays fared somewhat better only, with 2 doubles, 2 homers, 5 runs scored, 6 RBIs, and a .200 batting average, while slugging .378.

*****

The Yankees roared through the month of May, ending with a 29–13 record, six and a half games in front of the White Sox and Indians, with the Red Sox another game back. In the more tightly contested National League, the 19–10 Braves were one game better than the Cardinals, two in front of both the Reds and the Pirates, with the Dodgers, having slumped to a 19–16 mark, another game behind. The 15–21 Giants were sitting in sixth place, already seven and a half games out of first. Underscoring his newly found status as MLB's greatest star, Mantle exploded during May, scoring and driving in 35 runs, hitting 16 homers, walking 23 times, batting .414, getting on base over half the time, and slugging at an .879 pace. Although Brooklyn went into something of a tailspin, Duke Snider excelled too, although not quite at Mickey's astronomical rate. Snider scored 19 runs, hit 8 homers, drove in 21 runs, batted .383, had a .453 on-base percentage, and slugged at a .723 level. Willie Mays also improved, but his power numbers continued to lag. He scored 18 runs, managed 4 doubles, 6 triples, but only 2 homers, drove in 10 runs, batted .297, had a .407 OBP, and slugged .538.

As Mantle hit five homers during the first five games of May, Shirley Povich wrote, "The time has come, perhaps, to acknowledge that Babe Ruth's record of 60 home runs in a single season is in greater jeopardy than ever before." To Povich, Mantle was "taking such dead aim at the record that his challenge must be honored even with the season only three weeks old." Every previous contender, the columnist noted, had faded following the middle of the season, while being overwhelmed by the Babe's historic crushing of 17 homers in September of 1927. However, Mantle, he wrote, "is a very special challenger. He hits balls farther than anybody since Ruth, and some of his blows in Yankee Stadium have reached sectors that not even the Babe's wallops attained."

Significantly, during the initial 16 games of the 1956 season, Mantle, having hit nine home runs, had "apparently developed an assurance" previously lacking. Yankee coach Bill Dickey explained that Mantle's approach had changed. "When I say he's getting a piece of the ball, I mean he is laying off the sucker pitch. He doesn't have to hit balls on the nose to get himself home runs, he's that powerful. I told him if he could cut down on his strikeouts, he could boost his batting average 50 points." Helpful too was the fact that pitchers were disinclined to walk Mantle because Yogi Berra followed him in the lineup.

Summing up, Povich wrote, "No hitter was ever endowed with as many natural advantages to become a home run king as Mantle." Having proved himself "a good hitter," he "brought into play his bonus assets, the sheer muscle of his swing, and the rare ability to swing from either side of the plate without loss of power." Or, if necessary, he could leg "out a home run that might fall inside the park." But his power stood out, with Mantle "the only player who has ever hit one into the dead-center seats in Yankee Stadium." Regarding Mickey's gargantuan blast at Griffith Stadium three years earlier, the late Senators owner stated, "Maybe the wind did help him, but that wind has been blowing off and on for 51 years out her and nobody else ever put one over the fence."[11]

The *Los Angeles Times*' Frank Finch reported that Mantle displayed "no signs of cooling off despite a chronic knee injury that has hampered him from time to time." No matter, "ripping the cover off the ball in game after game," Mantle was "off to his fastest start since joining the Yankees." Presciently, Finch indicated, "Looks like Mickey's taking dead aim on that coveted rarity, the triple batting crown," last achieved by Ted Williams nine years earlier. "If Micky's (*sic*) knee doesn't cave in," Finch wrote, "he figures to rewrite a few records." Bob Addie was soon wondering, "Whatever happened to that school of thought which said that Mickey Mantle was only the third best centerfielder and hitter in New York behind Brooklyn's Duke Snider and the Giants' Willie Mays?" Shirley Povich wrote, "In New York where the rank of the centerfielders used to be (1) Willie Mays, (2) Duke Snider, (3) Mickey Mantle, it has now been rearranged to read Mantle, Snider, Mays."[12]

With nearly 30,000 fans in attendance at Yankee Stadium, Mantle helped the Yankees sweep a doubleheader from the Senators, powering two homers, "one of colossal proportions," giving him 20 homers in New York's first 41 games. The first, hit off Pedro Ramos in the fifth-inning, "was a skyscraper wallop to right that hit just below the top of the roof cornice high above the third deck." Barely missing going out of the ballpark, the homer attained "previously unplumbed territory." Yankee players commented, "I've never seen anything like it before." Mantle acknowledged, "It was the best I ever hit a ball lefthanded." The second homer, off Camilo Pascual, also in the fifth-inning, but in the nightcap, "carried halfway up into the right-field bleachers, just to the left of the bullpen."[13]

In his *Sports of the Times* column, Arthur Daley waxed on about "The Boy Grew Older." Evidently no longer considering himself a kid, Mantle was speaking and behaving "with the assurance of an old-timer." As Daley put it, "the once awed and frightened youngster from Commerce, Okla., has finally left boyhood behind and has flowered to full maturity at long last." Pulled from the rural heartland, the 19-year-old was playing in the Yankee outfield during the 1951 World Series. "He was lionized and subjected to the most extravagant raves . . . a bewildering, head-spinning process" for "a fundamentally shy introvert."[14]

Every spring, predictions could be heard that Mantle would fulfill "his potentialities and reach greatness." No matter how hard he tried, "he never quite made it," resulting in constant booing from the home crowd. To Daley, "the burden of succeeding Babe Ruth and Joe DiMaggio as the Yankee superstar was too much of a burden." But from Opening Day, New York infielder Jerry Coleman asserted, "Mickey attained maturity," swatting "two tremendous homers without even trying," boosting him. He had also displayed a greater willingness to go the other way when necessary, causing Coleman to declare, "The boy has come of age."[15]

*****

During May, *Collier's* published an article purportedly penned by Duke Snider, with assistance from the sportswriter Roger Kahn, "I Play Baseball for Money, Not Fun." After declaring, "The truth is that life in the major leagues is far from a picnic," Snider stated, "I feel that I'd be just as happy if I never played another baseball game again." Kids threw "skate keys and marbles" at his head as he approached outfield fences during games, while older fans hurled beer cans. Little knowledgeable sportswriters tossed brickbats. Travel, sleep deprivation, and dietary issues also troubled him. More positively, Snider referred to teammates who were "great friends, fellows like Pee Wee Reese and Carl Erskine," business contacts, nicer fans, and "even some sports writers." Plus, he had "made an awful lot of money." On the other hand, he had been compelled to put up with the antics of former manager Chuck Dressen.[16]

Striking back, Dressen charged that a slumping Snider would "dog it in the outfield," forcing the manager to react. "I tried to tell him in private and finally shamed him before his teammates. After all, Robinson, Furillo, Campanella, Gilliam, Newcombe, Hodges, Reese and all the rest were team men." But "Snider always was a pouter. In fact, his own teammates used to ride him because he'd sulk in the field." Calling Duke "a hardhead and a popoff," Dressen said, "Fellows like him ought to get down on their knees and thank the Lord for having the gift to play ball or they'd be out scrambling for a living."[17]

Shirley Povich compared Snider unfavorably with retired heavyweight boxing champion Rocky Marciano, who prided himself on refusing "to knock the sport which had given him wealth and fame." Snider, by contrast, was "less of a big leaguer," having taken "many pieces of silver . . . and then rapped the baseball business." Referring to Snider, Povich's colleague, Robert P. Jordan, wrote, "So everybody worries, Snider, you big bawlbaby." The *Los Angeles Times*' Braven Dyer sarcastically discussed how Snider "painted a most depressing picture of slave labor in the majors, and all for a paltry $50,000 plus per year, too." Dyer foresaw, "I have an idea some of the poor working people who pay to see Snider play in Brooklyn will let him have it pretty good now."[18]

On the playing field, Snider, coming out of a slump, got three hits, two of them homers, one the fifth grand slam of his career, to help Brooklyn beat New

York, 6–4, a day after Carl Erskine tossed his second no-hitter. The Dodger team was experiencing hitting doldrums, with only Junior Gilliam near the .300 mark. Gil Hodges was down to .192, while Snider's hot day bumped his average up to .270. Brooklyn publicity director Arthur E. (Red) Patterson declared, "Snider was an angry hitter in the West, and . . . angry hitters are no good." He had even "over-swung himself below .200" but was rebounding.[19]

*****

During June, Mantle, despite having another fine month, came back to earth. He scored 21 runs, hit 7 homers, gathered 17 RBIs, walked 16 times, had a .415 on-base percentage, slugged .598, and batted .324, pulling his season totals to .471, .757, and .378, respectively. The New York Yankees ended June with a 44–25 record, placing them only two games ahead of Chicago, five and a half in front of Cleveland, with Boston another two games back. In the National League, Milwaukee, sitting at 36–25, remained in first place, one game better than both Brooklyn and Cincinnati, with St. Louis three back. The New York Giants, with a 26–38 win-loss record, were in last place, eleven and a half games behind the Braves. Snider hit for power but not a high average during June, scoring 22 runs, getting 9 homers, driving in 14, walking 27 times—12, intentionally—and hitting .263, dropping his average for 1956 to .296. Mays scored 13 runs, hit 6 homers, drove in 11 runs, and batted .308.

At the beginning of the month, New Yorkers considered it "a matter of course that Mantle" would smash Babe Ruth's single-season home run record. "Some have even predicted 75 homers for the Oklahoma kid," columnist Bob Addie revealed. One of Mickey's closest friends, Yankee right fielder Hank Bauer, stated, "He's really grown up all of a sudden. You know, this is quite a strain, everybody nailing him every day and asking him what he thinks about the possibility of beating Ruth's record." Then, Bauer added, "I think Mantle's talent is just beginning to blossom. . . . He's smartened up at the plate with experience. There's your answer why he's knocking down buildings."

Mantle, Addie declared, had "been great in other things since he came up with the Yanks. He's at least as fast as anybody in baseball. He's a magnificent fielder with a great arm. He's by far the best bunter in baseball." Having become "more approachable," Mantle admitted, "I only hope I can keep it up. I don't allow myself to think about records. Suppose somebody does break Ruth's record. It wouldn't mean a thing. Ruth was Ruth."

Addie contended, "The Mantle story promises to be an exciting one all summer, and the biggest lift to baseball since the Ruthian era. . . . Mantle's long shots inevitably bring out the slide-rule because he has broken barriers no other human has ever penetrated in baseball." He continued, "Mantle is the man of the hour. At the moment, three New York papers are writing his life story and four national magazines have articles on him in the mill. Mr. Wonderful has arrived."[20]

The Sporting News featured its own examination, "Long-Shot Mantle Rocks Ruth Mark," with Willard Mullin sketching the Yankee slugger batting left-handed with "Target for Mickey" and "Ruth's 60 Homers." At some point, Dan Daniel predicted, Mantle would likely accomplish the unprecedented feat of knocking "a far ball out of Yankee Stadium." However, Babe Ruth's single-season home run record appeared a more difficult accomplishment, as both Hank Greenberg and Jimmie Foxx, each of whom hit 58, would attest. Working against Mantle was his propensity for injuries, while operating in his favor was "his ability to drive a baseball just about as far as we now believe a human can drive one." Another handicap, Daniel thought, was Mickey's "astonishing speed." Mantle, "an amazing batter" with "the build of a blacksmith and the speed of Mercury," was "the fastest player the majors have boasted in some time." That led to his readiness to drop down bunts, something Ruth seldom considered doing. With two strikes against him, Mickey would resort to drag bunts, notwithstanding his possessing "the most astonishing power and distance" since Ted Williams's heyday.[21]

Several former big leaguers expressed doubts that Mantle could match the Babe's record. One of them, Mel Ott, said, "I won't believe it until I see it," while acknowledging that Mantle had "gotten off to the most sensational start probably in baseball." But Ott pointed to Mantle's troubled knees, the pressure that would continue to mount, and the adoption of a slider by many pitchers that even Williams suggested had "knocked 15 points off his batting average."[22]

After going homerless for seven straight games in early June, Mantle hit six in seven games, with one on June 18 flying out of Briggs Stadium in Detroit, matching a feat accomplished by Williams back in 1939, Ted's rookie season.

This tape-measure shot soared over the 370-foot roof perched 110 feet above the baseball diamond.[23]

One result of Mantle's batting heroics was a shift in fans' response at Yankee Stadium, as well as wider, national coverage. Instead of receiving Bronx cheers, Mickey was being applauded. "The most talked-about player in the land," Mantle was also hailed in ballparks and written about in mass-circulation magazines. *Sports Illustrated* placed him on the cover of its June 18 issue, with the declaration, "The Year of the Slugger."[24]

The feature article, "The Mantle of the Babe," written by senior editor Robert Creamer, contained a preface celebrating sports' "overpowering onrush of youth." Creamer began the piece referring to the "thick-bodied . . . young man" with "his massive torso" operating through "a magnificently tuned set of reflexes." Employing "the exorbitant strength generated by his legs, back, shoulders and arms," Mantle drove "the ball immensely high and far toward the right-field roof, so high and far" as to amaze longtime Yankee Stadium patrons.

"The excitement surrounding Mantle," Creamer explained, "goes beyond numbers, beyond homers hit and homers and games to go. Like Ruth, his violent strength is held in a sheath of powerful, controlled grace. Like Ruth, he makes home run hitting simple and exciting at the same time. The distance he hits his home runs (the approved cliché is "Ruthian blast") takes away the onus of cheapness, a word often applied to the common variety of home run hit today, and leaves the spectator aghast, whether he roots for Mantle or against him." Listening to sportswriter Howard Cosell describing the homer Mantle blasted on Memorial Day, Tiger shortstop Harvey Kuenn exclaimed, "His strength isn't human. How can a man hit a ball that hard?" White Sox manager Marty Marion recalled a home run Mantle belted in "the far reaches of the upper stands in deep right-center field": "I never saw anything like it."[25]

The June 25 issue of *Life* magazine displayed the smiling Yankee star, holding a bat in his left-handed stance, with the description, "The Remarkable Mickey Mantle." The companion article, "A Prodigy of Power," emphasized that baseball fans reacted to Mantle's at bats as they had to Ted Williams and Babe Ruth. They anticipated Mickey's hitting "the longest, most prodigious homer in history." In unprecedented fashion, Mantle was a hard-hitting switch-hitter whose speed could convert "singles into extra base hits." And, as Joe Collins offered, "Mickey hits every one like they don't count under 400 feet."[26]

Sport magazine offered an article by Roger Kahn on one of New York City's other great center fielders, "The Bewildering World of Willie Mays." Baseball scribe Barney Kremenko called Mays "a genius. What Einstein was in his field, Willie is in baseball. That's all. He's a genius." Brooklyn Dodger Duke Snider said, "Willie is a helluva centerfielder," while former manager Leo Durocher called him "the greatest outfielder I've ever seen." Durocher had once said of the then rookie Mays, "I wouldn't trade him for Stan Musial, Ted Williams or even DiMag."[27]

*****

July proved to be another good month for Mantle, as he scored 22 runs, hit 7 homers, had 22 RBIs, walked 33 times, and batted .349 with a .513 on-base percentage, while his Yankees went 23-6, landing nine games ahead of the Indians, with the Red Sox having dropped thirteen and a half back. The 57–35 Braves stood two games ahead of the Reds, the Dodgers four behind, and the last-place Giants 23 back. Duke Snider scored 23 runs, hit 8 homers, drove in 17 runs, and walked 24 times, but hit only .250. Willie Mays had another middling month, scoring 16 times, getting 6 home runs, producing 15 RBIs, and batting .284, matching his season mark.

The cover of that month's *Baseball Digest* displayed a slugging Mantle and a smiling one too, with the question, "Can Mickey Make It?" A companion article by the *Cleveland Plain Dealer*'s Gordon Cobbledick was titled, "Yankee Stadium Could Beat Him!"[28]

Forced to wear a knee brace after suffering an injury during the opening game of a doubleheader against Boston in early July, Mantle, it was feared, might miss the All-Star Game. Brace and all, he not only played at Griffith Stadium but like other stars—Ted Williams, Stan Musial, and Willie Mays—he delivered a home run, although the National League prevailed, 7–3. Indicating he was experiencing no pain, Mantle admitted, "I still can't run."[29]

Approaching the end of July, Mantle had his sixth multi-homer game, one a grand slam, his first of the season, pushing his total to 34, a game ahead of Ruth's pace, as New York beat Cleveland, 13–6, at Municipal Stadium.[30]

While the Yankees possessed a substantial lead in the American League, experts wondered if any team could surpass the Braves in the other circuit. Displaying life, the Dodgers, led by Snider, Carl Furillo, and Roy Campanella, had won eight straight games to narrow the gap. Campy, despite still carrying a woeful batting average, had been "belting the fall of late," and Snider had hit four homers before experiencing another slide.[31]

Notwithstanding a nine-game homerless stretch, Mantle roared through August, scoring 24 runs, hitting 13 homers, driving in 29 runs, walking 20 times, batting .351 and slugging .763. Losing almost as many games as they won, the Yankees ended the month at 83–46, eight games ahead of the Indians, with the White Sox having dropped eleven and a half games back. The National League remained tight, the 78–49 Braves two and a half games in front of the Dodgers, with the Reds another game behind. Snider heated up, scoring 28 runs, homering 12 times, producing 30 RBIs, and batting .327. Mays had his best month of the season so far, with 22 runs scored, 9 homers, 21 RBIs, and a .293 batting average.

Mantle's assault on Babe Ruth's home run record continued, with Mickey remaining comfortably ahead of his great predecessor's pace. It made sense, the *New York Times*' John Drebinger indicated, that baseball fans failed to "become unduly excited" as a slugger appeared to threaten the Babe's mark. "They've been let down too often." In the 1930s, Hack Wilson, Jimmie Foxx, and Hank Greenberg all made runs of their own, as did Ralph Kiner and Johnny Mize during the following decade. Just the year before, Mays hit 51 homers. However, Mantle appeared "as a real threat," exciting the baseball world.

Referred to as "the Yankees' precocious youngster with the neck of a bull and the shoulders of a wrestler," Mantle was said to be "endowed by nature, both physically and mentally, with certain gifts" other sluggers lacked. He was a switch-hitter "with tremendous power from either side of the plate," while "the dramatics of a situation bother him hardly at all."[32]

Earlier skeptical of Mantle's chances, Baltimore manager Paul Richards had become a believer, declaring Mickey "a better hitter than Ruth . . . and a better center fielder even than Joe DiMaggio." Jimmie Foxx predicted Mantle would become the new home run king "if he stays healthy." Johnny Mize thought it likely "if he just keep (*sic*) on swinging." Claire Ruth, the Babe's widow, agreed.

"Mickey is quite a few games out in front, isn't he? I should say he has an excellent chance, wouldn't you?" Ralph Kiner, who had two shots at, if not Ruth's single-season home run total, then Wilson's National League mark, predicted, "He will not top the Babe's record" due to late-season pressure. However, he indicated that if anyone could do so, it was Mickey Mantle.[33]

Even his own manager conveyed doubts, declaring, "I don't think he can do it," following the next-to-last Yankee game in August when Mantle hit his 46th homer to remain slightly ahead of Ruth's pace. "Don't misunderstand me," Casey Stengel said. "He is a great player but it is asking an awful lot for a youngster to lead in all departments. And remember the Babe hit 17 homers in September." Referring to the fact that Mantle was leading the league in a welter of batting areas, Stengel offered, "But if I was he, I wouldn't be disappointed if I didn't reach Ruth's record. After all he's young. I never had a man who's led the league in all divisions. I would gain if he did."[34]

*****

As matters turned out, Casey was right on both counts. Mantle's home run onslaught slackened during September, although he went on to top the American League in statistic after statistic. Expressing dismay, as Stengel did, when Mantle opted early in the month to lay down a bunt, Shirley Povich wrote, "Few have ever had as glowing a chance to penetrate" what he called "the home run barrier" in the manner of "Mickey, and perhaps none ever had as great a potential." Povich indicated, "The successor to Babe Ruth's throne can't miss it, though, what could be the game's greatest immortality. It is pretty well established now that only the maudlin sentimentalists would resent Mantle's ascension to it. Never was the nation more eager to accept a new baseball hero, especially one who is cast in the model of the modest, blushing All-American boy. So, Mickey, please, no more bunts; at least for now."[35]

As Tom Meany reported, Stengel and virtually all other observers of the American League were waxing on regarding "the emergence of Mantle as a star this season." The manager noted Mickey's "natural power at the plate," his "speed on the base paths and in the outfield," his "overall quickness and coordination." While calling Joe DiMaggio "the greatest ball player which ever played for me," Stengel admitted Mantle could "break records" and was "the best switch hitter I ever saw.... with tremendous power from both sides of the plate." Casey still sought to turn Mantle into "the perfect ball player," although he had adopted a go-slow approach. Teammate Joe Collins declared, "His swing is so perfect and his power is so great that he" could hit a ball more than "400 feet, right off his fists."

While praising Mantle's greater selectivity at the plate, Stengel also underscored "his physical courage," suggesting, "Thing too many people overlook about him is that he's been doing all he has been doing this year as a cripple. He still hasta have his right leg bandaged before every game, and then he pulled a muscle on the back of the same leg under his knee, which was so sore you couldn't touch it." On top of that, the knee injured during the 1951 World Series still troubled him. Yankee trainer Gene Mauch, who massaged him prior to each game, declared, "I've seen plenty of athletes play when bandaged up, but nobody like Mantle who has to be bandaged constantly." Mantle taped himself, although Mauch was called on if Mickey couldn't reach the spot of the latest injury. As Tom Meany indicated, "The daily bandage Mickey wraps himself in extends from low on his right shin to the top of the thigh. It is bound so tightly that the marks of it are plain an hour after it has been removed." As the binding restricted circulation, Mantle declined to go to the batting cage on a doubleheader day, having been taped prior to the initial game. Otherwise, he would be wrapped for more than six hours, numbing his body.[36]

During the first ten Yankee games in September, Mantle failed to hit a homer. As he fell behind Ruth's scorching rush to baseball immortality 29 years earlier, a *Washington Post and Times Herald* editorial, "The Fraying Mantle," suggested that Mickey, young as he is," was "a tragic figure like Agamemnon, Oedipus and Hippolytus." After homering against Kansas City on September 13, Mantle went three games without doing so, then had three straight games with a homer, followed by another five contests without one. He belted home run number 52 with two games left in the season, then had only one official at bat during those games.[37]

Thus, September proved to be far and away Mantle's weakest month yet, with 20 runs scored, 5 homers, 12 RBIs, 17 walks, and a .270 batting average. No matter, his 1956 season was incandescent, as he appeared in a then career-best 150 games (10th), had 188 hits (4th), 22 doubles, 5 triples, 10 stolen bases (7th), 112 walks (2nd), and a .464 on-base percentage (2nd). He led the league with 132 runs scored, 52 homers, 130 RBIs, a .353 batting average, a .705 slugging average, 376 total bases, a 1.169 OPS, a 210 OPS+, and an 11.2 WAR. His New York Yankees ended with a 97–57 win-low record, despite dropping four of their final meaningless six games, ending up nine in front of Cleveland, twelve ahead of Chicago, with Boston thirteen back.

The blistering National League race concluded with Brooklyn prevailing with a 93–61, beating out Milwaukee, which led for much of the season, by a game, and Cincinnati, which finished two back. In September, Duke Snider scored 16 runs, hit 6 homers, drove in 18, walked 17 times, and batted .289. Willie Mays tore through the month, scoring 27 times, hitting 11 homers, driving in 21, and batting .336.

After being tied with Milwaukee for first on May 20, Brooklyn fell as far as fifth place as late as June 9, then spent much of July in third place, where the Dodgers were situated on September 5, although a game and a half out of first. From September 7, they were never more than a game behind or in front of the National League, taking first place for good by sweeping a doubleheader against Pittsburgh on the next-to-last day of the regular season. The pennant was only clinched by defeating the Pirates on September 30, 8–6.

Before that happened and amid the torrid pennant race, the *New York Times*' Arthur Daley recalled Duke Snider's previous year's smackdown, "Brooklyn fans don't deserve a pennant." Backing off only a bit, Snider soon declared, "Some Dodger fans don't deserve a pennant." Daley now indicated in a column titled "The Deserted Village" that Snider's original pronouncement may have been the correct one. As the Dodgers attempted to catch the front-running Braves, a mere 7,847 fans showed up at Ebbets Field to watch Brooklyn lose to Philadelphia, 7–3, despite a pair of homers by Snider off Robin Roberts, to drop a full game behind Milwaukee. The previous night, as Sal Maglie heroically pitched a no-hitter to keep Brooklyn in the race, just over 15,000 were in attendance.

Daley asked, "Is that civic pride? Is Brooklyn really the wackiest and most fanatical baseball town in the country?" He advised against thinking that Dodger owner Walter O'Malley's proposed construction of a "super-duper new ball park will solve this problem." The very same fans, Daley noted, would "holler bloody murder" on being unable to purchase World Series tickets if Brooklyn advanced to the postseason.[38]

A sweep of a doubleheader against Pittsburgh enabled Brooklyn to regain a one-game lead over Milwaukee, which lost 2–1, in twelve innings to St. Louis. A third straight victory over Pittsburgh the next day, fueled by a pair of homers, four RBIs, and a terrific catch by Snider, sealed the second straight pennant for the Dodgers, with 31,983 having shown up at Ebbets Field. Responding as if they had clinched their first title, the team's "old pros . . . whooped it up."[39]

*****

While Mickey Mantle became the first Triple Crown winner in the American League since Ted Williams in 1947, Yogi Berra had another excellent season, scoring 93 runs, hitting 30 homers, driving in 105 runs, and batting .298. Playing full-time, Bill Skowron had 23 homers, 90 RBIs, and a .308 batting average, while Gil McDougald hit .311. Hank Bauer scored 96 runs, hit 26 homers, drove in 84 runs, but hit only .241. Whitey Ford was 19–6, with a league-leading .760 win-loss percentage and 2.47 ERA. Twenty-three-year-old Johnny Kucks went 18–9, Tom Sturdivant was 16–8, Don Larsen, 16–8, and Bob Turley, 8–4, with a sky-high 5.05 ERA. Tom Morgan was only 6–7, the disappointing Mickey McDermott, 2–6. Thirty-six-year-old Tommy Byrne was 7–3 and Bob Grim, 6–1, while starting only six games.[40]

For the third straight season, the Yankees attracted just around 1.5 million fans, tops in the American League; the Orioles' attendance improved slightly but the Athletics, during their second year in Kansas City, had 400,000 fewer customers. In the National League, the Braves again drew more than two million fans, with the Dodgers attracting almost 200,000 more fans than the previous season. By contrast, the Giants' attendance fell to 629,179; a sizable percentage of that involved intra-city games with the Dodgers.

Coming off his third MVP season, 34-year-old Roy Campanella had his second miserable campaign in the last three, scoring only 39 runs, driving in but 73, and batting .219, although he managed to hit 20 homers. Finally displaying his own signs of aging, 38-year-old Pee Wee Reese scored 85 runs but hit only .257. Thirty-four-year-old Carl Furillo hit 21 homers, drove in 83 runs, and batted .289. Two years younger, Gil Hodges had 86 runs scored, 29 doubles, 32 homers, and 87 RBIs, but his batting average slid to .265. Sandy Amoros had 16 homers and batted .260, while Jim Gilliam scored 102 runs, stole 21 bases, batted .300, landed on the All-Star team, and finished fifth in the National League MVP contest. Thirty-seven-year-old Jackie Robinson bettered his 1955 year but in 357 official at bats had only 98 hits, 27 of them extra-base hits, including 10 homers, and drove in 43 runs, while batting .275. Duke Snider's batting average slipped to .292, although he scored 112 runs (2nd), 33 doubles (2nd), a league-leading 43 homers, 101 RBIs (4th), 324 total bases (2nd), and an NL-best 99 walks, 26 intentional passes, .399 OBP, .598 slugging average, .997 OPS, 155 OPS+, and 7.6 WAR.

Don Newcombe, named both the Cy Young Award winner—given for the initial time to the majors' top pitcher—and National League MVP, had a brilliant regular season. He won a league-high 27 games, losing only 7, equating to an NL-best .794 win-loss percentage, and a 3.06 ERA. Thirty-nine-year-old Sal Maglie, finishing second in both the Cy Young and NL MVP races, went 13–5 with a 2.87 ERA for Brooklyn after starting the season with Cleveland. Carl Erskine was 13–11, Roger Craig, 12–11, Clem Labine, 10–6, with a league-leading 19 saves. Young pitchers Don Drysdale, Don Bessent, and Ed Roebuck displayed promise, but Sandy Koufax and Ken Lehman proved disappointing.

The 67–86 New York Giants, sixth-place finishers, 26 games behind Brooklyn, had Red Schoendienst and Jackie Brandt batting .296 and .299, respectively, but in a virtually punchless manner. Don Mueller fell to .269. Bill White had 22 homers but only 59 RBIs and a .256 BA. By contrast, Willie Mays scored 101 runs, had 171 hits, got 27 doubles (10th) hit 36 homers (5th), drove in 84, batted .296, produced a .557 slugging average (5th), a .369 OBP (9th), a .926 OPS+ (4th) and gathered 322 total bases. He led the league with 40 steals and finished second in WAR (7.5). Johnny Antonelli had another 20-game season and a 2.86 ERA, while 38-year-old reliever Marv Grissom had a 1.56 ERA in over 80 innings, but the rest of the pitching staff was fair to miserable.

*****

Despite being afflicted with a hand infection that caused him to miss 18 games, the Cubs' Ernie Banks remained an All-Star, hitting 28 homers, driving in 85 runs, and batting .297. His teammate, Sam Jones, went 9–14 with a 3.91 ERA, but led the NL with 176 strikeouts. A new Cub, Monte Irvin, playing his last major league season, had 15 homers and batted .271. The Athletics' Harry Simpson had a career year, also making the All-Star team, leading the American League with 11 triples, hitting 21 homers, driving in 105 runs, and batting .293. In 225 official at bats, the Orioles' Bob Boyd batted .311. Despite missing the All-Star team for the first time in eight years, Larry Doby, now playing for the White Sox, scored 89 runs, hit 24 homers, drove in 102 runs, walked 102 times, and batted .268. New teammate Minnie Minoso scored 106 runs and drove in 88, had 29 doubles, a league-leading 11 triples, 21 homers, and a .316 batting average. New Cincinnati pitcher Brooks Lawrence went 19–10, with 11 complete games, making the All-Star team.

The Braves' Henry Aaron, who, during 1952, played with the Indianapolis Clowns, a Negro American League team, became an even bigger star, nearly helping to lead Milwaukee to the National League pennant. He scored 106 runs, hit 26 homers, drove in 92 runs, and led the NL with 200 hits, 14 triples, a .328 batting average, and 340 total bases. Throughout the season, the *Los Angeles Sentinel* columnist Eddie Burbridge applauded Aaron's performance and that of other Black major leaguers. Burbridge pointed to Roberto Clemente, the second-year Pirate player, who hit 30 doubles and batted .311.[41]

*****

Meeting for the seventh time spanning 16 World Series, and, more notably, the sixth time within a decade, the Brooklyn Dodgers and New York Yankees faced off, with the matchup unfolding precisely as it had the previous year in one sense. The home team won every game other than the clincher. Game One, played at Ebbets Field before 34,479 fans, was won by Brooklyn, 6–3, with Maglie outpitching Ford, who lasted only three innings. Triple Crown winner Mantle belted a two-run homer to deep right in the first, Billy Martin hit a solo shot, and Enos Slaughter had three hits and scored a run. Robinson and Hodges both homered off Ford, Hodges delivering a three-run shot.

In a slugfest, Brooklyn went up two games to none, with 36,217 individuals in the stands. Both starters, Brooklyn's Newcombe and New York's Larsen, were knocked out in the second, but the Dodgers' Bessent pitched seven innings of two-run ball to notch the win, while Morgan took the loss. Slaughter had another pair of hits and scored three runs, Joe Collins drove in two, and Berra belted a second-inning grand slam off Newcombe. Mantle went one for four, scoring one run. Both Gilliam and Reese drove in two, Hodges went three for three, with two doubles, and drove in four. Duke Snider hit a three-run second-inning homer off Byrne, going two for four, and scored three runs. Robinson and Furillo each had two hits and scored two runs.

Switching to Yankee Stadium for Game Three, New York prevailed, 5–3, with 73,977 present, as Ford rebounded from his opening game debacle, beating Craig. Reed and Furillo had two hits apiece, with Reese tripling and Furillo doubling, while Snider was hitless in three official at bats, driving in one run. Martin and Slaughter homered, Enos swatting a three-run sixth-inning dinger off Craig. Berra had two hits, while Mantle was one for four.

The Yankees evened the series in Game Four, beating the Dodgers, 6–2, with 69,705 at the Stadium. New York's Sturdivant had a complete game, while Brooklyn's Erskine only went four innings. Roy Campanella went two for two, with an RBI; Hodges drove in the other Dodger run, and Snider and Robinson each scored after doubling. Duke went one for four. Mantle got his second homer, scored twice, and went one for three, while Bauer slammed a two-run homer in the seventh inning off reliever Don Drysdale.

Game Five, performed at Yankee Stadium with 64,519 fans present, proved historic, with Don Larsen facing and retiring 27 batters in succession. Maglie, despite giving up only five hits, took the loss. Mantle produced what proved to be the winning run, homering off Maglie in the fourth, while Bauer plated Andy Carey in the sixth inning.

In Game Six, the Dodgers, before 33,224 fans, scored for the first time in 19 innings, scoring the only run in the bottom of the tenth, as Robinson drove in Gilliam. Snider walked three times and had one of four Brooklyn hits, while Bauer, Collins, and Berra each had two hits. Mantle walked once and was hitless in his three other trips to the plate.

Newcombe's World Series woes continued as he was rocked in Game Seven, with 33,782 showing up at Ebbets Field, getting knocked out after three innings, while Johnny Kucks pitched a three-hit shutout as New York won, 9–0. Snider had two hits, Furillo one. Berra scored three times, smacked two homers off Newcombe, drove in four, while Mantle had a double, walked once, and scored a run. Skowron hit a seventh-inning grand slam off Craig, and Elston Howard also homered off the Dodger starter.[42]

Berra led the Yankees with five runs scored, nine hits, three homers, ten RBIs, and a .360 batting average. Slaughter scored six runs, drove in four, and batted .350, while Martin scored five runs, hit two homers, and batted .296. Mantle scored six runs, had three homers, drove in four, and hit .250 to cap off his phenomenal season. Yankee pitchers, led by Ford, Kucks, Larsen, and Turley, posted a cumulative 2.48 ERA.

Hodges topped Dodger hitters with five runs scored, one homer, eight RBIs, and a .304 batting average. Snider scored five runs, had a homer, and drove in four, while also hitting .304. In what proved to be his final games with Brooklyn, Robinson scored five runs, hit a homer, had two RBIs, and batted .250. Maglie pitched well in his two starts, Labine threw twelve scoreless innings, and Bessent proved impressive as well. However, Erskine and Craig got roughed up, while Newcombe's two starts were simply disastrous, making him 0–4 in World Series competition, with an 8.59 ERA.

*****

Tributes to Mickey Mantle's brilliant season continued to pour forth. *The Sporting News* named him its American League Player of the Year and picked Milwaukee's Henry Aaron as the National League recipient. The top pitchers chosen were Chicago White Sox left-hander Billy Pierce and Brooklyn's Don Newcombe. *The Sporting News* also named its 32d annual All-Star team, leaving off "Stan Musial, Willie Mays, Al Kaline," and "Duke Snider, four of baseball's brightest luminaries and hardest hitters." The infield included catcher Yogi Berra, Cincinnati first baseman Ted Kluszewski, Chicago second baseman Nellie Fox, St. Louis third baseman Ken Boyer, Detroit shortstop Harvey Kuenn, outfielders Mantle, picked by 208 of 211 writers, Aaron, and Boston's Ted Williams, and pitchers Pierce, Newcombe, and Whitey Ford. Mantle was the lone player to be selected unanimously to the United Press' American League All-Star squad, which included fellow outfielders Williams and Detroit's Kaline, catcher Berra, Boston first baseman Mickey Vernon, Fox, Detroit third baseman Ray Boone, Kuenn, Pierce, and Ford.[43]

Amazingly, three out of 205 voters failed to place Mantle on their ballots delivered to the Baseball Writers' Association of America. He was joined in the outfield by Williams and Aaron. Other selections included Kluszewski, Fox, Boyer, Kuenn, Brooklyn's Newcombe, and Pierce. The second team was made up of St. Louis first baseman Musial, New York Giant second baseman Red Schoendienst, Milwaukee third baseman Eddie Mathews, Cincinnati shortstop Roy McMillan, Snider, Mays, Cincinnati outfielder Frank Robinson, Cincinnati catcher Ed Bailey, Maglie, and Ford.[44]

The Baseball Writers Association named the American League Most Valuable Player, with Mantle becoming only the second individual to receive all the first-place votes. Finishing behind Mantle were Berra, Kaline, Kuenn, Pierce, and Williams. Awards continued pouring in, including the announcement that Mickey had been chosen by sportswriters and broadcasters as 1956's outstanding male athlete. He easily outdistanced sprinter Bobby Morrow, winner of three gold medals at the Summer Olympics in Melbourne, heavyweight boxing champion Floyd Patterson, and basketball star Bill Russell, who led the University of San Francisco to the NCAA championship and the US Olympic team to a gold medal. Coming in fifth was Don Larsen of perfect no-hitter fame.[45]

The Sporting News named its Men of the Year, including Mantle as the top player in the major leagues. The newspaper indicated, "Without Mickey Mantle, it is questionable if the Yankees would have won the American League pennant, despite their long lead. With him, they had almost a one-man team," leading "the league in nearly every department and was among the leaders in those he did not lead." He did so and engaged in a season-long "assault on the home run record" notwithstanding "an ailing leg that bothered him all season." Additionally, 24-year-old Mantle had "a lot of time in which to surpass his own records and many others."[46]

The New York Chapter of the Baseball Writers Association of America named Mantle its player of the year, making him the tenth Yankee, including Lou Gehrig, Bill Dickey, Phil Rizzuto, Allie Reynolds, and Joe DiMaggio, who was twice selected, honored during the Mercer Award's 27-year history. The *New York Times*' Roscoe McGowan noted, "Mantle also completes the cycle of modern, great New York center fielders to get the Mercer award," Mays and Snider having been the last two recipients.[47]

Sportswriters and broadcasters picked Mantle to win the Hickok "professional athlete of the year," with Larsen, Patterson, Sal Maglie, and Jackie Burke, the winner of the Masters and Professional Golfers Association major tournaments, also finishing in the top five. *Sport* magazine would also name Mantle its "Man of the Year."[48]

Talk continued to abound about Mantle's chances of breaking Ruth's home run record. He predicted that Ruth's mark would likely fall within the next few years "but not by me. I had my chance this season and could not quite make it." He considered as many as a handful of present-day players, led by Duke Snider, as most apt to accomplish the feat. Expressing appreciation for Mantle's modesty, Shirley Povich indicated that during Mickey's first years with the Yankees, he operated "in the shadows of the skillful Snider . . . and the amazing Willie Mays."[49]

Mickey required "none of those conveniences," with no one able to match "the sheer power and distance of the Mantle swats." He also had the "special asset" of being a switch-hitter. Still, a very young man, his future appeared "very bright." Povich wrote, "High on everybody's list of those who could break Ruth's record, you'd have to put Mantle's name, no matter what the boy himself says."[50]

15

A Baseball Era Nears an End

During the off-season, Brooklyn's Boys of Summer lost another member, who, in many ways, was their most consequential player: Jackie Robinson. This occurred amid the kind of talk Duke Snider had spurred regarding their fans' allegiance. *Los Angeles Times* columnist Ned Cronin, perhaps privy to talk of a possible move out West, stated, "Brooklyn baseball fans are noisier than they are loyal. They built a mousetrap for the Dodgers to play in, but they certainly didn't build a better one. At least, nobody seems to be beating a path to it." The purportedly "'loyal' Dodger fans," Cronin charged, "didn't even give their club a sellout crowd in either of the last two games of the Series." In fact, "attendance was so miserable" amid "their great" pennant drive that Snider had asserted, "Brooklyn should be replanted in Texas, where it belongs."[1]

Brooklyn management, on December 13, 1956, announced the stunning, "implausible" trade of Robinson, "the dashing hero of six Dodger pennants triumphs," to the New York Giants for southpaw pitcher Dick Littlefield and cash, estimated to be between $30,000 and $50,000. Robinson, along with the Dodgers, "broke the color line in organized baseball," then he became Brooklyn's "sparkplug" and "the chief driving force behind a succession of winning Dodger teams," the *New York Times*' Joseph M. Sheehan remarked. Jackie "inevitably incurred the wrath of Giant fans" as he "became more prominently identified than any other individual with the Dodger success of the past decade."[2]

Not surprisingly, New York fans responded with dismay to news of the trade. One Dodger fan indicated, "I'm shocked to the core. This is like selling the Brooklyn-Battery Tunnel. Jackie Robinson is a synonym for the Dodgers. They can't do this to us." A Giant counterpart reacted, "I'm flabbergasted. First Durocher, now Robinson. How many enemies can we absorb?" Referring to Robinson's involvement "in the great experiment that opened the doors to dozens of his race," columnist Shirley Povich wrote, "It has been a pride-taking decade and he has been a credit to his race—the human race," a sentiment sportswriter Wendell Smith conveyed in a column years earlier.[3]

Expressing his own viewpoint, Robinson indicated, "Naturally, I'm disappointed. I've had wonderful years in Brooklyn, received wonderful treatment from the fans and made lasting friendships with the players." Then, Robinson said, "But we realize baseball is like that. We have no control over it."[4]

The *New York Times* delivered an ode, "A Pioneering Athlete: Jack Roosevelt Robinson." It began by declaring that Jackie, who had just received the Spingarn Medal, given by the NAACP annually to a distinguished Black American, "entered baseball as a social symbol" but would depart "as an authentically great and exciting player of the game." Robinson set a "trail" many other Black ballplayers followed, with only three major league teams presently fielding all-white lineups. But as the *Times* indicated, "few players of any race have had more impact of the game" with Robinson serving as "the acknowledged sparkplug of the Dodgers in their greatest era of success." He delivered "opportune hitting . . . flashy fielding and . . . daring sallies on the basepaths" to the delight of Dodger fandom. Moreover, "his intense will to win gave Jackie rare power to dominate a game or diamond situation," while "his fierce competitive spirit . . . at last unshackled" piqued controversies. Desiring "acceptance and respect," he earned those on the playing field and off.[5]

In an editorial, the *Times* referred to Robinson as having "made history" and been "one of the best players who ever wore spikes or stole second base." More significantly, the nation's leading newspaper called Robinson "a national symbol" who broke Organized Baseball's color barrier. And "the path that he opened has been walked by some splendid followers. The game is richer for its Campanella, Brooks Lawrence, Willie Mays, Ernie Banks, and a dozen others. But Robinson was the first."[6]

Soon opting to retire, Robinson explained why he was doing so in *Look* magazine, an article for which he was handsomely compensated. He revealed having agreed to join the Chock-Full-O'-Nuts restaurant chain as a vice president overseeing personnel relations. "I have to think of the future and the security of my family. At my age a man doesn't have much future in baseball and very little security. I've been thinking since I was 34 that I should be thinking of my future." Jackie said, "After you're reached your peak, there's no sentiment in baseball. You start slipping and pretty soon they're moving you around like a used car. You have no control over what happens to you. I don't want that."[7]

Even with Robinson's retirement, Black players, many but not all Negro League alumni—increasingly the case—continued to appear on most, although not all, major league rosters. Discussing the upcoming season, the *Los Angeles Sentinel*'s L.I. "Brock" Brockenbury indicated, "No one ever knows when another Willie Mays or Hank Aaron will pop out seemingly out of nowhere." The World Champion Yankees were represented by Elston Howard and seemingly disinclined to look "for others." Prior to adding Howard, the team argued it was unable to find Black ballplayers with "the character and ability" befitting the Yankees. Brockenbury flatly stated, "That is the absurdity to end all absurdities. Men like Minnie Minoso, Billy Bruton, Larry Doby, Monte Irvin, Hank Aaron, Frank Robinson, Roy Campanella, Junior Gilliam could fit into any system," no matter its "most ignorant and bigoted white players." The columnist then wrote, "I can understand why some of them couldn't stand Jackie Robinson (but it can't be on character, because there is not a cleaner-living athlete anywhere than Jackie), because he doesn't know how to 'stay in his place.'"

Neither the Detroit Tigers nor the Boston Red Sox had yet to field a Black player. Indicating, "Phooey!!" Brockenbury mentioned Robinson's begging Boston for a tryout in 1945 and his supposedly failing to impress the team's "bigwigs." Detroit, the columnist said, "is said to be worse in many respects than Jackson, Mississippi. But it is shocking to see the way Boston acts."[8]

*****

One week following the announcement of the trade of baseball pioneer Jackie Robinson, the 381-day-long bus boycott in Montgomery, Alabama, led by Dr. Martin Luther King Jr. and other civil rights activists, ended. On that day, the US Supreme Court upheld a federal court ruling in Montgomery that the Fourteenth Amendment prohibited legislation mandating public buses to be racially segregated. Backed by the Black community, King terminated the boycott, which had demonstrated the potency of mass nonviolent direct action. The following day, integration of Montgomery buses began, although violence and intimidation, including snipers shooting at buses and bombs laid by KKK members, hardly abated. Bombers targeted the homes of civil rights leaders, including Dr. King's. On January 23, Klansmen grabbed 24-year-old Willie Edwards Jr., a married Winn-Dixie driver with two young daughters. They forced Edwards, said to be dating a white woman, to leap from a bridge to his death.

Prominent white residents of Montgomery strengthened Jim Crow practices wherever they could. A new city ordinance declared it "unlawful for white and colored persons to play together or, in company with each other." It listed "any game of cards, dice, dominoes, checkers, pool, billiards, softball, basketball, baseball, football, golf, trace, and at swimming pools, beaches, lakes or ponds or any other game or games or athletic contests, either indoors or outdoors."

Dr. King joined other civil rights activists in establishing the Southern Christian Leadership Conference, based in Atlanta, Georgia. It was intended to aid local groups in battling Jim Crow edicts and discriminatory practices. Relying on nonviolent resistance, those leaders, many based in Southern Black churches, sought to redeem "the soul of America."[9]

*****

The team that had broken Organized Baseball's racial barrier, the Brooklyn Dodgers, and its league archrival, the New York Giants, confronted swirling rumors of possible franchise shifts. Such speculation had long existed. During the 1953 pennant chase, Dodger president Walter O'Malley fended off reports of a move out West. "Let me quickly say that the invitation is not being considered," he declared. "The Dodgers are mighty fortunate to be in

Brooklyn. I trust this statement will close speculation as irreparable harm could be done to the Pacific Coast franchise which we respect."[10]

On November 15, 1954, New York Giants' president Horace Stoneham pushed back at gossip regarding a franchise shift. "There is nothing, absolutely nothing to it," he declared. "Our lease" at the Polo Grounds "runs through 1964." Stoneham wondered, "why should the Giants be interested in moving" to California? "How could we possibly build up so strong a rivalry there as the one we enjoy here with the Dodgers? Why, one third of our season's crowds is attracted by the New York-Brooklyn series."[11]

NL President Warren C. Giles fended off a report about a possible Dodger shift, stating, "It never has been suggested to me that the Brooklyn club be moved to Los Angeles." He asked, "How could we have one club out there and the other seven way back here?" Initiating a campaign to "keep the Dodgers in Brooklyn," the Brooklyn Junior Chamber of Commerce pledged, "We are not going to let what happened to the Philadelphia Athletics, Boston Braves and St. Louis Browns hit the Dodgers."[12]

Responding to the latest scuttlebutt, O'Malley declared, "What the future holds, I don't know. But there is no league discussion scheduled to discuss moving the club and I have no present plans to move or sell." O'Malley admitted he had considered the possibility of heading out West "some time ago. At the time I was interested only in the extreme future."[13]

At one point, the Brooklyn boss acknowledged, "However, what the future holds for us I just wouldn't know. We are confronted by two serious problems. One is at the turnstiles. The other, which you might say dovetails with the first, has to do with the parking situation at Ebbets Field. We are giving a great deal of thought to both."[14]

During an informal session on August 19, 1955, with Robert Wagner, attended by some of the New York City mayor's aides, O'Malley warned that both the Dodgers and the Giants, unless new baseball stadiums were constructed, might have to relocate. Obviously having consulted with Stoneham, O'Malley stated, "If anybody went, the two teams would go." He added, "But that doesn't mean we couldn't play in the general area of New York City." Wagner responded, "We want to help you."

Just days earlier, O'Malley revealed the Dodgers' intention to play a series of games in Jersey City during 1957 and to abandon Ebbets Field following that season. The Dodgers were willing, O'Malley indicated, to put up $6 million to build a ballpark with a seating capacity of 50,000 and stood ready to purchase the necessary real estate. The team's financial backers, O'Malley offered, would "stand the gaff two more years" only. Stoneham telegrammed Wagner, expressing similar concerns about the Polo Grounds.[15]

The following spring, Stoneham acknowledged he had been considering moving his team to Minneapolis. He also expressed interest in designs by New York City planners to construct "a huge stadium on Manhattan's West Side [to] house the Giants."[16]

During a press conference at the Statler Hotel in Los Angeles on the evening of October 11, 1956, O'Malley explained why the Dodgers were not moving there. Over the past decade, Brooklyn had the MLB's highest attendance record other than the New York Yankees. "Substantial progress" was occurring regarding building a new ballpark in Brooklyn. His "good friend Phil Wrigley" owned a Pacific Coast League based in Los Angeles, "and I wouldn't be guilty of invading a friend's territory."[17]

But during late December, O'Malley conveyed "disappointment" on learning that a mere $25,000, not the $280,000 requested, had been allocated by the NYC Board of Estimates to the Brooklyn Sports Center Authority to conduct a study regarding a new ballpark. In early February, O'Malley informed municipal officials, "Unless something is done within six months, I will have to make other arrangements. There is still a short time left before we could be forced to take an irrevocable step to commit the Dodgers elsewhere." He insisted, "We want to stay in Brooklyn and our Dodger fans want us to stay in Brooklyn, and that's where we should be allowed to continue."[18]

During early January, the Brooklyn Dodgers bought a 44-seat passenger plane. Asked if that portended a westward move, O'Malley replied, "If any club should go to the West Coast, it would have to fly and it would have to own an airplane. But our future for the time being in in Brooklyn."[19]

As the Dodgers trained at Vero Beach, Florida, Brooklyn management announced having purchased Wrigley Field in Los Angeles and territorial rights, along with the swapping of Brooklyn's minor league team in Fort

Worth for Philip K. Wrigley's Pacific Coast franchise. The Dodgers, O'Malley indicated, continued to hope for "a new downtown sports center in Brooklyn," although scant progress had occurred. He also asserted, "I haven't been bluffing. I have had one objective in all my thinking—to put a new stadium in Brooklyn. I have tried to make people aware that a serious condition faced us in Brooklyn, an inadequate and outmoded park and especially the lack of parking facilities." While affirming, "We are not at a point now where we are considering shifting the franchise to Los Angeles," O'Malley soon indicated the team would likely conduct a series of exhibition games there in 1958.[20]

Mayor Wagner acknowledged being "deeply disturbed" by talk of the Dodgers' possible departure. He telegrammed O'Malley, "I realize that the problem of appropriate facilities poses serious problems for the Dodger management. As you know, I have been deeply concerned with the problem." Wagner hoped his administration could "aid in its solution." O'Malley stated, "We trust he will have the full support" from city officials for "time is running out."[21]

Toward the end of March, Wagner continued to believe New York City could retain the Dodgers notwithstanding "'cold war' threats by Walter O'Malley." But negotiations between the Brooklyn owner and Los Angeles Mayor Norris Poulson and parallel discussions involving Stoneham and San Francisco Mayor George Christopher proceeded apace.[22]

*****

That same month amid spring training, *Sports Illustrated* displayed on its cover the Yankee slugger running and featured an article by Gerald Holland, "The Real Mickey Mantle." The magazine also contained, along with commentary, accompanying sketches by the artist Robert Riger, who was impressed by "the consistency and rhythm of Mickey Mantle's power." Notable, the essay indicated, was the speed of the "fastest man in baseball." Then there was the defensive prowess, thanks to "one of the strongest arms in the major leagues" and "his wide range in center field." Baseball's "biggest attraction" was "watched by everyone, players and fans alike, when his turn comes to take his practice swing."[23]

Referring to Mantle as the Hero with a "great, powerful body," Holland pointed to Mickey's "magic numeral on" the back of his Yankee uniform but also "his right leg bandaged from ankle to thigh, a plastic shield protecting an arrested bone infection . . . osteomyelitis on his left ankle." Now 25, the Hero was

> already a legend. By his deeds and by his courageous triumph over his physical handicaps, he was Everybody's dream miraculously come to life. He was being hailed as baseball's alltime superstar. He could do everything: he could run with the speed of a jack rabbit, he could throw strikes to home plate from deep in the outfield; a switch-hitter, he could blast a ball farther than any man who ever lived. He was Elmer the great, Frank Merriwell and a blond Li'l Abner rolled into one. He was a Walter Mitty vision for every man to see. He was a baseball scout's favorite fantasy in the flesh: a spring that had been blooming on a sandlot in the back country, a free agent with no strings on him, a kid to whom $1,100 offered as a bonus for signing looked like all the money in Oklahoma.

The minimal amount had enabled his team, the world's wealthiest baseball club, to acquire him at little cost. It also allowed Mickey to avoid the fate of toiling in lead mines or mills. From an athletic vantage point, linking up with the New York Yankees provided "a proper arena for his magnificent talents and a proud tradition for him to rise to, the uniform of Ruth and Gehrig and DiMaggio to inspire him and the incomparable baseball wizardry of old Casey Stengel to draw out and to nourish his wondrous native skills."

Following his sixth season in the major leagues, "the Hero, Mickey Charles Mantle, had left the country boy far behind." He had become the Yankees "great center fielder . . . the Homer Run King," who had won both the Triple Crown and the MVP, as well as an array of other awards. He had also become involved in a series of business endeavors, "drove a brand-new Lincoln," had an agent and a lawyer to negotiate commercial deals and investments. Pals like Billy Martin, with whom he roomed for away games, and Whitey Ford, "knew where the laughs were."[24]

*****

Yet again, baseball experts tagged the Dodgers and Yankees as pennant favorites. A recent trade between the Yankees and Athletics appeared only to strengthen the World Series titleholders. The key figures in the 13-player deal included infielder Billy Hunter and outfielder Irv Noren, swapped to Kansas City, and pitchers Art Ditmar and Bobby Shantz, the 1952 AL MVP, going to New York.[25]

This time around, both Charles Dexter and Hal Middlesworth indicated that the Dodgers and Yankees had excellent pitchers, catchers, and infielders, along with good outfielders. Dexter did not view Jackie Robinson's departure as insurmountable, with Brooklyn's returning veterans, other than an ailing Carl Erskine, viewed as "top-ranking" and its farm system said to contain "promising prospects." The Giants, whether due to "bad luck or mismanagement," seemed "heading into the doldrums." The Yankees possessed "a wealth of pitching, a catcher without peer, plenty of candidates" at third base, and center fielder Mantle.[26]

Also likely to help the Yankees' bid to retain their title was rookie Tony Kubek, a heralded youngster capable of playing several positions in either the infield or outfield. Deemed New York's latest "wonder boy," the 20-year-old Kubek was said to have had the greatest impact on a Yankee training camp since Mickey six years earlier. Arthur Daley reported, "He has the other ballplayers raving and Casey Stengel talking more incoherently than usual, although he was yet to be listed on the team roster.[27]

Roscoe McGowen also picked Brooklyn, with its mixture of "old pros" and "accomplished youngsters," to repeat as the National League champion. Talk could be heard, McGowen said, of the Dodgers "growing old," with Snider, Hodges, Campanella, Furillo, and Reese all in their thirties, although Duke and Gil hardly seemed to have aged. Sal Maglie was soon to turn 40, and Erskine was "a slight question mark," while Don Newcombe, notwithstanding his October debacles, "still rates as No. 1." Other prospective starters included Johnny Podres, the 1955 World Series hero returning from military service, Roger Craig, ace reliever Clem Labine, and 20-year-old Don Drysdale. Sandy Koufax, whose control appeared to have improved, was another possible starter. All in all, the Dodgers remained "a championship team until it is proved otherwise," McGowen insisted.[28]

Arthur Daley placed Philadelphia, New York, and Chicago at the bottom of his projected NL standings, behind improving Pittsburgh. "The hard-luck team of the year," the New York Giants, had lost "budding stars" Jackie Brandt and Bill White, as well as "the gifted" prospect Willie Kirkland, to the US Army; both White and Kirkland would likely have been Negro League veterans had they been a little younger. St. Louis seemed slated for the last spot in the first division, with Cincinnati, Milwaukee, and Brooklyn ready to repeat their quest for the pennant and likely to finish in that order.[29]

One reason why Daley and other analysts were downgrading the Dodgers was the aging of the team roster, notwithstanding the recent addition of several younger players. Even with Robinson's absence, the core, dating back to 1949, included Reese, Hodges, Snider, Furillo, Campanella, Newcombe, and Erskine. Those eight had helped guide Brooklyn to five pennants in eight seasons, along with the 1955 World Series title. Now, as Daley put it, "the Brooks may not exactly qualify as the Nine Old Men, but they ain't boys." This stood in sharp contrast to their fierce American League rivals, the New York Yankees, who had adopted platooning, endured retirements or trades of longtime stars, drawn on aging veterans, added a superstar like Mantle, and incorporated other promising young players throughout Casey Stengel's tenure. The Yankee skipper bragged, "What few people has [sic] noticed is that I been winnin' while rebuildin' the ball club. Nobody ever done that before." Even longtime catcher Yogi Berra was only 31, in contrast to several key Dodgers.[30]

Stengel selected his own team to win the American League pennant while admitting that other teams had improved. He singled out Kubek, indicating he "can play any position, outfield or short. I'm not sick at the way he has done things." Casey also acknowledged he "never had so many in my life, not so many good ones, anyway," referring to the Yankee pitchers. Extolling his ball club's spirit, he stated, "Around here they either have that, or, if they don't there are other men for the jobs."[31]

Las Vegas betting odds made the Yankees "prohibitive favorites at odds of 2–5," with the Braves and Dodgers "co-favorites at 6–5," to win their respective pennants. Baseball experts made the Yanks the easy, all-but unanimous choice in the American League, while narrowly choosing the Braves over the Dodgers and the Redlegs. Shirley Povich wrote, "The Yankees, off by themselves. The

Dodgers in jeopardy but winning by as much as it takes." The additions of Kubek, Ditmar, and Shantz, he reasoned, only strengthened the league's "most powerful . . . most flexible . . . team with the most self-assurance." The Dodgers, "older but . . . not dead," also seemed improved due to Podres's return, although they needed to overcome the departure "of Jackie Robinson, their clutch guy." The Braves had the NL's "best and deepest pitching and the three most dangerous hitters on any club in Aaron, Mathews and Adcock." The Giants had a promising rookie in second baseman Andre Rodgers—the first player from the Bahamas to make the NL or AL—along with Willie Mays, Red Schoendienst, and Don Mueller. They had also just added Hank Sauer, the 1952 NL MVP who had hit 41 homers as recently as 1954 prior to two injury-plagued seasons.[32]

Thirty-one baseball analysts cast ballots for the *American Weekly*'s preseason poll, with all but one picking the Yankees in the AL but dividing their votes among the Braves, Redlegs, and Dodgers, with most picking Milwaukee in the NL. The baseball writers proved impressed with the Yanks' "devastating crew," led by "the powerful middle line of Yogi Berra, Gil McDougald and Mickey Mantle," along with a deep pitching staff. The Braves were believed to have the NL's top pitching staff, formidable hitters topped by Aaron, along with sadly earned "maturity and experience" from their blown lead the previous season. Brooklyn appeared weakened by the loss of Robinson, Campanella's injured hand, and Newcombe's World Series failures.[33]

*****

Just as the baseball world had fixated on Willie Mays, Duke Snider, and Mickey Mantle during the past three seasons as they conducted chases, however abbreviated in the first two instances, on Babe Ruth's single-season home run record, statistics continued to fascinate onlookers. Of current players who had competed in more than 500 games, 15 had lifetime batting averages of at least .300, topped by Ted Williams's .348 and Stan Musial's .340. The three great New York City center fielders were all in the mix, with Mickey Mantle perched at .308 and both Duke Snider and Willie Mays at .306. With 2,781 hits, Musial stood poised to move into the top ten, thereby surpassing George Sisler, Babe Ruth, Mel Ott, Al Simmons, and Rogers Hornsby. Both Musial and Williams were already in the top ten career home run leaders, Stan's 352 placing him ninth, while Ted's 418 landed him in fifth, behind only Ruth, Jimmie Foxx, Ott, and Lou Gehrig. Snider (276) and Gil Hodges (271) stood poised to join the 13-man list of 300-home run hitters. Moving up fast were Mantle and Eddie Mathews, each having delivered more homers than any 25-year-old player. Early Wynn (221), Warren Spahn (203), and Bob Lemon (201) were the only 200-win pitchers.[34]

Dissecting New York City's center fielders, A. S. "Doc" Young, a leading African American sports columnist, narrowed his discussion to Mays or Mantle regarding who was "the greatest." Contesting most recent analyses, Young opted for Mays, declaring him "the world's greatest player . . . because he can do more things well than any other player living." Referring to the previous season when Mays hit 36 homers and stole 40 bases, Young wrote, "There never has been another slugger in the game who possessed Willie's ability to pilfer the sacks." Young admitted that Mantle's 1956 campaign had been brilliant but called it Mickey's "first super season." He also acknowledged that Mantle might be "stronger than Mays," although Willie's home ballpark required "nothing short of a cannon shot" to "reach the center field wall."

While long depicted as "the mild-mannered, laugh-it-up, great-natural player," Mays was fiercely competitive, exuding "a burning zeal for victory." Returning to his comparison of Mays and Mantle, Young stated the switch-hitting Yankee had greater power but asked who was "a better center fielder? A more powerful, or accurate, thrower? A finer baserunner? A more competitive athlete?" Furthermore, Mantle remained brittle and benefited "from the Yankees' power-packed lineup. Mays, by contrast, had no teammates opposing pitchers feared, "power-wise." He remained, Young concluded, "baseball's greatest player," which he would definitively prove this season or "before he's finished."[35]

16

The New York City Dynasty Winds to a Close

At the start of the 1957 major league season, the biggest baseball news occurred away from the sports field. On April 18, the New York City Park Commission, with Robert Moses taking the lead, offered 78 acres in Queens' Flushing Meadows sector. The Dodgers could purportedly build their "dream-stage, plastic-domed ball park" accommodating 50,000 fans there, a dozen miles from Manhattan's midtown. Walter O'Malley responded, "I have an open mind. I am willing to listen to more about it." He also pointed to the Los Angeles freeway network's abutting a ballpark's proposed site in Chavez Ravine.[1]

Brooklyn leaders, including borough president John Cashmore, expressed outrage at Moses's plan. Cashmore asserted, "I'm still wholly for the proposal to keep the Dodgers in Brooklyn," as fans, enraged about a possible franchise shift, indicated, "It should never happen!" O'Malley indicated, "If and when this latest reported possibility ever achieves political maturity, I will be pleased to discuss it in detail."[2]

On the evening of May 10, the *New York Post* indicated O'Malley had informed officials in Los Angeles that the Dodgers "definitely will play all their 1958 home games at the" LA. Coliseum. Fearing "possible disastrous effects on Brooklyn home attendance," O'Malley refused "to dignify" that report.[3]

San Francisco Mayor George Christopher quickly revealed an agreement with Horace Stoneham suggesting the Giants' relocation to his city in 1958. Stoneham expressed a desire, "everything else being equal," to remain back

East. Following Commissioner Ford Frick's directive, he declared, "It is not the time to even discuss any franchise transfers."[4]

Following a unanimous vote by team owners, NL President Warren C. Giles explained, "If New York and Brooklyn request consent before Oct. 1 to relocate their franchises in San Francisco and Los Angeles, respectively," he was "authorized to grant it." New York Mayor Robert Wagner responded, "We want both clubs to stay in New York. . . . We feel they are part of the city and we'll continue to do all we can to make them want to stay here." But he warned that the municipality "will not be blackjacked into anything."[5]

*****

On May 17, the Prayer Pilgrimage to Washington for Freedom occurred in the nation's capital, with more than 30,000 participants congregating at the Lincoln Memorial. The purpose was to commemorate the 1954 US Supreme Court ruling, Brown v. the Board of Education, and to maintain the fight for the integration of segregated schools. A. Philip Randolph, Bayard Rustin, and SCLC's Ella Baker helped to organize the gathering, which featured talks, prayers, songs, and biblical offerings by leading Black figures. The gospel singer Mahalia Jackson offered "Keep-A-Trustin," while Harry Belafonte also performed. Speakers included NAACP Executive Director Roy Wilkins, Howard University President Mordecai Johnson, and Dr. Martin Luther King Jr., who demanded, "Give Us the Ballot."[6]

*****

Amid ongoing reports of possible franchise shifts, the MLB season, of course, continued with Chicago and Cincinnati atop their respective leagues. Chicago's 26–11 record was four games ahead of New York in the AL. Cincinnati's 26–14 mark was two games better than Brooklyn and another half-game ahead of Milwaukee, with New York eight and a half back in the NL. Heating up, Mickey Mantle scored 27 runs, hit 8 homers, had 20 RBIs, gathered 29 walks, and batted .376 that month. An improving Duke Snider had 16 runs scored, 6 homers, 15 RBIs, 15 walks, and a .284 batting average. Willie Mays scored 16 runs, hit 4 homers, drove in 14 runs, walked 14 times, and batted .352.

While Snider garnered some news on May 26 for swatting a homer that happened to be the 1500th hit of his career and helped to beat the Giants, 5–3, at Ebbets Field, Mantle and Mays received publicity for other reasons. Ten days earlier, at 2:30 in the morning, Mantle's teammate and friend Hank Bauer got into a fracas with another patron at the Copacabana, a nightclub favored by Yankees players, with several gathered to celebrate Billy Martin's 29th birthday. Asked if he had belted the man, Bauer, mired in a slump that had him batting .203, reacted, "Hit him? Why, I haven't hit anybody all year." Forty-year-old Edward Jones, the injured party and a Bronx delicatessen owner, admitted, "I love the guy, anyway," although his attorney envisioned a lucrative civil suit.[7]

Casey Stengel removed Whitey Ford, an attendee, from pitching that night, benched the .200 hitting Berra, kept Martin sidelined, and slid Bauer into his lineup's eighth spot. Mickey and Johnny Kucks had also been at the party, which had been attended by the players' wives, but not Jean Martin. Bauer was subsequently charged with felony assault.[8]

Mays was attracting nearly as much attention for his base-stealing as his other feats on the playing field. Like Jackie Robinson earlier, Mays appeared to be reintroducing "the art of base-stealing," having led the majors in 1956 and poised to do so again. Consequently, the *New York Times*' John Drebinger noted, "Willie almost single-handedly has added luster and liveliness to a second-division ball club, something his home run hitting alone could never accomplish."[9]

*****

On June 1, Representative Emanuel Celler, whose 11th congressional district included portions of southern Brooklyn, insisted on investigating the proposed franchise moves. Declaring open hearings starting during the middle of the month, Celler charged that O'Malley and Stoneman had "been inconsistent" in asserting, "Baseball is a sport," thereby "not subject to antitrust regulations." They insisted on their right to shift "franchises in the interest of dollars, selling to the highest bidder." Chairman Celler, a Brooklyn resident and Dodger devotee, quipped, "If that isn't business, I'd like to know what is." The House Judiciary Committee, he indicated, would seek financial information from the two teams, which had demanded "taxpayers' money . . . be spent" for new baseball stadiums.[10]

All the while, Los Angeles inhabitants were told that the Dodger transfer was "cinched" with O'Malley "ready to pack his pack" and civic leaders said to "Hail Bums." What also seemed increasingly certain was MLB's long-sought expansion, with Minneapolis, Toronto, Montreal, Dallas, Houston, and Denver prime targets. A supporter of expansion, Commissioner Ford Frick also favored creating a third major league. He foresaw "a major league setup" ranging across the United States that would unfold "in orderly and proper fashion," absent "loose and irresponsible talk."[11]

New York Times columnist Arthur Daley wondered what Mayor Wagner could offer to prevent franchise shifts. The "shrewd" O'Malley, Daley suggested, had actually "put baseball in an awkward spot," providing Congressman Celler with "solid ammunition for a change" and bolstering his argument "that baseball is more business than sport in relation to antitrust law." After all, the Boston Braves, St. Louis Browns, and Philadelphia Athletics were "dying franchises in need of transfusion." The Brooklyn ball club, by contrast, was "a money maker," and O'Malley appeared primed for a move not to become "healthy but to make him wealthy." Daley was more critical still of Stoneham, who loved the Giants but had allowed "his franchise go to seed" and apparently had received fewer assurances regarding a move.[12]

Following a meeting with Mayor Wagner on June 4, O'Malley indicated he had been "offered . . . 'nothing' in the way of a new park." At the session, both the Dodger owner and Stoneham informed Wagner they had "no commitments either to go or to stay." But O'Malley warned, "If the situation isn't changed in six weeks, I will be even more discouraged than I am now." He stated, "I have always in the past wanted to keep the Dodgers in Brooklyn where they belong, but now I'm not so sure." The mayor promised to continue meeting with the two baseball moguls, promising to do "all within reason" to help keep their teams in New York City. An unnamed city official, present at the meeting, appeared convinced that the Dodgers and Giants were relocating.[13]

Testifying to the House Judiciary Subcommittee on June 19, Commissioner Frick declared that "no one knows" if such a move were taking place. "They are in the process of negotiation and it may go this way or it may go that way." Congressman Celler questioned Frick's pronouncement that the "constant scrutiny of an interested and sometime enraged public" afforded a degree of regulation of baseball, stating, "Sometimes the public doesn't know what's going on in the sport." The subcommittee soon revealed that financial statements indicated the Dodgers had made a profit each year over a five-year span, amounting to $1,860,744, while the Giants had accumulated an overall profit of $242,602, with profits each of the past three years.[14]

On June 26, O'Malley declared before the House Judiciary Subcommittee, "The place for the Dodgers is in Brooklyn." He indicated the team would not leave provided it obtained land in the borough suitable for constructing a stadium with a seating capacity of 50,000, along with "adequate parking facilities at Atlantic and Flatbush Aves." But he backtracked, stating a decision would be made when the season concluded. Afterward, O'Malley exclaimed, "The jig is up in Brooklyn," and declared that the "only thing" able to keep the Dodgers there was "a new ball park in downtown Brooklyn." He responded, "I do not know the answer" when Congressman Cellar asked, "Will the Dodgers play in Los Angeles next year?"[15]

Celler quickly expressed his belief that the Dodgers were headed for Los Angeles. "There's no question about it. I think Mr. O'Malley has his mind made up to go. It's all cut and dried." Representative Kenneth B. Keating, a Republican member of Celler's subcommittee, blamed city officials for having "flubbed it."[16]

*****

During June, the New York Yankees, with a record of 44–25, regained their usual position at the top of the American League standings. That put them a game in front of the Chicago White Sox, with both the Cleveland Indians and the Boston Red Sox seven games back. Over in the National League, the Milwaukee Braves, at 42–29, were only a half-game better than the Cincinnati Reds, with the St. Louis Cardinals two and a half games back, the 37–32 Brooklyn Dodgers four behind, with the 36–36 New York Giants mired in sixth place, although only six and a half games out of first.

That month, Mantle scored 31 runs, hit 11 homers, had 30 RBIs, gathered 31 walks, 8 of them intentional, and batted .419; his season-long batting average stood at a blistering .359. Still not playing at his normal level, Snider had 15 runs, 6 homers, 19 RBIs, 11 walks, and a .279 B.A. to leave his batting average at .268. Mays collected 26 runs, 8 doubles, 6 triples, 6 homers, 24 RBIs, and 21 walks, while hitting .300, making his average for the 1957 season .321.

The impact of the Copacabana incident continued to linger, with five of the players involved—Mantle, Martin, Bauer, Berra, and Ford—saddled with fines of $1000 apiece by Yankee management. Kucks was fined half that amount, probably owing to his considerably lower salary. Displeased by being labeled a "bad boy," Martin wondered, "What makes a 'bad boy.' All I know is that I'll play my heart out for Stengel at all times. I am 100 per cent loyal to him." He was more distressed after being traded, along with three other players, to the Kansas City Athletics for three players, including pitcher Ryne Duren and outfielder Harry Simpson; the acquisition of Simpson doubled the number of Black players on the Yankee roster. That followed a recent melee Martin had been involved in against the Chicago White Sox. The New York front office was said to be unhappy with the purported influence Martin had over Mantle.[17]

In a lighter vein, the *Los Angeles Sentinel* posed the question, "Which is the fastest, a hard-hit baseball or Willie Mays?" Having watched Mays snare a "screaming line drive" by Pittsburgh's Roberto Clemente, the Giants' bullpen coach, Bucky Walters, insisted Willie "out-ran the baseball." With the catch lauded by baseball experts, Willie called it "the best I ever made," outdoing his famous grab of the Vic Wertz smash in Game One of the 1954 World Series. In the Pirates' contest with runs on first and second and only one out, Clemente slammed the ball toward left center field, Mays "turned and ran like a scalded rabbit, turning just as he approached the wall to stick up his gloves and snear the ball into the webbing." Driven into the wall, Mays "pushed himself away and rifled his ball" back "to the infield," not allowing the runners to advance.[18]

*****

On July 17, Horace Stoneham informed the House Antitrust Subcommittee that he would favor the Giants' relocation if San Francisco delivered a positive proposal, regardless of what the Dodgers decided. New York City, Stoneham insisted, "cannot support" three big league clubs as "the baseball population has been moving outside the city," and he admitted the city was unable to address his team's concerns. Those included "inadequate transportation and parking facilities."[19]

The Giants' owner soon announced, "This is our last year in the Polo Grounds—no matter where we go." He did indicate, "If the city would build a suitable stadium in the Baychester area and permit the Giants to play there at a reasonable rental, we would have to consider such a proposition." Stoneham stated, "I have been in this city for more than fifty years and sentimentally I have more attachment to the Giants than any of the stockholders. But I think, when I show them how much more money we can make elsewhere, they will recognize it."[20]

The columnist John Drebinger deemed Stoneham's comments, lacking artifice, to be "refreshing," no matter "how painful." The Giants, on September 29, would depart from the Polo Grounds, once home to "John McGraw, Christy Mathewson, Billy Terry, Carl Hubbell and Mel Ott." Drebinger discussed MLB's attendance problems as Cleveland was experiencing. Shortly following the Second World War, the Indians' "huge, modern stadium" had welcomed over 2.5 million fans one year, but during the present season they might not attract 600,000. Receipts from radio and television helped, but problems at the turnstiles continued. When even top teams involved in "a sizzling pennant race" brought out "3,000 in the afternoon and 9,000 at night, brother, you've had it," Drebinger reasoned. "The Polo Grounds is dead."[21]

The Dodgers' vice president, Buzzie Bavasi, admitted, "If you had asked me a month ago, I would have said 'not a chance.' You're asking me now. It looks as though the city fathers are making it necessary for us to move." Nevertheless, he indicated that the team continued to anticipate municipal plans "for a projected development at Atlantic and Flatbush Avenues" in Brooklyn. He seemed displeased with Robert Moses, who wanted the Dodgers to look at Flushing Meadows in Queens as a potential spot for a stadium. Moses, for his part, expressed concern that the team "never made a firm offer to pay a sufficient rental" for a ballpark.[22]

*****

By the end of July, the Yankees, with their 65–34 record, were three and a half games ahead of the White Sox in the American League, while the Red Sox had fallen 11 games behind. The 59–40 Cardinals and the 60–41 Braves were virtually tied in the National League, two ahead of the 57–42 Dodgers, four in front of both the Redlegs and the Phillies. The 44–57 Giants were 16 games behind.

During the month, Mantle scored 31 runs, hit 7 homers, drove in 20 runs, walked 42 times, and hit .295. Picking up his pace, Snider scored 24 runs, hit 11 homers, had 21 RBIs, walked the same number of times, and batted .326. Mays had 15 runs scored, 6 homers, 13 RBIs, 10 walks, and hit .307. Mantle and Mays were selected as starters for the All-Star Game, but Snider, for the first time in eight years, was not chosen. Mantle's teammate, Yogi Berra, was also picked as a starter, while AL manager Casey Stengel named six other Yankees: pitchers Bobby Shantz and Bob Grim, catcher Elston Howard, and infielders Bill Skowron, Bobby Richardson, and Gil McDougald. The National League roster included Brooklyn's pitcher Clem Labine, first baseman Gil Hodges, and left fielder Gino Cimoli, and New York's pitcher Johnny Antonelli, along with Mays.[23]

At the season's halfway point, Mantle was leading the American League with a .369 batting average, while having hit 22 homers. That was fewer than the National League batting leader, Milwaukee's Henry Aaron, who was batting .347 with 27 homers, on a pace with Babe Ruth's total in 1927. On July 23, Mantle hit for the cycle, including his 26th homer, a 465-foot smash at Yankee Stadium, as New York beat the White Sox, 10–6. Mantle's four hits enabled him to regain the AL batting lead, at .367, over Ted Williams, who led the home run chase by one.[24]

No matter, several old-timers viewed Mays as superior to Mantle, Snider, and every other present-day major leaguer. The *Los Angeles Sentinel* presented an article titled "Willie Mays Must Be the Mostest—Say Top Greats." It deemed Mays's "daring on the base paths and feats afield . . . unparalleled even by such former greats as Ty Cobb, Bob Meusel and . . . Joe DiMaggio." Frankie Frisch stated, "He and Joe DiMaggio are the greatest centerfielders I ever saw. But Joe couldn't run the bases as well; he wasn't as daring as Willie." Frisch added, "I would pay money just to see him (Mays) play. He brings the old days for a fellow like myself." The Hall of Fame inductee asked, "How about that arm? It's the greatest I ever saw." Another former player and manager, Jimmie Dykes, said Mays was "one of the greatest I ever saw," a superior center fielder to Tris Speaker with a much better arm. Dykes then offered, "I think Mays is a better all-around player than Ty Cobb. Ty couldn't field in Mays' class."[25]

In a column for the *New York Times*, John Drebinger declared that Mantle and Mays were "the two greatest ballplayers of today," leaving out of the discussion Duke Snider, who previously would have been considered. But Snider, although hitting better in July, was still not performing at the level of the other two New York City center fielders. Focusing on Mantle and Mays, Drebinger wrote,

> Mantle is a fine fielder, can throw hard and in getting down to first base is just about the fastest human on a ball field. But it is at the plate that the Oklahoma Kid outstrips all rivals. He could develop into the most devastating hitter the game ever has known. Mantle's ability to swing from either side of the plate alone gives him a tremendous advantage. The Switcher has exploded record shots in virtually all American League parks. Many pitchers have said they fear him far more than Ted Williams.

Those pitchers declared, "With control, you can stop Williams. But not this guy."

Drebinger indicated, "Willie is a terrific hitter himself" and was "smacking the ball with vigor this year." But like Ty Cobb, Mays excelled in other aspects of the game, attaining

> super status. He may not be able to run quite as fast as Mantle, but on the base paths he is by far the more alert and dashing player. He has the quicker reflexes. On three occasions this year, he stole second and third in the one inning. He has been well named as 'baseball's most exciting player.' And afield he has no match at all. Willie repeatedly has made seemingly impossible catches such as the 'miracle catch' in the 1954 world series.

Thus, Drebinger determined, "If you want the slugger who murders all pitchers, Mantle's your man. If, with a hitting club, you want the fellow who can do a number of other things better, Willie's got to be your choice. Casey Stengel probably has the best answer: 'I'd like to have both.'"[26]

With the Dodgers not positioned in their usual spot atop the National League, New York City's other great center fielder, Duke Snider, bemoaned the absence of Jackie Robinson, despite apparent admonitions by Brooklyn management to avoid such talk. "Sure, this club misses Robinson," Snider said. "He could tear a game apart and win it for you in so many ways. Even sitting on the bench he was a big help, with the things he could tell you." The Dodgers went on a run, taking nine of ten games, slugging 18 homers, 8 by Duke. On July 20, he powered the 300th homer of his career, helping Brooklyn beat Chicago, 7–5.[27]

*****

On August 20, 1957, all but one of the nine members of the board of directors running the New York Giants voted to approve relocation to San Francisco for the following major league season. This was the death knell for an institution that New York City had featured for almost three-quarters of a century. Long Organized Baseball's dominant franchise, the New York Giants had a storied history that included managers McGraw, Terry, Ott, and Durocher, and Hall of Fame players Mathewson, Frisch, Terry, Ott, and Hubbell. Stoneham expressed his intention of flying out West to sign a contract with the city of San Francisco by the next week. "It's a tough wrench," he acknowledged. "We're very sorry about leaving. I'm very sentimental about the Giants and New York City. But conditions were such we had to accept now or they might not be so favorable again."

Under a 12-point plan, a stadium was to be built in San Francisco with a 40,000–45,000-person seating capacity to be rented to the team through a 35-year lease. The city intended to "operate and collect revenue from a parking area" able to hold up to 12,000 vehicles. The team would operate stadium concessions. Explaining the necessity of the move, Stoneham stated, "Lack of attendance. We're sorry to disappoint the kids of New York, but we didn't see many of their parents out there at the Polo Grounds in recent years." San Francisco Mayor George Christopher, a strong backer of MLB on the West Coast, reported that the Giants, during the next year, would play at Seals

Stadium, which could seat 22,000 fans, while stadium construction occurred. National League President Warren C. Giles indicated that the Giants' decision would have no impact on that of the Dodgers, whose management supposedly continued to wrestle with the question of whether to stay or to go.[28]

Remaining concerned about the Dodgers' possible departure from Brooklyn, Congressman Emanuel Celler called the Giants' impending move "a sad commentary on the club owners' attitude" toward baseball. "It proves that their only motive is the money motive." He continued, "This is all the more reason why the business aspects of baseball should be included under the antitrust laws." Predicting his beloved Dodgers would follow suit, leaving New York City the sole preserve of Yankees' management, Celler asserted, "Congress has to attend to that, and Congress will attend to it."[29]

*****

As Walter O'Malley continued to deflect rumors regarding the Dodgers' intentions to relocate or remain in New York City, even in Brooklyn, his Dodgers struggled in their pennant chase. In the National League, Milwaukee, sporting a 79–48 record, stood seven games ahead of Brooklyn, with St. Louis another half-game back. The New York Giants' 62–70 placed them in sixth place, nineteen and a half games behind the Braves. Over in the American League, New York, with a major league best mark of 82–47, was five and a half games in front of Chicago.[30]

With his batting average reaching as high as .386 during the middle of the month, Mantle hit what proved to be his final 6 homers of the season, scored 21 runs, drove in 17, walked 23 times, and batted a scorching .438 in August. Snider had 18 runs scored, 8 homers, 18 RBIs, 14 walks, and hit .306. Mays scored 27 times, had 4 doubles, 3 triples, 9 homers, 25 homers, 14 walks, and a .379 batting average.

Soon to appear in *Sport* magazine was an article by Frank Graham, "Why Don't They Stop Knocking the Duke?" Other than possibly his teammate, Don Newcombe, Snider was "the most freely psycho-analyzed ballplayer in the major leagues," Graham indicated. "What's more, he is probably the most criticized and the most harshly judged." Many sportswriters and fans subscribed to the belief that Snider was "potentially one of the greatest players of all time," but he failed "to realize his potential" due to a lack of concern or effort or because he "cares too much, tries too hard, presses, and explodes in a black rage when he doesn't hit like Babe Ruth, field like Tris Speaker and run the bases like Ty Cobb." Notwithstanding impressive lifetime and World Series records, Snider endured unrelenting criticism. Compared unfavorably with Willie Mays, the embittered Dodger center fielder retorted, "I'm a big man now. Nobody appreciated me until Willie came along."[31]

*****

In early September, violence beckoned as the integration of Central High School in Little Rock, Arkansas, began. A federal court issued an injunction to halt Governor Orval Faubus's deployment of the Arkansas National Guard to prevent nine Black students from entering the school. Over a period of several days, a standoff occurred, a white mob gathered, spewing hateful, racist expletives, and President Eisenhower ordered Army troops and the Guardsmen, whom he federalized, to protect the African American youngsters. Dr. Martin Luther King Jr. telegraphed the president, "You should know that the overwhelming majority of southerners, Negro and white, stand firmly behind your resolute action."

*****

In early September, the industrialist Louis F. Wolfson, businessman and apparent Republican Party gubernatorial aspirant Nelson Rockefeller, and New York City's Corporation Counsel Peter C. Brown attempted to keep the Dodgers in Brooklyn. Wolfson offered to purchase the ball club for $5 million, to spend $2 million to obtain rights to new players, and still more to construct a stadium. Rockefeller had engaged in discussions with business associates regarding "every conceivable means of keeping the Brooklyn Dodgers in New York," including purchasing partial ownership rights and building a ballpark to also serve "as a youth and sports recreational center." Brown informed City Hall that the municipality "could legally acquire land for resale to the Dodgers for a stadium."[32]

On September 16, the Los Angeles City Council, by an 11–3 vote, approved tendering an offer to O'Malley to facilitate a franchise shift. The city would "make available approximately 300 acres of land in Chavez Ravine" and spend up to $2 million "to level the proposed new stadium site," while the Dodger owner would build "$500,000 worth of recreational facilities on 40 acres of the area for free public recreation." The county Board of Supervisors followed up by unanimously agreeing on a plan to construct nearly $3 million "worth of access roads to Chavez Ravine."[33]

Hoping to prevent the Dodgers from accepting the Los Angeles offer, Wagner and Rockefeller huddled together on September 18, prior to the mayor's scheduled meeting with O'Malley, which Rockefeller attended. But the Dodger boss publicly acknowledged, "The Los Angeles offer is generally acceptable to us." In a formal statement, O'Malley indicated, "It is an attractive offer and one which we must seriously consider."[34]

A meeting by the Board of Estimates on September 19 resulted in no support to what Controller Lawrence E. Gerosa derided "as a 'give-away' of taxpayers' money" to the Dodgers. That involved the city's condemnation, at a cost of $8 million, of a 12-acre plot located at Flatbush and Atlantic Avenues that O'Malley sought. Under the proposal, the land would be transferred to a corporation set up by Rockefeller for $2 million, with the corporation, in turn, leasing "the site to the Dodgers, rent-free, for twenty years." The team would cover "all real estate taxes and assessments" over the course of the lease and build an all-weather stadium available for civic and municipal events at the site. During the lease period, the Dodgers would be able to purchase the location for $2 million plus accrued interest.[35]

O'Malley rejected the Rockefeller plan, but snags developed concerning a move to Los Angeles. The City Council was not scheduled to meet until October 7, past the NL deadline for announcing franchise shifts.[36]

*****

In his *New York Herald Tribune* column, "Views of Sports," Red Smith penned an essay following the last game the Giants played at the Polo Grounds. "A Wake for the Giants" followed a 9–1 loss to Pittsburgh, with 11,606 fans present, several going on a rampage at the game's end, grabbing the bases and home plate, while the teams scurried to their clubhouses. Smith mentioned the Giants' initial manager, James Mutrie, exclaiming, "My big fellows! My

Giants!" The artful sportswriter wrote of fast baller Amos Rusie, Wee Willie Keeler, and Buck Ewing, but most of all Bobby Thompson's epic homer to win the 1951 NL pennant over the Dodgers. Smith also referred to attendees at the final game cheering Willie Mays final plate appearances. When the game ended, patrons poured onto the field, with boys grabbing at the pitching mound, outfield grass, green canvas situated behind home plate, outfield walls' sponge rubber, and bullpen bench roof. A sign indicated, "Stay, team, stay."[37]

Despite the paltry showing for the Giants' final game at the Polo Grounds, overall major league attendance surpassed 17 million for the first time since 1950. Virtually replicating their attendance over the past three years, the Yankees drew just under 1.5 million customers to lead the AL. In only their third year in Kansas City, the Athletics fell below 1 million, barely attracting 900,000, while the Baltimore Orioles drew just over 1 million. The Milwaukee Braves set a National League record, with an attendance total of 2,215,404, almost exceeding that of any other NL team. The Brooklyn Dodgers welcomed 1,028,258 to Ebbets Field, almost 200,000 fewer than the previous year. Only 653,923 came to the Giants' home ballpark, a seeming justification for their franchise shift.

The final standings saw the New York Yankees with their third straight American League title, posting a 98–56 record, eight games ahead of the Chicago White Sox, with the Red Sox 16 games behind, and the Detroit Tigers rounding out the first division, 20 games below New York. The 95–59 Milwaukee Braves also prevailed by eight games in the National League, beating out the St. Louis Cardinals, with the 84–70 Brooklyn Dodgers finishing 11 games behind. The disappointing Cincinnati Redlegs finished fourth, fifteen games back of the Braves, while the sixth-place, lame duck New York Giants, at 69–85, were 26 behind.

Riddled by injuries, Mickey Mantle had a basically unproductive final month of the regular season, scoring only 6 runs, going homerless, contributing but 3 RBIs, walking 9 times, and batting a mere .225, thus dispelling any chance for either a Triple Crown or repeating in any of its categories. Willie Mays had 15 runs, 3 doubles, 2 triples, 7 homers, 11 RBIs, 9 walks, and a .337 batting average. Duke Snider finished with 11 runs, 6 homers, 14 RBIs, 10 walks, and a .182 batting average. His pair of homers off Philadelphia's Robin Roberts on

September 22 were the last hit at Ebbets Field and gave him 40 for the fifth consecutive time, matching Ralph Kiner's NL record.

Despite missing ten games and being beset by nagging injuries, Mantle led the New York Yankees while compiling another brilliant season. He had 173 hits (4th in the AL), 28 doubles (7th), 6 triples (6th), 34 homers (3rd), 94 RBIs (6th), 16 steals (4th), career-best .365 batting average (2nd), .512 on-base percentage (2nd), .665 slugging average (2nd), 1.177 OPS (2nd), 210 OPS+ (2nd), and 315 total bases (2nd). Mantle led the American League with 121 runs scored, 146 walks, and 11.3 WAR. First baseman Bill Skowron hit 17 homers, drove in 88 runs, and batted .304. Shortstop Gil McDougald had 25 doubles, 9 triples, and 13 homers, in batting .289. Rookie utility man Tony Kubek batted .297, but catcher Yogi Berra, second baseman Bobby Richardson, third baseman Andy Cary, left fielder-catcher Elston Howard, and right fielder Hank Bauer all had mediocre years. Berra did hit 24 homers and drove in 82 runs, while Bauer managed 18 homers and 65 RBIs, but neither performed any longer at an exceptional or nearly exceptional level.

The Yankee pitching staff carried much of the team's load, with a team ERA of 3.00. Whitey Ford remained stellar although limited by injuries to 17 starts, as he went 11–5 with a 2.57 ERA. Picking up the slack, Tom Sturdivant went 16–6 with a 2.54 ERA, Bob Turley was 13–6 with a 2.71 ERA, and newly acquired Bobby Shantz was 11–5 with a league-leading 2.45 ERA. Johnny Kucks slumped to 8–10 with a 3.56 ERA, but Don Larsen was 14–4 despite an even higher ERA of 3.74. Both starting and relieving, Art Ditmar was 8–3 with a 3.25 ERA. Acting as closer, Bob Grim was 12–8 with a 2.63 ERA and 19 saves. Added late to the roster, 40-year-old Sal Maglie was 2–0 with a 1.73 and a shutout.

Amid all the questions of where the team would be residing the next year, the Brooklyn Dodgers fell to third place in the National League, still led at the plate by center fielder Duke Snider and first baseman Gil Hodges. Snider scored 91 runs (9th in the NL), hit 25 doubles, smacked 40 homers (3rd), and drove in 92 runs (8th), although his batting average dropped to .274 thanks to that lousy final month to the season. Hodges scored 94 runs, hit 28 doubles, had 27 homers, drove in 98 runs, and hit .299. Right fielder Carl Furillo rebounded with a dozen homers and a .306 B.A., and left fielder Gene Cimoli scored 88 runs, had 10 homers, and batted .293. Displaying more of the promise previously expected of him, shortstop Charlie Neal had 12 homers, drove in 62 runs, and hit .270. But second baseman Jim Gilliam hit only .250, catcher Roy Campanella hit just 13 homers, drove in 62 runs, and hit .242, and third baseman Pee Wee Reese, displaced at shortstop, batted .224.

In his first full season, 20-year-old Don Drysdale became Brooklyn's latest pitching star, delivering a 17–9 win-loss record, with a 2.69 ERA and 4 shutouts. Returning from the military, Johnny Podres was 12–9 with a league-leading 2.66 ERA and 6 shutouts. Twenty-four-year-old Danny McDevitt was 7–4 with a 3.25 ERA and 2 shutouts, while Ed Roebuck, one year older, was 8–2, with a 2.71 ERA. The ageless Sal Maglie was 6–6 with a 2.93 ERA but was traded late in the season. Twenty-one-year-old Sandy Koufax went 5–4 with a 3.88 ERA. Closer Clem Labine was 5–7 with a 3.44 ERA and 17 saves. Thirty-year-old Carl Erskine, suffering from a sore arm, was 5–3 with a 3.55 ERA but made only six starts. Roger Craig dropped to 6–9 with a 4.61 ERA, but the even more disappointing Don Newcombe was 11–12, despite a decent 3.44 ERA and 4 shutouts. Newcombe's World Series travails, coupled with alcoholism, were sending him into a deep downward spiral.

The soon-to-be departing New York Giants, sixth-place finishers, had center fielder Willie Mays excelling at the plate, on the base paths, and in the field, and not much else. Mays scored 112 runs (3rd), had 195 hits (4th), hit 26 doubles, 20 triples, and 35 homers (4th), drove in 97 runs (6th), stole 38 bases, and hit .333 (2nd). He also delivered a .407 OBP (2nd), .626 slugging percentage, 1.033 OPS (2nd), 173 OPS+, and 366 total bases (2nd). His triples, stolen bases, SLG, OPS, and WAR (8.3) led the NL. Right fielder Don Mueller managed only a .258 batting average, although that was better than several Giant regulars. Forty-year-old Hank Sauer, operating in left field, hit 26 homers and had 76 RBIs, while batting a point higher than Mueller. Red Schoendienst hit .307 before being swapped to the Braves.

Ruben Gomez was 15–13 with a 3.78 ERA, while Johnny Antonelli slid to 12–18, although his ERA was insignificantly better than Gomez's. Only Marv Grissom performed well from the bullpen, with a 2.61 ERA, splitting eight decisions.

The NL champion Milwaukee Braves featured right fielder Henry Aaron, who scored 118 runs, had 198 hits, delivered 27 doubles, 6 triples, 44 homers, 132 RBIs, a .322 batting average, and 369 total bases. His OBP was .378, slugging percentage, .600, OPS, .978, and OPS+ 166. He topped the National League in runs scored, homers, RBIs, and total bases. Third baseman Eddie Mathews scored 109 runs, had 28 doubles, 9 triples, 32 homers, 94 RBIs, a .292 batting average, and 309 total bases. Left fielder Wes Covington hit 21 homers and batted .284. After coming over from the Giants, second baseman Red Schoendienst hit .310 and proved a sparkplug. While having only 134 official-at bats, outfielder Bob Hazle batted .403. The Braves' top starters were Warren Spahn, Lew Burdette, and Bob Buhl. The 36-year-old Spahn went 21–11 with a 2.69 ERA, Burdette was 17–9 with a 3.72 ERA, and Buhl was 18–7 with a 2.74 ERA. Closer Don McMahon was only 2–3 but put up a 1.54 ERA and finished 19 games.[38]

Along with Mays and Aaron, other former Negro League performers and Black players, too young to have competed in Blackball, starred on the baseball diamond during the 1957 major league season. The Cubs' Ernie Banks scored 113 runs and hit 43 homers—both second to Aaron—drove in 102 runs, hit .285, had 344 total bases, third best in the league, made the All-Star team for the third straight year, and finished sixth in the NL MVP race. Avoiding the dreaded sophomore slump, Cincinnati's Frank Robinson scored 97 runs, had 197 hits—one behind Aaron—got 29 doubles and homers, drove in 75 runs, and batted .322, tying Aaron for third best in the league; he was again named an All-Star and finished ninth in the NL MVP tabulation. The White Sox's Minnie Minoso continued to play at an All-Star level while garnering MVP votes, scoring 96 runs, leading the AL with 36 doubles, driving in 103 runs, and batting .310. His teammate Larry Doby had 14 homers, 79 RBIs, and batted .288. The Orioles' Bob Boyd batted .318, while the Redlegs' George Crowe delivered 31 homers, 92 RBIs, and a .271 batting average. The Cardinals' Sam Jones was 12–9 with a 3.60 ERA but failed to win the strikeout title for the only time during a four-year stretch.

*****

For the third straight year, the World Series went seven games. In Game One, New York beat Milwaukee, 3–1, with 69,476 fans at Yankee Stadium watching Ford outduel Spahn, who was knocked out in the sixth inning. Mantle went two for four, while Bauer, Carey, and Coleman picked up the RBIs. Coleman also had two hits, as did the Braves' Covington; Aaron was one for four.[39]

Game Two went the other way, with Milwaukee, and right-hander Burdette, prevailing, 4–2, before 65,202 in attendance. New York starter Shantz was pounded out in the fourth inning. The Yankees' Bauer hit a solo homer, and Kubek had a pair of singles, but Mantle, Berra, and McDougald were hitless. Aaron again went one for four, tripling before scoring on a single by Adcock, who, like Covington, had two hits. Logan smacked a third-inning four-bagger off Shantz.[40]

Almost 46,000 were present at County Stadium but saw Milwaukee fall to New York, 12–3, in Game Three with Larsen starring over seven innings of relief, while Buhl got only two men out in the first-inning before leaving the game. Schoendienst had three singles, Logan two, and Aaron went two for five, with a two-run fifth-inning homer off Larsen. Kubek led the Yankee onslaught, with three runs scored, three hits, including two homers, and four RBIs. Mantle was two for three with a two-run homer. Bauer drove in a pair of runs.[41]

Rebounding in Game Four at County Stadium, with almost 46,000 present, Milwaukee scored three in the bottom of the tenth to beat reliever Grim. Despite relinquishing eleven hits, Spahn went all the way, while New York starter Sturdivant lasted only four innings. Mantle, who left the game in the tenth because of an injured right shoulder, was hitless in five at bats, Bauer had a hit and another RBI, while Berra, Kubek, and McDougal had two hits each. Howard tied the score during the top of the ninth with two outs, powering a three-run homer. Mathews and Aaron had two hits each, with Mathews driving in two runs and Aaron three, hitting his second homer of the series and collecting three RBIs. First baseman Frank Torre hit a fourth-inning homer. Mathews won the game with a solo shot to deep right off Grim in the bottom of the tenth.[42]

Winning his second game of the Series, Burdette shut out New York on seven hits at County Stadium, again with a full house of almost 46,000 individuals, edging Ford. The Yankees' Bauer and left fielder Enos Slaughter had two hits each, as did the Braves' Aaron and Pafko. First baseman Joe Adcock drove in the game's only run, scoring Mathews in the bottom of the sixth. Mantle got into the game only as a pinch-runner.[43]

Game Six went to New York, 3–2, before over 61,000 fans at the Stadium, with Turley going the distance, scattering four hits, while Milwaukee starter Buhl again flopped, leaving the game in the third-inning. Torre and Aaron homers provided the only Brave runs, with Henry going one for four and Torre getting two hits. Berra guided the Yankees with three hits, including a two-run, third-inning homer off Buhl, while an ailing Mantle missed the game. "If that fellow could hit, I'd played him, but he can't swing a bat. His shins is okay. It's his arm that's bad. I mightier put him on first base if he coulda raised him arm above his head, which he can't," Stengel explained.[44]

Milwaukee won the deciding contest, 5–0, before 61,207 fans at Yankee Stadium, as Burdette won a World Series-tying record third game. Mantle played but managed only a single in four at bats, while only Coleman got as many as two hits. Hazle, Aaron, and Crandall had two hits each, and Mathews drove in a pair of runs.[45]

As he had all season, Aaron led Milwaukee hitters, scoring five runs, getting eleven hits, slamming three homers, driving in seven runs, and batting .393. Brave batters hit a collective .209, with Mathews hitting .227, but he scored four runs, had three doubles, one homer, drove in four runs, and walked eight times. Spahn won one game; Burdette, as indicated, won three, including two shutouts.

Coleman topped New York's hitters, batting .364, while Berra batted .320. Bauer and Kubek each hit two homers; Mantle had one, finishing with a .263 batting average. Yankee batters hit a collective .248 while failing to deliver key hits when necessary. Other than Burdette, New York pitchers outshone their rivals, with Ford putting up a 1.13 ERA and Turley a 2.31 mark.

*****

On the day that Game Five of the World Series was played, the Los Angeles City Council voted 10–4 to approve an ordinance effectively ratifying the contract previously agreed to by the Dodgers. The following day, the Brooklyn management announced it was preparing for the move out West. NL President Warren C. Giles applauded the decision, declaring it demonstrated his circuit's "professional" makeup. This ended the Dodgers' formal association with Brooklyn, which dated back to 1890. Mayor Wagner indicated his intention to form a committee to solicit another NL ball club for his city. When asked during a press conference if O'Malley had operated in good faith, Wagner responded, "I can only say that in my conversations with him he said that he had no commitments, and I have to take the man's word."[46]

The *New York Times'* Arthur Daley delivered blistering commentary on the decisions by Stoneham and O'Malley to move their teams to California. Homing in on the Dodgers' design, Daley discussed the "bitter end it was to be for those faithful Brooklyn fans who enabled the Dodgers" profits to average $360,000 during a five-year period. Other ball clubs relocated due to "apathy, or incompetence." But "the only word that fits the Dodgers is greed." Although Ebbets Field became "a wretchedly outmoded baseball arena . . . with hopelessly inadequate parking facilities. . . . it still could ring a lively tune on the cash register." Regarding Los Angeles' agreement to make 300 acres of property available while New York City refused to offer a dozen, Daley wrote, "This is the biggest haul since the Brink's robbery—except that it's legal."[47]

He then asked, "Baseball is a sport, eh?" That might be true, Daley acknowledged, for the Red Sox's Tom Yawkey, the Cubs' Phil Wrigley, and perhaps two more owners. However, "the crass commercialism of O'Malley and . . . Stoneham . . . presents the disillusioning fact that it's big business, just another way to make a buck." Admitting to feeling "galling resentment," Daley wrote, "These are not true sporting deals. They go without even a good-by."[48]

*****

The Sporting News named 37-year-old Stan Musial and 39-year-old Ted Williams its National League and American League Player of the Year, respectively. It also selected Warren Spahn as NL Pitcher of the Year and Billy Pierce as his AL counterpart. The magazine chose Williams as its Major League Player of the Year.[49]

The United Press American League All-Star team included Mickey Mantle, a unanimous selection, Yogi Berra, and Gil McDougald. The Associated

Press major league All-Star squad included the same three Yankee players, along with five members of the World Series champion Milwaukee Braves: Red Schoendienst, Eddie Mathews, Henry Aaron, Warren Spahn, and Lew Burdette. The Dodgers' Gil Hodges and the Giants' Willie Mays made the second team. For the second straight year, Mantle was named the American League MVP, beating out Ted Williams—who beat out Mickey to take his fifth batting crown with a .388 average—by 24 votes, with Washington outfielder Roy Sievers a close third. Henry Aaron finished ahead in the National League MVP tabulations, only nine votes in front of Stan Musial, who won his seventh batting title, with Red Schoendienst, who led the NL with 200 hits, in third, followed by Mays. Warren Spahn was the near-unanimous winner of the second Cy Young Award.[50]

*****

The three great center fielders who had graced New York City baseball diamonds, each leading his team to the pinnacle of the national pastime, remained in the news as the offseason continued. The possibility of breaking Babe Ruth's home run records continued to fascinate fans of the sport, something that at one point, at least within the past three years, Willie Mays, Duke Snider, and Mickey Mantle had appeared capable of accomplishing. The *Washington Post and Times Herald* indicated that both Eddie Mathews of the Milwaukee Braves and Mantle, each just 25 years old, could threaten Ruth's lifetime total of 714 homers, while Eddie could set his sights on Mel Ott's more reachable National League mark of 511. Snider's 316 lifetime homers placed him in 11th place, 15 behind Hank Greenberg.[51]

Appearing in *This Week* magazine, Snider informed the journalist Milton Richman, "We'll never break Babe Ruth's record!" Referring to Mantle, Snider noted he had been ahead of Ruth's pace for much of the 1956 season but did not come close to matching Babe's finishing flourish of 17 homers in September 1927. Present-day ball players had to contend with both day and night games, a taxing combination Ruth had not encountered. Mantle and Mays probably had "the best chance of doing it," Snider offered, but their home ballparks were "not conducive to hitting 61 homers" and neither was Milwaukee's County Stadium for the most consistent home run hitter, Eddie Mathews, a player with "terrific power." Snider admitted that he himself was "too erratic to break any home run record."[52]

Duke concluded, "There are simply too many obstacles to overcome for anyone who has designs on Babe's all-time record." A ballplayer would require both "a terrific start and an even more spectacular finish," while disregarding "all that pressure," modern-day schedules, and different park configurations. "I don't advise you to hold your breath waiting."[53]

*****

As for Mays, he and his wife encountered racial prejudice in seeking to purchase a house in San Francisco's affluent Sherwood Forest neighborhood. Having agreed to a purchase price with Mays, the residential owner, pressured by neighbors, reneged. Expressing disappointment, Willie insisted he did not blame anyone. His wife Marghuerite declared, "Down in Alabama, where we come from, you know your place, and that's something, at least. But up here it's all a lot of camouflage. They grin in your face and then deceive you."[54]

17

Legacies

The decisions by the Brooklyn Dodgers' Walter O'Malley and the New York Giants' Horace Stoneham to relocate their franchises ended two Major League Baseball (MLB) eras, one that extended back more than half a century and another that lasted for just over a decade. This book focuses on that latter period, particularly its final four years. No longer the dominant team in professional baseball, the Giants had been surpassed by the Dodgers, who achieved preeminent status in the National League, only to be repeatedly rebuffed by the New York Yankees.

Starting in 1947 and continuing for the ensuing decade, New York City teams battled to win ball games, league championships, and World Series, along with the allegiance of fans in the Bronx, Brooklyn, Upper Manhattan, and across the vast metropolitan area. During those 11 years, the Yankees won every AL pennant, except for the two captured by the Cleveland Indians in 1948 and 1954. The Dodgers or Giants took every NL title, other than the ones the Boston Braves won in 1948, the Philadelphia Phillies two years later, and the Milwaukee Braves in 1957. This was truly a New York City dynasty, although heavily dominated by the Yankees, but the Dodgers won six pennants, the Giants two, and both of those NL teams won a World Series, while the Yanks prevailed in seven Fall Classics. Such dominance, sustained for more than a decade, remains unmatched to the very present.

Star power drove those great Yankee, Dodger, and Giant teams. At various points, Casey Stengel could call on center fielder Joe DiMaggio, shortstop Phil Rizzuto, catcher Yogi Berra, center fielder Mickey Mantle, and pitchers

Allie Reynolds, Vic Raschi, Eddie Lopat, and Whitey Ford, among others. The Brooklyn Dodgers lacked the kind of continuity in the managerial spot that Stengel, who replaced Bucky Harris in October 1948, afforded the Yankees, moving from Burt Shotton to Leo Durocher and on to Charlie Dressen, and then Walter Alston. Regardless, their starters included Jackie Robinson, who shattered Organized Baseball's appalling color barrier, Pee Wee Reese, Roy Campanella, Gil Hodges, Duke Snider, and pitcher Don Newcombe. Mel Ott managed the New York Giants through the first half of the 1948 season, then turned over the team to the talented but controversial Durocher. Giant lineups first featured Johnny Mize and Walker Cooper, then Bobby Thompson, Monte Irvin, Willie Mays, and Al Dark, with star pitchers Larry Jansen and Sal Maglie.

*****

Following six Yankee World Series triumphs—including four over the Dodgers and one over the Giants—in seven years, New York City's preeminence in MLB continued from 1954–1957. Fittingly, each of those teams prevailed during the first of those three years, starting with the Giants, followed by the Dodgers and then the Yankees, while none did in 1957, although the Yankees grabbed yet another pennant before losing to a non-New York City team, the Milwaukee Braves. That too was fitting, in one sense, as the Braves had relocated after the 1952 season, just as the Dodgers and Giants would do so five years later. Striking as well was the superstar status affirmed or confirmed through the brilliant performances in 1954 by the Giants' Willie Mays, in 1955 by the Dodgers' Duke Snider, and in 1956 by the Yankees' Mickey Mantle. During that year, each became arguably the best player in the game. While all excelled again in 1957, that season's stardom or anti-stardom revolved around the expansionist machinations of Walter O'Malley and Horace Stoneham culminating in the decision to move their historic franchises, thereby terminating the New York City dynasty altogether.

Thus, *A Baseball Era* heralds the ascent and descent of the New York City dynasty, an unparalleled period in major league history. The Yankees remained a powerhouse in the American League, winning another six pennants between 1958 and 1964, taking the World Series that first year, with Mantle again leading the AL in homers, when they were the only team in town, falling to third in 1959, then running off another five-year pennant-winning streak. Their unanticipated loss to the heavily underdog Pittsburgh Pirates was followed by Stengel's firing, despite his having won ten pennants in 12 years, along with seven World Series. New to the lineup that season was slugger Roger Maris, who beat out Mantle for the AL MVP award by three votes despite getting two fewer first-place votes and losing the home run title to him, 40–39. The powerful 1961 team, winning 109 regular season games under new manager Ralph Houk, continued to be led by Mantle, Maris, and Ford.

Maris accomplished what the great New York City center fielders highlighted in this book—Mantle, Snider, and Mays—had been unable to do: break Babe Ruth's single-season home run record. During that season, the American League played its initial 162-game regular season schedule, having expanded to ten teams by adding the Los Angeles Angels and the Washington Senators, who replaced the team that moved to Minneapolis as the Twins. After 154 games, Maris had belted 59 homers, but he added two more in the final eight games to end with a new mark of 61. He beat out Mantle, now the darling of Yankee Stadium fans, who managed a career-high 54 after a spirited chase that slackened as the bugaboo of injuries again crippled him, worsened by highly questionable medical treatment, during the final weeks of the season. Maris again was named MVP, with Mantle only four votes behind.

Repeating in 1962, the Yankees slipped past the San Francisco Giants in seven games to win the World Series, their last for a decade and a half. Maris had a decent but not spectacular season, while Mantle, notwithstanding injuries confining him to 123 games, hit 30 homers and batted .321, getting named MVP for the third time. The 1963 Yankees staved off extensive injuries to both Mantle and Maris, which kept them on the bench for much of the season, but Ford's 24 wins and 21 by Jim Bouton, along with an MVP campaign by former Negro Leaguer Elston Howard, enabled the team to win 104 games. The Yanks then dropped four straight in the World Series against the Dodgers, led by pitching stars Sandy Koufax, the former bonus baby, and Don Drysdale. The next season, with Berra now managing, was Mantle's last great one, enabling him to finish second in the MVP voting for the third time. After that, the Yankees experienced a tailspin, even falling into the cellar by 1966, as injuries and age diluted Mickey's once remarkable skills.

Before the Dodgers played their first game in Los Angeles, the team suffered a near mortal blow. On January 28, 1958, Roy Campanella, having toiled at both his liquor store and a nightclub, seemingly fell asleep while driving along a wet road on Long Island. His rental car hurtled into a telephone pole, flipping over, leaving Campy a quadriplegic.[1]

The Dodgers finished their first season in Los Angeles in seventh place, with Gil Hodges having a down year and Snider reduced to 106 games, while the absence of Ebbets Field diminished his homer total to 15 despite a .312 batting average. The young pitching staff, including Drysdale, Johnny Podres, and Koufax, proved disappointing. Carl Erskine approached the end of his fine career, while former MVP and Cy Young Award winner Don Newcombe was winless in seven decisions with a 7.86 ERA before being traded to Cincinnati. The Dodgers overperformed the next year, beating the Milwaukee Braves twice in a best-of-three playoff series, then topped the Chicago White Sox for the team's second World Series championship. Hodges rebounded, Snider had a fine year, and left fielder Wally Moon, coming over from St. Louis, was a terrific addition. Drysdale, Podres, and Roger Craig headed the pitching staff, while Koufax remained a work in progress. That year, the Boston Red Sox became the last major league team, prior to the expansion era, to add a Black player, Pumpsie Green, to their roster.

After finishing fourth in 1960, the Dodgers ended up second the next two years, losing to the Giants in a playoff series again in 1962. Those teams included outfielders Tommy Davis and Frank Howard, with both Snider and Hodges reduced to part-time duty; those two longtime Dodger sluggers would soon leave the team before each would eventually move over to a new NL team, the New York Mets. During 1961, Koufax finally displayed the skill set long predicted for him, winning 18 games and setting an NL strikeout record, breaking Christy Mathewson's mark of 267 by two. Koufax's injury the next year while on pace to win the Cy Young Award that would go to 25-game winner Drysdale undoubtedly cost the Dodgers the pennant. Sandy's unmatched brilliance over the next four seasons would help lead to three pennants—in 1963, 1965, and 1966—along with the World Series title in the first two of those years. Koufax's golden but ailing arm compelled him to retire after the 1966 World Series, just prior to his receipt of a third Cy Young.

Far more successful than the Dodgers during their first year out West, the Giants finished third in 1958, featuring Willie Mays, second in the MVP voting, first baseman Orlando Cepeda, a 20-year-old rookie sensation, and Johnny Antonelli, who remained the team's pitching star. Another third-place finish followed, along with another brilliant season from both Mays and Cepeda and the astonishing hitting performance of 21-year-old rookie Willie McCovey. Antonelli was again stellar, as was 21-game-winner Sam Jones, coming over from the Cardinals. Dropping to fifth in 1960, the Giants saw McCovey experience a terrible sophomore slump and Antonelli shift to a closer role during his final year with the team, although Mays and Cepeda remained All-Stars. Cepeda won both the homer and RBI titles, while Mays played like, well, Willie Mays. Second-year pitcher Juan Marichal displayed signs of brilliance but proved inconsistent.

The Giants won their first pennant in San Francisco in 1962, with Mays, Cepeda, and right fielder Felipe Alou providing the bulk of the hitting, while Jack Sanford, Billy O'Dell, Billy Pierce, and Marichal comprised a strong starting pitching contingent. Over the next three years, the Giants finished third, fourth, and second, with Mays still at the top of his game, Cepeda, excellent before missing most of the 1965 season due to injury, McCovey, operating as a power-hitting behemoth, and Marichal, becoming a dominant pitcher. Slamming 52 homers, Mays won his second MVP, beating out Koufax, who had won the award two years earlier. Although he continued to be named to All-Star teams, Willie's hitting prowess began to slacken by 1967, never again reaching the heights he had previously attained.

At different points during the mid-1950s, Willie Mays, Duke Snider, and Mickey Mantle were each viewed as not only the greatest center fielder but the finest player in the major leagues, in addition to being a candidate to eclipse Babe Ruth's single-season home run record. They were seen as powerful, high-average hitters and excellent fielders. Mantle was considered the fastest runner in the game, Snider a skilled runner, and Mays an exceptional one. For the four years—1954-1957—featured in this book, Mays, Snider, and Mantle vied for supremacy among New York City center fielders as their teams strove for and reached the pinnacle of American sports at the time. Each was proclaimed, for one year at least during that critical period, the very best player in the game as he led his respective team to a World Series championship.

Five years older than the other two, Snider reached his peak during the heyday of the New York City baseball dynasty. The different dimensions of the Dodger's home stadiums in Los Angeles, injuries, and age eroded his considerable skills, something that Mantle and Mays also eventually confronted. Mantle's peak was perhaps the greatest of the three, with his Triple Crown season among the most magnificent in major league history, while injuries precluded a repeat Triple Crown the next year and ended his 1961 home run duel with Maris. Notwithstanding an inordinately high threshold for pain and indomitable courage, Mantle's incredible abilities too suffered the ravages of time and his own refusal to care for his health due to nightlife endeavors and alcoholism. Mays's brilliance lasted the longest and was scarcely matched in the history of MLB, surpassed among everyday players perhaps only by Ty Cobb, Honus Wagner, Ruth, Ted Williams, Stan Musial, and Barry Bonds. He had individual seasons close to Mantle's greatest during the mid-1950s and again a decade later, a testimony to his enduring athletic brilliance.

Who was the greatest? Snider, Mantle, and Mays all ended up in the Hall of Fame, although Duke's entry, inexplicably, took 11 tries before finally occurring in 1980 when he received 86.5 percent of the votes by the Baseball Writers' Association of America. This came a year after Mays, receiving 94.7 percent of the ballots, was voted in through his initial appearance on the ballot. Mantle had attained the honor first, in 1974, getting 88.2 percent of the votes, entering the Hall with his good friend and longtime teammate Whitey Ford.

Snider's difficulty in obtaining entry through the ballot box was in keeping with that of many greats, including those who played in the Negro Leagues. Fittingly, Jackie Robinson, in 1962, became the first former Negro Leaguer to be elected to the Hall of Fame. Four years later, during his own Hall of Fame address, Ted Williams stunned the audience by asserting,

> Baseball gives every American boy a chance to excel, not just to be as good as someone else, but to be better than someone else. This is the nature of man and the name of the game, and I've always been a very lucky guy to have worn a baseball uniform, to have struck out or hit a tape major home run. And I hope that someday the names of Satchell Page and Josh Gibson in some way can be added as a symbol, the great Negro players that are not

here, only because they were not given a chance. And I know Casey Stengel feels the same way, and I'm awfully glad to be with him on this big day. I also know I'll lose a dear friend if I don't stop.[2]

Spurred by Williams's impassioned oration and considerable pressure from the growing number of historians of Negro League baseball, such as Robert Peterson, the Hall of Fame formed a new committee focusing on Blackball. Thus, the full class of 1971 included Leroy "Satchel" Paige, the legendary Negro Leaguer and one of the greatest pitchers ever, who, at the age of 42, helped the Cleveland Indians win the 1948 World Series. Over the next few years, a small number of players whose bulk of their careers was in the Negro Leagues joined Paige in Organized Baseball's Valhalla, including Josh Gibson, Buck Leonard, Monte Irvin, Cool Papa Bell, Judy Johnson, Oscar Charleston, Martin Dihigo, Pop Lloyd, and, finally, Rube Foster, ten years after Paige, far too late for the founder of the Negro National League and its one-time greatest pitcher and manager.[3]

This almost did not occur, as MLB initially sought to fend off pleas by the likes of Williams and Blackball historians with a proposal for a separate wing at the Hall of Fame. The ten-person committee chosen to select one Blackball participant annually "as part of a new exhibit commemorating the contributions of the Negro Leagues to baseball" chose Paige, who responded, "I was just as good as the White boys. I ain't going in the back door to the Hall of Fame." Robinson urged Paige to boycott the induction ceremony scheduled for the summer of 1972. "It's not worth a hill of beans. It's the same thing all over again," Robinson stated.[4]

All of this was keeping with MLB's longstanding racist practices, which had allowed for Jim Crow practices to afflict the national pastime. The Hall of Shame included bigots like Cap Anson and Commissioner Kenesaw Mountain Landis, who ensured throughout his lengthy tenure (1920–1944) that the nation's then most popular sport mirrored the disgraceful practices that beset too many individuals residing in the world's leading democracy.

The Hall of Fame tabulations for Snider, Mantle, and Mays demonstrated how imprecise and, at times, untrustworthy they could be. Why it took so long for a great all-around player like Snider, who helped lead his Dodgers to six pennants and two World Series championships, to be voted in remains unfathomable. So too are the relatively small number of voters who refused to back Mantle and Mays, both of whom compiled statistics that are still among the game's most remarkable, including Mickey's ten World Series appearances and seven World Series titles, despite a ravaged body that sometimes resulted in his missing championship contests or playing hurt in such key contests. No matter, in 65 games, he had a record 42 runs scored, 40 RBIs, and 18 homers.

In the most statistically oriented sports entity, MLB, Snider, Mantle, and Mays shone brightly, both in particularly resplendent seasons and over lengthy careers. Over 18 years, six of which were quite shortened, Duke had 1,259 runs scored, 2,119 hits, 358 doubles, 85 triples, 407 homers, 971 walks, a .295 batting average, .380 on-base percentage, .540 slugging percentage, .919 OPS, and 140 OPS+, along with eight All-Star selections and three top four MVP vote totals. Despite the move to Los Angeles and injuries, Snider, who had five consecutive 40-homer seasons, slammed more homers than any big leaguer during the 1950s. He led the NL in runs scored (3 times), hits (1), homers (1), RBIs (1), walks (1), OBP (1), slugging (2), OPS (2), OPS+ (1), total bases (3), and WAR (2). Four of his six World Series were brilliant, with his 36 games resulting in 21 runs, 8 doubles, 11 homers, 26 RBIs, 13 walks, a .351 OBP, a .594 SLG, and a .945 OPS. Twice, he belted a then record-tying 4 homers in a Series.

Mantle's career stats, compiled notwithstanding his injuries, were still more luminous. Playing 18 years, he scored 1,676 runs, collected 2,415 doubles, produced 344 doubles, hit 72 triples, smashed 536 homers, drove in 1,509 runs, walked 1,733 times, batted .298, and had a .421 OBP, .557 SLG, .977 OPS, 172 OPS+, and 110 WAR. Mickey hit 40 or more homers four times, twice rapping more than 50. He led the AL in runs (5), triples (1), homers (4), RBIs (1), batting average (1), walks (5), OBP (3), slugging (4), OPS (6), OPS+ (8), total bases (3), WAR (6), and oWAR (Offensive WAR, 9). Named to the All-Star team every year but twice, he won 3 MVPs, finishing in the top five on six other occasions.

With a career spanning more than a quarter of a century, which included appearances in the Negro American League, other Blackball games, and four World Series, Mays, in the face of continued racism confronting African

American players, produced some of the gaudiest statistics of any major leaguer. His lifetime totals included 2,068 runs scored, 3,293 hits, 525 doubles, 141 triples, 660 homers, 1,909 RBIs, 1,468 walks, 339 steals, a .301 batting average, .384 OBP, .557 slugging average, .940 OPS, 155 OPS+, and 156.2 WAR. Willie hit more than forty homers six times, twice delivering more than 50. He led the NL in runs scored (2), hits (1), triples (3), homers (4), stolen bases (4), batting average (1), on-base percentage (2), slugging (5), OPS (5), OPS+ (5), total bases (3), WAR (10), oWAR (7), and dWAR (defensive WAR, 1). Named to the All-Star team for 22 straight years, he won the Rookie of the Year Award and two MVP awards, attaining ten other top-six MVP vote totals. In addition, Mays received 12 consecutive Gold Gloves for his stellar defense, although that award was not initiated until his fifth full season.

*****

In addition to their success on the baseball diamond, the Dodgers proved a resounding hit at the box office, drawing large crowds over four years at Los Angeles Memorial Coliseum and then, starting in 1962, at Dodger Stadium, which proved tremendously helpful to the team's pitching staff, including Koufax and Drysdale. After finishing second to the Braves in attendance after attracting over 1.845 million fans, the Dodgers were first in the NL for the remainder of Koufax's tenure, which ended following the 1966 World Series. Attendance reached as high as 2,755,184, the first year at Dodger Stadium, and was nearly as impressive when the Koufax-led Dodgers made their third World Series appearance in four years during Sandy's final season.

Away from the Polo Grounds, the Giants drew approximately 1.273 million and 1.422 million customers in their two years at Seals Stadium, then shattered the team record, attracting 1,795,356 fans in their initial season at Candlestick Park. They continued to draw well until 1968, when they dipped below 900,000, not pulling in as many as 1 million patrons again until 1971, when the team won the NL West, a new division carved out due to more expansion two years earlier. But in 1972, when a slumping Mays was shipped off to the Mets, attendance slid to less than 650,000.

While they remained a powerhouse, the New York Yankees continued to draw well, pulling in almost 1.75 million during the AL's first expansion year, 1961. However, in 1966, when the team slid to the bottom of the league standings, attendance dropped too, with the Yankees finishing out of the top two in AL attendance for the first time in 41 years. The Yankees, nevertheless, drew more than 1 million annually for Mantle's final years with the ball club, although averaging fewer fans per game, several thousand below the number they had during his first several years in the major leagues. Their too-long reluctance to bring on board Black players, as well as their continued disinclination to add many even after former Negro Leaguer Elston Howard, a 12-time All-Star and the 1963 AL MVP, proved to be such a fine player, undoubtedly contributed to the demise of the latest Yankee dynasty.

   The ending of the New York City baseball dynasty coincided with changes in fortunes for the American civil rights movement. After a lull, it received a jolt of inspiration, energy, and momentum from young activists at the beginning of the 1960s, who participated in sit-ins, freedom rides, mass rallies, voting rights campaigns, and marches. Many soon gravitated to calls for Black power and militant stances, seemingly more in line with Malcolm X than Dr. King as the nation was beset by white resistance, racial conflagrations, rising expectations, divisions induced by a war waged thousands of miles from its shores, and dashed hopes. MLB was hardly immune to mounting racial, political, and cultural tensions during a decade seemingly far removed from New York City's golden period when Willie, Duke, and Mickey reigned supreme.

Notes

Introduction

1 Roger Kahn, *The Boys of Summer* (New York: Harper Perennial Modern Classics, 2006).

2 Larry Lester, *Black Baseball in New York City: An Illustrated History, 1885–1959* (Jefferson City, NC: McFarland Publishing, 2017); Sean Lahman, "How Negro League Teams' Legacies Shaped Baseball History in New York City," *Rochester Democrat & Chronicle*, March 31, 2021, https://www.democratandchronicle.com/story/sports/2021/03/31/negro-league-baseball-teams-new-york-get-major-league-status/7058608002/.

3 "MLB to Officially Recognize Negro Leagues, Rectifying 'A Longtime Oversight in the Game's History,'" *Boston Globe (Online)*, December 16, 2020.

4 Anthony Castrovince, "What to Know about Negro League Stats Entering MLB Record," MLB Advanced Media, LP, May 29, 2024, https://www.mlb.com/news/faq-negro-leagues-stats-major-league-record#:~:text=Following%20the%202020%20announcement%20that,Leagues%20numbers%20into%20the%20official; Philip Lee, *Black Stats Matter: Integrating Negro League Numbers into Major League Records* (Jefferson City, NC: McFarland and Company, 2023).

5 Robert C. Cottrell, *Two Pioneers: How Hank Greenberg and Jackie Robinson Transformed Baseball* (Washington, DC: Potomac Books, 2012); "Monarch Owner to File Protest," *Los Angeles Times*, October 24, 1945, p. 10.

6 William C. Rhoden, *Forty Million Dollar Slaves: The Rise, Fall, and Redemption of the Black Athlete* (New York: Crown, 2007); Roberta J. Newman and Joel Nathan Rosen, *Black Baseball, Race Enterprise and the Fate of the Segregated Dollar* (Jackson, MS: University Press of Mississippi, 2014).

7 "N.Y. Cubans Win Title," *New York Times*, September 29, 1947, p. 25; "Cubans Win Title," *Washington Post*, September 29, 1947, p. 15.

8 Roger Kahn, *The Era 1947–1957: When the Yankees, the Giants, and the Dodgers Ruled the World* (Boston: Ticknor & Fields, 1993); Harvey Frommer, *New York City Baseball: The Golden Age, 1947–1957* (Boulder, CO: Taylor Trade Publishing, 2013); Carl E.

Prince, *Brooklyn's Dodgers: The Bums, the Borough, and the Best of Baseball, 1947–1957* (New York: Oxford University Press, 1997).

Chapter 1

1. Frederick G. Lieb, *The Boston Red Sox: An Informal History* (New York: G.P. Putnam's Sons, 1947); Robert C. Cottrell, *Blackball, the Black Sox, and the Babe: Baseball's Crucial 1920 Season* (Jefferson City, NC: McFarland & Company, 2002).

2. Frederick G. Lieb, *The Philadelphia Athletics: An Informal History* (New York: G.P. Putnam's Sons, 1945); Frederick G. Lieb, *The Philadelphia Phillies* (New York: G.P. Putnam's Sons, 1953).

3. Warren Brown, *The Chicago Cubs: An Informal History* (New York: G.P. Putnam's Sons, 1946); Warren Brown, *The Chicago White Sox* (New York: G.P. Putnam's Sons, 1952).

4. Frederick G. Lieb, *The St. Louis Cardinals: An Informal History* (New York: G.P. Putnam's Sons, 1944); Frederick G. Lieb, *The Baltimore Orioles: The History of a Colorful Team in Baltimore and St. Louis* (New York: G.P. Putnam's Sons, 1955).

5. Frederick G. Lieb, *The Pittsburgh Pirates: An Informal History* (New York: G.P. Putnam's Sons, 1948); Shirley Povich, *The Washington Senators* (New York: G.P. Putnam's Sons, 1954).

6. Frederick G. Lieb, *The Cincinnati Reds: An Informal History* (New York: G.P. Putnam's Sons, 1948).

7. Frederick G. Lieb, *The Detroit Tigers: An Informal History* (New York: G.P. Putnam's Sons, 1946).

8. Or five-time, if one considers Lajoie, rather than Cobb, to have won the controversial 1910 batting title. See George Vass, "Baseball Records: Fact or Fiction," *Baseball Digest* (June 2005): 26–7.

9. Franklin Lewis, *The Cleveland Indians* (New York: G.P. Putnam's Sons, 1949).

10. Robert Peterson, *Only the Ball Was White: A History of Legendary Black Players and All-Black Professional Teams* (New York: Oxford University Press, 1992); Leslie A. Heaphy, The *Negro Leagues, 1869–1960* (Jefferson, NC: McFarland & Company, 2013); Todd Peterson, *The Negro Leagues Were Major Leagues: Historians Reappraise Black Baseball* (Jefferson, NC: McFarland & Company, 2019).

11. Cottrell, *Blackball, the Black Sox, and the Babe*; John Thorn, "Whitman, Melville, and Baseball." (Jefferson City, NC: McFarland, 2002).

12 Thomas F. Gossett, *Race: The History of an Idea in North America* (Dallas: Southern Methodist University Press, 1963); Theodore Brantner Wilson, *The Black Codes of the South* (Tuscaloosa, AL: University of Alabama Press, 1965).

13 Robert C. Cottrell, *The Best Pitcher in Pitcher: The Life of Rube Foster, Negro League Giant* (New York: New York University Press, 2001); Sol White, *Sol White's History of Colored Baseball with Other Documents on the Early Black Game, 1886-1936* (Lincoln, NE: Bison Books, 1996).

14 Isabel Wilkerson, *The Warmth of Other Suns: The Epic Story of America's Great Migration* (New York: Random House, 2010).

15 Cottrell, *The Best Pitcher in Pitcher*; Paul Debono, *The Chicago American Giants* (Jefferson City, NC: McFarland & Company, 2011).

16 Cottrell, *Two Pioneers*; Janet Bruce, *The Kansas City Monarchs: Champions of Black Baseball* (Lawrence, KS: University of Kansas Press, 1986).

17 Jim Bankes, *The Pittsburgh Crawfords* (Jeffersons City, NC: McFarland & Company, 2001).

18 Brad Snyder, *Beyond the Shadow of the Senators: The Untold Story of the Homestead Gays and the Integration of Baseball* (New York: McGraw-Hill, 2003).

19 James E. Overmyer, *Black Ball and the Boardwalk: The Bacharach Giants of Atlantic City, 1916–1929* (Jefferson City, NC: McFarland & Company, 2014); Neil Lanctot, *Fair Dealing and Clean Playing: The Hilldale Club and the Development of Black Professional Baseball, 1910–1932* (Jefferson, NC: McFarland & Company, 1994).

Chapter 2

1 "Champions of the World," *New York Times*, October 26, 1888, p. 3; "Still Champions," *San Francisco Chronicle*, October 30, 1889, p. 6; Frank Graham, *The New York Giants: An Informal History of a Great Baseball Club* (New York: G.P. Putnam's Sons, 1952); Noel Hynd, *The Giants of The Polo Grounds: The Glorious Times of Baseball's New York Giants* (Dallas: Taylor Publishing, 1996).

2 Chris Epting, *The Early Polo Grounds* (Charleston, SC: Arcadia Publishing Library Editions, 2009).

3 Lyle Spatz and Steve Steinberg, *1921: The Yankees, the Giants, and the Battle for Baseball Supremacy in New York* (Lincoln, NE: University of Nebraska Press, 2010).

4 Frank Graham, *The Yankees: An Informal History* (New York: G. P. Putnam's Sons, 1947); *The New York Yankees: One Hundred Years, The Official Retrospective* (New York: Ballantine Books, 2003).

5 "Babe Ruth Is Sold to Yanks by Bostonians," *San Francisco Chronicle*, January 6, 1920, p. 14.

6 David J. Gordon, "The Rise and Fall of the Deadball Era," *Baseball Research Journal* (Fall 2018), https://sabr.org/journal/article/the-rise-and-fall-of-the-deadball-era/; Marty Appel, *Pinstripe Empire: The New York Yankees from before the Babe to after the Boss* (New York: Bloomsbury USA, 2012).

7 Cottrell, *Blackball, the Black Sox, and the Babe*.

8 John Horne, "The Babe's Called Shot," *National Baseball Hall of Fame*, https://baseballhall.org/discover-more/stories/baseball-history/called-shot.

9 Stanley Cohen, *Yankees 1936–39, Baseball's Greatest Dynasty: Lou Gehrig, Joe DiMaggio and the Birth of a New Era* (New York: Skyhorse, 2018).

10 Lew Freedman, *DiMaggio's Yankees: A History of the 1936–1944 Dynasty* (Jefferson City, NC: McFarland & Company, 2011).

11 Frank Graham, *The Brooklyn Dodgers: An Informal History* (New York: G.P. Putnam's Sons, 1945).

12 Michael Schiavone, *Dodgers vs. Yankees: The Long-Standing Rivalry between Two of Baseball's Greatest Teams* (New York: Sports Publishing, 2020).

13 "10 Black Baseball Sites in NYC," *Untapped New York*, https://untappedcities.com/2021/02/18/black-baseball-sites-nyc/.

14 Lester, *Black Baseball in New York City: An Illustrated History, 1885–1959*.

Chapter 3

1 "124 Still in Service," *Washington Post*, January 17, 1946, p. 10; Bob Feller, *Baseball Digest* (May 1946): cover; Ted Williams and Joe DiMaggio, *Baseball Digest* (July 1946): cover; Steve Treder, "1946: Major League Baseball's 1491," *The Hardball Times*, September 29, 2024, https://tht.fangraphs.com/tht-annual-2018/1946-major-league-baseballs-1491/.

2 Robert Weintraub, *The Victory Season: The End of World War II and the Birth of Baseball's Golden Age* (Boston: Little, Brown and Company, 2013).

3 Cottrell, *Two Pioneers*.

4 David E. Hubler and Joshua H. Drazen, *The Nats and the Grays: How Baseball in the Nation's Capital Survived WWII and Changed the Game Forever* (Lanham, MD: Rowman & Littlefield, 2015).

5   President Franklin D. Roosevelt, "Annual Message to Congress," January 6, 1941, Washington, DC, https://www.fdrlibrary.org/documents/356632/390886/readingcopy.pdf/42234a77-8127-4015-95af-bcf831db311d.

6   President Franklin D. Roosevelt, "Executive Order 8802: Prohibition of Discrimination in the Defense Industry," June 25, 1941, https://www.archives.gov/milestone-documents/executive-order-8802.

7   Edgar Rouzeau, "Black America Wars on Double Front for High Stakes," *Pittsburgh Courier*, February 7, 1942, p. 5.

8   Greg Robinson, *By Order of the President: FDR and the Internment of Japanese Americans* (Cambridge, MA: Harvard University Press, 2001).

9   Alex L. Swan, "The Harlem and Detroit Riots of 1943: A Comparative Analysis," *Berkeley Journal of Sociology* 16(1971–72): 75–93.

10 Matthew Delmont, *Half American: The Epic Story of African Americans Fighting World War II at Home and Abroad* (New York: Viking, 2022).

11 Cottrell, *Two Pioneers*; "Negro Major Clubs to Play Baseball," *New York Times*, January 23, 1945, p. 14.

12 Cottrell, *Two Pioneers*; Arnold Rampersad, *Jackie Robinson* (New York: Alfred A. Knopf, 1997).

13 Bill Ladson, "Monte Irvin Was Close to Breaking Color Barrier," *The Negro Leagues* (Negro Leagues Baseball Museum), https://www.mlb.com/history/negro-leagues/features/monte-irvin-was-close-to-breaking-color-barrier.

14 Cottrell, *Two Pioneers*; "Red Sox Test 3 Negroes," *New York Times*, April 17, 1945, p. 31.

15 "Florida Rule Bans Jackie," *Los Angeles Times*, March 22, 1946, p. 6; "Batting King Jackie Robinson Knocks at Major League Door," *Washington Post*, September 15, 1946, p. M6; Red Smith, "Model Ball Player," *New York Herald Tribune*, August 4, 1946.

16 Smith, "Model Ball Player."

17 Erin Blakemore, "How the GI Bill's Promise Was Denied to a Million Black WWII Veterans," *History*, June 21, 2023, https://www.history.com/news/gi-bill-black-wwii-veterans-benefits.

18 "Federal Help Sought for Blinded Veteran," *New York Times*, July 25, 1946, p. 23; "Louisiana: Quiet Week," *Time* XLVIII (August 26, 1946); Richard Gergel, *Unexampled Courage: The Blinding of Sgt. Isaac Woodard and the Awakening of President Harry S. Truman and Judge J. Waties* (New York: Sarah Crichton Books, 2019).

19 "Mexican Leaguers Raid U.S. Teams," *New York Times*, February 19, 1946, p. 29; Richard McKelvey, *Mexican Raiders in the Major Leagues: The Pasquel Brothers vs.*

Organized Baseball, 1946 (Jefferson City, NC: McFarland & Company, 2006); Robert Elias and Peter Dreier, *Major League Rebels: Baseball Battles over Workers' Rights and American Empire* (Lanham, MD: Rowman & Littlefield, 2022).

20. "'Contract Breakers' Warned by Chandler," *Los Angeles Times*, March 11, 1946, p. A6.

21. Cottrell, *The Year without a World Series*.

22. John B. Old, "Tour Hikes '46 Income to $175,000," *The Sporting News*, November 6, 1946, pp. 1–2.

23. Cottrell, *Two Pioneers*.

24. "Negro Homer King, Josh Gibson, Dies," *Washington Post*, January 21, 1947, p. 12.

Chapter 4

1. "Major League Miscellaneous Year-by-Year Averages and Totals," Baseball Reference, https://www.baseball-reference.com/leagues/majors/misc.shtml; "Majors Pass Attendance Record of 18,534,444 Set in '46," *The Sporting News*, September 17, 1947, p. 1; Red Barber, *1947: When All Hell Broke Loose in Baseball* (New York: Da Capo Press, 1984).

2. Cottrell, *Two Pioneers*; Louis Effrat, "Chandler Bars Durocher for 1947 Baseball Season," *New York Times*, April 10, 1947, p. 1; "Durocher—Always on the Spot," *Sport Magazine* (April 1947), cover.

3. Arthur Daley, "Baseball's Showmen—the Dodgers," *New York Times Magazine*, June 8, 1947, pp. 18, 32, 34.

4. *The Team That Forever Changed Baseball and America: The 1947 Brooklyn Dodgers*, ed. Lyle Spatz (Lincoln, NE: University of Nebraska Press, 2012); Duke Snider, *The Duke of Flatbush* (New York: Kensington Publishing Corporation, 1988); Tommy Holmes, "Jackie Robinson No Longer Unique," *Brooklyn Eagle*, July 22, 1947, p. 11; "A Rookie to Be Proud Of," *Brooklyn Eagle*, September 16, 1947, p. 8.

5. J.G. Taylor Spink, "Rookie of the Year . . . Jackie Robinson Gains Award on Basis of All-Around Ability," *The Sporting News*, September 17, 1947, p. 3.

6. Cottrell, *Two Pioneers*; Jules Tygiel, *Baseball's Great Experiment: Jackie Robinson and His Legacy* (New York: Oxford University Press, 2008).

7. Jackie Robinson, *Time* L (September 22, 1947): cover; "Rookie of the Year," *Time* L (September 22, 1947).

8. "Rookie of the Year."

9. "Doby Makes Debut as Indians Lose, 6–5," *New York Times*, July 6, 1947, p. 85.

10 *Bridging Two Dynasties: The 1947 New York Yankees*, ed. Lyle Spatz (Lincoln, NE: University of Nebraska Press, 2019).

11 John Drebinger, "Yanks Win Series, Page Taking Final from Dodgers, 5–2," *New York Times*, October 7, 1947, p. 1.

12 "Recommendations Made in the Report on Civil Rights and Their Preamble," *New York Times*, October 30, 1947, p. 14; Steven F. Lawson, *To Secure These Rights: The Report of President Harry S. Truman's Committee on Civil Rights* (Boston: Bedford/St. Martin's, 2003).

13 President Harry S. Truman, "Special Message to the Congress on Civil Rights," February 2, 1948, Harry S. Truman Library Museum, https://www.trumanlibrary.gov/library/public-papers/20/special-message-congress-civil-rights.

14 Al Wolf, "Tribe Takes World Series with 4–3 Win," *Los Angeles Times*, October 12, 1948, p. 1.

15 Jackie Robinson, "What's Wrong with Negro Baseball?" *Ebony* (June 1948): 16–24.

16 Louis Moore, "Bill Bruton's Fight for the Full Integration of Baseball," *Black Perspectives*, May 9, 2019, https://www.aaihs.org/bill-brutons-fight-for-the-full-integration-of-baseball/.

17 President Harry S. Truman, "Executive Order 9981: Desegregation of the Armed Forces," National Archives, July 26, 1948, https://www.archives.gov/milestone-documents/executive-order-9981; Anthony Leviero, "Truman Orders End of Bias in Forces and Federal Jobs; Addresses Congress Today," *New York Times*, July 27, 1948, pp. 1, 4; John E. Taylor, *Freedom to Serve: Truman, Civil Rights, and Executive Order 9981* (New York: Routledge, 2013).

18 President Harry S. Truman, "Executive Order 9980," *National Archives*, July 26, 1948; Harry S. Truman Library Museum, https://www.trumanlibrary.gov/library/executive-orders/9980/executive-order-9980.

19 President Harry S. Truman, transcript of address before the NAACP, June 29, 1949, Truman Library Institute, https://www.trumanlibraryinstitute.org/historic-speeches-naacp/#:~:text=We%20must%20take%20the%20Federal,responsibility%20to%20his%20fellow%20countrymen.

20 Leviero, "Truman Orders End of Bias in Forces and Federal Jobs; Addresses Congress Today."

21 "Mrs. Effa Manley Says Eagles Got $15,000 for Doby," *The Morning Call* (Paterson, NJ), May 22, 1948, p. 9.

22 John Klima, *Willie's Boys: The 1948 Birmingham Black Barons, the Last Negro League World Series, and the Making of a Baseball Legend* (Kutztown, PA: Trade Paper Press, 2009); Willie Mays, *Say Hey: The Autobiography of Willie Mays* (New York: Simon & Schuster, 1988).

23 "Negro League Dissolved," *New York Times*, December 1, 1948, p. 40.

24 J.G. Taylor Spink, "Looping the Loops," *The Sporting News*, October 20, 1948, p. 2.

25 "Irvin Signed for St. Paul," *New York Times*, December 28, 1948, p. 27.

26 Transcript of the meeting of President Harry S. Truman with Fahy Committee and Four Service Secretaries, January 12, 1949, National Archives Catalog, NAID: 257688205, https://catalog.archives.gov/id/257688205.

Chapter 5

1 Dan Daniel, "Yankees Call Casey to the Bat as Pilot," *The Sporting News*, October 20, 1948, p. 3.

2 Bill Bishop, "Casey Stengel," *Society for American Baseball Research*, https://sabr.org/bioproj/person/casey-stengel/.

3 Dan Daniel, "Casey Faces Toughest Yank Job Since '18," *The Sporting News*, October 20, 1948, p. 3; J.G. Taylor Spink, "Pennant Expect to Fly from New Poles: Flag Rating for Red Sox and Brooks," *The Sporting News*, April 20, 1949, p. 3.

4 Peter Golenbock, *Dynasty: The New York Yankees, 1949–1964* (New York: Prentice Hall Direct, 1975).

5 Dan Daniel, "Yank Hopes Totter on DiMaggio's Heel," *The Sporting News*, April 20, 1949, p. 2; Red Smith, "Casey Didn't Say Anything," *New York Herald Tribune*, September 10, 1949.

6 Dan Daniel, "Yankees Set New High in Drama in Throbbing Finish," *The Sporting News*, October 5, 1949, p. 6.

7 "Yankees and Dodgers Win Pennants in Final Games," pp. 1, 21; Dan Daniel, "Few Dual Flag Finishes as Red-Hot as '49," *The Sporting News*, October 5, 1949, p. 5.

8 J.G. Taylor Spink, "Don Won 17 for Dodgers; Roy Hit .306 for Browns," *The Sporting News*, October 26, 1949, p. 5; Irwin Winehouse, *The Duke Snider Story* (New York: Julian Messner, Inc., 1965).

9 Cottrell, *Two Pioneers*; John Lardner, "Reese and Robinson: Team Within a Team," *New York Times Magazine*, September 18, 1949, pp. 17, 19–20; Jackie Robinson, *Sport Magazine* (August 1949), cover. Harold C. Burr, "Dodgers' Jackie Robinson Wins Most Valuable Player Award," *Brooklyn Eagle*, November 18, 1949, p. 1.

10 Frank Graham, "New Yorkers Jittery about the Lip and His 'Kind of Team,'" *The Sporting News*, October 26, 1949, p. 2: Bill Roeder, "Giants Resent Lippy's Lashing—Cooper," *The Sporting News*, June 29, 1949, pp. 1–2.

11 John Drebinger, "Yanks Win Series, Beating Dodgers in Fifth Game, 10–6," *New York Times*, October 10, 1949, pp. 1, 27.

12 J.G. Taylor Spink, "Thar She Blows! Rickey Boils, Spouts," *The Sporting News*, October 19, 1949, pp. 1–2; Dan Daniel, "Weiss Wonders about Dodger Farm System," *The Sporting News*, October 26, 1949, pp. 1, 4; Dan Daniel, "Rickey Blasts Weiss for Claims for Yank Clubs," *The Sporting News*, November 2, 1949, p. 4.

13 Tom Meany, "Fall-Guy Casey Chuckles 'April Fool,'" *The Sporting News*, October 12, 1949, p. 5.

14 Carl. T. Felker, "Experts Strong for Dodgers, Red Sox," *The Sporting News*, April 19, 1950, pp. 1–2.

15 Dan Daniel, "Rizzuto Sparking Yanks in Streak," *The Sporting News*, June 7, 1950, p. 1; Red Smith, "It Never Happened Before," *New York Herald Tribune*, August 13, 1950.

16 Stan Baumgartner, "Bonus Kids Paying Off on Hill for Phils," *The Sporting News*, May 10, 1950, pp. 1–2.

17 Jackie Robinson, *Life* 28 (May 8, 1950): cover.

18 Joe King, "A Goat Grows in Brooklyn; Who Is It?: Mahatma's Blast Has Alibi Ring," *The Sporting News*, August 23, 1950, pp. 1–2; Jimmy Breslin, *Branch Rickey* (New York: Viking, 2011).

19 "Right Near the End of August," *The Sporting News*, August 23, 1950, p. 2.

20 "Yanks Win, 5–2; Take Series," *New York Times*, October 8, 1950, p. 1.

21 Austin Stevens, "President Praises Negro Troop Gain; Renews F.E.P.C. Bid," *New York Times*, May 23, 1950, pp. 1, 9; "Text of Truman's Statement on Equality," *New York Times*, May 23, 1950, p. 9.

Chapter 6

1 Jane Leavy, *The Last Boy: Mickey Mantle and the End of America's Childhood* (New York: Harper, 2010).

2 Dan Daniel, "Two-Way Slugger Fitted for Clipper's Shoes," *The Sporting News*, April 4, 1951, pp. 3–4; "Dodgers Slow Up Mickey—Then He Lowers Boom," *The Sporting News*, April 25, 1951, p. 4; Mickey Mantle, *The Mick: An American Hero: The Legend and the Glory* (New York: Jove, 1986).

3 Willard Mullin, "He'll Pass," *The Sporting News*, April 25, 1951, p. 1; J.G.T. Spink, "Looping the Loops: Yankees' Meteoric Mickey," *The Sporting News*, April 25, 1951, pp. 1, 4.

4   J.G. Taylor Spink, "Musial and Fain Named as Top Players: Roe, Feller Gain Awards as Hill Stars," *The Sporting News*, October 10, 1951, pp. 1–2.

5   Joe King, "$3,000,000—Player Value of Dodgers," *The Sporting News*, August 8, 1951, pp. 1–2.

6   "'Best N.L. Team since Cubs of '29,'" *The Sporting News*, August 8, 1951, p. 2.

7   Joe King, "Campanella Not Antique But Modernizer: Set Club Homer Mark for Catchers Last Season," *The Sporting News*, July 18, 1951, p. 3; "Reese: 'He's Good Even When He Isn't Perfect,'" *The Sporting News*, July 18, 1951, p. 3.

8   Clay Felker, "Mays Dynamite at Bat, Magnet in Field," *The Sporting News*, August 15, 1951, pp. 3–4. "Mays, Black Baron Star, Is Going Up," *Birmingham News*, June 22, 1950, p. 18; "Willie in Center for Giants 339 Days after High School Graduation," *Minneapolis Star*, May 25, 1951, p. 35.

9   Joe King, "Diamond Dossier: Shopworn Refuge from Mexico Now an 18-Karat Hill Gem," *The Sporting News*, June 20, 1951, p. 15.

10 Joe King, "The Lip Learns Old Soldiers Never Die: He's Haunted by Stalwarts Shipped Away," *The Sporting News*, May 9, 1951, pp. 1–2.

11 Joe King, "Bats May Carry Dodgers to Flag Romp," *The Sporting News*, May 30, 1951, pp. 1–2; Darvass, "Fearsome Flatbush Foursome," *The Sporting News*, May 30, 1951, p. 1; Joe King, "Mail Threats Spur Jackie to Bat Volley," *The Sporting News*, May 30, 1951, pp. 1, 4; "Jackie Lays Mail Threats to 'Crank,'" *The Sporting News*, May 30, 1951, p. 4.

12 Joe King, "High-Flying Giants Dive at Box Office," *The Sporting News*, September 5, 1951, p. 1–2; *The Team That Time Won't Forget: The 1951 New York Giants*, eds. Bill Nowlin and C. Paul Rogers III (Society for American Baseball Research, 2015).

13 Jackie Robinson, *Sport* (October 1951), cover.

14 Joshua Prager, "Was the '51 Giants Comeback a Miracle, or Did They Simply Steal the Pennant?" *Wall Street Journal*, January 31, 2001, p. 1; Joshua Prager, *The Echoing Green: The Untold Story of Bobby Thompson, Ralph Branca and the Shot Heard Round the World* (New York: Pantheon Books, 2006).

15 Red Smith, "Miracle of Coogan's Bluff," *New York Herald Tribune*, October 4, 1951.

16 Photograph of Joe DiMaggio awaiting ball in center field, with Mickey Mantle sprawled on the turf, *New York Times*, October 6, 1951, p. 1; "Yanks' Joy Over Triumph Is Tempered by Loss of Mantle for Remaining Games," *New York Times*, October 6, 1951, p. 10.

17 John Drebinger, "Yanks Win Series as Bauer's Triple Tops Giants, 4 to 3," *New York Times*, October 11, 1951, pp. 1, 52.

18 Roger Birtwell, "Clubs Using Negroes Finished 1-2-2-4-4," *The Sporting News*, February 6, 1952, pp. 3–4.

19 Jack McDonald, "The Georgia Peach Bats for Negroes—Tells How Colored Fans Can Help," *The Sporting News*, February 6, 1952, p. 4.

20 "Bombing Kills Negro Leader; Wife Hurt in Florida Home," *New York Times*, December 27, 1951, pp. 1, 22; Gregory Marquette, *The Bomb Heard Around the World: The Lives and Deaths of Harry T. and Harriette V. Moore* (Top Cat II Production Publishing Group, 2019).

Chapter 7

1 "Mantle Remains in 4-F Status," *Los Angeles Times*, August 19, 1952, p. C1; "Mantle Physical Oct. 6," *New York Times*, September 2, 1952, p. S2.

2 Christopher Jennison, *Wait 'Til Next Year* (New York: W.W. Norton & Company, Inc., 1974); Doris Kearns Goodwin, *Wait Till Next Year: A Memoir* (New York: Simon & Schuster, 1997).

3 James P. Dawson, "Irvin Breaks Ankle, Jolting Giants' Pennant Hopes," *New York Times*, April 3, 1952, p. 47; "Giants' Willie Mays Accepted for Armed Services in 2d Test," *Washington Post*, January 17, 1952, p. 13; Al Wolf, "Sportraits," *Los Angeles Times*, February 2, 1952, p. B2.

4 Arthur Daley, "Sports of the Times: Who Replaces Newk?" *New York Times*, January 7, 1952, p. 23.

5 Roscoe McGowen, "Marines Recall Coleman of Yanks and Merriman of Reds to Service," *New York Times*, January 11, 1952, p. 25; Adam Lazarus, *The Wingmen: The Unlikely, Unusual, Unbreakable Friendship Between John Glenn and Ted Williams* (New York: Citadel Press, 2023).

6 Will Grimsley, "Services Hitting Big Leagues Hard," *Washington Post*, February 2, 1952, p. 10.

7 "Pressure Off, Mantle Set for Big Year," *Los Angeles Times*, March 2, 1952, p. A14.

8 John Drebinger, "Yankees' Advantage in Pitching May Be Decisive Factor in Series," New York Times, September 29, 1952, p. 18.

9 "Snider Gets His Revenge on Reynolds," *Los Angeles Times*, October 2, 1952, pp. C1-2.

10 "Locker-Room Injury Hampers Erskine; Dodgers Praise Raschi, Rebuke Selves," *Los Angeles Times*, October 3, 1952, p. C2.

11 John Drebinger, "Yanks Win, 3–2, Tie Dodgers; Series to Be Decided Today," *New York Times*, October 7, 1952, pp. 1, 35; John Drebinger, "Yanks Take Series, Defeating Dodgers in 7th Contest, 4–2," *New York Times*, October 8, 1952, pp. 1, 38; "Stengel Equals Record," *New York Times*, October 8, 1952, p. 38.

12 Shirley Povich, "Yanks Win, 3–2; Mantle, Berra Match Snider Clouts: Duke's 2 Homers Tie Ruth, Gehrig," *Washington Post*, October 7, 1952, p. 1; Al Wolf, "Horns for Hodges—Wreath for Reynolds," *Los Angeles Times*, October 8, 1952, p. C1.

13 "Mantle Killed Us, Moans Robinson," *Los Angeles Times*, October 8, 1952, p. C2.

14 "Mantle Receives 3D Draft Physical," *New York Times*, October 23, 1952, p. 45; "Army Doctors Complete Examination of Mickey Mantle; Delay Decision," *Los Angeles Times*, October 24, 1952, p. C2; "Career Goes On: Mantle Rejected Again by Army—Knee Defect," *Los Angeles Times*, November 4, 1952, p. C1.

Chapter 8

1 "Ruth Involved in Projected Shift of Browns to Coast," *Washington Post*, July 26, 1951, p. 8; "Breadon Says His Cardinals Will Stay in St. Louis," *Washington Post*, August 3, 1947, p. C1.

2 Al Wolf, "Franchise Shift by Major Loops Seems Unlikely," *Los Angeles Times*, August 29, 1947, p. 10; Shirley Povich, "This Morning," *Washington Post*, September 6, 1947, p. 14.

3 Arthur Daley, "Sports of the Times: A Horrifying Prospect," *New York Times*, June 23, 1950, p. 41.

4 "Griffith Says Coast Faces Wait for Majors," *Los Angeles Times*, October 16, 1951, p. C1.

5 "New Proposal Dims PCL's Major Hopes," *Los Angeles Times*, November 29, 1951, p. C1.

6 Shirley Povich, "This Morning," *Washington Post*, March 15, 1953, p. C1; "High Brass Tells Veeck and Perini to Follow Rules," *Los Angeles Times*, March 16, 1953, p. C1; "Boston Up in Arms over Braves' Shift," *New York Times*, March 17, 1953, p. 32; Louis Effrat, "Transfer of Browns to Baltimore Rejected by American League Club Owners," *New York Times*, March 17, 1953, p. 32; Louis Effrat, "Braves Moves to Milwaukee; Majors' First Shift Since '03," *New York Times*, March 19, 1953, pp. 1, 38; J.G. Taylor Spink, "Braves to Milwaukee, Browns to Baltimore," *The Sporting News*, March 18, 1953, pp. 1, 4.

7 "Television Influenced His Move, Perini Says," *Washington Post*, March 19, 1953, p. 19; Lester Smith, "Braves Set Sail on Sea of Red Ink," *The Sporting News*, March 25, 1953, pp. 1, 8.

8 Louis Effrat, "Braves Move to Milwaukee; Majors' First Shift Since '03," *New York Times*, March 19, 1953, pp. 1, 38; "Milwaukee Roars Hello to Braves," *New York Times*, April 9, 1953, p. 1.

9   "Eddie Mathews," *Baseball Digest* (February 1953): cover; Harold Sheldon, "Long Distance Mathews," *Baseball Digest* (February 1953): 25–6.

10 Andrew Paul Mele, *"Tearin' Up the Pea Patch": The Brooklyn Dodgers, 1953* (Jefferson City, NC: McFarland Publishing, 2015).

11 Dan Daniel, "Mantle Make Home Run History at 21," *The Sporting News*, April 29, 1953, p. 13.

12 Charles Dexter, "Can Mickey Carry the Big Load?" *Baseball Digest* (April 1953): 5–9; "Mickey Mantle: New Pride of the Yankees," *Sport* (April 1953): cover.

13 "Kansas City May Try to Land Browns," *Washington Post*, July 18, 1953, p. 11; J.G. Taylor Spink, "Webb Sees K.C. as Major League Entry," *The Sporting News*, July 22, 1953, pp. 1–2; "Veeck Is Out West Seeking Ballpark," *New York Times*, August 19, 1953, p. 33; "Latest Guess—Browns to Canada," *Los Angeles Times*, September 23, 1953, pp. 1–2; Joe Trimble, "Webb Favors Major Loop Team in West," *Los Angeles Times*, July 14, 1953, pp. C1, 4; Joe Reichler, "Thinks A's Should Also Shift West," *Washington Post*, July 14, 1953, p. 13; Jack Geyer, "Veeck Says L.A. Won't Get Browns," *Los Angeles Times*, July 21, 1953, pp. C1, 3; "Bill Veeck Says Los Angeles, San Francisco 'Not for Us,'" *Los Angeles Times*, August 26, 1953, p. C1.

14 Jerry Liska, "League to Study 7-City List Veck Says Seeking Browns," *Washington Post*, September 10, 1953, p. 19; Joseph M. Sheehan, "Baltimore Gets St. Louis Browns as Syndicate Buys Veeck Interest," *New York Times*, September 30, 1953, pp. 1, 40; Shirley Povich, "A.L. Votes for Shift, 8–0, Veeck Sells Out," *Washington Post*, September 30, 1953, pp. 1, 17.

15 John Drebinger, "Yankees' 4 Homers Beat Dodgers, 11–7, for 3–2 Series Edge," *New York Times*, October 5, 1953, 35.

16 John Drebinger, "Yanks Take Fifth Series in Row, a Record," *New York Times*, October 6, 1953, pp. 1, 35; Dan Daniel, "'My Boy' Martin Surprised Even Casey in Series," *The Sporting News*, October 14, 1953, pp. 1, 6.

17 Harold Rosenthal, "Classy Farm Crop Backs Yankee Reign," *The Sporting News*, October 21, 1953, pp. 1–2; Louis Effrat, "Yankees Purchase Contracts of Two Negro Players from Kansas City Club," *New York Times*, October 14, 1953, p. 37.

18 Dan Daniel, "Dan Topping Denies Jim Crow Charge in Yankees' Failure to Call Up Power," *The Sporting News*, August 19, 1953, p. 4.

19 Joseph M. Sheehan, "Yankees Get Byrd and Eddie Robison in 13-Man Deal with Athletics," *New York Times*, December 17, 1953, p. 57.

20 Arthur Daley, "Sports of the Times: Grand Larceny," *New York Times*, December 18, 1953, p. 45.

21 Susan Goldman Rubin, *Brown v. Board of Education: A Fight for Simple Justice* (New York: Holiday House, 2016).

Chapter 9

1. Roscoe McGowen, "Dodgers Once Again Hear 'Wait 'Til Next Year,'" *New York Times*, October 6, 1953, p. 36.

2. Louis Effrat, "In Moment of Triumph, Stengel Talls of 'Good Chance' for Bombers in 1954," *New York Times*, October 6, 1953, p. 35.

3. "It Looks Like Yanks, Dodgers Will Meet Again in 1954 Series," *Los Angeles Times*, October 7, 1953, p. C1.

4. "Dressen Quits in Squabble with Dodgers over Contract," *Los Angeles Times*, October 15, 1953, pp. C1, 3.

5. "Exit Mr. Dressen," *Washington Post*, October 15, 1953, p. 18; "Reese Heads List for Dodger Job," *Washington Post*, October 17, 1953, p. 12; "Five Strong Candidates in Running," *Washington Post*, November 16, 1953, p. 14; "Alston Appointed Dodger Manager," *Los Angeles Times*, November 25, 1953, p. C1.

6. Hyamn C. Turkin, "Lip Gives Army-Bound Willie a 5-Star Rating," *New York Daily News*, May 29, 1952, p. C20; Grantland Rice, "Baseball Will Miss Willie," *Birmingham News*, May 28, 1952, p. 31; Wendell Smith, "Wendell Smith's Sports Beat," *Pittsburgh Courier*, June 7, 1952, p. 12.

7. Red Smith, "A Chapter Closes," *New York Herald Tribune*, May 29, 1952.

8. Arthur Daley, "Sports of the Times: Farewell to Willie," *New York Times*, May 29, 1952, p. 22; Daley, "Sports of the Times: The Year in Review," *New York Times*, December 21, 1952, p. S4.

9. Daley, "Sports of the Times: Farewell to Willie," p. 22.

10. "Giants Hear the Bad News: Willie Mays Stays in Army," *Washington Post*, March 17, 1953, p. 23; Shirley Povich, "Say, Hey, Willie, Hurry Back to Those Giants," *Washington Post*, May 21, 1953, p. 16.

11. Povich, "Say, Hey, Willie, Hurry Back to Those Giants."

12. "Willie Mays Hurt at Camp," *New York Times*, July 28, 1953, p. 24; "Players Must Serve Hitch Like All Gi's," *Washington Post*, July 28, 1953, p. 14.

13. "Willie Mays Gets out of Army on New Regulation," *Washington Post*, November 8, 1953, p. C6; Al Wolf, "Willie Mays' Army Release Due in Time for Giants' Spring Work," *Los Angeles Times*, January 15, 1954, p. C2.

14. Shirley Povich, "This Morning," *Washington Post*, January 28, 1954, p. 17.

15. "Willie Mays Gets Release Feb. 26 to Rejoin Giants," *Washington Post*, February 7, 1954, p. C3; Red Smith, "Giants in Gay Daze over Return of Mays," *Washington Post*, February 13, 1954, p. 13; Al Wolf, "Cubs, Giants, Orioles and Indians Begin Spring Work," *Los Angeles Times*, February 21, 1954, p. B10.

16 Al Wolf, "Franchise Shift L.A.'s Only Hope for Major Ball Team," *Los Angeles Times*, February 16, 1954, p. C2.

17 Roger Kahn, "Superman of the Giants: Willie Mays—That's All," *New York Herald Tribune*, March 27, 1954.

18 "Mays Released, Flies to Giants," *Washington Post*, March 2, 1954, p. 16; Louis Effrat, "Mays Marks Return to Giants with 400-Foot Homer at Phoenix," *New York Times*, March 3, 1954, p. 33; Louis Effrat, "Giants Subdue Yannigans as Mays and Katt Drive Home Runs at Phoenix," *New York Times*, March 5, 1954, p. 23; "Tribe Wallops Giants, 23–10," *Washington Post*, March 8, 1954, p. 9; "Orioles Rap Giants for Third in Row," *Los Angeles Times*, March 9, 1954, p. C3; "Mays Clouts Two Homers; Giants Win," *Los Angeles Times*, March 13, 1954, p. 9; Louis Effrat, "Antonelli Stars in 9-to-6 Victory," *New York Times*, March 19, 1954, p. 26.

19 Braven Dyer, "Sports Parade," *Los Angeles Times*, March 24, 1954, p. C1.

20 Arthur Daley, "Sports of the Times: Report of a Tourist," *New York Times*, March 28, 1954, p. S2; Dan Daniel, "'Great to Be Cardinal—Ex-Yank Raschi," *The Sporting News*, March 17, 1954, p. 5.

21 C.C. Johnson Spink, "Raschi Sale Jolts Complacency of 'Fat Cat' Yanks," *The Sporting News*, March 3, 1954, pp. 1, 6.

22 Willard Mullin, "Little Rays of Hope," *The Sporting News*, March 24, 1954, p. 1; John Drebinger, "Martin Ordered to Report for Army Induction Monday," *New York Times*, March 4, 1954, p. 35; "Pitcher Abandons Retirement Plan," *New York Times*, March 20, 1954, p. 18.

23 Louis Effrat, "Hearn and Liddle Aid in 4–2 Victory," *New York Times*, April 1, 1954, p. 45; Louis Effrat, "Giants' 13 Blows Down Indians, 6–1," *New York Times*, April 4, 1954, p. S1.

24 Carl Lundquist, "Ex-GIs Could Scramble Major Races," *The Sporting News*, April 7, 1954, pp. 1–2.

25 John Drebinger, "Yanks and Dodgers Choices Despite Big Question Marks," *New York Times*, April 11, 1954, pp. S1-2; Roscoe McGowen, "Mantle Operation Is Successful, But He Is Warned on Knee Strain," *New York Times*, February 4, 1954, p. 32; "Mantle Rivals DiMaggio as an Invalid," *Washington Post*, February 9, 1954, p. 14.

26 Drebinger, "Yanks and Dodgers Choices Despite Big Question Marks," pp. S1-2; Harold Sheldon, "I'm Going After 25!" *Baseball Digest* (April 1954): 5.

27 Drebinger, "Yanks and Dodgers Choices Despite Big Question Marks," pp. S1-2.

28 Tom Meany, *Milwaukee's Miracle Braves* (New York: A.S. Barnes and Company, 1954). See also Tom Meany, "How Mathews Compares to Babe Ruth," *Baseball Digest* (June 1954): 13–15.

29 Dan Daniel, "Three New Men Boost Stengel's Hopes for No. 6," *The Sporting News*, April 14, 1954, pp. 1, 6; Casey Stengel, "Man of the Year," *Sport* (March 1954), cover.

Chapter 10

1 Bill Madden, *1954: The Year Willie Mays and the First Generation of Black Superstars Changed Major League Baseball Forever* (New York: Da Capo Press, 2014); James S. Hirsch, *Willie Mays: The Life, the Legend* (New York: Scribner, 2010).

2 John Drebinger, "Giants Defeat Dodgers as Five Home Runs Highlight Polo Grounds Opener," *New York Times*, April 14, 1954, p. 36; Roscoe McGowen, "Rival Managers Briefed by Frick," *New York Times*, April 14, 1954, p. 36; Arthur Daley, "Sports of the Times: Another Opening Day," *New York Times*, April 15, 1954, p. 41.

3 "President Opens Baseball Season, Sees 3-Hour Game," *New York Times*, April 14, 1954, p. 1.

4 Joseph M. Sheehan, "Baltimore Hails Return to Majors; Orioles Respond by Beating White Sox," *New York Times*, April 16, 1954, p. 25.

5 Roscoe McGowen, "Maglie Magic Works Again as Giants Top Dodgers at Ebbets Field," *New York Times*, April 19, 1954, p. 26.

6 Eddie Burbridge, "Layin' It on the Line," *Los Angeles Sentinel*, April 22, 1954, p. B1.

7 "Mays' Homer Wins in 14th," *Washington Post and Times Herald*, May 1, 1954, p. 17; "Five Homers Set New Record," *Los Angeles Times*, May 3, 1954, p. C1.

8 "House Unit to List 10 Army Athletes," New York Times, May 3, 1954, p. 19; "Army to Check Assignments of Athletes after Induction," *Washington Post and Times Herald*, May 4, 1954, p. 26; Jack Walsh, "Yanks Blast Committee for Error on Bauer," *Washington Post and Times Herald*, May 5, 1954, p. 29; Jack Walsh, "Ray Robinson's 'Desertion' Rehashed by Athlete Probers," *Washington Post and Times Herald*, May 8, 1954, p. 15; "Name 4 in House Quiz on 'Coddling,'" *Los Angeles Sentinel*, May 13, 1954, p. C5.

9 John Drebinger, "Polo Grounds Turned Back, 5-4," *New York Times*, May 7, 1954, p. 28; John Drebinger, "Mays' Drive Helps Vanquish Pirates," *New York Times*, May 9, 1954, pp. 1-2; "Maglie Beats Pirates, 5-1; First to Win Five in National," *Washington Post and Times Herald*, May 10, 1954, p. 22.

10 John Lardner, "Lardner's Week: The Fifty Per Cent Color Line," *Newsweek* 43 (May 10, 1954): 95; Lee Lowenfish, "The Rise of Baseball's Racial Quota System in the 1950s," *Nine* (Spring 2008): 52–61.

11 Joseph M. Sheehan, "Janses Triumphs by 6-3 as Irvin Hits 2 Polo Grouns 4-Baggers," *New York Times*, May 14, 1954, p. 27.

12 "Mays, Hearn Errors Smooth Cubs' Path, 4-3," *Los Angeles Times*, May 16, 1954, p. B9; "Milwaukee, Giants Split," *Washington Post and Times Herald*, May 17, 1954, p. 22.

13 Shirley Povich, "This Is Morning," *Washington Post and Times Herald*, May 18, 1954, p. 27.

14 U.S. Supreme Court, *Brown v. Board of Education*, 347 US 483 (May 17, 1954; Luther A. Huston, "High Court Bans School Segregation; 9-To-0 Decision Grants Time to Comply," *New York Times*, May 18, 1954, pp. 1, 14.

15 John Drebinger, "Polo Grounders Rally to Win, 5–4," *New York Times*, May 25, 1954, p. 30; William J. Briordy, "22-Hit Drive Routs Pittsburgh, 21 To 4," *New York Times*, May 26, 1954, p. 38; William J. Briordy, "Williams' Homer Decides Game, 2–1," *New York Times*, May 27, 1954, p. 35.

16 John Drebinger, "4 Homers in 8th Mark 17–6 Victory," *New York Times*, May 29, 1954, p. 19; "Dodgers Win over Giants," *Los Angeles Times*, May 31, 1954, p. C2; Arthur Daley, "Sports of the Times: Polo Grounds Chatter," *New York Times*, May 31, 1954, p. 17.

17 "Joe Black of Dodgers Sent to Montreal Royals," *Los Angeles Sentinel*, June 3, 1954, p. B1.

18 Shirley Povich, "This Morning," *Washington Post and Times Herald*, June 3, 1954, p. 31; John Drebinger, "Thompson, Mays Pace 13–8 Victory," *New York Times*, June 4, 1954, p. 30.

19 Bob Addie, "Sports Addition," *Washington Post and Times Herald*, June 6, 1954, p. C2.

20 Braven Dyer, "Sports Parade," *Los Angeles Times*, June 22, 1954, p. C1; "Mays, Dark Lead Giants over Cards," *Washington Post and Times Herald*, June 22, 1954, p. 25.

21 Shirley Povich, "This Morning," *Washington Post and Times Herald*, June 23, 1954, p. 25.

22 John Drebinger, "Three Home Runs Help Braves Vanquish Polo Grounders, 5 to 2," *New York Times*, June 24, 1954, p. 35; John Drebinger, "Liddle Sets Back Milwaukee, 2 to 1," *New York Times*, June 25, 1954, p. 24; Joseph M. Sheehan, "Early Drive Trips Chicagoans, 6 to 2," *New York Times*, June 26, 1954, p. 8; Hirsch, *Willie Mays*.

23 Al Wolf, "Sportraits," *Los Angeles Times*, June 27, 1954, p. B7.

24 Arthur Daley, "Sports of the Times: Casting a Ballot," *New York Times*, June 27, 1954, p. S2.

25 Shirley Povich, "This Morning: He's Willie 'The Wonderful' Mays to Giants," *Washington Post and Times Herald*, June 27, 1954, p. C1.

26 Shirley Povich, "This Morning: He's Willie 'The Wonderful' Mays to Giants," *Washington Post and Times Herald*, June 27, 1954, p. C1.

27 Shirley Povich, "This Morning," *Washington Post and Times Herald*, June 28, 1954, p. 19; Shirley Povich, "This Morning," *Washington Post and Times Herald*, June 29, 1954, p. 23.

28 Joe King, "Crowds Thrill to Mays' Great Play in Clutch," *The Sporting News*, July 7, 1954, p. 5.

29 "Giants Beat Cubs, 3–2, in Tenth, Mays Starts," *Washington Post and Times Herald*, June 28, 1954, p. 22.

30 Arthur Daley, "Sports of the Times: Leo Rereads the Book," *New York Times*, June 29, 1954, p. 32.

31 Eddie Burbridge, "Layin' It on the Line," *Los Angeles Sentinel*, July 1, 1954, p. B1.

32 Shirley Povich, "This Morning," *Washington Post and Times Herald*, July 1, 1954, p. 31; Shirley Povich, "This Morning," *Washington Post and Times Herald*, July 4, 1954, p. C1.

33 Bob Addie, "Sport Addition," *Washington Post and Times Herald*, July 1, 1954, p. 33.

34 Walter Winchell, "Memos of a Midnighter," *Washington Post and Times Herald*, July 1, 1954, p. 55.

35 Shirley Povich, "This Morning," *Washington Post and Times Herald*, July 2, 1953, p. 33; Bob Addie, "Sports Addition," *Washington Post and Times Herald*, July 4, 1954.

36 Shirley Povich, "This Morning," *Washington Post and Times Herald*, June 30, 1954, p. 25; John Drebinger, "Two-Run Uprising Trips Brooks, 4–3," *New York Times*, June 30, 1954, p. 33.

37 "Mays Ahead of Ruth by Three Games," *Los Angeles Times*, July 9, 1954, p. C1.

38 Shirley Povich, "This Morning," *Washington Post and Times Herald*, July 9, 1954, p. 31.

39 Gilbert Millstein, "'Natural Boy' of the Giants," *New York Times Magazine*, July 11, 1954, pp. 16, 40–1; "Hat Trick," *New York Times Magazine*, July 11, 1954, p. 41.

40 John Drebinger, "American League's 17 Hits End National's All-Star Game Streak at Four," *New York Times*, July 14, 1954, p. 34.

41 Dorothy Kilgallen, "Willie, Won't You Sign with Me?" *Washington Post and Times Herald*, July 16, 1954, p. 58.

42 Willie Mays, *Time* LXIV (July 26, 1954): cover.

43 Joe Reichler, "If Baseball Career Is Your Aim—Forget Center Field," *Washington Post and Times Herald*, July 25, 1954, p. C5.

44 Whitney Martin, "Mays' 60-Home Run Target Comparable to 4-Minute Mile," *Washington Post and Times Herald*, July 31, 1954, p. 13.

45 John Drebinger, "Dodgers Trounce Giants for Sweep of Series and Now Trail by Half Game," *New York Times*, August 16, 1954, p. 20; Charles Einstein, *Willie's Time: A Memoir* (New York: Penguin, 1992), p. 100.

46 John Drebiner, "Antonelli Hurls 20th Victory, 4–1," *New York Times*, August 31, 1954, p. 15; Shirley Povich, "This Morning," *Washington Post and Times Herald*, August 31, 1954, p. 16; Joe King, "Mays, Antonelli MVP Standouts in N.L.," *The Sporting News*, September 15, 1954, pp. 1–2.

47 "Kluszewski Homers Twice but Phils Beat Reds, 9–3," *Washington Post and Times Herald*, September 1, 1954, p. 27; Shirley Povich, "This Morning," *Washington Post and Times Herald*, September 3, 1954, p. 31.

48 Al Wolf, "Sportraits," *Los Angeles Times*, September 7, 1954, p. C2.

49 Douglas Wallop, *The Year the Yankees Los the Pennant* (New York: Norton, 1954).

50 Willar Mullin, "Ruins All," *The Sporting News*, September 22, 1954, p. 1.

51 Willie Mays, *Baseball Digest* (September 1954): cover; Willie Mays, as told to Milton Richman, "I'd Play for Nothing," *Los Angeles Times*, September 12, 1954, p. K12.

52 John Drebinger, "Giants Clinch 1954 Pennant as Maglie Tops Brooks, 7–1," *New York Times*, September 21, 1954, pp. 1, 32; "Mays Gets 3 Hits to Clinch Batting Crown," Los Angeles Times, September 7, 1954, p. C1.

53 Tallulah Bankhead, "What Is So Rare as a Willie Mays?" *Look* 18 (September 21, 1954).

54 Al Wolf, "Giants Top Indians in 10th, 5 to 2," *Los Angeles Times*, September 30, 1954, pp. 1, 29; Roscoe McGowen, "Heroics of Mays, Rhodes, Grisson Regarded as Routine by Happy Giants," *New York Times*, September 30, 1954, p. 40.

55 McGowen, "Heroics of Mays, Rhodes, Grisson Regarded as Routine by Happy Giants."

56 John Drebinger, "78,102 See Finale," *New York Times*, October 3, 1951, p. S1.

57 Louis Efrat, "Lopez Lauds 'Hot' Giants, Who Did Everything Right against 'Cold' Indians," *New York Times*, October 3, 1954, p. S2.

58 Arthur Daley, "Sports of the Times: He Generates Excitement," *New York Times*, October 5, 1954, p 31.

59 C.C. Johnson Spink, "Moon and Grim Named Top Rookies," *The Sporting News*, October 6, 1954, pp. 1–2; J.G. Taylor Spink, "Mays and Avila No. 1 Players of '54," The Sporting News, October 13, 1954, pp. 1, 6; "Mays Voted Most Valuable Player in NL," *Los Angeles Times*, December 17, 1954, p. C1; "Mays and Berra Head All-Stars," *New York Times*, December 18, 1954, p. 19; "Moon Named Top Rookie in Majors," *Los Angeles Times*, December 20, 1954, p. C3; "Mays Is Selected 'Athlete of Year,'" *New York Times*, December 22, 1954, p. 33; Edgar G. Brands, "Major Citations Swept by Giants," *The Sporting News*, January 5, 1955, pp. 1–2.

Chapter 11

1. Kahn, *The Boys of Summer*.

2. Jackie Robinson, "A Kentucky Colonel Kept Me in Baseball, Part II," *Look* 19 (February 8, 1955): 82.

3. "Negro Girl Convicted," *New York Times*, March 19, 1955, p. 36.

4. Lanse McCurley, "House of Mack—A House Divided," *The Sporting News*, November 10, 1954, pp. 1, 6; Ernest Mehl, "Johnson Firm Believer in Own Destiny," *The Sporting News*, November 17, 1954, pp. 3, 6; Ernest Mehl, "Persistence Won Obstacle Race for Kaycee," *The Sporting News*, November 17, 1954, pp. 5-6; Jack Gallagher, "Money Galore—and Fans Who Always Support Teams," *The Sporting News*, December 1, 1954, pp. 1-2.

5. Jack Gallagher, "Money Galore—and Fans Who Always Support Teams," *The Sporting News*, December 1, 1954, pp. 1-2; Hal Lebovitz, "Greenberg Asks for Ten Clubs in A.L.," *The Sporting News*, November 17, 1954, pp. 1-2.

6. Dan Daniel, "National League to Discuss Plans to Invade Coast," *The Sporting News*, November 17, 1954, p. 2; "'Majors Will Invade Coast within Three Years'—Lane," *The Sporting News*, November 17, 1954, p. 2.

7. Roscoe McGowen, "'No Trade Offers for Jackie'—But It's a Long Time to April," *The Sporting News*, November 17, 1954, p. 2.

8. Arthur Daley, "Sports of the Times: It Figured," *New York Times*, November 24, 1954, p. 29.

9. Roscoe McGowen, "Dodgers' New Year Needs: A New Campy and Newcombe," *The Sporting News*, January 5, 1955, p. 2.

10. "Lippy Says Willie Mays Better than Stan Musial," *Los Angeles Times*, January 19, 1955, p. C1.

11. Dan Daniel, "Delving into New Year with Dan," *The Sporting News*, January 5, 1955, pp. 3-4.

12. Al Wolf, "Sportraits," *Los Angeles Times*, February 6, 1955, p. B7.

13. Arthur Daley, "Sports of the Times: Under the Sheltering Palms," *New York Times*, February 27, 1955, p. S2.

14. Shirley Povich, "This Morning," *Washington Post and Times Herald*, April 7, 1955, p. 31.

15. Shirley Povich, "Those 'Superlative Bums' Should Take It All," *Washington Post and Times Herald*, April 3, 1955, p. C1; Povich, "This Morning," April 7, 1955, p. 31.

16 Dan Parker, "Baseball Forecast for 1955," *Washington Post and Times Herald*, April 10, 1955, pp. AW10-12.

17 John Lardner, "A Baseball Fan's Favorites," *New York Times Magazine*, April 10, 1955, p. 27.

18 Cover with Willie Mays, Lorraine Day, and Leo Durocher, *Sports Illustrated* (April 11, 1955).

19 Duke Snider, *Sport Life* (September 1951): cover.

20 Duke Snider, *Baseball: 1953* (1953): cover; "Duke Snider: Brooklyn Dodgers," *Sport* (September 1954): cover.

21 Arthur Mann, "The Dodgers' Problem Child," *Saturday Evening Post* (February 20, 1954): 27, 111, 113; Charles Dexter, "The Duke's a King Now," *Baseball Digest* (November 1952): 6.

Chapter 12

1 Shirley Povich, "This Morning," *Washington Post and Times Herald*, May 26, 1955, p. 35.

2 Willard Mullin, "The Peer of Punch," *The Sporting News*, May 25, 1955, p. 3; Roscoe McGowen, "Duke Proves Dynamo in Dodger Drive," *The Sporting News*, May 25, 1955, p. 3.

3 "Mantle Hammers Three Home Runs," *Los Angeles Times*, May 14, 1955, p. B1; Jack Walsh, "Mantle Gets on Base for 15th Straight Time but Is It a Record? Nobody Seems to Know," *Washington Post and Times Herald*, May 23, 1955, p. 18; Bob Addie, "Bob Addie's Column," *Washington Post and Times Herald*, May 27, 1955, p.64; Joe Falls, "Ed Robinson Hammers 2; Mantle Hits One a 'Mile'," *Washington Post and Times Herald*, June 7, 1955, p. 18.

4 Bob Addie, "Bob Addie's Column," *Washington Post and Times Herald*, May 28, 1955, p. 12.

5 "Snider's 3 Homers Pace Dodger Win," *Los Angeles Times*, June 2, 1955, p. C1; Joseph M. Sheehan, "Brooklyn's Duke Making Bid for Batting's Triple Crown," *New York Times*, June 7, 1955, p. 43.

6 Sheehan, "Brooklyn's Duke Making Bid for Batting's Triple Crown," p. 43.

7 Eddie Burbridge, "Layin' It on the Line," *Los Angeles Sentinel*, June 9, 1955, p. B1.

8 "Majors Have Hurt Negro Ball," *Washington Post and Times Herald*, July 10, 1955, p. C6.

9 Al Wolf, "Sportraits," *Los Angeles Times*, July 20, 1955, p. C2.

10 *Brown v. Board of Education*, 347 U.S.483.

11 "Slain Youth's Body Seen by Thousands," *New York Times*, September 4, 1955, p. S9; "Mississippi Jury Acquits 2 Accused in Youth's Killing," *New York Times*, September 24, 1955, p. 1; Timothy B. Tyson, *The Blood of Emmett Till* (New York: Simon & Schuster, 2017).

12 Al Wolf, "Sportraits," June 12, 1955, p. 88.

13 Wolf, "Sportraits," June 12, 1955, p. 88.

14 Shirley Povich, "This Morning," *Washington Post and Times Herald*, June 14, 1955, p. 21.

15 Al Wolf, "Sportraits," *Los Angeles Times*, June 20, 1955, p. C2; Eddie Burbridge, "Layin' It on the Line," *Los Angeles Sentinel*, June 23, 1955, p. B1.

16 Arthur Daley, "Sports of the Times: Not a Secret Ballot," *New York Times*, June 26, 1955, p. S2; Al Wolf, "Sportraits," *Los Angeles Times*, June 28, 1955, p. C2.

17 "Duke Snider: The Sluggers in Full Cover," *Sports Illustrated* (June 27, 1955): cover; "Duke or Willie? A Vote for Snider," *Sports Illustrated* (June 27, 1955).

18 "Mays Ruins Dodgers by Himself, 6–1," *Los Angeles Times*, June 30, 1955, p. C1; Shirley Povich, "This Morning," *Washington Post and Times Herald*, June 29, 1954, p. 29.

19 Al Wolf, "Sportraits," *Los Angeles Times*, July 6, 1955, p. C2.

20 Shirley Povich, "This Morning," *Washington Post and Times Herald*, July 20, 1956, p. 20.

21 "Duke Snider Hopes 'Nobody Ever Breaks Ruth's Record,'" *Washington Post and Times Herald*, August 7, 1955, p. C1.

22 "Snider, Banks Run Ahead of Ruth's Mark," *Washington Post and Times Herald*, August 7, 1955, p. C2; Al Wolf, "Sportraits," *Los Angeles Times*, August 14, 1955, p. B7; John Drebinger, "Storming That Magic '60,'" *New York Times*, August 10, 1955, p. 29.

23 "Snider Blast Dodger Fans Then He Takes It All Back," *Washington Post and Times Herald*, August 27, 1955, p. 12.

24 "Snider Blast Dodger Fans Then He Takes It All Back."

25 Arthur Daley, "Sports of the Times: The Duke's Pop-Off," *New York Times*, August 30, 1955, p. 21.

26 Duke Snider, *Sport* (September 1955): cover; Al Stump, "Duke Snider's Story," *Sport* (September 1955).

27 Al Stump, "Duke Snider's Story," *Sport* (September 1955).

28 Arthur Daley, "Sports of the Times: The Unkindest Cut of All," *New York Times*, August 17, 1955, p. 35; Arthur Daley, "Sports of the Times: Return of a Firebrand," *New York Times*, September 9, 1955, p. 29.

29 Bob Addie, "Bob Addie's Column," *Washington Post and Times Herald*, July 17, 1955, p. C2; Ned Cronin, "Cronin's Corner," *Los Angeles Times*, September 3, 1955, p. B3.

30 Kahn, "The Ten Years of Jackie Robinson," pp. 12, 76.

31 Roger Kahn, "The Ten Years of Jackie Robinson," *Sport* (October 1955): 12, 76–8, 82.

32 Arthur Daley, "Sports of the Times: The Long Road Home," *New York Times*, September 13, 1955, p. 35.

33 "Snider, Kaline Selected as Outstanding Players," *New York Times*, October 16, 1955, p. S11; Bob Broeg, "Snider, Roberts, Kaline, Ford Best in '55," *The Sporting News*, October 19, 1955, pp. 1–2; "Two Dodgers Placed on AP All-Star Team," *Los Angeles Times*, November 14, 1955, p. 38.

34 "Two Dodgers Placed on AP All-Star Team."

35 Red Smith, "The Case of Willie Mays," *Baseball Digest* (November-December 1955): 15–16.

36 Jimmy Cannon, "Why Durocher Was Fired," *Baseball Digest* (November-December 1955): 74, 76; "Managers' Box Score," *Baseball Digest* (November-December 1955): 75.

37 "Managers' Box Score," p. 75.; Broeg, "Snider, Roberts, Kaline, Ford Best in '55."

38 John Drebinger, "Yanks Win First; Collins' 2 Homers Beat Dodgers, 6–5," *New York Times*, September 29, 1955, pp. 1, 40.

39 "Dodgers Tie Series, 2–2, by Defeating Yanks, 8–5," *New York Times*, October 2, 1955, p. 1; Al Wolf, "Plenty of Room for Series Laurels," *Los Angeles Times*, October 2, 1955, p. B7; Arthur Daley, "Sports of the Times: The Spell Is Broken," *New York Times*, October 2, 1955, p. S2.

40 Will Grimsley, "'The Duke Wrecked Us,' Says Casey," *Los Angeles Times*, October 3, 1955, p. C3.

41 Ted Smits, "Snider Vows He Will Play Today," *Los Angeles Times*, October 4, 1955, pp. C1.

42 John Drebinger, "Dodgers Capture 1st World Series; Podres Wins, 2–0," *New York Times*, October 5, 1955, pp. 1, 42.

43 Franklin Lewis, "The Yankees Were Dis-Mantled," *Baseball Digest* (November-December 1955): 49–50.

44 Louis Effrat, "Bombers, Conceding Better Team Won, Show No Sadness in Dressing Room," *New York Times*, October 5, 1955, p. 44.

45 Effrat, "Bombers, Conceding Better Team Won," p. 44.

46 Al Wolf, "Sportraits," *Los Angeles Times*, October 7, 1955, p. C2.

47 Wolf, "Sportraits," October 7, 1955, p. C2.

48 Edgar G. Brands, "No. 1 Men of the Year," *The Sporting News*, January 4, 1956, pp. 1–2.

49 The City of Montgomery, No. 41464, Recorder's Court, December 5, 1955, Frank Johnson Papers, Manuscript Division, Library of Congress; Jeanne Theoharis, *The Rebellious Life of Mrs. Rosa Parks* (Boston: Beacon Press, 2013).

50 Martin Luther King, Jr., *Stride Toward Freedom: The Montgomery Story* (New York: Harper & Brothers, Publishers: 1958).

51 "Negro Leader Slain in Georgia Dispute," *New York Times*, February 19, 1956, pp. 1, 49.

Chapter 13

1 "Baseball-Hungry Fans Ask for Answers to Questions."

2 Charles Dexter, "It'll Be Dodgers—N.L. Analysis Rates Cards 3D," *Baseball Digest* (April 1956): 32, 36; Hal Middlesworth, "____ and Yanks Again!: Red Sox Top A.L. Challengers," *Baseball Digest* (April 1956): 33.

3 "Strength, Weakness of Clubs in Majors," *Washington Post*, April 1, 1956, p. C2.

4 "National League," *Washington Post and Times Herald*, April 1, 1956, p. C2.

5 Shirley Povich, "Yankees, Dodgers Again Have Too Much Class," *Washington Post and Times Herald*, April 8, 1956, p. C1.

6 Dan Parker, "Baseball Forecast: 30 Experts from Coast to Coast," *Washington Post and Times Herald*, April 15, 1956, p. AW6-7, 9.

7 Roscoe McGowan, "Dodgers Should Retain League Title," *Washington Post and Times Herald*, April 15, 1956, p. M9.

8 Frank Finch, "Here's the Pitch," *Los Angeles Times*, April 16, 1956, p. C2.

9 Arthur Daley, "Sports of the Times: In the Pink," *New York Times*, February 26, 1956, p. S2; Arthur Daley, "Sports of the Times: Within Range," *New York Times*, November 14, 1955, p. 36; "Bob Addie's Column," *Washington Post and Times Herald*, March 18, 1956, p. C3.

10 "Mantle Sidelines by Sore Arm, Leg," *Washington Post and Times Herald*, March 14, 1956, p. 27; John Drebinger, "Yankees Down Athletics," *New York Times*, March 22, 1956, p. 41.

11 Shirley Povich, "Mantle Just Bursting into Full Magnificence," *Washington Post and Times Herald*, March 25, 1956, p. C1.

12 Povich, "Mantle Just Bursting into Full Magnificence," p. C1.

13 Bob Addie, "Bob Addie's Column," *Washington Post and Times Herald*, March 29, 1956, p. 43.

14 Shirley Povich, "This Morning," *Washington Post and Times Herald*, March 30, 1956, p. 59.

15 "Mantle Will Be Out 3 or 4 Days with Injury," *Washington Post and Times Herald*, March 30, 1956, p. 59; Shirley Povich, "This Morning," *Washington Post and Times Herald*, April 1, 1956, p. C1.

16 "Bruton Says Mays Has Finest Throwing Arm," *Washington Post and Times Herald*, March 6, 1956, p. 20.

17 Frank Finch, "Mays Best Bet to Bust Babe's Mark," *Los Angeles Times*, March 12, 1956, p. C2; "This Could be Willie's Big Year," *Washington Post and Times Herald*, March 18, 1956, p. C6.

18 Louis Effrat, "Tribe Triumphs at Tucson by 10–5," *New York Times*, March 30, 1956, p. 29; "Mays Clouts 3 Homers, Drives in 9," *Los Angeles Times*, April 1, 1956, p. B6.

Chapter 14

1 "Stengel Will Start Lumpe at Shortstop," *Washington Post and Times Herald*, April 16, 1956, p. 10; "Mantle Raps 2 Home Runs as Sluggers Rule Openers," *Los Angeles Times*, April 18, 1956, pp. C1-2.

2 "Alston Picks Robinson," *Washington Post and Times Herald*, April 16, 1956, p. 10.

3 "One for Mickey," *Washington Post and Times Herald*, April 18, 1956, p. 19; Bob Addie, "Bob Addie's Column," *Washington Post and Times Herald*, April 18, 1956, p. 21.

4 Shirley Povich, "This Morning," *Washington Post and Times Herald*, April 19, 1956, p. 31.

5 Addie, "Bob Addie's Column," April 20, 1956, p. 65.

6 "Mantle's Bat Paces Yanks to 7–1 Victory," *Los Angeles Times*, April 21, 1956, p. B1; "Casey Claim Mickey Can Break Record," *Los Angeles Times*, April 22, 1956, p. 10.

7 "Casey Claims Mickey Can Break Record," *Los Angeles Times*, April 22, 1956, p. B10.

8 Joseph M. Sheehan, "5 in Eight Decide: Yanks Win after 8–0 Lead Fades," *New York Times*, April 22, 1956, p. 201; Arthur Daley, "Sports of the Times: A Reformed Man," *New York Times*, April 22, 1956, p. 202.

9 Daley, "Sports of the Times: A Reformed Man, p. 202.

10 Dan Daniel, "Mantle Has Reached Cross-Roads of Career," *The Sporting News*, April 25, 1956, p. 13.

11 Shirley Povich, "This Morning," *Washington Post and Times Herald*, May 7, 1956, p. 13.

12 Frank Finch, "Here's the Pitch," *Los Angeles Times*, May 8, 1956, p. C2; Bob Addie, "Bob Addie's Column," *Washington Post and Times Herald*, May 27, 1956, p. C3; Shirley Povich, "This Morning," *Washington Post and Times Herald*, May 27, 1956, p. C1.

13 Joseph M. Sheehan, "Mantle Hits 19th and 20th Homers to Help Yankees Defeat Senators Twice," *New York Times*, May 31, 1956, p. 30.

14 Arthur Daley, "The Boy Grew Older," *New York Times*, May 31, 1956, p. 30.

15 Daley, "The Boy Grew Older," p. 30.

16 Duke Snider with Roger Kahn, "I Play Baseball for Money, Not Fun," *Collier's* (May 1956): 42.

17 Bob Addie, "Bob Addie's Column," *Washington Post and Times Herald*, May 11, 1956, p. 59.

18 Shirley Povich, "This Morning," *Washington Post and Times Herald*, May 20, 1956, p. C1; Robert P. Jordan, "Magazine Rack," *Washington Post and Times Herald*, May 13, 1956, p. E5; Braven Dyer, "Sports Parade," *Los Angeles Times*, May 21, 1956, p. C1.

19 "Brooklyn Righthander Record Second No-Hit," *Washington Post and Times Herald*, May 13, 1956, p. C1; John Drebinger, "Snider Hits Two Homers, One a Grand Slam, as Dodgers Again Defeat," *New York Times*, May 14, 1956, p. 41; Shirley Povich, "This Morning," *Washington Post and Times Herald*, May 16, 1956, p. 47.

20 Bob Addie, "Bob Addie's Column," *Washington Post and Times Herald*, June 2, 1956, p. 8.

21 Dan Daniel, "Long-Shot Mantle Rocks Ruth Mark," *The Sporting News*, June 13, 1956, pp, 1–2.

22 Braven Dyer, "Sports Parade," *Los Angeles Times*, June 6, 1956, p. C1; "Ott 'Doubts' Mantle Will Top Ruth," *Washington Post*, June 13, 1956, p. 44; Braven Dyer, "Sports Parade," *Los Angeles Times*, June 16, 1956, p. B1.

23 "Mantle Homer Equals Mark at Detroit," *Los Angeles Times*, June 19, 1956, p. C1.

24 Louis Effrat, "What a Change Mantle Hath Wrought in Fans," *New York Times*, June 22, 1956, p. 26; "Mickey Mantle: The Year of the Slugger," *Sports Illustrated* (June 18, 1956): cover.

25 Robert Creamer, "The Mantle of the Babe," *Sports Illustrated* (June 18, 1956).

26 "Mickey Mantle: The Remarkable Mickey Mantle," *Life* (June 25, 1956): cover; "The Prodigy of Power," *Life* (June 25, 1956): 100–2, 105–6.

27 Roger Kahn, "The Bewildering World of Willie Mays," *Sport* (June 1956).

28 "Can Mickey Make It?" *Baseball Digest* (July 1956): cover; Gordon Cobbledick, "Yankee Stadium Could Beat Him!" *Baseball Digest* (July 1956): 11–12.

29 Bob Addie, "Injured Mantle Gets Knee Brace, May Miss All-Star Game Tuesday," *Washington Post and Times Herald*, July 6, 1956, p. 53; National Sluggers Triumph, 7 to 3," *Los Angeles Times*, July 11, 1956, pp. A1, 3.

30 "Mickey's Total 34 with First Grand Slam," *Washington Post*, July 31, 1956, p. 15.

31 Shirley Povich, "This Morning," *Washington Post and Times Herald*, July 31, 1956, p. 15.

32 John Drebinger, "Sports of the Times: Can the Kid Make It?" *New York Times*, August 16, 1956, p. 32.

33 "The Homeric Mantle," *Washington Post and Times Herald*, August 16, 1956, p. 14; "Pressure Will Keep Mantle from Breaking Mark—Kiner," *Los Angeles Times*, August 25, 1956, p. A2.

34 "Casey Doubts Mickey' Will Break Record," *Washington Post and Times Herald*, August 31, 1956, p. 33.

35 Shirley Povich, "This Morning," *Washington Post and Times Herald*, September 3, 1956, p. 16.

36 Tom Meany, "His Boy Mantle," *Baseball Digest* (October 1956): 41–8.

37 "The Fraying Mantle," *Washington Post and Times Herald*, September 13, 1956, p. 14.

38 Arthur Daley, "Sports of the Times: The Deserted Village," *New York Times*, September 27, 1956, p. 45.

39 "Dodgers Win Flag by Beating Bucs, 8–6, in Final Contest," *Los Angeles Times*, October 1, 1956, p. A1; "Dodgers Act as if They Just Won First Pennant," *Los Angeles Times*, October 1, 1956, p. A2.

40 Michael Shapiro, *The Last Good Season: Brooklyn, the Dodgers, and Their Final Pennant Race Together* (New York: Doubleday, 2003).

41 Eddie Burbridge, "Layin' It on the Line," *Los Angeles Sentinel*, August 16, 1956, p. 8; Eddie Burbridge, "Layin' It on the Line," *Los Angeles Sentinel*, September 13, 1956, p. A10.

42 John Drebinger, "Yanks Champions; Kucks' 3-Hitter Tops Dodgers, 9–0," *New York Times*, October 11, 1956, pp. 1, 53.

43 J.G. Taylor Spink, "Mantle and Aaron Top Players of Year," *The Sporting News*, October 10, 1956, pp. 1–2; C.C. Johnson Spink, "A.L. Places Seven on '56 All-Star Team," *The Sporting News*, October 17, 1956, pp. 1–2; "Mantle Highest in All-Star Votes," *Los Angeles Times*, October 25, 1956, p. C2.

44 "American League Places Six on Major All-Stars," *Los Angeles Times*, October 31, 1956, p. C5.

45 "Mantle Unanimous Choice as Most Valuable Player," *Los Angeles Times*, November 15, 1956, p. C1; "Mantle Selected Athlete of Year," *Los Angeles Times*, December 23, 1956, p. B2.

46 Edgar G. Brands, "Mantle, Tebbetts, Paul Top Majors," *The Sporting News*, January 2, 1957, pp. 1–2.

47 Roscoe McGowen, "Mantle Is Voted Player of Year," *New York Times*, January 20, 1957, pp. 1, 4.

48 "Mantle Receives $10,000 Trophy," *New York Times*, January 22, 1957, p. 49; "Mickey Mantle: Man of the Year," *Sport* (March 1957): cover.

49 "Mantle Says Ruth Mark to Fall Soon," *Los Angeles Times*, December 25, 1956, p. C3; Shirley Povich, "This Morning," *Washington Post and Times Herald*, December 26, 1956, p. A17.

50 Povich, "This Morning," December 26, 1956, p. A17.

Chapter 15

1 Ned Cronin, "Cronin's Corner," *Los Angeles Times*, October 13, 1956, p. A3.

2 Joseph M. Sheehan, "Giants Get Robinson for Pitcher and Cash," *New York Times*, December 14, 1956, pp. 1, 38.

3 "Brooklyn's Fans Rocked by Trade," *New York Times*, December 14, 1956, p. 46; Shirley Povich, "This Morning," *Washington Post and Times Herald*, December 17, 1956, p. A19; Wendell Smith, "The Sports Beat," *Pittsburgh Courier*, April 26, 1947.

4 "Dodgers Send Robinson to Giants in Surprise Trade," *Los Angeles Times*, December 14, 1956, p. C1.

5 "A Pioneering Athlete: Jack Roosevelt Robinson," *New York Times*, December 14, 1956, p. 38; "Jackie Robinson Gets Spingarn Medal December 8," *Los Angeles Times*, November 29, 1956, p. B1.

6 "The Robinson Trade," *New York Times*, December 15, 1956, p. 23.

7 "Robinson to Retire; Giants' Trade Void," *New York Times*, January 6, 1957, p. 1; James F. Lynch, "Jackie Robinson Quits Baseball; Trade Is Voided," *New York Times*, January 6, 1957, Section 5, pp. 1–2; Jackie Robinson, "Why I'm Quitting Baseball," *Look* (January 22, 1957): 91–2.

8 L.I. "Brock" Brockenbury, "Tying the Score," *Los Angeles Sentinel*, February 14, 1957, p. C4.

9. Adam Fairclough, *To Redeem the Soul of America: The Southern Christian Leadership Conference and Martin Luther King Jr.* (Athens, GA: University of Georgia Press, 1987).

10. "Now It's Brooklyn Rumored Coming Here," *Los Angeles Times*, August 27, 1953, p. C2; Michael D'Antonio, *Forever Blue: The True Story of Walter O'Malley, Baseball's Most Controversial Owner, and the Dodgers of Brooklyn and Los Angeles* (New York: Riverhead Books, 2009); Robert E. Murphy, *After Many a Summer: The Passing of the Giants and Dodgers and a Golden Age in New York Baseball* (Lincoln, NE: University of Nebraska Press, 2009).

11. Louis Effrat, "Talk of Giants Moving to Coast Idle Gossip, Stoneham Asserts," *New York Times*, November 16, 1954, p. 37.

12. "Rumor Dodgers Might Shift to L.A. Spike by NL Chief," *Los Angeles Times*, November 17, 1954, p. C3.

13. "O'Malley Says Present Plans Call for Dodgers to Stay in Brooklyn," *Los Angeles Times*, November 20, 1954, p. B2; John Drebinger, "Dodgers Consider Going to Coast for Spring Exhibitions in 1956," *New York Times*, November 20, 1954, p. 14.

14. Drebinger, "Dodgers Consider Going to Coast for Spring Exhibitions in 1956," p. 14.

15. "Dodgers, Giants May Move Teams," *Los Angeles Times*, August 20, 1955, p. B1.

16. "Stoneham Considers Moving Giants," *Washington Post and Times Herald*, May 20, 1956, p. C5.

17. Paul Zimmerman, "Bums Unavailable for Move to L.A.," *Los Angeles Times*, October 12, 1956, p. C1.

18. Frank Finch, "Sale of Angels Spurs L.A. Big League Hopes," Los Angeles Times, February 22, 1957, p. 1.

19. "Dodgers Buy 44-Passenger Plane to Transport Club, Farm Teams," *New York Times*, January 5, 1957, p. 13.

20. Finch, "Sale of Angels Spurs L.A. Big League Hopes," p. 1; Roscoe McGowen, "Dodgers Buy Los Angeles Club, Stirring Talk of Shift to Coast," *New York Times*, February 22, 1957, p. 1.

21. "Mayor Promises Help," *New York Times*, March 2, 1957, p. 26.

22. "Mayor Confident Dodgers Won't Go," *New York Times*, March 27, 1957, p. 33.

23. Mickey Mantle running, *Sports Illustrated* (March 4, 1957): cover; Gerald Holland, "The Real Mickey Mantle," *Sports Illustrated* (March 4, 1957).

24. Holland, "The Real Mickey Mantle."

25. "Yanks, Bums Choices Again as Big League Drills Begin," *Los Angeles Times*, March 1, 1953, p. C3; "The Big Switch," *Washington Post and Times Herald*, February 23, 1957, p. A10.

26 Charles Dexter, "Another Dodger," *Baseball Digest* (April 1957): 16; Hal Middlesworth, "—and Yankee Year!" *Baseball Digest* (April 1957): 17, 19–21, 29–30, 34.

27 Shirley Povich, "This Morning," *Washington Post and Times Herald*, March 7, 1957, p. D1; Arthur Daley, "Sports of the Times: A Rare Prize," *New York Times*, March 31, 1957, p. 198; Dan Daniel, "Kubek, Rodgers Tabbed as Top Rookies," *The Sporting News*, April 17, 1957, pp. 1, 6.

28 Roscoe McGowen, "Aging Dodgers Should Retain Flag," *Washington Post and Times Herald*, April 14, 1957, p. K9.

29 Arthur Daley, "Sports of the Times: Out on a Limb," *New York Times*, April 14, 1957, p. S2.

30 Arthur Daley, "Sports of the Times: The Advancing Years," *New York Times*, April 16, 1957, p. 41.

31 "Casey Predicts Flag for Yanks," *Los Angeles Times*, April 10, 1957, p. C1.

32 "Yankees 2–5 Favorites on Betting Line," *Los Angeles Times*, April 11, 1957, p. C2; "Yanks, Braves Picked to Win Pennants in Voting by Writers and Broadcasters," *New York Times*, April 13, 1957, p. 14; Shirley Povich, "It Will Be Dodgers, Yankee Again," *Washington Post and Times Herald*, April 14, 1957, p. C1.

33 Dan Parker, "Baseball Forecast for 1957," *Washington Post and Times Herald*, April 14, 1957, pp. AW5, 23–4.

34 Joseph M. Sheehan, "Williams and Musial Taking up More Space in Record Books," *New York Times*, January 20, 1957, p. 180.

35 A.S. "Doc" Young, "Who's the Greatest—Mays or Mantle?" *Los Angeles Sentinel*, March 28, 1957, p. A12.

Chapter 16

1 "Dodgers Get Tract Offer in Queens," *Los Angeles Times*, April 19, 1957, p. C1; "Dodgers Get Plan for Site in Queens," *New York Times*, April 19, 1957, p. 1.

2 "Moses' Plan Irks Dodger Rooters," *New York Times*, April 20, 1957, p. 19.

3 "Dodgers Will Move to Coast, Paper Says," *Washington Post and Times Herald*, May 11, 1957, p. A13; "S.F. Mayor, Stoneham in Agreement," *Los Angeles Times*, May 12, 1957, p. C1.

4 "S.F. Mayor, Stoneham in Agreement," p. C1.

5 "Dodgers' Shift to L.A. Given O.K.," *Los Angeles Times*, May 29, 1957, p. 1; Clayton Knowles, "Wagner Striving to Keep Dodgers and Giants Here," *New York Times*, May 30, 1957, p. 1.

6 Jay Walz, "Negroes Hold Rally on Rights in Capital," *New York Times*, May 18, 1957, pp. 1, 23.

7 "Snider Makes 1500th Hit," *Washington Post and Times Herald*, May 27, 1957, p. C1; McCandlish Phillips, "Yankee Is Linked to Fight in Café," *New York Times*, May 17, 1957, p. 37.

8 Phillips, "Yankee Is Linked to Fight in Café," p. 37; "Ford, Berra Benched after Night-Club Row," *Los Angeles Times*, May 17, 1957, p. C1; "Hank Bauer Held in Brawl in Café," *New York Times*, May 22, 1957, p. 24.

9 John Drebinger, "Stolen Base Is Returned to Baseball by Willie the Wonder," *New York Times*, May 24, 1957, p. 37.

10 "Solon Orders Probe of Major Loop Shifts," *Los Angeles Times*, June 2, 1957, p. D1.

11 Gladwin Hill, "Los Angeles See Dodgers on Way," *New York Times*, June 2, 1957, p. 44; Joe Reichler, "More Expansion Seen Likely in Majors," *Washington Post and Times Herald*, June 2, 1957, p. C3.

12 Arthur Daley, "Sports of the Times: The Passing Baseball Scene," *New York Times*, June 4, 1957, p. 62.

13 "N.Y. Loses Round in Bid for Dodgers," *Los Angeles Times*, June 5, 1957, pp. 1, 3; "Top New York Official Sure Bums to Move," *Los Angeles Times*, June 6, 1957, p. C3.

14 "Dodger Transfer Still in Negotiation—Frick," *Los Angeles Times*, June 20, 1957, pp. C1-2; "Bum, Giant Books Show Net Profit," *Los Angeles Times*, June 21, 1957, p. C1.

15 "O'Malley: 'Jig Is up in Brooklyn,'" *Los Angeles Times*, June 27, 1957, p. C1.

16 "Celler Convinced L.A. to Get Bums," *Los Angeles Times*, June 28, 1957, p. C1.

17 "Yanks' 'Sinning Six' Fined Total of $5500," *Washington Post and Times Herald*, June 4, 1957, p. A16; "Bombers Feel 'Playboy' Fines Will Put Club in 'Play Ball' Mood," *New York Times*, June 5, 1957, p. 42; "Kansas City Obtains Martin from Yanks," *New York Times*, June 16, 1957, Section 5, pp. 1, 3.

18 "Mays Faster than Baseball?" *Los Angeles Sentinel*, June 20, 1957, p. B4.

19 Richard E. Mooney, "Stoneham Favors Giants' Transfer," *New York Times*, July 18, 1957, p. 1; "O'Malley Hopes to Remain in City," *New York Times*, July 18, 1957, p. 37.

20 Louis Effrat, "Giants to Quit Polo Grounds This Year, Stoneham Says," *New York Times*, July 19, 1957, p. 1.

21 John Drebinger, "Sports of the Times: San Francisco or Bust," *New York Times*, July 21, 1957, p. S2.

22 "Dodgers Disclaim Firm Moving Plan," *New York Times*, July 25, 1957, p. 25.

23 "Mantle and Ted Williams Will Start for American League in All-Star Game," *New York Times*, July 1, 1957, p. 28; "Stengel Names AL All-Stars," *Los Angeles Times*, July 2, 1957, p. C3; "3 Dodgers Named to All-Star Team," *New York Times*, July 4, 1957, p. 29.

24 "Hank Aaron Ties Ruth Homer Mark after 77 Games," *Washington Post and Times Herald*, July 11, 1957, p. C1; Joseph M. Sheehan, "Mantle Is Star of 10–6 Triumph," *New York Times*, July 24, 1957, p. 17.

25 "Willie Mays Must Be the Mostest—Say Top Greats," *Los Angeles Sentinel*, July 4, 1957, p. B1.

26 John Drebinger, "Sports of the Times: Mantle vs. Mays," *New York Times*, July 28, 1957, p. 134.

27 Shirley Povich, "This Morning," *Washington Post and Times Herald*, July 15, 1957, p. A12; "Snider Clouts 300th as Dodgers Triumph," *Los Angeles Times*, July 21, 1957, p. C1.

28 Bill Becker, "Giants Will Shift to San Francisco for 1958 Season," *New York Times*, August 20, 1957, pp. 1, 30.

29 "Giants' Move Hailed but Not by Celler," *Washington Post and Times Herald*, August 20,1 957, p. A16.

30 "Dodger Rumors Denied," *New York Times*, August 30, 1957, p. 21.

31 Frank Graham, "Why Don't They Stop Knocking the Duke?" *Sport* (September 1957): 12–13, 94–96.

32 "Wolfson Adds to His Bid for Dodgers: A Stadium Plus 2 Million for Players," *New York Times*, September 7, 1957, p. 16; Charles G. Bennett, "Nelson Rockefeller Offers Aid to Keep Dodgers in the City," *New York Times*, September 11, 1957, pp. 1, 18.

33 Paul Zimmerman, "Deal for Dodgers Get L.A. Council Approval," *Los Angeles Times*, September 17, 1957, p. 1; Paul Zimmerman, "Supervisors Move to Speed up Dodger Deal," *Los Angeles Times*, September 18, 1957, p. 1.

34 Charles G. Bennett, "Mayor Sees O'Malley on Rockefeller Bid Today," *New York Times*, September 18, 1957, pp. 1, 21.

35 Paul Crowell, "City Board Is Cool to Bid on Dodgers," *New York Times*, September 20, 1957, pp. 1, 17.

36 Paul Crowell, "Rockefeller Bid to Help Dodgers Ends in Failure," *New York Times*, September 21, 1957, p. 1; Frank Finch, "O'Malley Must Decide While L.A. Ponders," *Los Angeles Times*, September 28,1 957, p. A1.

37 Red Smith, "Views of Sports: A Wake for the Giants," *New York Herald Tribune*, September 30, 1957.

38 John Klima, *Bushville Wins!: The Wild Sage of the 1957 Milwaukee Braves and the Screwballs, Sluggers, and Beer Swiggers Who Canned the New York Yankees and Changed Baseball* (New York: Thomas Dunne Books, 2012).

39 John Drebinger, "Ford of Yankees Tops Braves, 3–1, as Series Starts," *New York Times*, October 3, 1957, pp. 1, 35.

40 John Drebinger, "Braves' Burdette Beats Yanks, 4–2, and Evens Series," *New York Times*, October 4, 1957, p. 1, 15.

41 "Yanks Win 3d Game, 12–3," *New York Times*, October 6, 1957, p. 1.

42 John Drebinger, "Braves Tops Yanks in 10th Inning, 7–5, for 2–2 Series Tie," *New York Times*, October 7, 1957, pp. 1, 30; Louis Effrat, "Bombers Face Prospect of Losing Mantle for Fifth Series Contest," *New York Times*, October 7, 1957, p. 31.

43 John Drebinger, "Braves Win, 1 to 0, and Lead Yankees in Series, 3 to 2," *New York Times*, October 8, 1957, pp. 1, 43.

44 John Drebinger, "Turley of Yanks Beats Braves, 3–2, and Evens Series," *New York Times*, October 10, 1957, pp. 1, 43; Shirley Povich, "Mantle out of Crucial Sixth Game," *Washington Post and Times Herald*, October 9, 1957, p. A16; Arthur Daley, "Sports of the Times: Heading toward a Photo-Finish," *New York Times*, October 10, 1957, p. 44.

45 John Drebinger, "Braves Beat Yanks, 5–0, to Win Series," *New York Times*, October 11, 1957, pp. 1, 33.

46 Gladwin Hill, "Dodger Pact Wins Los Angeles Vote," *New York Times*, October 8, 1957, p. 1; Emanuel Perlmutter, "Dodgers Accept Los Angeles Bid to Move to Coast," *New York Times*, October 9, 1957, pp. 1, 37.

47 Arthur Daley, "Sports of the Times: It's His Own Description," *New York Times*, October 14, 1957, p. 37.

48 Daley, "Sports of the Times: It's His Own Destruction," p. 37.

49 "Williams, Musial Picked as Top Players," *The Sporting News*, October 9, 1957, pp. 1–2; Bob Burnes, "Ted, Lane, Hutch Majors' Top Men," *The Sporting News*, January 1, 1958, pp. 1–2.

50 "Three Yanks Land Berths on UP Team," *Los Angeles Times*, October 24, 1957, p. C9; "Five Braves and Three Yankees on Major League All-Star Team," *New York Times*, November 7, 1957, p. 61; Roscoe McGowen, "Yank Outfielder Gets 233 Points," *New York Times*, November 23, 1957, p. 28; Roscoe McGowen, "Milwaukee Star Gets 239 Points," *New York Times*, November 23, 1957, p. 30.

51 "Ruth, Ott Homer Marks under Fire," *Washington Post and Times Herald*, November 3, 1957, p. C3.

52 Duke Snider, "We'll Never Break Babe Ruth's Record," This Week (1957), appearing in *Baseball Digest* (November–December 1957): 61–4.

53 Snider, "We'll Never Break Babe Ruth's Record," pp. 61–4.

54 George Skelton, "Column: Baseball Legend Willie Mays Instrumental in California Fight against Housing Discrimination," *Los Angeles Times*, June 22, 2024, https://www.latimes.com/california/story/2024-06-22/column-baseball-legend-willie-mays-led-charge-against-housing-discrimination.

Chapter 17

1 Roy R. Silver, "Campanella Paralyzed in Crash; Broken Neck Is Expected to Heal," *New York Times*, January 29, 1958, pp. 1, 17.

2 Ted Williams, Hall of Fame induction speech, 1966, https://speakola.com/sports/ted-williams-hall-of-fame-induction-speech-1966.

3 Cottrell, *The Best Pitcher in Baseball*.

4 Frederic J. Frommer, "Baseball's First Plan for Negro League Stars," *Washington Post*, January 21, 2023, https://www.washingtonpost.com/sports/2023/01/21/mlb-hall-fame-negro-leagues/.

5 In 1981, Terry Cashman recorded "Talkin' Baseball," an ode to the national pastime, with a particular emphasis on "Willie, Mickey, and the Duke." Wonderfully evocative of Major League Baseball, its lyrics open with the Philadelphia Whiz Kids, Bobby Thompson, and Yogi Berra, then move on to Kluszewski, Campanella, Musial, Feller, Rizzuto, Maglie, and Newcombe, before shifting to Mays, Mantle, and Snider. Next up are Stengel, Aaron, Jackie Robinson, Frank Robinson, Kiner, Eddie Gadel, Williams, and Parnell, before "Talkin' Baseball" comes back to the three great New York City center fielders. After a brief splash into the then contemporary game, Cashman jauntily returns to "Willie, Mickey, and the Duke."

Selected Bibliography

Appel, Marty. *Pinstripe Empire: The New York Yankees from before the Babe to after the Boss*. New York: Bloomsbury USA, 2012.

Bankes, Jim. *The Pittsburgh Crawfords*. Jeffersons City, NC: McFarland & Company, 2001.

Barber, Red. *1947: When All Hell Broke Loose in Baseball*. New York: Da Capo Press, 1984.

Bridging Two Dynasties: The 1947 New York Yankees, ed. Lyle Spatz. Lincoln, NE: University of Nebraska Press, 2019.

Brown, Warren. *The Chicago Cubs: An Informal History*. New York: G.P. Putnam's Sons, 1946.

Brown, Warren. *The Chicago White Sox*. New York: G.P. Putnam's Sons, 1952.

Bruce, Janet. *The Kansas City Monarchs: Champions of Black Baseball*. Lawrence, KS: University of Kansas Press, 1986.

Cohen, Stanley. *Yankees 1936-39, Baseball's Greatest Dynasty: Lou Gehrig, Joe DiMaggio and the Birth of a New Era*. New York: Skyhorse, 2018.

Cottrell, Robert C. *The Best Pitcher in Pitcher: The Life of Rube Foster, Negro League Giant*. New York: New York University Press, 2001.

Cottrell, Robert C. *Blackball, the Black Sox, and the Babe: Baseball's Crucial 1920 Season*. Jefferson City, NC: McFarland & Company, 2002.

Cottrell, Robert C. *Two Pioneers: How Hank Greenberg and Jackie Robinson Transformed Baseball*. Washington, DC: Potomac Books, 2012.

D'Antonio, Michael. *Forever Blue: The True Story of Walter O'Malley, Baseball's Most Controversial Owner, and the Dodgers of Brooklyn and Los Angeles*. New York: Riverhead Books, 2009.

Delmont, Matthew. *Half American: The Epic Story of African-Americans Fighting World War II at Home and Abroad*. New York: Viking, 2022.

Elias, Robert and Peter Dreier. *Major League Rebels: Baseball Battles over Workers' Rights and American Empire*. Lanham, MD: Rowman & Littlefield, 2022.

Epting, Chris. *The Early Polo Grounds*. Charleston, SC: Arcadia Publishing Library Editions, 2009.

Freedman, Lew. *DiMaggio's Yankees: A History of the 1936-1944 Dynasty*. Jefferson City, NC: McFarland & Company, 2011.

Frommer, Harvey. *Five O'Clock Lightning: Babe Ruth, Lou Gehrig, and the Greatest Baseball Team in History, the 1927 New York Yankees*. Lanham, MD: Taylor Trade Publishing, 2015.

Frommer, Harvey. *New York City Baseball: The Golden Age, 1947-1957*. Boulder, CO: Taylor Trade Publishing, 2013.

Gergel, Richard. *Unexampled Courage: The Blinding of Sgt. Isaac Woodard and the Awakening of President Harry S. Truman and Judge J. Waties*. New York: Sarah Crichton Books, 2019.

Golenbock, Peter. *Dynasty: The New York Yankees, 1949-1964*. New York: Prentice Hall Direct, 1975.

Goodwin, Doris Kearns. *Wait Till Next Year: A Memoir*. New York: Simon & Schuster, 1997.

Gossett, Thomas F. *Race: The History of an Idea in North America*. Dallas: Southern Methodist University Press, 1963.

Graham, Frank. *The Brooklyn Dodgers: An Informal History*. New York: G.P. Putnam's Sons, 1945.

Graham, Frank. *The New York Giants: An Informal History of a Great Baseball Club*. New York: G.P. Putnam's Sons, 1952.

Graham, Frank. *The Yankees: An Informal History*. New York: G. P. Putnam's Sons, 1947.

Heaphy, Leslie A. *The Negro Leagues, 1869-1960*. Jefferson, NC: McFarland & Company, 2013.

Hirsch, James S. *Willie Mays: The Life, the Legend*. New York: Scribner, 2010.

Hubler, David E. and Joshua H. Drazen. *The Nats and the Grays: How Baseball in the Nation's Capital Survived WWII and Changed the Game Forever*. Lanham, MD: Rowman & Littlefield, 2015.

Hynd, Noel. *The Giants of The Polo Grounds: The Glorious Times of Baseball's New York Giants*. Dallas: Taylor Publishing, 1996.

Jennison, Christopher. *Wait 'Til Next Year*. New York: W.W. Norton & Company, Inc., 1974.

Kahn, Roger. *The Era 1947-1957: When the Yankees, the Giants, and the Dodgers Ruled the World*. Boston: Ticknor & Fields, 1993.

Kahn, Roger. *The Boys of Summer*. New York: Harper Perennial Modern Classics, 2006.

Klima, John. *Bushville Wins!: The Wild Sage of the 1957 Milwaukee Braves and the Screwballs, Sluggers, and Beer Swiggers Who Canned the New York Yankees and Changed Baseball*. New York: Thomas Dunne Books, 2012.

Klima, John. *Willie's Boys: The 1948 Birmingham Black Barons, the Last Negro League World Series, and the Making of a Baseball Legend*. Kutztown, PA: Trade Paper Press, 2009.

Lanctot, Neil. *Fair Dealing and Clean Playing: The Hilldale Club and the Development of Black Professional Baseball, 1910-1932*. Jefferson, NC: McFarland & Company, 1994.

Lawson, Steven F. *To Secure These Rights: The Report of President Harry S Truman's Committee on Civil Rights*. Boston: Bedford/St. Martin's, 2003.

Lazarus, Adam. *The Wingmen: The Unlikely, Unusual, Unbreakable Friendship Between John Glenn and Ted Williams*. New York: Citadel Press, 2023.

Leavy, Jane. *The Last Boy: Mickey Mantle and the End of America's Childhood*. New York: Harper, 2010.

Lee, Philip. *Black Stats Matter: Integrating Negro League Numbers into Major League Records*. Jefferson City, NC: McFarland and Company, 2023.

Lester, Larry. *Black Baseball in New York City: An Illustrated History, 1885-1959*. Jefferson City, NC: McFarland Publishing, 2017.

Lewis, Franklin. *The Cleveland Indians*. New York: G.P. Putnam's Sons, 1949.

Lieb, Frederick G. *The St. Louis Cardinals: An Informal History*. New York: G.P. Putnam's Sons, 1944.

Lieb, Frederick G. *The Detroit Tigers: An Informal History*. New York: G.P. Putnam's Sons, 1946.

Lieb, Frederick G. *The Boston Red Sox: An Informal History*. New York: G.P. Putnam's Sons, 1947.

Lieb, Frederick G. *The Cincinnati Reds: An Informal History*. New York: G.P. Putnam's Sons, 1948.

Lieb, Frederick G. *The Pittsburgh Pirates: An Informal History*. New York: G.P. Putnam's Sons, 1948.

Lieb, Frederick G. *The Baltimore Orioles: The History of a Colorful Team in Baltimore and St. Louis*. New York: G.P. Putnam's Sons, 1955.

Madden, Bill. *1954: The Year Willie Mays and the First Generation of Black Superstars Changed Major League Baseball Forever*. New York: Da Capo Press, 2014.

Mantle, Mickey. *The Mick: An American Hero: The Legend and the Glory*. New York: Jove: 1986.

Martin Luther King, Jr., *Stride Toward Freedom: The Montgomery Story*. New York: Harper & Brothers, Publishers: 1958.

Marquette, Gregory. *The Bomb Heard Around the World: The Lives and Deaths of Harry T. and Harriette V. Moore*. Top Cat II Production Publishing Group, 2019.

Mays, Willie. *Say Hey: The Autobiography of Willie Mays*. New York: Simon & Schuster, 1988.

McKelvey, Richard. *Mexican Raiders in the Major Leagues: The Pasquel Brothers vs. Organized Baseball, 1946*. Jefferson City, NC: McFarland & Company, 2006.

Meany, Tom. *Milwaukee's Miracle Braves*. New York: A.S. Barnes and Company, 1954.

Mele, Andrew Paul. *"Tearin' Up the Pea Patch": The Brooklyn Dodgers, 1953*. Jefferson City, NC: McFarland Publishing, 2015.

Murphy, Robert E. *After Many a Summer: The Passing of the Giants and Dodgers and a Golden Age in New York Baseball*. Lincoln, NE: University of Nebraska Press, 2009.

Newman, Roberta J. and Joel Nathan Rosen. *Black Baseball, Race Enterprise and the Fate of the Segregated Dollar*. Jackson, MS: University Press of Mississippi, 2014.

The New York Yankees: One Hundred Years, The Official Retrospective. New York: Ballantine Books, 2003.

Overmyer, James E. *Black Ball and the Boardwalk: The Bacharach Giants of Atlantic City, 1916-1929*. Jefferson City, NC: McFarland & Company, 2014.

Peterson, Robert. *Only the Ball Was White: A History of Legendary Black Players and All-Black Professional Teams*. New York: Oxford University Press, 1992.

Peterson, Todd. *The Negro Leagues Were Major Leagues: Historians Reappraise Black Baseball*. Jefferson, NC: McFarland & Company, 2019.

Povich, Shirley. *The Washington Senators*. New York: G.P. Putnam's Sons, 1954.

Prager, Joshua. *The Echoing Green: The Untold Story of Bobby Thompson, Ralph Branca and the Shot Heard Round the World*. New York: Pantheon Books, 2006.

Prince, Carl E. *Brooklyn's Dodgers: The Bums, the Borough, and the Best of Baseball, 1947-1957*. New York: Oxford University Press, 1997.

Rampersad, Arnold. *Jackie Robinson*. New York: Alfred A. Knopf, 1997.
Rhoden, William C. *Forty Million Dollar Slaves: The Rise, Fall, and Redemption of the Black Athlete*. New York: Crown, 2007.
Riley, James A. *The Biographical Encyclopedia of the Negro Baseball Leagues*. New York: Carroll & Graf Publishers, Inc., 1994.
Robinson, Greg. *By Order of the President: FDR and the Internment of Japanese Americans*. Cambridge, MA: Harvard University Press, 2001.
Rubin, Susan Goldman. *Brown v. Board of Education: A Fight for Simple Justice*. New York: Holiday House, 2016.
Schiavone, Michael. *Dodgers vs. Yankees: The Long-Standing Rivalry between Two of Baseball's Greatest Teams*. New York: Sports Publishing, 2020.
Shapiro, Michael. *The Last Good Season: Brooklyn, the Dodgers, and Their Final Pennant Race Together*. New York: Doubleday, 2003.
Snider, Duke. *The Duke of Flatbush*. New York: Kensington Publishing Corporation, 1988.
Snyder, Brad. *Beyond the Shadow of the Senators: The Untold Story of the Homestead Gays and the Integration of Baseball*. New York: McGraw-Hill, 2003.
Spatz, Lyle and Steve Steinberg. *1921: The Yankees, the Giants, and the Battle for Baseball Supremacy in New York*. Lincoln, NE: University of Nebraska Press, 2010.
Taylor, John E. *Freedom to Serve: Truman, Civil Rights, and Executive Order 9981*. New York: Routledge, 2013.
The Team That Forever Changed Baseball and America: The 1947 Brooklyn Dodgers, ed. Lyle Spatz Lincoln, NE: University of Nebraska Press, 2012.
The Team That Time Won't Forget: The 1951 New York Giants, eds. Bill Nowlin and C. Paul Rogers III. Society for American Baseball Research, 2015.
Theoharis, Jeanne. *The Rebellious Life of Mrs. Rosa Parks*. Boston: Beacon Press, 2013.
Tygiel, Jules. *Baseball's Great Experiment: Jackie Robinson and His Legacy*. New York: Oxford University Press, 2008.
Tyson, Timothy B. *The Blood of Emmett Till*. New York: Simon & Schuster, 2017.
Wallop, Douglas. *The Year the Yankees Los the Pennant*. New York: Norton, 1954.
Weintraub, Robert. *The Victory Season: The End of World War II and the Birth of Baseball's Golden Age*. Boston: Little, Brown and Company, 2013.
White, Sol. *Sol White's History of Colored Baseball with Other Documents on the Early Black Game, 1886-1936*. Lincoln, NE: Bison Books, 1996.
Wilkerson, Isabel. *The Warmth of Other Suns: The Epic Story of America's Great Migration*. New York: Random House, 2010.
Wilson, Theodore Brantner. *The Black Codes of the South*. Tuscaloosa, AL: University of Alabama Press, 1965.
Winehouse, Irwin. *The Duke Snider Story*. New York: Julian Messner, Inc., 1965.

Index

Aaron, Henry "Hank"   120–2, 141, 159–60, 209, 211–12, 225, 234, 243–5, 247
   MVP   247
   Negro Leaguer   6, 209, 217, 243
Adcock, Joe   97, 225, 244–5
Addie, Bob   127, 131–2, 157–8, 186, 190, 192, 196–7, 199–200
Alexander, Grover Cleveland   10, 65
Allen, Johnny   24
Allen, Newt
   Negro Leaguer   16
Alston, Walter   5, 108, 138, 143, 147, 150, 156, 167, 169, 174–6, 183–4, 250
   on Jackie Robinson   168
Amoros, Sandy   143–4, 159, 161, 173–5, 180, 184, 208
   Negro Leaguer   120, 145, 181
Anson, Adrian "Cap"   122
   on Organized Baseball's color barrier   14–15, 283
Antonelli, Johnny   112, 116, 122–4, 126–7, 133, 135, 138, 140–1, 145, 148, 161, 170, 180, 182–3, 190, 208, 234, 242, 253
Appling, Luke   33
Armstrong, Major General George E.   89
Ashburn, Richie   65
Austin, Frankie
   Negro Leaguer   56
Avila, Bobby   134, 139, 141

Bagby, Jim   12
Bailey, Ed   83, 212
Baker, Gene   145
   Negro Leaguer   181
Baker, Home Run   10, 21, 23
Bankhead, Dan
   Negro Leaguer   47–8, 66
Bankhead, Tallulah
   "What is so rare as a Willie Mays?"   137
Banks, Ernie   122, 141, 159, 165, 170, 208–9, 216, 243
   Negro Leaguer   6, 83, 113, 145, 181
Banta, Jack   62
Barney, Rex   52, 62–3, 66
Baseball Digest   31, 97, 137, 202
   "Can Mickey Make It?"   202
Baseball Magazine (Dell)   152
Baseball's Great Experiment   40, 46, 125
Bauer, Hank   65, 67, 70–1, 76–7, 84, 99, 100, 102, 107, 116, 122, 139, 144, 171, 174, 176, 180, 182, 186, 192, 199, 207, 210, 229, 232, 241, 244–5
Bavasi, Emil "Buzzie"   107, 233
Bearden, Gene   52–3
Bell, Cool Papa
   Negro Leaguer   16–17, 255
Bender, Charles "Chief"   10, 19–20
Berra, Yogi   4, 51, 61, 65, 70, 81, 84, 86–8, 97, 99, 101–2, 116, 121, 129, 134, 139, 141, 144, 148, 155, 162,

171–6, 179–83, 189–90, 192, 196, 207, 210–12, 224–5, 229, 232, 234, 241, 244–7, 249, 251
Bessent, Don   144, 170, 173–5, 208–11
Birtwell, Roger
   on Black players   78
Black, Joe   37, 49, 56, 85–6, 100, 126, 143, 163
Black baseball in New York City   1
   1947 Negro League World Series   49–50
   Brooklyn Eagles   28
   Brooklyn Royal Giants   2, 27
   Cuban Stars   2, 28
   Harlem Stars   28
   New York Black Yankees   2, 28
   New York Cubans   2, 28
   New York Lincoln Giants   2, 27
Black Sox   10–11
Blackwell, Ewell   45, 87, 114–15
Bolden, Ed   17
Bollweg, Don   104
Bonham, Tiny   25
Boone, Ray   211
Borowy, Hank   25
Bourdeau, Lou   52–3
Bouton, Jim   251
Bowman, Emmett   12
Boyd, Bob   209, 243
   Negro Leaguer   49, 79, 181
Boyer, Ken   211–12
Boys of Summer   1, 4, 51, 62, 142, 180, 215
Branca, Ralph   45, 52, 62–3, 66, 71–2, 75, 86
Brandt, Jackie   108, 208, 224
Bresnahan, Roger   19
Brewer, Dr. Thomas Hency
   assassination of   177
Brockenbury, L.I. "Brock"
   on Black players   217
Brooklyn Dodgers   3–6, 11, 25–8, 32, 37–40, 43–52, 54, 59–66, 69, 71–5, 78, 81–8, 91–2, 94, 96–7, 99–102, 107–9, 111–12, 114–15, 119–22, 125–33, 135, 137–8, 140, 143–4, 147, 149–77, 179, 181–4, 186, 189, 195, 202–3, 206–7, 209–10, 215–16, 218–21, 223–5, 227, 230–4, 236–41, 245–7, 249–52, 255–7
Brown, Bobby   51, 63–4, 67, 77, 83, 111
Brown, Mordecai "Three-Finger"   10
Brown, Ray
   Negro Leaguer   17
Brown, Willard
   Negro Leaguer   37, 41, 47, 56
Brush, John T.   19
Bruton, Bill   97, 187
   Negro Leaguer   120, 217
Bryant, Clay   108
Buffalo Soldiers   36
Buhl, Robert   83, 96, 243–5
Burbridge, Eddie   122, 159, 209
Burdette, Lew   5–6, 96, 243–5, 247
Burns, Thomas   26
Bush, Bullet Joe
   Negro Leaguer   16
Byrd, Bill   56
Byrd, Harry   104, 116, 147
Byrne, Tommy   61, 65, 144, 172, 181, 207

Caldwell, Ray   12
Camilli, Dolf   26
Campanella, Roy   1, 4, 51, 62–3, 66, 72–3, 82, 85, 88–9, 97, 99, 102, 116, 120–1, 124, 128–9, 131, 138, 143–4, 147–8, 150–1, 153, 156, 161, 163, 169–73, 176, 180–4, 189, 198, 203, 207, 210, 216–17, 223–5, 242, 250, 252
   Negro Leaguer   3, 6, 37, 64, 68, 71, 78, 112, 159
Cannon, Jimmy   171
   on Willie Mays   133
Carey, Andy   139, 144, 155, 176, 180, 210, 244
Carey, Max   151, 184
Carter, Spoon
   Negro Leaguer   17
Caruthers, Bob   25

Casey, Hugh   26, 32, 45, 52
Cashman, Terry
    "(Talkin' Baseball) Willie, Mickey, and Duke"   296
Cashmore, John   227
Celler, Emanuel   229–31, 237
Cepeda, Orlando   252–3
Cerv, Bob   116–17, 155, 173, 176
Chance, Frank   10
Chandler, Commissioner A.B.
    "Happy"   40, 44
Chandler, Spud   24–5, 32, 41
Chapman, Ben   24
Chapman, Ray   12, 22
Charleston, Oscar
    Negro Leaguer   17–18, 72, 255
Chesbro, Jack   21
Christopher, Mayor George   221, 227, 236–7
Cicotte, Eddie   10–11
Cimoli, Gene   184, 234, 241–2
Clarke, Webbo
    Negro Leaguer   50
Clarkson, Buzz
    on Mays and Henry Aaron   160
Clemente, Roberto   108, 159, 187, 209, 232
Cobb, Ty   11, 122, 151, 234–5, 238, 254
    on Black players   79
    on Duke Snider   166
    on Willie Mays   166
Cobbledick, Gordon   202
Cochrane, Mickey   10
Coleman, Jerry   67, 83, 144, 197, 244–5
Coleman, Rip   176
Collier's
    "I Play Baseball for Money, Not Fun" (Snider with Roger Kahn)   198
Collins, Eddie   10
Collins, Joe   76, 139, 144, 172, 202, 205, 210
Colvin, Claudette   145–6
Combs, Earle   23–4
Combs, Jack   10
Connor, Roger   19

Cooper, Walker   48, 63, 72, 74, 250
Cosell, Howard   201
Coveleski, Stan   12
Covington, Wes   243–4
Cox, Billy   71–2, 87–8, 99, 101–3, 110, 143, 147, 153–4
Craig, Roger   144, 173, 175, 180, 190, 208, 210–11, 223, 242, 252
Crandall, Del   83, 96–7, 245
Cravath, Gavvy   10
Creamer, Robert
    "The Mantle of the Babe"   201–2
Cronin, Joe   12, 32
Cronin, Ned   167–8, 215
Crosetti, Frankie   24
Crowe, George
    Negro Leaguer   145, 209, 271
Cuban Stars   27
Curry, Homer "Goose"
    on Black major leaguers and Blackball   159

Daley, Arthur   44–5, 83, 95, 104, 224
    on Duke Snider   128, 147, 166–7, 169, 206
    on Horace Stoneham   246
    on Mickey Mantle   149, 193–4, 197, 223
    on Walter O'Malley   206–7, 230, 246
    on Willie Mays   83, 110, 114, 121, 128, 130, 141, 162
    on Yankees and Black players   104
Daly, Tom   25–6
Dandridge, Ray
    Negro Leaguer   18
Daniel, Dan   60, 117, 148
    on Mickey Mantle   148, 194, 200
Dark, Al   53, 72, 75–7, 85, 100, 121–4, 126, 138, 141, 144, 172, 182–3, 250
Daubert, Jake   26
Davis, Piper   56
Davis, Tommy   252
Day, Leon
    Negro Leaguer   2, 18, 28, 37

Dean, Dizzy   11, 110
Derringer, Paul   11
Dexter, Charles   182, 223
　on Mickey Mantle   98
Dickey, Bill   24, 31, 212
　on Mickey Mantle   69–70, 98, 186, 191, 196
Dihigo, Martin
　Negro Leaguer   2, 17–18, 27–8, 255
DiMaggio, Joe   1, 4, 24–5, 31–2, 44, 48–9, 51, 53, 60–1, 63–5, 67, 69, 71, 73, 76–7, 81, 84, 88, 94, 98, 108, 113, 116, 124, 129, 131–2, 134, 149, 157, 159, 163, 166–7, 173, 197, 203, 205, 212, 222, 234, 249–50
Ditmar, Art   223, 225, 241
Dittmer, Jack   97
Doby, Larry   6, 53, 56–7, 78, 89, 112, 120, 134, 136, 139–40
　Negro Leaguer   3, 6, 18, 41, 47, 49, 135, 145, 181, 209, 217, 243
Doerr, Bobby   33, 52, 94
Donald, Atley   24–5
Donlin, Mike   19
Double Victory Campaign   34–5
Doyle, Larry   20
Drebinger, John   86, 115, 116
　on Duke Snider   116
Dressen, Charlie   4–5, 66, 75, 82, 86, 88–9, 107–8, 119, 147, 153, 250
　on Duke Snider   154, 198
　on Horace Stoneham   233
　on Jackie Robinson   168
　on Mickey Mantle   88, 203, 235–6
　on Willie Mays   121, 125, 229, 235–6
Drysdale, Don   180, 189–90, 208, 210, 223, 242, 251–2, 257
Duany, Claro
　Negro Leaguer   49
Du Bois, W.E.B.   39
Duncan, Frank   41
Dunn, Jack   26
Duren, Ryne   232
Durocher, Leo   4–6, 26, 32, 44–5, 51–2, 63, 67, 73–4, 82, 92, 109, 116, 119, 121, 128, 141, 144, 150–1, 156, 161, 163, 171, 180, 216, 236, 250
　on Willie Mays   73, 110–11, 113–14, 127, 129–31, 133, 135, 140, 148, 162, 202
Durr, Clifford   176
Durr, Virginia   146, 176
Dyer, Braven   27
　on Duke Snider   198
　on Willie Mays   113–14, 127
Dyer, Eddie   3
Dykes, Jimmie
　on Willie Mays   235

Easter, Luke
　Negro Leaguer   17, 56, 68, 78, 89, 103
Ebbets Field   5, 26, 28, 32, 45, 60, 65, 75, 86–7, 91–2, 102, 109, 121, 133, 137–8, 155, 158, 163–5, 172, 179, 189, 206–7, 209–10, 219–20, 229, 240–1, 246, 252
Ebony
　"WHAT'S WRONG WITH NEGRO BASEBALL?" by Jackie Robinson   54
Edwards, Bruce   32, 45–6, 51
Edwards, Willie Jr
　murder of   218
Effrat, Louis
　on Willie Mays   115, 187
Eisenhower, President Dwight David   36, 105, 189, 238
Elliot, Bob   45, 53, 64, 85
Ennis, Del   65
Epstein, Ben
　on Mantle's power   191
Erskine, Carl   52, 62, 66, 71–2, 82, 85–7, 99–102, 116, 121, 138, 144, 147–8, 155, 161, 164, 170, 173, 175, 180, 182–3, 198–9, 208, 210–11, 223–4, 242, 252
Ewing, Buck   19, 240

Farmer, James   35
Faubus, Orval   238

Federal League 26
Feller, Bob 5–6, 31, 33, 40–1, 44, 54, 69–70, 136, 139–40, 187
  on Jackie Robinson 38, 41
Ferris, Dave 33
Field, Wilmer 56
Ford, Whitey 4, 65, 67–8, 71, 81, 83, 98–9, 102, 116, 121, 122, 139, 144, 155, 171–2, 174–6, 181, 192, 207, 209–12, 222, 229, 232, 241, 244–5, 250–1, 254
Foster, Rube
  Negro Leaguer 12, 16, 27, 255
Foster, William
  Negro Leaguer 16–17
Foutz, Dave 25
Foxx, Jimmie 10, 98, 105, 187, 191–2, 200, 203, 226
  on Mickey Mantle 203
Frazee, Harry 21–2
Freedom to Serve: Equality of Treatment and Opportunity int he Armed Services 68
Frick, Ford 94–5, 115, 228, 230–1
Frisch, Frankie 20, 236
  on Willie Mays 234–5
Furillo, Carl 32, 45, 49, 52, 62, 66, 71–2, 82, 88, 99, 101–3, 110, 116, 138, 143–4, 147, 155–6, 161, 169–70, 172–5, 180, 182–4, 187, 189, 198, 203, 207–8, 210, 223–4, 241

Gaines, Jonas 56
Galehouse, Denny 52
Gallagher, Jack
  "The Land of the Rich" 146
Garagiola, Joe 47
Garcia, Mike 116, 136, 139–40
Garcia, Silvio
  Negro Leaguer 50
Gaven, Mike
  on Duke Snider 154
Gaynor, Dr. Sidney 81–2
Gehrig, Lou 1, 11, 22–5, 60, 88, 98, 173, 184, 212, 222, 226

Gerosa, Lawrence E. 239
Gibson, Josh
  Negro Leaguer 3, 16–17, 37, 41, 159, 254–5
Giles, Warren C. 115, 219, 228, 237, 246
Gilliam, Jim 99, 101–2, 116, 138, 143–4, 147, 155, 161, 173, 175, 180, 184, 189, 198–9, 208, 210, 242
  Negro Leaguer 99, 120, 145, 151, 181, 217
Gomez, Lefty 24
Gomez, Ruben 100, 116, 124, 126, 133, 138, 140, 145, 170, 183, 242
Goodman, Billy 65
Gordon, David J
  Deadball era 22
Gordon, Joe 24–5, 32, 53
Gordon, Sid 32, 52, 63, 94, 97, 145
Grace, Willie 50
Graham, Frank
  "Why Don't They Stop Knocking the Duke?" 237, 238
Grant, Frank
  Negro Leaguer 2, 12, 15
Great Migration 15, 28
Green, Pumpsie 252
Greenberg, Hank 12, 33, 40, 44, 60, 135, 146, 187, 200, 203, 247
Greenlee, Gus 16
Griffith, Clark 95
  on Josh Gibson 17
  on Mickey Mantle 185
Grim, Bob 116–17, 139, 141, 144, 172–3, 175–6, 181, 207, 234, 241, 244
Grimes, Burleigh 26
Grimley, Will
  on Korean War and the draft 83
Grimm, Charlie 10, 96, 116
Grissom, Marv 121, 138, 140, 145, 150, 170, 180, 208, 242
Grove, Lefty 10

Hadley, Bump 24–5
Hairston, Sam 69

Hall of Fame 2–3, 10, 76, 193, 236, 254–6
Hanlon, Ned 25–6
Harris, Bucky 51, 60, 250
Harris, Gail 145
Harris, Vic
 Negro Leaguer 17
Hartnett, Gabby 72
Hartung, Clint 75
Harvey, Bob 56
Hatten, Joe 45, 52, 66
Hazle, Bob 243, 245
Hearn, Jim 67, 73, 75, 77, 86, 100, 116, 124, 170, 183
Heath, Jeff 53
Hegan, Jim 54
Heinrich, Tommy 24–5, 32, 48–9, 51, 61, 63, 108, 149
Hemsley, Rollie
 Negro Leaguer 41
Herbert, Ray 83
Hermanski, Gene 52, 62, 64, 153
Hern, Gerald
 "Spahn and Sain and pray for rain" 53
Higbe, Kirby 26, 42
Hildebrand, Oral 24–5
Hill, Pete
 Negro Leaguer 12, 16
Hoak, Don 132–3, 138, 144, 147, 175
Hodges, Gil 11, 45, 51, 62, 66, 71–2, 75, 82, 85, 88, 99, 101–3, 126, 139, 143–4, 147, 150, 156, 161, 163, 169–70, 173–5, 180, 182–4, 198–9, 208–11, 223–4, 226, 234, 241, 247, 250, 252
Hodges, Russ 75
Holland, Gerald
 "The Real Mickey Mantle" 221–2
Holmes, Tommy 53
Hooper, Bob 136
Hopper, Clay
 on Jackie Robinson 38–9
Hornsby, Rogers 22, 225
 on possibility of baseball integration 47

Houtteman, Art 83, 116, 136, 139
Howard, Elston 103–4, 120, 149, 161, 172, 175–6, 180, 211, 234, 241, 244
 Negro Leaguer 144, 181, 217, 251, 258
Howard, Frank 252
Hoyt, Waite 23–4
Hubbell, Carl 20–1, 109, 135
Huggins, Miller 21, 23, 60
Hughes, Jay 26
Hughes, Jim 138
Hunter, Billy 144, 149–50, 223
Huston, Tillinghast, L. 21

Irvin, Monte 1, 4, 63, 67, 72–3, 75–8, 81–2, 85, 121–4, 126–7, 132, 138, 145, 150, 155, 158, 250
 Negro Leaguer 6, 18, 37–8, 41, 49, 57, 63, 68, 73, 78, 89, 100, 145, 181, 209, 217, 255
Isacson, Leo 55

Jackson, Randy 182–3
Jackson, "Shoeless" Joe 10–12, 192
Jansen, Larry 46, 48, 52, 63, 67, 75–7, 86, 110, 116, 123, 250
Jethroe, Sam 78, 89
 Negro Leaguer 49–50, 68
Johnson, Ban 21
Johnson, Grant
 Negro Leaguer 27
Johnson, Judy 2, 16, 18, 255
Johnson, Walter 11–12, 104
Jones, Sad Sam 23
Jones, Sam
 Negro Leaguer 69, 181, 209, 243, 253
Jones, Sheldon 52
Jones, Willie 65, 158–9

Kahn, Roger 5, 198
 "The Bewildering World of Willie Mays" 202
 Boys of Summer 4, 52, 143
 on Willie Mays 114–15
 "The Ten Years of Jackie Robinson" 168

Kaline, Al   141, 194, 211–12
Katt, Ray   145
Kauff, Benny   20, 26
Keating, Kenneth B.   231
Keefe, Tim   19
Keeler, Wee Willie   21, 25, 240
Keller, Charlie   24–5, 32
Kelley, Joe   25
Kellman, Leon   49
Kelly, George   20
Kelso, Dave   76
Keltner, Ken   52–3
Kendrick, Bob   2
  on Monte Irvin   37–8
Kennedy, Brickyard   25–6
Kimbro, Henry
  Negro Leaguer   41, 49
Kinder, Ellis   61
Kiner, Ralph   48, 52–3, 97, 122, 124, 187, 203, 241
  on Mickey Mantle   204
  on Willie Mays and Duke Snider   167
King, Clyde   71
King, Joe   71, 74
  on Willie Mays and Duke Snider   130
King, Martin Luther Jr.   176–7, 218, 228, 238
Kirkland, Willie   224
Kluszewski, Ted   134–6, 141, 164–5, 211–12
Konstanty, Jim   6, 66–7, 88, 144, 172, 176, 181
Koufax, Sandy   144, 147, 170, 175, 180, 182, 184, 190, 208, 223, 241, 251–3, 257
Kubek, Tony   223–5, 241, 244–5
Kucks, John   161, 173, 207, 210–21, 229, 232, 241
Kuenn, Harvey   201, 211–12
Kurowski, Whitey   33
Kuzava, Bob   71, 102

Labine, Clem   75, 100–2, 143–4, 161, 170, 173–5, 180, 182, 184, 208, 211, 223, 234, 242
Lacy, Sam   36–7

Lajoie, Nap   12
LaMarque, Jim
  Negro Leaguer   49
Lanier, Max   33, 40, 86, 100
Lardner, John   62, 151
  "The Fifty Per Cent Color Line"   123
Larsen, Don   144, 147–9, 167, 172–3, 175–6, 181, 207, 209–13, 241, 244
Lavagetto, Cookie   32, 108
Law, Vernon   111, 123
Lawrence, Brooks
  Negro Leaguer   120, 209, 216
Lazzeri, Tony   23–4, 122, 184
Lee, Reverend George
  assassination of   160
Lemon, Bob   5–6, 53–4, 116, 136, 139–41, 226
Lemon, Jim   83
Leonard, Buck
  Negro Leaguer   2, 17, 37, 41, 66, 255
Leonard, Dutch   41
Lester, Larry
  Fighting Jim Crow baseball   36–7
Liddle, Don   116, 140, 145, 170, 180, 183
Life magazine
  "A Prodigy of Power"   201
  "The Remarkable Mickey Mantle"   201
Lindell, Johnny   49, 51
Littlefield, Dick   215
Lloyd, John Henry "Pop"
  Negro Leaguer   2, 12, 16, 18, 27–8, 255
Lockett, Lester
  Negro Leaguer   56
Lockman, Whitey   63, 67, 75, 77, 85, 100, 122, 124, 126, 133, 144–5, 170, 182
Loes, Billy   83, 85, 87–8, 100, 102, 116, 132, 138, 144, 147, 161, 170, 172, 175, 183
Logan, Johnny   97, 244
Long, Dale   190
Lopat, Eddie   51, 61, 63, 65, 67, 71, 76, 81, 84, 86–8, 99, 101, 116, 139, 144, 148, 161, 167, 250

Lopez, Al   60, 116, 139–40
Lovett, Tom   25
Lumpe, Jerry   189
Lundquist, Carl
    on returning Korean War
        veterans   115

Mack, Connie   10, 19–20, 43, 60, 146
Mackey, Biz
    Negro Leaguer   17–18, 40–1, 72
MacPhail, Larry   44–5, 55, 81
Maglie, Sal   1, 4, 40, 67, 73–5, 77, 86, 100,
    109, 116, 121–4, 126–7, 132, 137–8,
    145, 150, 170, 180, 206, 208–13,
    223, 241
Malarcher, David
    Negro Leaguer   16
Manfred, Commissioner Robert D
    on Negro Leagues   2
Manley, Abe
    Negro Leaguer   18, 56–7
Manley, Effa
    on Jackie Robinson   56
    Negro Leaguer   2, 18, 28, 56–7
Mann, Arthur
    on Snider   153
Manning, Max   56
Mantle, Mickey   1, 4–5, 7, 69, 73, 76–7,
    81, 84, 86–8, 97–9, 101–2, 107, 114,
    116–17, 121, 124, 127, 129, 132,
    134, 137, 139, 144, 147–51, 154–5,
    157–9, 162–5, 167–70, 172–6,
    179–213, 249–58
    1951 season   69, 71
    1951 World Series   76–7
    1952 season   81, 84
    1952 World Series   86–9
    1953 season   97–9
    1953 World Series   101–2
    1954 season   107, 114, 116–17, 121,
        124, 127, 129, 132, 134, 137, 139
    1955 season   144, 150–70
    1955 World Series   172–5
    1956 season   5, 179–213
    1956 World Series   209–11
    1957 season   221–3, 229, 232–7,
        240–1
    1957 World Series   244–5
    All Star   159, 167, 202, 212, 234, 246,
        256
    American League Most Valuable Player
        Award   212, 247, 251, 256
    Arthur Daley on   149, 193–4, 197
    A.S. "Doc" Young on   226
    on Babe Ruth   191, 199–200
    "The Boy Grew Older"   197
    Ben Epstein on   191
    Bill Dickey on   69–70, 98, 186, 191,
        196
    Bob Addie on   132, 157, 186, 190,
        192, 196–7, 199–200
    Casey Stengel on   157, 184–6, 191–4,
        204–5, 245
    Charles Dexter on
        "Can Mickey Carry a Big
            Load?"   98
    Chuck Dressen on   88
    Claire Ruth on   203
    compared to Babe Ruth   98, 184,
        190–2, 196–7, 199–201, 203–4, 213
    compared to Eddie Mathews   97
    compared to Jimmie Foxx   191–2
    compared to Joe DiMaggio   98, 116,
        149, 184, 197, 203
    compared to Joe Jackson   191–2
    compared to Lou Gehrig   98, 184
    compared to other New York City
        center fielders   128–9, 132, 135,
        149, 151, 157, 159, 179, 197, 235,
        253
    compared to Stan Musial   192
    compared to Ted Williams   185, 192,
        200–1
    compared to Tony Lazzeri   184
    compared to Willie Mays   73, 127,
        132, 226, 235–6
    Copacabana fiasco   229, 232
    covers
        Baseball Digest "Can Mickey Make
            It?"   202

Life "The Remarkable Mickey
  Mantle" 201
Sport "New Pride of the
  Yankees" 98
Sports Illustrated "The Year of the
  Slugger" 202
Dan Daniels on 194, 200
Draft status 70, 81–4, 89
Duke Snider on 213, 247
Frank Finch on 184, 196
Gene Mauch on 205
Gerald Holland on
  "The Real Mickey Mantle" 221–2
Hall of Fame 255–6
Hank Bauer on 186, 199
Harvey Kuenn on 201
Hickok Belt Award 213
Home run chase of Babe Ruth's single-
  season record 194–6, 199–200,
  202–5, 213, 225, 247, 251
injuries 70, 76–7, 81–4, 89, 114, 116–
  17, 169, 172, 186–7, 192, 200, 202,
  205, 222, 226, 240–1, 244–5, 251
Jackie Robinson on 88
Jerry Coleman on 197
J.G.T. Spink on 70
Jimmie Foxx on 203
Jim Turner on 186
Joe Collins on 205
Joe Reichler on 134–5
John Drebinger on 203, 235
John Lardner on 151
Joseph M. Sheehan on 159
Life magazine
  "A Prodigy of Power" 201
Mel Ott on 200
minor leaguer 69
Ned Cronin on 167–8
New York City Chapter of the Baseball
  Writers of America Player of the
  Year Award 212
Paul Richards on 203
power of 69–70, 98, 135, 151, 164,
  184–6, 189–94, 196–7, 199–201,
  203–5, 221–2, 225–6, 235

Ralph Kiner on 204
Robert Creamer on
  "The Mantle of the Babe" 201
Robert Riger sketches 221
Roscoe McGowan on 212–13
Shirley Povich on 124, 127, 132,
  149–50, 184–5, 190, 195–6, 204,
  213
  "Mantle Just Bursting into Full
    Magnificence" 184
speed of 194, 196, 202, 204, 221, 235,
  253
The Sporting News
  "Long-Shot Mantle Rocks Ruth
    Mark" 200
The Sporting News American League
  Player of the Year 211
The Sporting News Player of the
  Year 212
Stan Musial on 184–5
stardom 1, 4, 7, 81, 84, 97–8, 139,
  148, 155, 170, 179–213, 241, 247,
  249–57
switch-hitter 70, 184, 201–5
Tallulah Bankhead on 137
Ted Williams on 193
Tom Meany on 205
Triple Crown 5, 189–226, 254
Washington Post and Times Herald
  "The Fraying Mantle" 205
  "One for Mickey" 190
Willard Mullin on
  "He'll Pass" 70
  "Ruth's 60 Homer" 200
  "Target for Mickey" 200
Marion, Marty 33, 40, 201
Marquard, Rube 20
Marquez, Luiz 69
Marshall, William 48, 63
Martin, Billy 87, 101–2, 107, 110, 114,
  122, 144, 149, 161, 167, 173–4, 176,
  179–80, 182–3, 209–11, 222, 229, 232
Martin, Whitney
  on Mays's pursuit of Babe Ruth's single-
    season home run record 135

Mathews, Eddie   6, 97–8, 116–17, 124, 153, 156, 165, 212, 225–6, 233, 243–5, 247–8
Mathewson, Christy   1, 19–20, 43, 233, 236, 252
Matlock, Leroy
   Negro Leaguer   16
Mays, Carl   12, 23
Mays, Marghuerite   248
Mays, Willie   1, 4–7, 69, 72–3, 75–8, 81–3, 85, 89, 108–41, 144–71, 179–84, 187, 190, 195–7, 199, 202–3, 206, 208, 211–13, 216–17, 225–6, 228–9, 232, 234–5, 237–8, 240, 242–3, 247–8, 250–7
   1948 Negro League World Series   56
   1951 season   100
   1951 World Series   75–8
   1952 season   82–3, 85, 89, 108–18
   1953 season   110
   1954 season   5, 82, 85, 112–41
   1954 World Series   140–1
   1955 season   144–71 *passim*
   1956 season   179–84, 187, 190, 195–7, 199, 202–3, 206, 208, 211–13, 225
   1957 season   228–9, 232, 234, 237, 240, 242
   Al Lopez on   140
   All Star   134, 159, 170, 202, 234, 247, 253, 256
   Al Simmons on   73
   Al Stump on   166
   Al Wolf on   128, 136, 162
   Arthur Daley on   83, 110, 114, 121, 128, 130, 141, 149, 162
   A.S. "Doc" Young on   226
   Barney Kremenko on   202
   Batting title   137
   Ben Wade on   164
   Billy Bruton on   187
   Bob Addie on   127, 131–2, 158, 196–7
   Braven Dyer on   113
   Bucky Walters on   232
   Buzz Clarkson on   160
   Carl Furillo on   110
   Carl Lunquist   115
   Casey Stengel on   157–8
   Clay Felker on   73
   comparison with Bob Meusel   235
   comparison with Duke Snider   128, 131, 144, 150, 156, 162–4, 166–7, 187, 238
   comparison with Henry Aaron   160
   comparison with Joe DiMaggio   73, 132, 134–5, 202, 234
   comparison with Larry Doby   134–6
   comparison with Mickey Mantle   127, 132, 226, 234–5
   comparison with other New York City center fielders   129, 132, 135, 137, 149, 151, 154, 157–9, 196–7, 213
   comparison with Pete Reiser   73, 130
   comparison with Stan Musial   131, 148, 202
   comparison with Ted Williams   202
   comparison with Tris Speaker   132, 134–5, 235
   comparison with Ty Cobb   150, 235
   covers
      Baseball Digest   137
      Time   134
   Dick Walsh on   183
   Dorothy Kilgallen   134
   on Duke Snider   131
   Duke Snider on   151, 202, 238
   Eddie Burbridge on   159
   Frank Finch on   184
   Frankie Frisch on   234–5
   Gary Schumacher on   127
   Gilbert Millstein on
      "Natural Boy"   133–4
   Grantland Rice on   73, 109
   Hall of Fame   254–6
   Homer "Goose" Curry on   159
   Home run chase of Babe Ruth's single-season record   134–5, 165, 187, 225, 247, 251, 253
   "I'd Play for Nothing" by Willie Mays (with assistance of Milton Richman)   137

injuries   111, 128
Jackie Robinson on   110, 112, 131
Jimmie Dykes on   235
Joe King on   130
John Drebinger   116, 121, 125, 229, 235
John Lardner on   151
Joseph M. Sheehan on   158–9
Ken Smith   114
Leo Durocher on   73, 113–14, 129–31, 140, 148, 202
Look magazine
  "Willie Mays: Spirit of the Giants"   127
Los Angeles Sentinel
  "Which is the fastest, a hard-hit baseball or Willie Mays?"   232
  "Willie Mays Must Be the Mostest—Say Top Greats"   234
Louis Effrat on   115
Mayo Smith on   156
National League Most Valuable Player Award   253, 257
National League Rookie of the Year Award   73
Negro Leaguer   6, 56, 69, 73, 78, 112, 159–60, 181, 216–17, 243
Pee Wee Reese on   131, 157
Racial prejudice   248, 256–7
Ralph Kiner   167
Red Smith on   109, 112, 170–1
Return from military service   82
Roger Kahn on
  "The Bewildering World of Willie Mays"   202
Shirley Povich on   110–11, 124, 127–9, 132–3, 136, 162, 197, 213
The Sporting News national league player of the year   141
Sports Illustrated
  "Duke or Willie?"   162–3
stardom   1, 4, 7, 120, 133–5, 138, 140–1, 144, 150, 165, 170, 179, 182–3, 187, 208, 212, 226, 242, 250, 253–4

Tallulah Bankhead on
  "What is so rare as a Willie Mays?"   137
Tom Sheehan on   73
Ty Cobb on   167
US military service   81–3, 89, 108, 110–11, 113, 122–3
Walt Alston on   156
Walt Winchell on   132
Wendell Smith on   109
Whitney Martin on   135
McCarthy, Joe   31, 52, 60, 88, 92
McClellan, Dan
  Negro Leaguer   12
McCormick, Frank   11
McCormick, Mike   53
McCovey, Willie   253
McDermott, Maury   181, 183, 207
McDevitt, Danny   242
McDougald, Gil   71, 77, 86, 88, 99, 102, 116, 121, 139, 144, 171, 173–4, 176, 180, 182, 207, 225, 234, 241, 244, 246
McGinnity, Joe   19, 20, 26
McGowen, Roscoe
  on Brooklyn Dodgers   147–8, 224
  on Duke Snider and Willie Mays   156–7
McGraw, John   1, 19–20, 26, 43, 64, 233, 236
McKechnie, Bill   11
McMahon, Don   243
McMillan, Roy   212
Meany, Tom   117
  on Casey Stengel   64
  on Mickey Mantle   204–5
Medwick, Joe "Ducky"   26, 40, 158
Melton, Cliff   135
Meusel, Bob   23, 234
Meusel, Irish   20
Mexican League   40
Meyer, Jack "Chief"   20
Meyer, Russ   67, 100, 102, 138, 174
Middlesworth, Hal   182, 223

Millstein, Gilbert
  on Willie Mays   133
Minoso, Minnie   124, 139
  Negro Leaguer   6, 28, 49–50, 56, 78, 89, 103, 145, 151, 181, 209, 217, 220
Mitchell, Dale   53
Mize, Johnny   21, 32, 45, 48, 52–3, 63, 65, 67, 87–8, 104, 114, 187, 250
  on Mickey Mantle   203
Monroe, Marilyn   108
Moon, Wally   121, 141, 252
Moore, Harry T. (Harriette)
  assassinations of   79
Moore, Louis
  on treatment of Black players   54–5
Moore, Wilcy   23
Morgan, Tom   71, 116, 139, 176, 207, 210
Moses, Robert   227, 233
Mossi, Don   136, 139
Mueller, Don   67, 75, 78, 85, 100, 122, 124, 127, 137–8, 144, 150, 161, 170, 180, 182–3, 208, 225, 242
Mullin, Willard
  cartoon sketch of Casey Stengel   137
  cartoon sketch of Duke Snider   156
  cartoon sketch of Mickey Mantle   70, 200
  cartoon sketch of "Yankee Domination"   114
Murphy, Johnny   24–5
Murphy, Robert
  and American Baseball Guild   40
Musial, Stan   11, 32–3, 50, 52–3, 62–3, 66, 72, 98, 122, 124, 129, 131, 141, 148, 158–9, 162, 164, 185–6, 192, 202, 211–12, 225–6, 246–7, 254
Mutrie, Jim   19, 239–40

Narleski, Ray   136
Neal, Charlie   242
Nehf, Art   20
Neun, Johnny   31
Newberry, Jimmie
  Negro Leaguer   56

Newcombe, Don   1, 62–6, 72, 75, 83, 85–6, 107, 111, 116, 122–3, 138, 143–4, 147–8, 150–1, 161, 163, 170, 172, 175, 180, 182–3, 189, 198, 208–12, 223–5, 237, 242, 250, 252
  Negro Leaguer   3, 6, 37, 64, 71, 73, 78, 89, 112, 120, 145, 159, 181
Newhouser, Hal   33, 53, 60, 136, 139
New York Giants   1, 4–6, 9, 11–12, 16, 19–21, 23, 25–7, 32, 40, 43–4, 46, 48–9, 51–2, 56, 59–60, 63, 65, 67, 69–70, 72–8, 81–6, 92, 94, 97, 100, 107–41, 144–6, 148–50, 154–8, 161, 163–6, 170–1, 176, 180–4, 195, 197, 199, 202, 207–8, 215, 218–20, 223–5, 227, 229–34, 236–7, 239–40, 242–3, 247, 249–53, 257
New York Times
  Editorial on Jackie Robinson   216
  "A Pioneering Athlete: Jack Roosevelt Robinson"   216
New York Yankees   1, 4–7, 11–12, 20–7, 31, 33, 43, 48–9, 51–2, 57, 59–61, 63–5, 67, 69–71, 73–4, 76–8, 81–8, 91–2, 97–104, 107, 114–17, 119–22, 126–7, 129, 134, 136–7, 139, 143–4, 147–50, 153, 155–7, 160–1, 167–9, 171–6, 179–213, 220, 222–6, 229, 231, 234, 237, 240–1, 244–5, 249–51, 257–8 *passim*
Noble, Ray
  Negro Leaguer   69, 73
Noren, Irv   88, 107, 144, 148, 176, 223

O'Brien, Darby   26
O'Doul, Lefty   108
Olmo, Luis   62–3
Oms, Alejandro   27–8
O'Neil, Buck
  Negro Leaguer   3
Ott, Mel   20–1, 52, 200, 226, 233, 247, 250

Pafko, Andy   71–2, 75, 82, 85, 87–8, 97, 99, 163, 244

Pager, Joshua
   "Was the Giants Comeback a Miracle . . . ?"   76
Paige, Satchel   5–6, 42, 56, 78, 89, 103, 108
   Negro Leaguer   2–3, 6, 16, 28, 37, 41, 255
Parker, Dan   150
Parker, Tom   56
Parks, Rosa   146, 176
Parnell, Mel   61
Pascual, Camilo   189, 197
Patterson, Arthur E. (Red)   199
Pearson, Monte   24
Peck, Jim   42
Peckinpaugh, Roger   21
Pendleton, Jim
   Negro Leaguer   97
Pennock, Herb   23–4
Perini, Lou   95–6
Perry, Alonzo   56
Pesky, Johnny   33
Peterson, Robert   255
Pfeffer, Jeff   26
Pierce, Billy   211–12, 246, 253
Pinkney, George   25
Pipgras, George   24
Pipp, Wally   23
Plank, Eddie   10, 19–20
Podres, Johnny   100, 102, 116, 126, 130, 138, 144, 148, 170, 173–5, 223, 225, 242, 252
Pollet, Howie   33
Polo Grounds (reconstructed, 1913)   5, 20, 28–9, 49, 74–5, 77, 92, 109–10, 113–14, 121–3, 125, 127, 129–30, 135, 140, 158, 163, 179, 190, 219–20, 233, 236, 239–40, 257
Pompez, Alex
   Negro Leaguer   2
Poulson, Mayor Norris   221
Povich, Shirley   94–5, 124, 150, 156, 182, 224–5
   "Mantle Just Bursting into Full Magnificence"   184–5
   on Black players   111–12
   on Duke Snider   162, 164, 198
   on Jackie Robinson   216
   on Mickey Mantle   124, 127, 132, 149–50, 184–5, 190–1, 195–6, 204, 213
   on New York City center fielders   197
   on Willie Mays   110–11, 127–9, 133, 136, 150
Powell, Bill   24
Powell, Jake   56
Power, Vic   103, 120, 187
Prayer Pilgrimage   228
President's Committee on Civil Rights   42
   To Secure These Rights   50

Rackley, Marv   52, 62
Radcliffe, Ted "Double Duty"   28
Randolph, A. Philip   34, 55, 256
Raschi, Victor   48, 51, 61, 63, 65, 67, 77, 81, 84, 86–8, 99, 102, 114, 116–17, 122, 148–9, 167, 250
Redding, Dick "Cannonball"   16, 27
Reese, Pee Wee   1, 4, 32, 48–9, 62, 66, 71–2, 74, 82, 85–8, 99, 101, 108, 116, 139, 143–4, 147, 150, 156, 161, 168–70, 172–5, 180, 182–4, 189, 198, 208, 210, 223–4, 242, 250
   on Duke Snider   131, 156–7
   on Jackie Robinson   45
   on Willie Mays   110
Reichler, Joe
   on MLB center fielders   134–5
Reiser, Pete   26–7, 32, 45–6, 48, 73, 130
Renna, Bill   104
Reynolds, Allie   48–9, 51, 61, 63, 65, 67, 71, 76–7, 81, 84, 86–9, 99, 101–2, 116, 121, 129, 139, 148–9, 161, 167, 192, 212, 250
Rhoden, William C
   on Negro Leagues   3
Rhodes, Dusty   132, 138, 140, 145, 150, 183
Rice, Grantland
   on Willie Mays   109

Richards, Paul
  on Mickey Mantle 203
Richardson, Bobby 234, 241
Rickey, Branch 11, 44–6, 64, 66, 72, 84, 95
  on Duke Snider 154
  on signing Jackie Robinson 3, 37–8, 46, 54, 56–7, 71, 168
Rickey, Branch Jr
  on Duke Snider 153
Rigney, Bill 181, 183–4
Rizzuto, Phil 49, 65, 77, 116
Roberts, Robin 6, 65, 67, 85, 124, 155, 189, 206, 240–1
Robinson, Eddie 104, 144
Robinson, Frank 212
  Negro Leaguer 217, 243
Robinson, Jackie 1, 4–5, 38–9, 44–9, 52, 54, 57, 62–4, 66, 72–5, 78, 82, 85–8, 91, 98–9, 102–3, 112–13, 120, 124, 127, 129, 131–2, 139, 143–5, 147–8, 150, 151, 155–6, 161, 163, 168–70, 172–3, 175–6, 180–4, 189, 198, 208–11, 218, 223–5, 229, 250
  Baseball's Great Experiment 39, 46, 216
  Bob Feller on 41
  Burt Shotton on 62
  Clay Hopper on 38–9
  on Duke Snider 131
  Duke Snider on 236
  Effa Manley on 56
  Hall of Fame 254–5
  John Lardner on 151
  Negro Leaguer 3, 6–7, 16, 21, 37, 40–1, 44, 50, 64, 68, 71, 78, 89, 112, 123, 125, 159, 216
  Racial harassment of 45, 47, 54–5, 74, 217
  retirement of 215–17
  Shirley Povich on 112
  Tallulah Bankhead on 137
  "The Ten Years of Jackie Robinson" (Roger Kahn) 168
  Walt Alston on 189

  on Willie Mays 110, 131
  "WHAT's WRONG WITH NEGRO BASEBALL?" 54–5
Robinson, Wilbert 1, 26, 64
Rockefeller, Nelson D. 238–9
Rodgers, Andre 225
Rodney, Lester
  on Jim Crow baseball 37–8
Roe, Preacher 52, 63, 66, 71–2, 82, 85–7, 100–2, 109, 138, 143, 147, 163
Roebuck, Ed 161, 175, 208, 242
Rogan, Wilber "Bullet"
  Negro Leaguer 16
Rolfe, Red 24
Roosevelt, President Franklin Delano 34–5
Rosen, Al 116, 134, 139, 141
Ruffing, Red 24–5
Ruppert, Jacob 21
Rustin, Bayard 42
Ruth, George Herman "Babe" 1, 5, 9, 11, 21–4, 44, 88, 94, 98, 117, 128–9, 131, 133–5, 157, 164–5, 167, 173, 184–5, 187, 190–7, 199–205
Rutherford, Johnny 87

Sain, Johnny 5–6, 52–3, 84, 86–7, 99, 101–2, 104, 115–16, 139, 152, 161
Sallee, Slim 20
Sanford, Jack 253
Santop, Louis
  Negro Leaguer 2, 12, 18, 27
Sauer, Hank 85, 122, 124, 225, 242
Sawyer, Eddie 66, 86
Schlichter, H. Walter
  Negro Leaguer 12
Schoendienst, Red 180, 208, 212, 225, 242–4, 247
Schumacher, Garry 72
Schupp, Ferdie 20
Selkirk, George 24–5
Seminick, Andy 65
Shantz, Bobby 84, 223, 225, 234, 241, 244
Shawkey, Bob 21, 23

Shea, Spec   48–9
Sheehan, Joseph M
    on Duke Snider   158
    on Duke Snider, Mickey Mantle, and Willie Mays   159
    on Jackie Robinson   215
    on Willie Mays   73
Sheldon, Harold
    "Long Distance Mathews"   97
Shocker, Urban   23
Shotton, Burt   44–5, 51, 62, 66, 250
    on Jackie Robinson   62
Shuba, George   85, 101, 122
Sievers, Roy   164, 247
Simmons, Al   10, 73, 225–6
Simmons, Curt   6, 66, 83
Simpson, Harry
    Negro Leaguer   69, 145
Sisler, Dick   65–6
Sisler, George   22, 225
Skowron, Bill   116–17, 144, 155, 171, 173–4, 176, 180, 207, 211, 234, 241
Slaughter, Enos   33, 209–11, 245
    Spiking of Jackie Robinson   47
Smith, Al
    Negro Leaguer   50, 145, 159, 181
Smith, Ford   49
Smith, Hal   147
Smith, Harry A.   12
Smith, Hilton   16, 49
Smith, Ken
    on Willie Mays   114
Smith, Lamar "Ditney"
    assassination of   161
Smith, Red   61, 65
    on Jackie Robinson   38–9
    on 1951 New York Giants' winning pennant   76
    on 1957 New York Giants' last home game   239
    on Willie Mays   109, 112, 171
Smith, Wendell
    Fighting Jim Crow baseball   36–7
    on Jackie Robinson   216
    on Willie Mays   109

Snider, Duke   1, 4–5, 45, 51, 61–2, 64, 66, 71–2, 82, 85–7, 98–9, 101–3, 116, 124, 128–33, 135, 137–9, 141, 143–4, 147, 149–77, 179–80, 182–4, 195–9, 202–3, 206–8, 210–13, 215, 223–6, 228–9, 232, 234, 237–8, 240–1, 247–8, 250–6
    All-Star   152–4, 159, 212
    Al Stump on   166–7
    Al Wolf on   161–2, 175
    Arthur Daley on   162, 166, 206–7
    Arthur E. (Red) Patterson on   199
    Background   151
    "Baseball's Powerman" (*Sport Life*)   152
    Ben Wade on   163–4
    Billy Bruton on   187
    Bob Addie on   157–8, 196–7
    Boys of Summer   1, 62, 82, 143, 155–77
    Branch Rickey on   154
    Braven Dyer on   198
    Casey Stengel on   157, 173–5
    Charlies Dressen on   198
    compared to Mickey Mantle   132
    compared to other New York City center fielders   135, 149, 151, 154, 157, 159, 196–7, 213, 234–5, 253–4
    compared to Stan Musial   131
    compared to Willie Mays   128–32, 144, 150, 156, 162–4, 166–7
    covers
        Baseball   152
        Sport   166
        Sport Life   152
        Sports Illustrated   162
        Sports Stars   152
    Frank Graham on
        "Why Don't They Stop Knocking the Duke?"   237–8
    Hall of Fame   254–6
    Home run chase of Babe Ruth's single-season record   164–5
    "I Play Baseball for Money, Not Fun" (with Roger Kahn)   198

on Jackie Robinson   168, 236
Jackie Robinson on   131
John Lardner on   151
Joseph Sheehan on   158–9
McGowen, Roscoe on
  "Duke Proves Dynamo in Dodger
    Drive"   156
minor leaguer   152
Mullin, Willard   156
  "GANG WAY! MAKE ROOM F'R
    ROYALTY!"   156
MVP vote   152–4, 169–70 (Top Ten:
  1950, 1952, 1953, 1954, 1955)
Pee Wee Reese on   131, 156–7
Problems with authority   153–4
Ralph Kiner on   167
Shirley Povich on   150, 162, 198, 213
The Sporting News Player of the
  Year   170, 176
on Willie Mays   202
Southworth, Billy   11
Spahn, Warren   6, 53, 73, 96, 110, 126–7,
  226, 243–7
Speaker, Tris   9, 12, 26, 98, 129, 132,
  134–5, 235, 238
Spencer, Darryl   183
Spink, J.G. Taylor
  on Jackie Robinson   46
  on Larry Doby   57
  on Mickey Mantle   70
Spooner, Karl   144, 150, 170, 174–5, 180, 183
The Sporting News   46–7, 62, 66, 70, 137
  "Duke Proves Dynamo in Dodger
    Drive"   156
  "Long-Shot Mantle Rocks Ruth
    Mark"   200
Sport Life
  "Baseball's Powerman"   152
Sport magazine
  "Durocher—Always on the Spot"   44
Sports Illustrated
  "The Bewildering World of Willie
    Mays" (Roger Kahn)   202
  "The Year of the Slugger"   201
St. Claire, Ebba   123
Stanky, Eddie   53, 67, 86

stardom   1, 4, 7, 66, 88, 98–9, 103, 124,
  130, 138–9, 144, 152–77, 180,
  182–4, 212, 250, 253
1947 season   152
1948 season   152
1949 pennant race   61
1949 season   62, 152
1949 World Series   64
1950 season   66, 152
1951 season   72, 152
1952 season   85, 152
1952 World Series   86–8, 154
1953 season   98–9, 152–3
1953 World Series   101–3, 154
1954 All-Star game   134
1954 season   113–39 *passim*
1955 season   5, 143–4, 147, 155–77
1955 World Series   172–4
1956 season   195–213 *passim*
1956 World Series   179, 210–11
1957 season   223–48 *passim*
Tallulah Bankhead on   137
Temper   153, 165–6, 206
Ty Cobb on   166–7
Walt Alston on   156, 167
Stearnes, Turkey
  Negro Leaguer   2, 16
Steele, Ed   56
Stengel, Casey   4–5, 59–61, 64–5, 69–71,
  81–2, 86, 88, 92, 97, 99, 102, 107,
  115–17, 119, 136–7, 139, 144, 149,
  161, 167, 173, 175, 184, 222–4,
  229, 232, 234, 236, 249–51, 255
  on Mickey Mantle   107, 184–6,
    191–4, 204–5, 245
  on MLB center fielders   157
Stephens, Vernon   61
Stirnweiss, Snuffy   48
Stobbs, Chuck   98, 186
Stoneham, Horace   171, 219–21, 227–8,
  230, 232–3, 236, 246, 249–50
Stovey, George   14–15
Strong, Nat   27
Stump, Al
  Writing about Snider   166
Sturdivant, Tom   176, 181, 207, 210, 241, 244

Sundra, Steve 24–5
Suttles, George "Mule"
  Negro Leaguer 2, 17, 28

Taylor, Candy Jim
  Negro Leaguer 17
Terry, Adonis 25
Terry, Bill 1, 20–1, 108, 233, 236
Terwilliger, Wayne 145
Thompson, Bobby 1, 48, 63, 67, 72, 75–6, 85, 100, 240, 250
Thompson, Fresco 108, 109
Thompson, Hank
  Negro Leaguer 41, 47, 49, 67–8, 73, 78, 89, 100, 120–4, 126, 138, 145, 181, 183
Thurman, Bob
  Negro Leaguer 56, 181
Till, Emmett
  murder of 160–1
Time magazine
  "Rookie of the Year" 47
  on Willie Mays 134
Topping, Dan 59, 103
Torre, Frank 244–5
Triandos, Gus 147
Troupe, Quincy
  Negro Leaguer 49
Truman, President Harry S
  Executive Order 9980 55
  Executive Order 9981 55
Turley, Bob 83, 104, 121, 144, 147–50, 162, 172–3, 175–6, 181, 207, 211, 241, 245
Twain, Mark 13

US Supreme Court 14, 42, 218
  Brown v. Board of Education 105, 125
  Brown v. Board of Education (implementation order) 160

Veeck, Bill 95–6, 100–1, 146
Vernon, Mickey 41, 121, 211

Waddell, Rube 10
Wade, Ben 163

Wagner, Honus 11, 254
Wagner, Mayor Robert 219–21, 228, 230, 239, 246
Waitkus, Eddie 65
Walker, Dixie 26, 32, 45–6
Walker, Edsall
  Negro Leaguer 17
Walker, Harry 33
Walker, Moses Fleetwood 14–15
Walker, Rube 74
Wallace, Henry A. 34, 55
Wallop, John Douglass
  The Year the Yankees Lost the Pennant 136
Walsh, Dick 183
Walters, Bucky 11, 232
Ward, John Montgomery 19
Ware, Archie
  Negro Leaguer 50
Warren, Earl 105, 125, 160
Washington, Johnny
  Negro Leaguer 49
Washington Post and Times Herald
  "The Fraying Mantle" 205
Weaver, Buck 10–11
Webb, Del 100–1
Weiss, George 59–60, 64, 114, 161
  on Yankees and Black players 104
Welch, Mickey 19
Wells, Willie
  Negro Leaguer 2, 17–18, 28
Wheat, Zach 26
White, Bill 180, 208, 224
White, Sol
  Negro Leaguer 2, 12, 15–16, 27
Whitman, Walt 13
Wiesler, Bob 176
Wilhelm, Hoyt 86, 100, 126–7, 133, 138, 140, 145, 150, 170, 180
Wilkinson, J.L
  Negro Leaguer 3, 16, 37
Williams, Davey 100, 122, 150
Williams, "Smokey" Joe
  Negro Leaguer 2, 17, 27
Williams, Ken 22

Williams, Ted   25, 31–3, 40, 44, 48, 52–3, 61, 70, 83, 94, 98, 111, 115, 124, 129, 130, 158, 163, 166–7, 185, 192, 200–2, 207, 211–12, 225–6, 234–5, 246–7
   on Mickey Mantle   193
   on Negro League stars and Hall of Fame   254–5
Wilson, Artie   56
Wilson, Hack   135, 165, 187, 203
Wilson, Jud
   Negro Leaguer   2, 17
Winchell, Walter
   on top center fielders   132
Wolf, Al   94
   on Brooklyn Dodgers   175–6
   on Duke Snider   162
   on Larry Doby   136
   on Willie Mays   128, 136, 161–2
Wolfson, Louis F.   238
Woodling, Gene   84, 88, 99, 102, 107, 116, 121, 139, 147, 161
Wright, Johnny
   Negro Leaguer   17
Wrigley, Phil   101, 220, 246
Wyatt, Whit   26

Yankee Stadium   28–9, 54, 61, 76, 87, 92, 101, 153, 155, 157, 172, 174, 192, 194, 196–7, 200–2, 210, 234, 244–5, 251
Young, A.S. "Doc"
   on Mays   226
Young, Cy   9, 19
Youngs, Ross   20

About the Author

A longtime history professor, **Robert C. Cottrell** is the author of numerous books, among them biographies of the dissident journalist I. F. Stone, Negro League pioneer Rube Foster, and ACLU founder Roger Nash Baldwin. His books on the national pastime include *Blackball, the Black Sox, and the Babe: Baseball's Crucial 1920 Season*; *Two Pioneers: How Hank Greenberg and Jackie Robinson Transformed Baseball—and America*; and *The Year Without a World Series: Major League Baseball and the Road to the 1994 Players' Strike*. Rowman & Littlefield previously published Cottrell's *Sex, Drugs, and Rock 'n' Roll: The Rise of America's 1960s Counterculture*; *1968: The Rise and Fall of the New American Revolution*; and *All-American Rebels: The American Left from the Wobblies to Today*, among other works. Cottrell lives in Northern California with his wife and daughter.